Pilkington Brothers and the Glass Industry

First published in 1960, *Pilkington Brothers and the Glass Industry* is a comprehensive economic history of the glass industry in Britain. It charts the story of Pilkington Brothers and the manufacture of window and plate glass in Britain up to 1914. The epilogue to the book discusses the events that impacted the glass industry from 1914–1959.

The volume gives an extensive account of the family background of the Pilkington family; the historical background to the flat glass industry in Britain; the challenges posed and opportunities opened up by—arrival and removal of competitors, excise duty and window tax, international competition from Belgium and tariffs on imports, new techniques and technological advancement, and labour crises and trade unionism. This book will be of interest to students and researchers of business, economics, and history.

Due to modern production methods, it has not been possible to include some fold-out maps within the book. Any purchasers of the book will be able to receive a free pdf of the relevant pages by contacting Routledge Customer Services. https://www.routledge.com/contacts/customer-service

Pilkington Brothers and the Glass Industry

T. C. Barker

First published in 1960
by George Allen and Unwin Ltd.

This edition first published in 2024 by Routledge
4 Park Square, Milton Park, Abingdon, Oxon, OX14 4RN

and by Routledge
605 Third Avenue, New York, NY 10017

Routledge is an imprint of the Taylor & Francis Group, an informa business

Publisher's Note
The publisher has gone to great lengths to ensure the quality of this reprint but points out that some imperfections in the original copies may be apparent.

Disclaimer
The publisher has made every effort to trace copyright holders and welcomes correspondence from those they have been unable to contact.

A Library of Congress record exists under LCCN: 61019137

ISBN: 978-1-032-85197-6 (hbk)
ISBN: 978-1-003-51704-7 (ebk)
ISBN: 978-1-032-85199-0 (pbk)

Book DOI 10.4324/9781003517047

PILKINGTON BROTHERS
AND THE
GLASS INDUSTRY

T. C. BARKER

Lecturer in Economic History
London School of Economics and Political Science

Ruskin House
GEORGE ALLEN & UNWIN LTD
MUSEUM STREET LONDON

PRINTED IN GREAT BRITAIN
in 11 on 12 pt. Baskerville type
BY SIMSON SHAND LTD
LONDON, HERTFORD AND HARLOW

PREFACE

A WELL-KNOWN historian, writing from personal experience, has come to the conclusion that 'there is no more hazardous field of operations for an author to choose than business history, for there are possibilities of misunderstandings at every stage'. Several other writers would, I feel sure, endorse this opinion. I count myself all the more fortunate, for I have had the most friendly and encouraging support and assistance from the directors and staff of Pilkington Brothers Limited. I have been given a completely free hand up to the final chapter, which was written in close consultation. Our only difference was over the whereabouts of footnotes—and as I suspect that my preference for the foot of the page would not be welcomed by most readers, I had no hesitation in agreeing to banishing these references to the back of the book.

First of all I must thank the directors of Pilkington Brothers Limited, all of whom have been actively helpful at every stage in the production of this book.

It is impossible to mention by name all the members of Pilkingtons' staff past and present from whom I have had help in writing this book. I should, however, like particularly to thank Mr M. N. Leathwood and Dr W. B. Price for comments on technical and other aspects of the manuscript and Dr Price for reading the galley proofs and helping to make the index. Mr T. Appleton collected together many of Pilkingtons' historical records and obtained information from a considerable number of employees and pensioners who must, alas, remain unnamed. Mr D. Matthews drew the plans of the works and Miss F. Stretch the graphs used in this book, and Mr J. Birchall gave much help in adapting the pictures and photographs for our purposes. Mr E. B. LeMare, Mr R. F. Taylor and Mr F. B. Waldron helped to supply information for the later chapters, and Mr J. A. Hartley gave me much assistance among the intricacies of the company's legal documents. I also owe a considerable debt to Mr J. F. Rigby, secretary of the company, and his staff, particularly Miss Williams and Mrs Barlow, for their assistance.

Sir Hugh Chance kindly gave me permission to consult the archives at Spon Lane, Smethwick, and supplied information about Chance Brothers Ltd. Mr D. E. C. Eversley, who has worked on the Chance records, has given me much helpful advice, and has also commented on the book as a whole.

I am indebted to Mr R. C. Jarvis, the Librarian of H.M. Customs and Excise, for much help with the glass excise records and for his observations upon parts of the manuscript, and to H.M. Commissioners to consult and quote from these official sources. I am also indebted to Lord Salisbury for permission to use the Salisbury Papers and to Dr J. F. A. Mason for drawing my attention to letters among them. Dr Neville Williams gave me much assistance at the Public Record Office, as did Mr R. Sharpe France, the

Archivist, and his staff at the Lancashire Record Office, and Mr H. C. Caistor and his staff at St Helens Central Library.

Mr Michael Brett allowed me to use newscuttings in the possession of the Plate Glass Merchants' Association, Mr G. L. Chater documents relating to his firm, and Mr H. Salmond of James Hetley and Co. photographs of members of the Pilkington family (two of which are reproduced in this book) and information about his grandfather's service with Pilkingtons.

I owe a particular debt to the late F. A. Bailey, whose premature death has robbed Lancashire of one of its best and most widely informed regional historians.

Mr J. Charnock has provided much information about the history of Horwich and the illustration of Stock's Farm which is to be found opposite page 32. Mr R. K. Robertson took a number of the photographs. Mr Richard Pilkington M.P. provided genealogical information. Dr R. Dickinson has also given much genealogical help and has been largely responsible for charts 1–4; the books has also gained much from discussions on various topics with him and with Dr D. W. F. Hardie. Dr Marian Bowley has criticised the manuscript in the light of her special knowledge of the building industry. I have also received helpful comments from Professor William Ashworth, Dr W. H. Chaloner, Professor R. S. Edwards, Dr J. R. Harris, Mr S. A. Harris, Professor David S. Landes, Mr P. J. O'Leary, Dr L. S. Pressnell and Mr W. M. Stern, all of whom have read either the manuscript or the proof in whole or in part. I must also record my indebtedness to discussions with Dr P. Lesley Cooke, Mr J. Ginswick, Mr J. M. Hemphill, Mr P. Mathias and Mr H. Townshend, as well as with members of the Economic History staff of the London School of Economics who never fail to provide a constant guard against complacency in any shape or form.

My final debt is due to my wife for her patience and assistance.

The London School of Economics   T.C.B.
and Political Science
August 1959

CONTENTS

Richard Pilkington's successful claim to the manor of Allerton and other property near Liverpool, 1759. The history of the family at Horwich. Their short-lived venture into bleaching there 1786–96. Sale of the Allerton property. William Pilkington became a doctor at St Helens. Like most other doctors of his day he kept a shop and sold wines and spirits. The wine and spirit business prospered and, in 1813, he gave up his medical practice. Two of his sons, Richard and William, having been apprenticed to Liverpool firms, joined him in the wine and spirit business. In 1826 the duty on spirits was halved and William Pilkington and Sons began to rectify and compound spirits themselves.

The introduction of coal-fired furnaces for glassmaking at the beginning of the seventeenth century caused the industry to move to the coalfields. The Tyne, the chief source of coal, became the centre of the glass industry and held this position until the middle of the nineteenth century. Auxiliary furnaces were built in districts which could not be supplied easily from the north-east. Lancashire was such a district. The first coal-fired furnace was built in the south-east of the county. By 1700 a furnace had been built near St Helens. Early history of plate glass, a luxury product made in London. Small-scale attempts to make this thicker glass by casting instead of blowing. The first factory to cast plate glass on a large scale built at Ravenhead, St Helens, largely owing to the intervention of John Mackay, a local coalowner. The works' early failures and later successes. The Mackays became partners in the Eccleston Crown Glassworks, started in 1792.

J. W. Bell (who had come to the neighbourhood as a flint glassmaker) and five other local men formed a partnership in 1826 to make window glass, the firm being known as the St Helens Crown Glass Company. William Pilkington, Dr Pilkington's second son, was probably brought in by his brother-in-law, Peter Greenall. At first William Pilkington considered the venture merely as an investment, but he was drawn into its management when Bell became involved in a dispute with the excise authorities and the other partners, except Greenall, withdrew.

leading manufacturers. Great expansion in the 1850s; extensions at St Helens and acquisition of the Eccleston factory. The firm began to make cathedral glass and branched out into the coal and chemical industries.

The removal of duties on home-produced glass was accompanied by a reduction of the tariff on imports. From 1853 cheap Belgian glass started to come into Britain in some quantity and when Belgian exports were diverted from America during the Civil War, competition became more intense and continued to grow very rapidly. The Belgians were soon sending to Britain as much window glass as Chances, Pilkingtons and Hartleys themselves made. This competition led to retrenchment. Crown glass went out of production, Siemens' gas producers saved fuel, and a cut in freight charges between St Helens and the Mersey reduced transport costs. Retirement of Richard and William Pilkington. They were each succeeded by two of their sons.

The second generation put new life into the firm. More land was purchased next to the works and further extensions built. Pilkingtons wrested supremacy from Chances by quickly installing tank furnaces (which allowed round-the-clock working) and by venturing successfully into plate glass in a new works, built at Cowley Hill, St Helens. Pilkingtons alone among plate glass manufacturers were able to weather very intense competition in plate glass towards the end of the century because window glass was still profitable and because of lower production costs. Two outstanding features of these years were very heavy capital investment and rapidly-growing exports. In 1894, Pilkingtons became a limited company, though still confined to the family. Several members of the third generation were introduced to the Board.

The later 1860s witnessed a campaign to increase labour efficiency. Strikes broke out at Sheet Works in 1870 and 1878 and at Plate Works in 1890. Knights of Labor and trade unionism. Recreational activities and welfare services.

In the late 1850s Pilkingtons started to mine coal in the immediate vicinity of their works and were soon opening seams farther afield. In 1876 their St Helens Colliery was merged with the neighbouring Ravenhead Colliery to form the St Helens Collieries Company Limited. The glassworks thus safeguarded their fuel supplies and obtained preferential rates.

PLATES

GRAPHS, CHARTS AND PLANS

INTRODUCTION

I F a business history is to achieve any significance as a contribution to the field of economic study, it must pay as much attention to placing the particular firm in its correct economic setting as to describing that firm's growth readably and accurately. There is, however, no satisfactory history of British window and plate glass manufacture from which to create this setting. From time to time articles and chapters on glass technology and its history have appeared in various specialist journals and encyclopaedias, but most books dealing with the subject are concerned with its antiquarian and aesthetic aspects and are addressed to the connoisseur, rather than to the reader with historical and economic interests. The absence of any comprehensive economic history of glass manufacture made it necessary, in the preparation of the present book, to carry out general research into the growth of this branch of the industry in order to indicate the main features of the development of window and plate glass manufacture in Britain before Pilkingtons' appearance on the scene in 1826. It was then possible to set the rise of Pilkingtons against the background of the failure of their nearest rival and, somewhat later, the almost universal decline of the older glass firms in the north-east—for long the centre of the industry. In this way, glass manufacture in Britain tended early to undergo a species of natural rationalization, and, from 1860 onwards, Pilkingtons' chief competition came not from other concerns in this country but from foreign rivals, particularly Belgian. As Pilkingtons continued to increase in importance, the history of the firm became very largely that of British flat glass manufacture as a whole. Thus, in writing the history of the firm, the author had, in effect, to write the history of a branch of the industry.

Manufacture of window glass in Britain has always been confined to a small number of concerns, and that of plate glass to an even smaller number; the highly specialized nature of the technologies involved and the relatively large amounts of capital invested always discouraged multiplication of small enterprises. This, in its turn, facilitated understandings among manufacturers, and the high proportion of capital locked up in plant and stocks made such understandings, from the manufacturers' point of view, particularly desirable, especially when trade was slack. From the beginning of the seventeenth century onwards, intermittent evidence is to be found of agreements to fix prices, partition markets, and limit output. Pilkingtons inherited this tradition of commercial amity and became from the outset a member of an association which gave every appearance of being long-established and was certainly nation-wide. The minutes of the association's meetings add an extra charge to the already undermined view that manufacturers, in the first half of the nineteenth century, were apostles of ruthless, individualistic competition.

Until 1838 the association confined its attention to fixing prices. In that year, however, agreements were extended to output limitation. These output agreements were based upon returns which the various firms had made to the excise authorities during the preceding years. The excise duty on glass (repealed 1845) and the tax on windows (repealed 1851) exerted a considerable influence on the industry's development. The window tax had, as would be expected, the effect of reducing demand on the domestic market; the excise duty seems to have had little effect on demand but nevertheless had a considerable influence on the development of the industry in other ways. Two excise prosecutions—neither of which involved Pilkingtons—proved to be turning points in Pilkingtons' history; and the drawback paid upon exported glass unquestionably helped to establish in the country a new type of window glass manufacture which was soon to eclipse, and ultimately to supersede entirely, existing methods of production.

Removal of the duties on British-made glass was accompanied by the reduction, and then the complete repeal, of duties on imported glass. There followed a period of growing foreign competition, first in window glass, and then in the thicker and more costly plate glass, which Pilkingtons began to make in the 'seventies. Belgian manufacturers had the advantage of cheap water communication into London, the largest single market for glass in the country and the centre for its distribution to the Home Counties, East Anglia, and most of Southern England. As generally happens when commercial competition becomes acute and cannot be curbed, increased urgency was given to technological advance. Inventions in the field of window glass manufacture, quickly adopted by Pilkingtons, greatly strengthened their position when plate glass sales encountered growing Belgian competition in the 'eighties and when, in the 'nineties, they were drastically affected by losses in the North American market. In the face of this challenge, technological innovation occurred in plate glass manufacture but was confined to methods of finishing. There was no major innovation in casting until just after the First World War. Then Fords at Detroit, requiring rapidly-increasing supplies of plate glass for their cars, developed a continuous process for its production. This was achieved with the assistance of experts from Pilkingtons, who were sent to Detroit specially for the purpose. Pilkingtons thereby obtained an international advantage in plate glass manufacture which they subsequently maintained. In the mass production of window glass, however, which also came of age in the 'twenties, Pilkingtons lagged behind manufacturers abroad, particularly in America, in technological development.

Pilkingtons, from modest and hesitant beginnings, through decades of foreign competition and more than a century of far-reaching technological and economic changes, to the present organization which makes all the flat glass in Britain and has manufacturing interests in South America and all the principal countries of the Commonwealth, has remained a family concern. Beginning as a partnership, it grew to its present proportions as a private limited company. It is now managed by the fourth generation of the family. The Pilkingtons share with such world-famous industrial families as the Du Ponts and the Solvays the distinction of producing a succession of men ready, and fitted by their ability, to assume the increasing responsibility of controlling a great and growing enterprise. It is a commonplace that all too often the impetus of industrial or commercial ventures spends itself by the third generation. At that remove from the usually energetic founder, the successors are very often educated in a scheme of values which ensures that they seek a way of life that leads them far from factory and boardroom. Inevitably, in such cases, the divorce between the uninterested heirs and the origin and source of their wealth becomes complete. The business becomes a public company, managed by salaried officials. Often, of course, this is a law of economic necessity, since the resources of the family group must often prove inadequate to finance further expansion; mortality and severities of fiscal policy also play their part in the evolution of industrial as of other concerns. These general considerations make all the more notable the history of the Pilkington enterprise. By forgoing lives of ease and leisure and by continuing to plough back a very high proportion of the profits of their business, the Pilkington generations have been able to maintain the private status of their company and, at the same time, to finance its continued expansion. The real capital value of Pilkingtons is thus the collective personal fortunes of the members of the family; that total, which is not known since no shares have been offered publicly for sale, must be impressive indeed and comparable with the capitals of many large publicly-financed companies.

The Victorians used to argue a great deal about the relative merits of private concerns, with control in the hands of those who owned the capital, and public companies, with easier access to additional capital but usually with division between investor and management. Although this debate may seem a dead issue in an era characterized by public investment and the 'Managerial Revolution', the history told in the chapters which follow shows how at least one large private concern has come to hold a secure and significant place in the economy of this new age.

CHART 1

THE PILKINGTON CLAIM TO LANDS IN ALLERTON AND ELSEWHERE NEAR LIVERPOOL

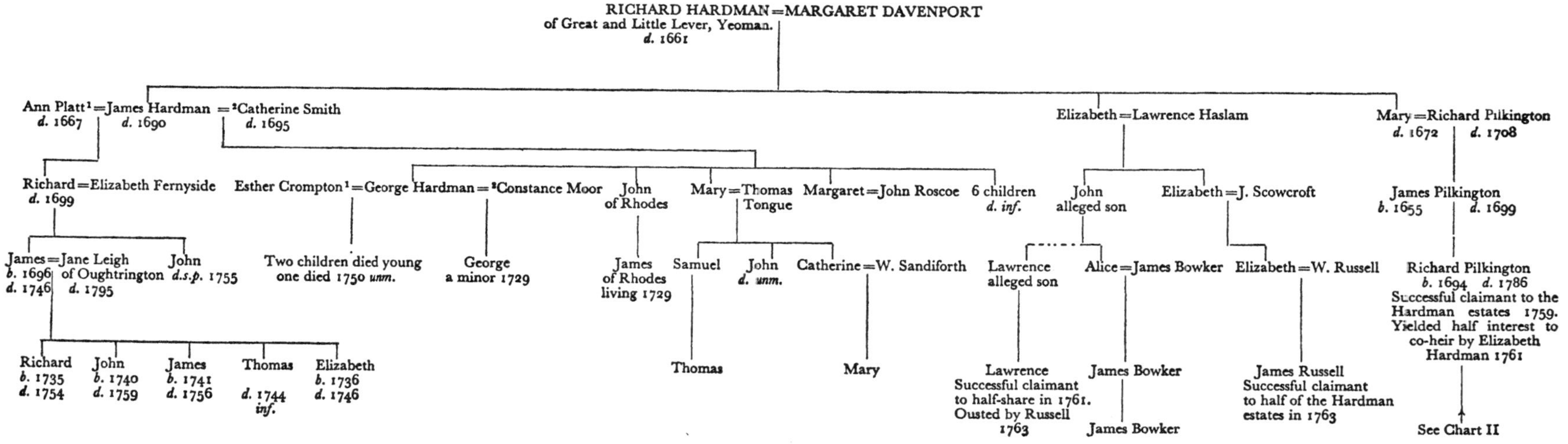

RICHARD HARDMAN = MARGARET DAVENPORT
of Great and Little Lever, Yeoman.
d. 1661

Ann Platt[1] = James Hardman = [2]Catherine Smith
d. 1667   d. 1690   d. 1695

Elizabeth = Lawrence Haslam

Mary = Richard Pilkington   d. 1708
d. 1672

James Pilkington
b. 1655   d. 1699

Richard Pilkington
b. 1694   d. 1786
Successful claimant to the
Hardman estates 1759.
Yielded half interest to
co-heir by Elizabeth
Hardman 1761

See Chart II

Richard = Elizabeth Fernyside
d. 1699

Esther Crompton[1] = George Hardman = [2]Constance Moor   John of Rhodes

George
a minor 1729

James of Rhodes
living 1729

Mary = Thomas Tongue

Margaret = John Roscoe

6 children
d. inf.

Elizabeth = J. Scowcroft

John
alleged son

Alice = James Bowker

Elizabeth = W. Russell

James = Jane Leigh
b. 1696, of Oughtrington d.s.p. 1755
d. 1746

Two children died young
one died 1750 unm.

Samuel

John
d. unm.

Catherine = W. Sandiforth

Lawrence
alleged son

Lawrence
Successful claimant
to half-share in 1761.
Ousted by Russell
1763

James Bowker

James Russell
Successful claimant
to half of the Hardman
estates in 1763

Richard   John   James   Thomas   Elizabeth
b. 1735   b. 1740   b. 1741   d. 1744   b. 1736
d. 1754   d. 1759   d. 1756   inf.   d. 1746

Mary

Thomas

James Bowker

(Based upon Ronald Stewart-Brown: *A History of the Manor and Township of Allerton*, Liverpool, 1911)

CHAPTER I

THE FAMILY BACKGROUND

THE Pilkington family was engaged in industry and trade for many years before 1826 when one of its members was drawn, almost by accident, to accept a partnership in a company which had just been formed for the purpose of making window glass. Like so many other successful business men, confronted by an expanding economy full of openings and opportunities, several generations of the Pilkington family allowed their actions to be determined very largely by events. The first of these actions—and undoubtedly our starting point—was a most rewarding claim, in 1759, to the manor of Allerton and other estates close to the rising port of Liverpool.

As may be seen from the accompanying pedigree, this claim was based upon a marriage, which had taken place a century before, between Richard Pilkington and Mary, one of the two daughters of Richard Hardman of Great Lever, near Bolton.[1] John Hardman (born in 1698), the grandson of Mary's only brother, made his fortune in trade at Liverpool, and in 1736 he and his brother, James, a successful woollen merchant at Rochdale, together bought the manor of Allerton for £7,700.[2] James Hardman died in 1746 leaving his half of this property to his sons. John Hardman lived on to continue his triumphal progress: he purchased Aigburth Hall and other lands in Garston for £5,000 in 1753 and was elected as one of the Members of Parliament for the Borough in the following year. But in 1755 he died, childless, and left all his property to his late brother's two surviving sons who were already heirs to their father's moiety of Allerton. But theirs was a sickly family. Three children had already died before reaching the age of fifteen and premature death awaited the other two. When the last survivor died in March, 1759, the whole question of the succession was left open to doubt, for the branch of the family which stemmed from Richard Hardman's only son, James, through his first wife, Ann Platt, was completely extinct. It was therefore necessary to go back three generations to discover the true heirs.

James Hardman had married a second time and the strongest claim lay with the children of this second marriage. As the pedigree shows, James Hardman had several children by his second wife, Catherine Smith, and four of them had issue. But, either through ignorance of their rights, death, or distance, none of them arrived to press their claims. It was, therefore, left to the descendants of Richard Hardman's two daughters to divide the estate between them.

First to appear was Richard Pilkington of Horwich, grandson of one of these daughters. He was over sixty years of age and had obviously taken a deep personal interest in the rising fortunes and dwindling issue of his wealthy relatives in Liverpool and Rochdale. As soon as he learnt, possibly in the newspaper, of the passing of the 'last direct heir . . . by whose death a considerable estate devolves to some of their distant relatives',[3] he lost no time in gaining possession of what he considered to be his rightful inheritance. He took proceedings to substantiate his claim at the Lancaster Assizes in August, 1759.

This property, all situated just to the south of Liverpool, was a rich prize, even after the heirs of Richard Hardman's other daughter had appeared and acquired their share of it.[4] It consisted of nearly 600 acres, 220 of which were arable and most of the rest pasture.[5] Richard Pilkington of Horwich was now a considerable landowner, fully entitled to style himself, as he did in a legal petition of 1761, as a gentleman.[6]

He could not have described himself as such before 1759. His grandfather he himself classed as a yeoman,[7] and he still rented the small farm in Horwich, called the White House, which had been the family home since his grandfather's day, when his predecessors had probably first moved into the district.[8] There he farmed his small holding, being called upon to play a part in township affairs from time to time. He had served as overseer in 1727—an office his grandfather had filled before him, in 1691—had signed a list of highways appointments in 1748–9 and, five years later, in 1754, had become churchwarden and constable.[9] He was obviously among the more prominent of the local inhabitants though still in quite humble circumstances.[10]

Although the rents from their newly-acquired property must have supplemented considerably the slender family income at Horwich, there is no indication that the acquisition of the Liverpool estates resulted immediately in any radical alteration in the way of life to which the Pilkingtons had long been accustomed. The new lords of the manor of Allerton continued to live at the White House in Horwich, partly, no doubt, because they only possessed a moiety of the Liverpool property which made occupation difficult, and partly because it was agreed that James Hardman's widow, Mrs Jane Hardman, should continue to reside at Allerton Hall. The new landlords confined their visits to two per year when they went to collect the rents.

As Richard Pilkington himself was well over sixty, it seems probable that these journeys and many other family affairs (including legal matters)[11] were attended to by his sons. The death of the eldest, James, in 1768, caused the main burden of responsibility to fall upon the shoulders of his second son, Richard, a joiner and house carpenter by trade,[12] then aged 37.

Richard Pilkington junior had married on January 6, 1761, Eleanor Pendlebury, a yeoman's daughter,[13] and shortly afterwards took a lease of Stock's Farm in Horwich.[14] His wife bore him six children: Elizabeth (1761), Richard (1763), William (1765), Hannah (1767), James (1769) and Eleanor (1771). Richard Pilkington senior lived to see two of his grandchildren reach their majority. He died in his 93rd year at the end of March, 1786, in the formal words of the obituary, 'sincerely esteemed and regretted by all who knew him'.[15]

Richard Pilkington junior kept a diary.[16] From his pithy, day-to-day entries we are able to piece together a reasonably full picture of the family's affairs from June, 1784. Our diarist led an extremely varied and active life, combining farming with his trade of carpentry and a multitude of other interests. On some days we find him weeding the potatoes, spreading dung, carting gravel, mowing clover or 'mowing Rushes for Bedding', or (as he quaintly put it) 'windowing our corn'. On others, he is following his trade, 'working in [the] Shop making a Door', repairing a gate, making a wheelbarrow or a ladder, repairing the parlour chimney piece, or even making a 'new little carriage'. At other times he is acting as a commissioner for the turnpike road which ran through Horwich, or serving on the Grand Jury in Manchester. In April, 1785, he was chosen as a Governor of Rivington Grammar School and a few months later was appointed to be its Treasurer. This office entailed his absence from home for ten or twelve days every year, travelling up to Durham and back to collect the rents, an expedition which he described, with characteristic economy of words, as 'the North Journey'. Like his predecessors, he was a Nonconformist, and a staunch supporter of the Independent Chapel at Horwich. Every Sunday he faithfully entered in his diary the text upon which the sermon had been preached. For a number of years, the ministers at Horwich New Chapel were his brothers-in-law; and his nephew, the Rev James Pilkington of Derby, was to earn some distinction as a Nonconformist divine and county historian.[17]

To be made Treasurer of Rivington Grammar School, Richard Pilkington must not only have been a man of integrity but must also have possessed at least a nodding acquaintance with the mysteries of accountancy. He was equipped to engage in business should the opportunity arise and he already possessed the necessary capital, or the means of raising it. The times were ripe. By the later 'seventies a combination of growing demand and technological change had given an enormous impetus to the already developing cotton textile industry. The traditional spinning and weaving districts of South Lancashire, and particularly the lower slopes of the Pennines where water power was available, became the scene of unprecedented business opportunity. Living in the heart of this industrial gold rush, Richard Pilkington would have been foolish had he not turned his business knowledge and capital to advantage and gone prospecting.

He appears to have started by making a small and safe investment in land. In January, 1778, he bought for £60 his brother-in-law's third share in a lease for lives of a 57-acre estate.[18] From this humble beginning he proceeded to venture farther into the land market until, by the time he came to make his will in September, 1797, he possessed three separate estates in and around Horwich.[19] Some of this land was soon put to industrial as well as to agricultural use. In 1781 he paid £35 to Thomas Nightingale of Horwich, a weaver, for a 99 years lease of a two-acre meadow.[20] Three years later, he had erected buildings on this land and spent upwards of £20 in installing a carding engine, a machine then coming rapidly into use as the basis of many of the rudimentary early cotton factories making cotton twist.[21] Nightingale then sold to him all the land and buildings on condition that they each held an equal share in the upper room of the building 'for the purpose of working the . . . engine therein'.[22]

Richard Pilkington now went a stage further and took up bleaching, a particularly lucrative branch of the industry for which the hilly slopes which lay within the shelter of Rivington Pike were well suited. At the beginning of 1784 the excise duty was removed from all soap and starch used for cotton finishing: the existence of a copy of the Act among his papers[23] suggests that this official inducement may have been responsible, at least in part, for Richard Pilkington's *début* as a bleacher. On June 14, 1785, he recorded in his diary that he was laying the foundation of a buckhouse[24] and for the next eighteen months he turned all his carpentering skill to building and equipping this buckhouse, together with what he called the dry house and cloth room. In December, 1785, the millwrights fixed a water-wheel and on January 16, 1786, he recorded that he 'Began to Bouck in Clough'. By the following May the slaters were at work on the cloth room, early in June the cloth press and smoothing frame were finished, and in October the dry house was built.

But this process of bleaching, which involved repeated bucking and crofting, took many months. It was about to be replaced by Berthollet's much more rapid method, employing chlorine, which reduced the time to a day or two. At first the chlorine gas was absorbed in water containing potash and sold to bleachers in liquid form. This *Eau de Javel*, as it was called, was first in use in the Manchester area in 1788.[25] Richard Pilkington started to buy it not long afterwards. On November 15, 1790, he recorded in his diary: 'At Bolton, bought a Bottle of Chimical Licquor'; and on April 23rd: 'We began to make Chimical Licquor'. At the beginning of 1792 he hired a man, part of whose duties were 'to make Chimical'. By 1793 he must have been making *Eau de Javel* on some scale, for in October of that year five casks of pulverized manganese were sent to him from Liverpool.[26] In April of the following year he was 'fixing to make Chimical a New way', possibly a reference to an early attempt to absorb the chlorine in slaked lime to make bleaching powder, a process which, we know, was being tentatively tried out in the district about that time.[27]

The replacement of a slow and tedious, but nevertheless simple, process which found employment for many bleachers, by a more complicated one requiring more expensive equipment and technical knowledge, tipped the scales against the small man and led to the rise of a few large firms. Richard Pilkington obviously tried to march with the times by using the 'chimical licquor'. But in 1794 he was embroiled in a land dispute with his brother-in-law, Ralph Pendlebury,[28] and in the following year he had the misfortune to be involved in the bankruptcy of his son, James, who in 1793 had become a partner in a firm of fustian manufacturers at Bolton which failed.[29] Although we lack the details, Richard Pilkington appears to have been hard hit.

On February 25, 1796, he agreed with Messrs Ridgway and Son, bleachers, to sell 'all the Buildings, Dams, Pits and Utensils used in the Bleaching Business' at Stock's Farm for £300 and to receive in exchange the 99 years lease of 'a piece of ground known by the name of the Millhole' (part of the property he sold).[30] Three months later he was pressing the Ridgways for payment. He recorded in his diary on June 1st: 'At Mr Ridgways to demand our Money. Got none'. The following day, however, he got the draft for his £300 'and borrowed £200 from Rathbone in Bolton'. On June 3rd he used some of this money to pay off the mortgage on his son's bankrupt business.

The sale of the bleaching concern at Stock's Farm was, apparently, not sufficient to set the family clear of their financial difficulties. On March 19th, less than a month after his agreement with the Ridgways, Richard Pilkington went to Bolton to see his solicitor about selling the Liverpool estates and on June 24th he paid a second visit to look over the terms of the sale.[31] Nor was that all. On May 6th he recorded: 'An auction sale at our House of our Horses, Carts and some House goods'; on the 27th: 'Began to remove our Household Goods to Chapple House'; and on the 28th: 'Carting Goods to Chapple House. Slept there last Night, first time'.

At first sight this removal and the sale at Liverpool suggests that the family's industrial ventures in Horwich and Bolton had landed them in desperate straits indeed. But from the whole confused situation there are indications that their predicament was not so serious as a quick glance would suggest. The sales at Stock's Farm were as much the result of the Ridgways' influence in controlling the local land market as a sign of the Pilkingtons' failure to become successful bleachers. Thomas Ridgway, in addition to being a bleacher, was agent for Henry Blundell of Ince Blundell who owned most of Horwich at that time. Ridgway had already used this key appointment to obtain the lease of three estates, including the White House; when the lease of Stock's, nearby, expired in 1796, he arranged for it to be taken by his own family and not renewed by the existing tenant. Richard Pilkington, therefore, had to find accommodation elsewhere. He removed to New Chapel Farm.

That he could raise £680 to purchase this farm,[32] despite his other embarrassments, makes it clear that, though passing through difficult times, he was by no means facing any privation. This is brought out by his will, made on September 5, 1797, less than a month before he died. It is true that this was sworn at under £1,000, considerably less than that of his father, who left a personal estate of something under £2,600.[33] But whereas his father's landed property was confined entirely to the Liverpool estates, he himself was able to bequeath three farms at Horwich upon one of which, Knowles's, stood 'erections and buildings' for bleaching which had been put up since the farm was purchased.[34] Moreover, Allerton had still to be sold. The purchase money was to be held in trust for his son William and his three daughters; each of them was to receive £1,000 and the residue was to be deemed part of the personal estate. All this does not suggest a man in any real financial difficulties. Nevertheless, there can be no doubt that his bleaching business came to a sorry end and was ultimately a source of impoverishment rather than of gain. Richard Pilkington died on October 1, 1797,[35] a failure so far as his business pursuits were concerned.

No more is heard of the Pilkingtons venturing into industry at Horwich. Richard Pilkington's eldest son, Richard, who had certainly joined his father in the bleaching concern,[36] confined his attention to farming.[37] It was left to another member of the family to achieve success in the industrial field.

Richard Pilkington's second son, William, embarked upon a career which carried him away from the family home and away from cotton. He was to become a doctor at St Helens.

Medicine at that time was a rather crude, cruel and casual profession. Although the eighteenth century saw considerable advances in medical knowledge—in anatomy and in practical methods of nursing and hygiene, for example—doctors, in general (surgeons as distinct from the few exclusive physicians), still relied upon trial and error, and patients suffered from their varying aptitudes for cutting, sawing and bleeding. Medical men did not really come into their own until the discovery of anaesthetics and the advent of antiseptic surgery. At the time we are considering, they were usually described as 'surgeons and apothecaries', the latter title covering the sale of herbs, pills, drugs and medicines. Port and other wines and spirits were also regularly prescribed to patients and, it would seem, their sale often formed an essential sideline. One Lancashire doctor, for instance, ordered as much as thirty-five gallons of port at a time, even though his practice was quite a small one.[38] 'It is abundantly clear from the literature of the period', writes the historian of the Surgeons' Company, 'that the ordinary surgeon could not make a living if he confined his activities to the treatment of external diseases and accidents. He was compelled to treat internal diseases, to keep a shop and to sell drugs and to practise midwifery though at the best his training had been in Anatomy and Surgery alone.'[39]

A doctor's training was realistic, if rudimentary. He was first apprenticed to a practising surgeon and apothecary, usually somewhere near his home, often to his own father. After serving for five or six years, he went to London to walk the hospitals for twelve months (for a fee of twenty-four guineas) or six months (for a fee of eighteen guineas) and to attend lectures, which cost up to ten guineas per course.[40] He was not usually allowed to perform any operation and was only permitted to observe and to ask questions of the surgeon in charge. He had to wait until he returned to the country again, armed with a certificate— not for competence but for attendance—before he could use the knife himself. In a cottage bedroom, perhaps, he sought to put into practice the knowledge he had gained months or perhaps years before, while watching a skilled surgeon operating in a London hospital.

How Richard Pilkington came to apprentice his son to Dr William Fildes at St Helens, we can only conjecture. As a regular traveller between Horwich and Liverpool to collect rents, he passed through St Helens after having taken the road through Wigan and over Billinge Hill. Since the opening of the Sankey Canal shortly before 1760, St Helens had become the bustling centre of a rapidly-developing coalmining district, and the largest plate glass works in the kingdom and two copper smelting plants had been opened there during the 'seventies. As he journeyed down from Billinge, through St Helens and along the turnpike road in the direction of Prescot and Liverpool, Richard Pilkington could hardly have failed to be impressed by the widespread signs of growth: the opening of factories, the sinking of pit shafts, the building of houses and the increase of population. St Helens was obviously a place with a future. And since the process of development was as yet only in an early stage, it was still possible to gain a secure footing at the outset and share in the growing prosperity.

We do not know when William Pilkington was apprenticed; possibly it was in 1779 when he reached the age of 14. He was certainly serving Dr Fildes in St Helens by August 3, 1781, for he received payment of a bill on behalf of his master on that date.[41] We hear nothing more of him until May 5, 1785, when Richard Pilkington recorded succinctly in his diary: 'Wigan Fare. Our William went to his master'. By this time his apprenticeship had been almost completely served and he was ready to walk the hospitals. On October 5, 1785, his father noted the receipt of a letter from him in London, where he had become a student at St George's. He attended lectures on anatomy given by Mr Cruickshank and Mr Baillie, and he was present during the spring of 1786 at the celebrated Dr Fordyce's course on the practice of physic. His passes into these lectures were not destroyed and have come down to us. On April 21st he received an attendance certificate, signed among others by the famous John Hunter, to prove that he had 'diligently attended the Practice of Surgery in this Hospital for these Six Months last past'. His training over, the young doctor, still only in his twenty-first year, returned to Lancashire.

It is not clear whether he returned to St Helens at once. An entry in his

CHART II
THE DESCENDANTS OF RICHARD PILKINGTON, 1694-1786

RICHARD PILKINGTON=ELIZABETH BROWNLOW
1694-1786

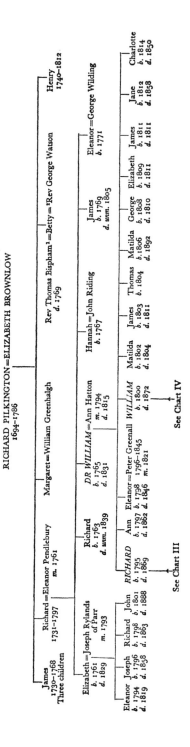

- James 1730-1768 Three children
- Richard=Eleanor Pendlebury 1731-1797 m. 1761
- Margaret=William Greenhalgh
- Rev Thomas Bispham¹=Betty¹=²Rev George Watson d. 1769
- Henry 1740-1812

Children of Richard=Eleanor Pendlebury:
- Elizabeth=Joseph Rylands of Parr b. 1761 d. 1829 m. 1793
- Richard b. 1763 d. unm. 1839
- DR WILLIAM=Ann Hatton b. 1765 d. 1831 m. 1794 d. 1815

Children of Rev Thomas Bispham / Betty:
- Hannah=John Riding b. 1767
- James b. 1769 d. unm. 1805
- Eleanor=George Wilding b. 1771

Children of Elizabeth=Joseph Rylands:
- Eleanor b. 1794 d. 1819
- Joseph b. 1796 d. 1858
- Richard b. 1798 d. 1863
- John b. 1801 d. 1888

Children of DR WILLIAM=Ann Hatton:
- RICHARD b. 1795 d. 1869 — See Chart III
- Ann b. 1797 d. 1862
- Eleanor=Peter Greenall b. 1798 d. 1846 1796-1845 m. 1821
- WILLIAM b. 1800 d. 1872 — See Chart IV

Children of Hannah=John Riding:
- Matilda b. 1802 d. 1804
- James b. 1803 d. 1811
- Thomas b. 1804
- Matilda b. 1806 d. 1892
- George b. 1808 d. 1810
- Elizabeth b. 1809 d. 1811
- James b. 1811 d. 1811

Children of Eleanor=George Wilding:
- Jane b. 1812 d. 1858
- Charlotte b. 1814 d. 1850

father's diary on August 25, 1786—'I have Pead upwards of £300 in cash for our Wm'—may refer to the cost of his training rather than to that of setting him up in practice. Later entries in the diary, telling of his collecting the debts on April 6, 1787—the context making it clear that they were family debts in the Horwich area—and giving medical attention to his brother, Richard, on April 30, 1787, suggest that he may not even then have removed to St Helens. The first definite evidence of his presence there after the completion of his training is found in the records of the St Helens Independent Chapel. In March, 1788, he and John Walker gave six guineas, the largest single donation, towards a relief fund.[42] Twelve months later, Dr Pilkington, then in partnership with Walker, occupied the house in Chapel Lane where Dr Fildes had previously lived.[43] His former master having died, Pilkington and Walker had taken over the practice.

On January 4, 1789, Richard Pilkington made the first of a series of visits to St Helens to see his son. At first he put up at the Raven Inn; later he stayed at his son's house. It was a difficult time in which to set up in practice and the bills owing to the young doctor remained long unpaid. On May 30, 1790, he wrote to his father complaining that money was 'verrey scarce'. Although he had sent John Walker on a tour of his debtors, he still required financial help. He added, as a postscript, that he was trying to economize at home:

'I have given sally notis and she is willing to go when the year is up which will be towards the end of next month. I shall drop a few lines when one of my sisters is to come.'[44]

It was his eldest sister, Elizabeth, who went to keep house for 'brother doctor', as he was called. Like her brother, she moved chiefly in Nonconformist circles, becoming friendly with the minister and congregation of the Independent Chapel. In this way she got to know Joseph Rylands, a weaver who lived at Parr Flat, a small hamlet a little to the east of St Helens. In due course he proposed marriage to her and was accepted. They were married at the end of September, 1793. On his next visit to St Helens, Richard Pilkington stayed with his new son-in-law and gave him £100, part of Elizabeth's marriage dowry.[45] Joseph and Elizabeth Rylands had a number of children. Their third son, John, born in 1801, was to become one of the most famous textile manufacturers in the kingdom.

In 1794 Dr Pilkington married Ann Hatton, who bore him thirteen children between 1795 and 1814. Their names appear at regular intervals in the baptism registers at the Independent Chapel. Richard, the first child, was born on August 20, 1795. After two daughters, Ann (baptised on January 29, 1797) and Eleanor (born May 11, 1798), came their second son William, born on May 14, 1800, their third, James, born on April 24, 1803, and their fourth, Thomas, born November 24, 1804. As may be seen from the accompanying pedigree, the others arrived at intervals until 1814. Although five of these children died in infancy, eight survived to bring up families of their own.

While the Pilkingtons at St Helens were rapidly increasing in numbers, the family at Horwich was dying out. James Pilkington, Dr William's younger brother, after his bankruptcy had joined the Royal Artillery and was, for a time, lodged in Maidstone gaol for debt.[46] He died in 1805, unmarried. Richard, the older brother and head of the family, lived to the good age of 76 but also died a bachelor. Thus by the early years of the nineteenth century the vital centre of the family had shifted from the Pilkingtons' traditional home in south-east Lancashire to the rising town of St Helens.

Like surgeons elsewhere, Dr William Pilkington was also an apothecary. He kept a shop. Perhaps he inherited it from his predecessor, Dr Fildes. He was soon dealing in wines and spirits. On Christmas Day, 1789, his father received a cask of rum from St Helens and, on the following May 6th, recorded the safe arrival of 'Licquors from St Hellin'. No doubt when John Walker was sent out to collect the debts, he called upon hale and hearty wine and spirit drinkers as well as upon the sick and ailing who had received professional attention.

In 1813 the rising turnover of the shop and, perhaps, the threat of a host of medical men returning from the wars then obviously drawing to a close, caused Dr Pilkington to decide to retire from his medical practice and to concentrate his attention on the wine and spirit business.[47] His elder sons were growing up and he would soon be able to count on their help. Richard, the eldest boy, had been apprenticed on April 28, 1810, to William Ewart and William Taylor, merchants and brokers in Liverpool, and the second son, William, was to follow his brother to Liverpool in September, 1815, and to serve his time at the distillery of Robert Preston.[48] Richard completed his apprenticeship on April 29, 1817, and in the following July became a partner in his father's business. William only served five of the seven years of his apprenticeship. In May, 1820, he, too, became a partner in what was thereafter known as William Pilkington and Sons.[49]

William Pilkington, junior, was a man of outstanding ability, a person who succeeded wherever he chose to apply himself. He was a gifted leader who, aided by a remarkable breadth of vision and a practical turn of mind, was able to dominate events. He is the hero of our story. As it unfolds, we shall have occasion to quote from several of the letters which he wrote. They are all masterpieces of clear thinking and forthrightness, tactfully expressed. They reflect a most powerful personality.

The earliest of these letters which still survives was written on December 15, 1827, to his uncle Richard at Horwich, and concerned the management of two farms there which had passed to the St Helens branch of the family at Richard Pilkington's death in 1797. The introduction is a model of polite firmness:

'I hope you will excuse the liberty I have again taken in addressing you upon the old subject but when you consider the situation in which we are at present with our affairs in Horwich and our wish to manage in future without an agent, you will perceive the necessity of a little exertion on our parts to improve the system and I hope that you will be induced to overlook for the present this further piece of trouble which you may think we are imposing upon you.'

Having adroitly cleared the decks, he then went into action, detailing the particular changes which he intended to carry out.[50]

It is significant that William and not his elder brother, Richard, wrote on behalf of the St Helens branch of the family. It is an indication that his business talents were already being recognized by the other members of the family. Indeed, two years earlier, in December, 1825, he had acted as family spokesman when he addressed a petition to the Commissioners of Excise on behalf of William Pilkington and Sons.[51] This petition shows that the wine and spirit business was benefiting very considerably at that time from a reduction in the duties.

In May, 1823, a Parliamentary committee had reported in favour of adopting a uniform method and rate of taxing spirits throughout the United Kingdom. For English distillers, this entailed a considerable reduction in the duty payable.[52] Two years elapsed before the necessary legislation was introduced. It provided for the halving of the English spirit duty from January 5, 1826.[53]

All these proposals for and rumours about the cheapening of the price of spirits, culminating in the Act of 1825, encouraged wine and spirit merchants to prepare to extend the scale of their operations. William Pilkington and Sons decided that the increase in demand would make it worth their while to embark upon the distillation of spirits, to manufacture what they sold; or, more exactly, to embark upon the final stages of the distillation process, rectifying and compounding.[54] Plant which they installed in buildings near the junction of Bridge Street and Church Street[55] came into use for the first time on October 28, 1823. Two years later they removed the stills and other apparatus to a site behind their premises in Church Street where the business could be more conveniently conducted.[56] By December, 1825, their orders, wrote William Pilkington, were already 'very considerable and likely to be still greater in consequence of the intended reduction of the duties.'

By the middle of the 1820s, therefore, the Pilkington family had again become manufacturers on some scale and an outstanding man of business was in control. The prospects for the wine and spirit concern seemed to be very bright indeed and there was every indication that the Pilkington brothers, Richard and William, would concentrate their energies upon extending this market, to the exclusion of all other interests. But, early in 1826, William Pilkington was prevailed upon to become one of the members of a partnership which had just been formed to manufacture window glass at St Helens. At first, it would seem, he looked upon the venture solely as a useful outlet for part of his share in the now considerable profits of William Pilkington and Sons. Two of the other partners in the new firm were glassmakers and a third had agreed to supervise the business side. There seemed to be no reason for William Pilkington to become involved in active management. To be a sleeping partner, however, was wholly alien to his character; and, as the fortunes of the recently-opened glassworks took a turn for the worse, he was called in to inject new life into their management. But before we can understand the problems which then confronted him, a complete stranger to glass manufacture, we must trace the growth of this branch of the glass industry in order to appreciate its structure, organization and possibilities at the time when he entered it.

1 Stock's Farm,
Horwich, leased
by Dr Pilkington's
father in 1761

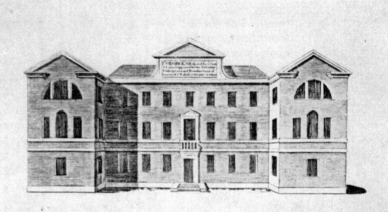

THESE are to *certify*, that Mr. *Wm Pilkington*

hath diligently attended the Practice of SURGERY in this *Hospital* for these *Six Months* last past. *Witness* our Hands the 21

Day of *April* 1786. *Manning*
John Hunter
C Hawkins
Wm Walker

Dr Pilkington's
attendance
certificate from
St George's Hospital,
London, 1786

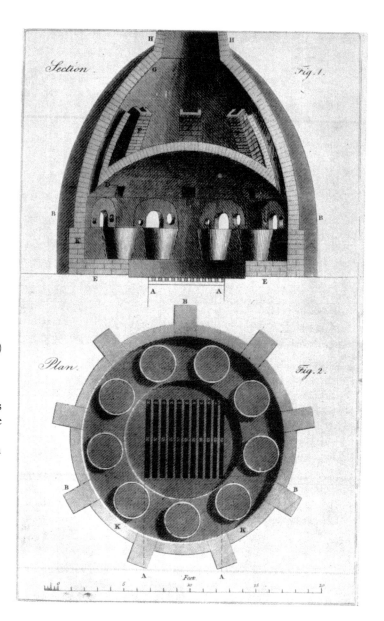

2 A coal-fired glass
furnace.
Fresh air was fed
to the grate (A–A)
from outside the
glasshouse *via* an
underground
tunnel. The flames
from the fire made
upon the grate
reverberated down
from the dome
(D–D).
(From *Pantalogia,
A New Cyclopaedia*,
1813)

Casting Plate Glass
at Ravenhead.
(From *An Illustrated
Itinerary of the County
of Lancaster*, 1842)

CHAPTER 2

THE HISTORICAL BACKGROUND
TO THE FLAT GLASS INDUSTRY IN BRITAIN

'The chief circumstance which seems to determine the seats of the glass manufacture is the neighbourhood of coal, of which very large quantities are necessary, but the facilities for obtaining other
materials, such as sand . . . have also in some cases had an important influence.'
—From a Parliamentary Report of 1865

B EFORE the coming of canals and railways made it easier to transport fuel
—it has been said that to carry coal overland for ten miles usually doubled
or trebled its price[1]—furnace industries had to be sited either in the midst
of, or with easy access to, forests or coalfields. It paid the glassmaker to build his
furnace where fuel was cheap and then to transport to it the smaller weights of
sand, alkali, clay and other materials he required. In the early days when
people were not particularly troubled if their window glass was somewhat discoloured, the level of impurity of all these materials did not matter much. Local
supplies could be used. Sand from a brook or river was good enough for the
Wealden glassmakers, wood and bracken yielded satisfactory alkali and the
pots were made from local clay.[2] Later, when brilliant, colourless glass was demanded and sand with a much lower iron oxide content had to be sought,
glassmakers still found it paid to carry their sand to their coal, even though
long distances were sometimes involved. When the works at Ravenhead near
St Helens were opened in the later eighteenth century, for instance, white sand
was brought all round the coast from Lynn in Norfolk.[3] This sand was also being
used at that time by Newcastle glassmakers.[4]

Clearly, the transition from wood to coal, as the fuel employed to stoke the
glass furnaces, was a development of crucial importance so far as the siting of
the industry was concerned. During the reign of Queen Elizabeth I, increasing
demands were made upon the country's supplies of wood, particularly by the
iron smelters who were rapidly extending the scale of their operations. Fuel
prices rose and by 1581 they were declared to have grown 'very great and
unreasonable'.[5] This trend of events caused the owners of furnaces to look for
an alternative fuel. They began to investigate the possibility of firing with coal,
which could be obtained cheaply in coalmining areas and in those parts of the

C   33

country which had good communication by water with those areas.[6] Since the requirements of the iron smelters were far greater than those of the early glass-makers, research upon coal as a fuel was chiefly concerned with devising a means of smelting iron. By the early seventeenth century attempts were made to separate the coal, with all its impurities, from the iron ore by using the rever-beratory principle of furnace design. In this type of furnace the fuel and the ore are kept quite apart, the flames being made to strike back from the arched roof of the furnace upon the materials to be smelted.[7] These early experiments failed so far as iron was concerned;[8] but the reverberatory furnace that was developed on the Dudley estate[9] was found to meet the glassmaker's needs. Using certain types of coal, and placing a cover over his pots, he could melt his materials without filling the molten glass with impurities. He was not slow to apply with at least a measure of success the principle which the iron smelter had been un-able to use. By the early months of 1612 'green glass for windows'—no doubt an apt description—was being imperfectly made at a coal-fired furnace in South-wark.[10]

In its ultimate form the new furnace and glasshouse design differed in several respects from its predecessors.[11] A long, underground tunnel fed fresh air from outside the glasshouse to the grate in the centre of the furnace. As may be seen from the diagram facing page 33, the furnace itself was built around this central grate in the shape of an inverted funnel. Half-way down the neck of the funnel was built a curved dome (or crown), which reflected the flame from the fire down again on to the pots which were ranged round the waist of the furnace on a circular course of brickwork. The pots were often covered (or caped) as a protection against soot, smoke and black drops which fell from the crown. The smoke and hot air escaped *via* flues close to the outer wall and through the chim-ney at the top. A furnace of this type could be erected in the centre of a square building with its chimney piercing the roof. In the case of British window glass manufacture, however, it was more usual to construct the outer building of the same shape as the furnace itself, allowing the glassmaker just enough room be-tween the furnace and the wall to blow and manoeuvre his cylinders or tables. To what extent the pioneers were themselves able to develop the cone-shaped glasshouse which later became the most outstanding physical feature of the industry, is open to debate. It was certainly in use by 1700.[12]

But any uncertainty about the details of design ought not to be allowed to detract from the fundamental importance of the innovation itself. Although a group of men who held an earlier furnace patent (but not the group who were eventually credited with having produced a working model) agreed that they had gained some assistance from the results of unsuccessful experiments which had been conducted in France,[13] the new furnace seems to have been a wholly English development. At all events, the glass produced from coal-fired furnaces was a matter which a French visitor saw fit to comment upon in 1738, and the glasshouse *à l'anglaise* was only used in bottleworks across the Channel half a century later. So late as 1784 a Frenchman claimed to have discovered what he called the 'secret' of the English furnace, no *faithful* copy being at that date in operation in France.[14]

Although the English appear to have possessed a distinct advantage in furnace design, they still relied for the greater part on skilled, foreign craftsmen to work the molten glass—or metal, as it was called—which their furnaces heated. In the early seventeenth century when coal-fired furnaces were introduced, foreign names loomed very large among the makers of window glass. The Bungards, a Norman family, who seem to have been the most influential men in this branch of the trade,[15] asserted that they had come to England about 1550 'when the Art of Window glass making was lost in this kingdom',[16] a claim which was almost certainly exaggerated.[17] The more famous Lorraine gentlemen glassmakers, the Henseys, Tytterys and Tyzacks came over in the middle of the 1560s.[18] As a consequence of the French wars of religion, exports of glass were interrupted and additional glasshouses were required in England to make good the shortage.[19] At the same time, increased taxes and irksome restrictions inside Lorraine,[20] and the promise of high wages from England, induced the continental glassmakers to cross the Channel. They erected their furnaces chiefly in the thickly-wooded lands of the Weald which had long been the scene of glassmaking on a small scale.[21] This invasion of foreign workmen aroused the hostility of the English and the depredations in their native woodlands served as a popular battle-cry against the newcomers.[22] It was an unfair line of attack: the glassmakers only used the branches of trees, which grew again,[23] and their glasshouses were very few in number compared with the host of ironworks which were responsible for the bulk of the damage. In 1589 there were said to be only fourteen or fifteen glass furnaces of all kinds in the whole of England[24] and a little later only eight were making broad or spread glass, a crude form of cylinder glass then in general use for window panes.[25] Nevertheless the foreign glassmakers seem to have been elbowed out of their early centre of operations in the vicinity of Guildford. We find them at Buckholt, near Salisbury and on the North Staffordshire–Shropshire border in the middle of the 1580s.[26] At the end of the century they had also reached the Nailsworth district and the Forest of Dean.[27] Here they continued to blow glass at their little furnaces fired with wood, an extraordinary and rather nomadic race of people.

With the appearance of the new furnace, employing a cheaper and more plentiful kind of fuel, the days of wood firing were numbered. The end came more swiftly than even the most pessimistic would have ventured to forecast. On May 23, 1615, King James I passed the death sentence on furnaces using wood. Anxious, as he pointed out, to preserve the forests, he decreed that in future glass was to be made in coal-fired furnaces alone.[28] The control of the furnace was already in the hands of those who held Letters Patent for its use.[29]

By the royal proclamation of 1615, the patentees were given monopolistic control not only of the furnaces but of the industry as well.

The history of glassmaking in England between 1615 and the outbreak of the Civil War is dominated by one man: Sir Robert Mansfield or, as he came to be known, Sir Robert Mansell.[30] One of the furnace patentees, he soon bought out the other partners and thus gained absolute authority over the entire glass industry of the country. He was a courtier and a sailor, holding after 1618 the office of Vice-Admiral of England. He had no previous knowledge of glassmaking. Indeed, his venture into the industry surprised the King who characteristically observed that it was unusual for one who had gained such a reputation for prowess at sea to tamper with fire, since fire and water were two contrary elements.[31] But, despite Mansell's frequent absences on naval service prior to 1621, he took his new responsibility very seriously. The glass made at the furnace in Southwark in 1612 had been 'uneven and full of spots';[32] obviously much had to be done before glassmaking by the new method was perfected and Mansell spent upwards of £30,000 before he was able to obtain consistently satisfactory results from coal-firing.[33] Under his direction the manufacture of window glass was eventually settled in a part of the country which was to remain the chief centre of production for nearly 250 years.

At first his works were situated in London where he used Scottish coal brought down the coast by sea. This was relatively free from sulphur and therefore less liable to discolour the glass. As a contemporary put it, Scottish coal was 'the best flamer and consumeth away into white ashes, as having in it more unctiousnesse than sulpharousnesse'.[34] But it was extremely expensive and Mansell was, therefore, obliged to seek sites for his furnaces elsewhere in order to have access to other sources of coal.[35] He first tried the Isle of Purbeck in Dorset, but 'the coal proved altogether unuseful', so he erected furnaces at Milford Haven in Pembrokeshire some distance to the west of the Mansell estates at Margam. There he enjoyed no greater success; the coal did not prove serviceable nor was 'the transportation of glass possible to be had'. Next he moved to a site near the Trent but manufacture in Nottinghamshire was no more economic than it had been elsewhere.[36] Finally, 'for his last refuge, contrary to all mens opinions', he set up furnaces at Newcastle-upon-Tyne at a cost of some £2,000.[37] Here, at last, he succeeded.

The Northumberland and Durham coalfield was the first of the English coalfields to be intensively exploited. It was very advantageously situated, for the rich measures extended to the coast and the coal could be easily removed by sea. Shipments from Newcastle to London (the chief market in Britain), as well as to the continent and elsewhere, grew at an unprecedented rate, from some 35,000 tons a year in the 1560s to 400,000 tons in 1625.[38] Nowhere in the country could coal be had in such abundance or perhaps so cheaply as at New-castle when Mansell came to site his window glass furnaces there about 1618.[39] Of his sources of sand and alkali for these works, we know little beyond the fact that 'ashes and materials for glass' were shipped from London.[40] We do know, however, that clay was the only requirement which he had difficulty in obtaining. At first he had to bring it 'at an infinite charge' from Stourbridge and, later, from the continent. Eventually he found suitable deposits in North-umberland.[41]

This, then, was the genesis of the glass industry in the north-east, which soon became the great centre for the manufacture of English window glass. By 1624, between three and four thousand cases of glass were reaching London from Newcastle ever year.[42] When the Scots invaded the north in 1640 and seized the Newcastle glasshouses, three furnaces were at work and 1,200 cases of glass waited to be shipped.[43] After the Long Parliament put an end to Mansell's monopoly,[44] others thought it worth while to venture into the trade. In the middle of the 1640s, for instance, Edmund Harris, a London merchant, erected two new glasshouses on the Tyne at Newcastle not far from the Ouseburn, where Mansell's furnaces still stood.[45] 'On the North side of the River', wrote William Gray in 1649, 'is Ewes Burne, over which is a wood Bridge, which goeth down to a place called the Glass-Houses, where plaine Glasse for win-dowes are made, which serveth most parts of the Kingdom'.[46] From this original nucleus, the industry spread out along Tyneside. Glass was being made at South Shields by 1650;[47] outside the Close Gate, to the west of Newcastle, by 1684,[48] and at Howden Pans by 1698.[49] In the latter part of the century Stour-bridge achieved some prominence for its window glass, but that branch of the industry did not take such firm root there.[50] In 1736 Newcastle still continued to provide the glass that was 'most in use in England.'[51]

Early in the eighteenth century, the Cooksons, a Penrith family, first became associated with glassmaking on the Tyne. When Isaac Cookson died in 1743, he was stated to be 'one of the most considerable Glass Manufacturers in those parts'.[52] A hundred years later Isaac Cookson and Company, who owned ex-tensive works both at South Shields and in Newcastle, paid £61,500 a year in excise duty, a greater amount than was paid by any other firm and just under one-tenth of the total sum paid for all the glasshouses in England. By that time, the glassmakers of the north-east contributed £204,000 in duty to the Exchequer annually, about twice as much as any other district in the country.[53] Although these excise returns can be misleading—the different branches of the industry paid different rates of duty—nevertheless they serve our purpose if we use them as a rough guide. There is certainly justification for the claim, made by the glass-makers of the Tyne and Wear in 1833, that they manufactured more window glass than all the other houses in Britain put together.[54] But by that time they were facing a serious challenge: manufacturers elsewhere were rapidly gaining upon them. Of particular significance was the remarkable growth of the industry in south-west Lancashire.

Although Newcastle was well placed for the operation of coal-fired furnaces, it was by no means the ideal centre for distributing fragile finished wares throughout the country. Lying close to the north-eastern corner of England, the Tyne was easily reached by collier from London or from anywhere along the east coast. Some of these vessels even plied round the coasts of Kent, to Sussex and beyond. They therefore provided a regular means of conveying glass to those parts of England which lay within easy reach of the North Sea or the English Channel. But the western half of England and the Midlands lay beyond the area that could be easily supplied. To meet the needs of what he called these 'most remote places of the kingdom from London', Mansell erected nine other furnaces to manufacture window glass 'for the ease of the subjects' charge in carriage and avoiding hazard of breaking and to the end that all the subjects might be served alike.'[55]

The north-west of England, the part of the country farthest removed by sea from Newcastle, was certainly a region which was likely to require at least one of these auxiliary furnaces to supply the local demand. Glassmaking was no new industry in that part of the country. It had been carried on at Wilderspool in Roman times[56] and in Delamere Forest in the Middle Ages.[57] Various references to glaziers and glassmen seem to indicate that there was quite a brisk trade in glass in the north-west immediately prior to the Proclamation of 1615.[58] But unfortunately these are indefinite terms which may refer to those who were actually engaged in the manufacture of glass or, as seems more likely, only to dealers in glassware. We have, however, one example of the term glassman almost certainly used to mean glassmaker. It occurs among entries in the Ormskirk Parish Register[59] on December 10, 1600:

'A stranger slayne by one of the glassmen beinge A Frenchman then workinge at Bycarstaff.'

This is the only furnace fired by wood which we can identify with any degree of certainty in Lancashire. There may have been others.[60] Indeed, it is highly probable that there were others at that time.

The Stockport Parish Registers include a series of entries relating to glass-makers, beginning in January, 1615/6.[61] These men worked at a furnace at Houghton, just inside the Lancashire border, the site of which is still remembered by the name Glasshouse Fold.[62] From the date at which the Parish Register entries start, this was almost certainly one of Mansell's nine auxiliary works.

At first glance, with later history in mind, it may seem strange that this early coal-fired furnace was not sited in south-west Lancashire, where vast quantities of sand were available as well as coal. The Shirdley Hill sand, a deposit some ten feet thick which is to be found a little below the surface over a considerable area to the north of present-day St Helens, is admirably suited for glassmaking on account of its low iron oxide content. Indeed, it is one of the very few places in the whole country where such high grade sand and coal occur together.[63] Why, then, was the south-eastern corner of the county preferred, which lacked this considerable advantage?

The answer seems to be twofold. As we have noticed, the early glassmakers were not very particular about the quality of their product—and they had a virtual monopoly in the area which they supplied. They could therefore use any sand, no matter how discoloured it made the glass. Provided they could find deposits of sand in sufficient quantity, close to their source of fuel, they seem to have been quite satisfied. No doubt the sand of the Stockport neighbourhood was good enough for their rough and ready purposes.

Secondly, with transport charges so high, geographical location was immensely important. It was essential to site glasshouses at places where as many glaziers as possible could be supplied. A furnace at Stockport lay in the heart of a relatively highly-populated district. South-west Lancashire, on the other hand, was not yet the busy centre of commercial activity that it was later to become. Liverpool was little more than a small fishing port enjoying a limited trade with Ireland and with a sparsely-populated hinterland. There was no great demand for glass thereabouts nor any export trade to justify the erection of an auxiliary furnace in that part of the county. It was not until the first half of the eighteenth century, when Liverpool rose to rival, and later to surpass, Bristol as the leading port on the English west coast, that we hear much about glassmaking on or near Merseyside.

The industry grew with the market. This was partly a local market: as more houses, factories, warehouses, shops and buildings of all kinds were built, more window glass was required. Much of the glass, however, was loaded on ships at Liverpool to be carried away, some round the coast, some over the sea. By 1770, more than 250 tons of glass of all kinds were being shipped oversea from the port per annum.[64] Almost half a century later, in 1812, one manufacturer of window and flint glass (that is, tableware and the like) was sending more than two-thirds of his output to America.[65] There is no reason to believe that other proprietors of glassworks in the vicinity of Merseyside were any less fortunate in securing orders from the United States which only possessed three or four window glass factories in 1800 and did not begin to develop this branch of the industry until after 1812.[66]

The rise of the glass industry in south-west Lancashire occurred, therefore, at roughly the same time as the development of Liverpool itself. Two glasshouses are mentioned in Houghton's list of 1696, one described as 'near Lever-

39

pool' and the other at Warrington.[67] The first glasshouse in Liverpool itself dates from 1721, or just before that, and a second was in operation by 1729. There was a marked increase in the amount of glassmaking activity at the port from about 1750.[68] If the Warrington glasshouse of 1696 was situated within the limits of Warrington parish, it does not appear to have survived far into the eighteenth century. There are no references to active glassmakers in the Warrington parish registers from 1720, when occupations start to be given, until 1758 when the firm of Peter Seaman and Company had just been formed to manufacture bottles and flint glass in the town.[69] During the first half of the eighteenth century glass was also blown near Ormskirk[70] and at Prescot and Thatto Heath.

The two last-mentioned glasshouses are of particular interest to us because of their situation near the south-western limits of the coalfield: they were the forerunners of the glassworks at St Helens. The distinctive cone of the Prescot glasshouse, the property of Thomas Cobham, is clearly to be seen in an old print dated 1743. It lay to the west of the town, half way down the hill, just off the road to Liverpool.[71] Window glass was made there: some of the panes were described as 'the best of that sort in England' when they were sold in London in 1734.[72] The glasshouse was said to be new in 1719[73] and appears to have had a life of about thirty years. Dr Richard Pococke, who visited Prescot in 1751, recorded in his diary that it had been purchased by a competing house at Stourbridge 'in order to shut it up'.[74]

The bottleworks at Thatto Heath, between Prescot and St Helens, outlived its Prescot contemporary by about a hundred years. The origins of glassmaking in and about Thatto Heath are obscure, though we have a clear and apparently reliable statement which fixed within a year or so the date at which the bottleworks were opened. According to this statement, which was made at the time of a poor law case in 1745, John Hensey, a working partner with his two brothers in the glass concern at Prescot, removed from there and 'built Thattow Heath Glasshouse' about the year 1721.[75] This tallies with a note in Nicholas Blundell's diary that on July 22, 1721, he bought some bottles from Thatto Heath.[76] But we also have evidence of earlier glassmaking activity in the district. The bottleworks were situated on the southern side of the brook which crossed the Heath and were, therefore, in Sutton township. We have the testimony of the Leaf family, who claim to have established the glasshouse near Warrington about 1650, that they later owned glassworks in Sutton.[77] John Leaf is first mentioned in the Sutton Township Book[78] in 1696, and he served a township office for the first time in 1701. John Leaf, junior, described as a glassmaker of Sutton, is mentioned in a marriage bond in 1705[79] and John Leaf, senior, also described as a glassmaker of Sutton, died there in 1713.[80] Although the evidence is far from conclusive, there would seem to be a strong indication that this glasshouse of the Leafs' in Sutton was, in fact, the one referred to in

Houghton's list of 1696 as making flint, green and ordinary glass 'near Lever-pool'.

It was probably situated, like Hensey's later works, in the immediate vicinity of Thatto Heath.[81] From the point of view of raw materials, such a situation was ideal for glassmaking. Not only were coal, sand and clay[82] readily available, but rock salt, an ingredient of the bottlemaker's batch, could also be obtained without difficulty.[83] At the close of the seventeenth century coal was being taken in increasing quantity from the south-western fringe of the Lancashire coalfield to feed the furnaces at the Cheshire saltworks. It would not have been difficult to return with a load of rock salt. This was, indeed, the beginning of the coal and salt connection which eventually gave rise to the Merseyside chemical industry of which glassmaking became an integral part.[84]

Although sites close to the collieries and within easy reach of the precious deposits of Shirdley Hill sand were obviously more suitable for glassmaking than those at Liverpool or Warrington, the lack of good communication between the coalfield and the Mersey prevented the manufacturer from making the most of these natural advantages. It was not until the opening of the Sankey Canal—a Liverpool creation—in the later 1750s that the great barrier to the expansion of the industry in St Helens was broken down. Direct communication by water with the coalfield induced a group of wealthy and influential gentlemen to build on the higher ground at Ravenhead, overlooking Thatto Heath, the largest glassworks in the country. These works are of particular interest to our story, for they were later acquired by Pilkingtons.

The Ravenhead works were built for the purpose of manufacturing plate glass. This was a type of glass which was made thicker than ordinary window panes so that it could bear grinding, using sand, and polishing, using rouge, by which means an even, lustrous finish was imparted. While window glass was coming more and more into general use during the seventeenth and eighteenth centuries, plate glass remained a luxury product and as in the case of all luxury products in England, London was its chief market. Although some plate glass was used for the windows of coaches where thicker panes were required, most of it was silvered and made into mirrors. Indeed, its name seems to have been derived from the old description for mirrors: looking glass plates. It was under that name that Mansell introduced this branch of the manufacture into England shortly before 1621, finding employment for upwards of 500 people.[85]

Only the purest ingredients—the best soda and lime, and thoroughly washed white sand—went into the manufacture of this kind of glass, and the whole batch was very carefully prepared and calcined (fritted) before being placed into the melting pots. Being thick glass, any discolouration was very noticeable. Any spots in the glass itself or unevenness of the surface meant that these glasses,

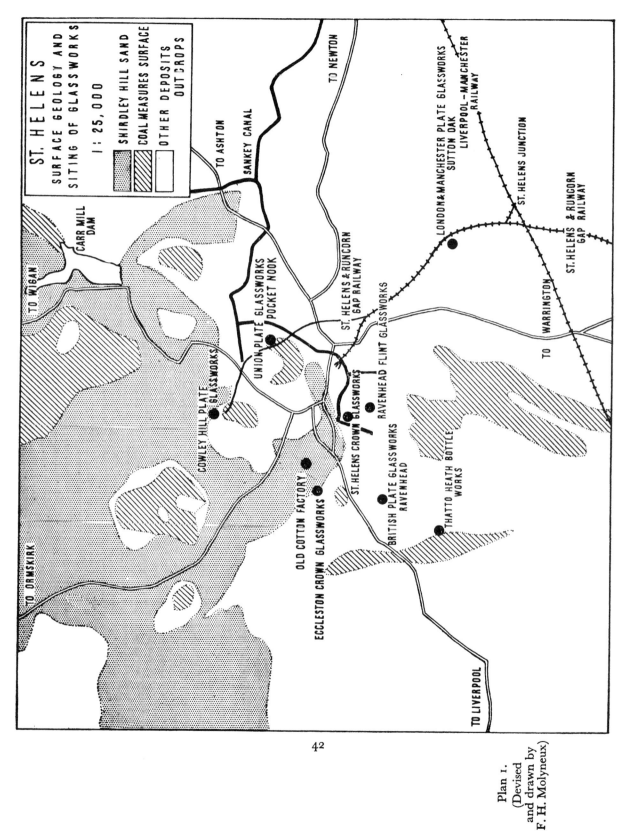

ST. HELENS

SURFACE GEOLOGY AND
SITING OF GLASSWORKS

1 : 25,000

SHIRDLEY HILL SAND
COAL MEASURES SURFACE
OTHER DEPOSITS
OUTCROPS

TO NEWTON

TO ASHTON

SANKEY CANAL

CARR MILL DAM

TO WIGAN

LONDON & MANCHESTER PLATE GLASSWORKS
SUTTON OAK

LIVERPOOL – MANCHESTER RAILWAY

ST. HELENS JUNCTION

ST. HELENS & RUNCORN
GAP RAILWAY

UNION PLATE GLASSWORKS
POCKET NOOK

ST. HELENS & RUNCORN
GAP RAILWAY

TO WARRINGTON

TO ORMSKIRK

COWLEY HILL PLATE GLASSWORKS

RAVENHEAD FLINT GLASSWORKS

ST. HELENS CROWN GLASSWORKS

OLD COTTON FACTORY

BRITISH PLATE GLASSWORKS
RAVENHEAD

THATTO HEATH BOTTLE WORKS

ECCLESTON CROWN GLASSWORKS

TO LIVERPOOL

42

Plan I.
(Devised
and drawn by
F. H. Molyneux)

chiefly used for mirrors, would fetch much lower prices. The emphasis, therefore, was always upon high quality. An eighteenth century price list divided
plate glass into five categories: a fine watery colour, the best; a reddish colour,
'Much coveted by pale-faced people'; a greenish colour, a yellowish colour and
a blackish colour, the last being 'worst of all'. 'But', added the compilers, 'even
all these, when ground down, will do for Coach-glass and many other un-
silvered purposes . . .'.[86]

Until the end of the seventeenth century, although plate glass was made with
much purer materials than window glass, the glassmaker manipulated his
molten glass, or metal, in much the same way when he was making both varie-
ties. In both cases he blew the glass into a cylinder which he slit along its length
and then flattened out into a pane. This method had serious disadvantages,
chief of which was that it imposed a strict limit upon the size: the cylinder
could not be blown more than fifty inches long without a loss of thickness which
would make grinding impossible.[87] This disadvantage could, however, be overcome if the metal, instead of being made into a pane *via* a cylinder, was run
straight on to a flat table, rolled out, and allowed to cool. The resulting plate
of glass would not be transparent, since both surfaces would be marred, but this
defect could be removed by the usual finishing processes of grinding and
polishing.

The French were the first to make plate glass by casting. The inventor of the
process was probably a man called Bernard Perrot.[88] As a result of his researches
several Frenchmen of note, acting through one Abraham Thévart, were in
December, 1688, granted Letters Patent which gave them a monopoly of glass
manufacture by the casting process for the French home market and, later, for
export as well. They were troubled by the cost of their fuel in much the same
way that Mansell had been. Like Mansell, they first tried to manufacture glass
in the immediate vicinity of the capital of their country but they, too, had to
remove the scene of their operations in quest of cheaper fuel. They went to St
Gobain in Picardy where wood was plentiful and cheap. There, after many
vicissitudes which drove the original partnership into bankruptcy, the process
was finally developed with success. By 1725 output probably reached about
700 tons annually, by 1750 about 850 tons, and after 1760 upwards of 1,150
tons.

In theory, the casting process was so much more straightforward than the
complicated method of making a flat piece of glass by way of a cylinder, that it
seems curious that plate glass was not made in this way long before the end of
the seventeenth century. In practice, however, casting, grinding and polishing
required a very large capital outlay, a strong deterrent to even the wealthier
investors. Instead of the customary small glasshouse, a large casting hall was
needed, complete with an extensive melting furnace in the centre, a number of
sizeable annealing ovens round the walls, a casting table upwards of ten feet

long and six feet wide, and cuvettes (or cisterns) in which the metal could be transferred from the furnace to the casting table together with a crane to carry them. Then there were all the workpeople's houses to be provided, the machinery required for grinding and polishing, and the warehouse accommodation. Above all, a large sum of money was permanently tied up in materials and stock, each plate of glass being an expensive—and fragile—item. All these factors made the manufacture of this kind of glass a most costly and risky venture. It is not surprising that St Gobain lacked a serious English rival for eighty years.

That is not to say that the English never made any attempt to compete with the French in the early days, particularly in wartime when imports of French manufactures were restricted. In 1691 Robert Hookes and Christopher Dodsworth (the former described as a gentleman and the latter as a merchant) obtained a patent which, among other things, included 'the Art of Casting Glasse and particularly Looking Glasse Plates, much larger than ever was Blowne in England or any Forreigne Parts'.[89] On October 5th of that year a number of men who were interested in the glass trade, Dodsworth prominently included, presented a petition to Parliament that they should be incorporated into the Company of Glass Makers with powers to raise stock and purchase land.[90] The proposal that Hookes and Dodsworth should be the first wardens of this Company makes it reasonably certain that this was an attempt to raise capital to erect the necessary large-scale plant for casting. The fate of this project is uncertain. No bill passed through Parliament and no English St Gobain came into being. Yet the patentees and other glasshouse proprietors do seem to have banded together. In June, 1692, they were advertising for sale 'all sorts of exquisite Looking-Glass plates, Coach-Glasses, Sash and other lustrous Glass for Windows and other Uses'.[91] Nine years later, in 1701, large looking glass plates, six feet long and six feet wide, 'the like never made in England before', were being sold at the Vauxhall glasshouse in London.[92] Not long afterwards an interchange of broadsides between two competing London firms called forth the extravagant assertion that—

> 'The Trade of Looking-Glass-Plates is so considerably improv'd that they serve not only for Furniture and Ornament in Her Majesty's Dominions at Home, but are likewise in great Esteem in Foreign Parts; the Venetians themselves buying these Plates and preferring them before their own.'[93]

Even if we accept this boast at a mere fraction of its face value, we are still left with the impression of considerable recent progress in this branch of the industry.

How long plate glass continued to be cast in England is far from clear, but it is certain that the process was completely abandoned before it was revived later in the eighteenth century. One proprietor, a descendant of two of the petitioners of 1691, confessed in 1773 that he had destroyed his apparatus for casting 'long since'.[94] The Vauxhall glasshouse, so proud of its large looking-glass plates in

1701, made none of them seventy years later. The proprietor had 'a sufficient trade in the less sizes' and 'did not choose to run so great a risk' as the casting process involved. Several merchants testified that no large plates of glass could be obtained from English glass firms; all their supplies came from St Gobain.

By the later eighteenth century the demand was great and rising fast, as it became more and more the fashion for the well-to-do to specify large windows for their houses. By 1773 it was estimated that between £60,000 and £100,000 worth of plate glass was imported from France every year. One merchant alone handled £10,000 worth annually. He thought that most of it was smuggled into the country and alleged that 'a kind of trading company' had been formed for that purpose, There was obviously money in this branch of the glass business, and as the demand continued to grow, a large-scale manufactory on the lines of St Gobain became a much more attractive economic proposition than it had been in 1691.

The whole matter came to a head in the early 'seventies when a company, known as the British Cast Plate Glass Manufacturers, was formed. Its origins are obscure for none of the records relating to its formation has survived. But we are able to piece together local knowledge and information from other sources. Since the proprietors needed to raise about £50,000 in order to finance the project, like the men of 1691 they deemed it advisable to seek an Act which would grant them incorporation and limited liability.[95] The *Journals of the House of Commons* are therefore a useful source of information about the promotion of the concern.

A Frenchman, Philip Besnard, who had been engaged in the casting of plate glass at St Gobain for fifteen years, appeared before the Commons' Committee as a technical expert. According to him, a large factory for casting glass would succeed in England because all the raw materials required, with the exception of barilla, the source of soda,[96] were obtainable in the country. The cost of production would be lower than in France because English fuel (coal) was cheaper. The factory could be built and equipped, he thought, for £12,000 and the entire outlay would be in the region of £50,000.

Two of the petitioners for the Bill bore the surname of Mackay. One of them, John Mackay, was unquestionably responsible for causing the factory to be sited at Ravenhead and it is by no means impossible that he may have been one of the prime movers in the whole scheme. He was a Scot who had emigrated to London. He was still living in Holborn when, in May, 1761, he took out a patent for a new method of making salt, with Jonathan Greenall of Parr near St Helens.[97] His interest in salt drew him northwards to the St Helens district from where the saltworks derived their supplies of coal. After leasing coal mines in Parr in 1763, he started to exploit those measures which lay below Ravenhead and Thatto Heath a few years later.[98] He sank pits and opened up the coal mines, raising part of the capital by mortgaging the estate to Charles Woodcock of Brentford Butts for £2,500 and to Thomas Lawrence of St Clement Danes, Samuel Pococke of Haybourne, Berkshire, and Alexander Mackintosh of Lombard Street, London, for a further £2,000.[99] Ravenhead Colliery was opened in 1770, and in May, 1771, Mackay advertised that his Thatto Heath Colliery would be open by the end of the year.[100]

Like the other local coal proprietors, he looked to the Cheshire saltfield and to the works and the export trade of Liverpool for the bulk of his sales. But he also saw that if he could attract a large furnace industry to settle on his newly-acquired estate, he would create a considerable local market for the output of his collieries. We know, from the terms of agreement which he signed with a copper smelting firm (later induced by him to establish furnaces on his land), that he went to great lengths to make his terms acceptable: the low price and high grade of coal and other attractive features were all carefully specified.[101] If Mackay went to such pains to attract a furnace industry in 1779–80, he would certainly have gone to even greater trouble to make his sites attractive six or seven years earlier when his collieries had been only recently opened.

Besnard told the Commons that he had arrived in England in the autumn of 1771, just about the time that Mackay's second colliery came into production. Unfortunately there is no clue to enable us to solve the mystery of how Mackay became concerned at this critical juncture with Besnard and the group of men who eventually promoted the British Cast Plate Glass Manufacturers. Among them Admiral Philip Affleck, a naval man with East India connections, was later stated to have been the prime mover.[102] We know that after going north, Mackay still maintained connections with the capital: his mortgages to Londoners leave that point in no doubt. We do not know how strong these connections were, but the fact that a later mortgagee of Ravenhead was none other than the famous actor David Garrick is significant.[103]

Probably these London friends helped him to make out an appealing case for Ravenhead as the best site for the proposed works. He certainly needed all the support he could get, for proximity to Liverpool and the American trade was not, in this branch of the glass industry, a bargaining counter: the chief market for plate glass was London, two hundred miles away, and if any oversea market was to be sought, it was much more likely to be in the east than in the west.[104] Perhaps the knowledge that direct communication by inland waterway would soon be opened between Ravenhead and London may have been a weighty selling point: it was Pickford's boats which eventually carried much of the firm's glass from the works to their warehouse near Blackfriars Bridge. But even given direct communication by water with the capital, this only placed Ravenhead on the same footing as Newcastle, which had the advantage of being the traditional manufacturing centre for flat glass. No doubt, as Besnard suggested, the price of coal was the decisive factor and Mackay saw to it that he offered the most attractive terms.

The new company obtained incorporation for twenty-one years by an Act of Parliament passed in April, 1773.[105] This permitted the proprietors to raise a joint stock of £40,000 in £500 shares and empowered them to raise an additional £20,000 with the consent of three-quarters of the shareholders. The foundations of the great casting hall at Ravenhead, 113 yards long and 50 yards wide, were laid in 1773[106] and glass was cast there for the first time three years later.[107]

The first fifty years of the company's history fall into two sharply-contrasted phases: miserable failure was followed by brilliant success, the turning point being the year 1792 when Robert Sherbourne was appointed to manage the works.

We hear no more of Besnard. The introduction of the new process was left to a number of other men from St Gobain,[108] a drain which caused the St Gobain company to adopt counter-measures to put a stop to further desertions. The original superintendent appears to have been Jean Baptist Francis Graux de la Bruyère, who was born at St Gobain in 1739 and died at Ravenhead on December 5, 1787. According to his epitaph, 'he was the first who brought to perfection [in Britain] . . . the cast plate glass manufacture'.[109] He may have been responsible for the introduction of the new process at Ravenhead but it cannot be pretended that he brought it to perfection. On the contrary, he ran the company to the verge of bankruptcy. Under his management there was a very high proportion of waste. In the eleven years to the time of his death, only 452 tons of saleable glass were made out of a total of 1,385 tons of metal.[110] One cause of trouble was that the French were still not accustomed to using coal in their furnaces; it was not until Sherbourne's time, for instance, that caped pots were successfully introduced to protect the metal from the great number of black drops which fell from the roof of the furnace. There were also various other technical difficulties to be surmounted before production reached a satisfactory pitch of efficiency.[111]

The company's difficulties were considerably aggravated by the workings of the excise, another problem which the French glassmakers never had to face in their own country.[112] The tax was levied by weight upon the metal in the pot, an allowance being made for wastage. It was found that for blown glass of all kinds, an allowance of a quarter of the metal and four inches at the bottom of the pot was sufficient compensation for metal lost in the course of manufacture. But in the case of glass that was cast, even had the process been efficiently worked, the wastage was far greater, nearer to a half than a quarter. To make matters worse, in 1777, only a year after the Ravenhead Works went into production, the excise rate was doubled as a war measure.[113] The proprietors appealed to the Commissioners of Excise to increase the allowance from a quarter to a half, but the Commissioners refused on the justifiable grounds that the losses were really due to 'the inexperience and improper management of the

47

workmen'.[114] In vain the proprietors sought to reverse this decision, urging, with equal justification, that 'the extraordinary waste of metal and materials is unavoidable and peculiar to the manufactory'.[115] The Excise Commissioners would not relent and, as the American war lingered disastrously on and a severe trade depression was experienced, the company saw its burden of debt grow heavier and heavier. In the four years 1780–3, they paid out £44,000 (a quarter of which went in duty) and sold glass worth only £40,000. These sales consisted almost entirely of unpolished plates, £28,000 worth being sold in London and £11,000 worth directly from Ravenhead. Only £1,000 worth of finished glass was sold throughout these four years, all of it in London.[116] This showed not only that there was gross inefficiency in casting, but also that the finishing process, the lucrative part of the operation, had hardly been embarked upon. This was indeed far from perfection—so far, in fact, that on May 18, 1784, the company, having spent in all more than £100,000, decided that all casting was to be stopped in order to avoid careering further into debt. The great works at Ravenhead lay idle, apart from the *blowing* of smaller plates, and was still idle a year later.[117]

Once again the Excise Commissioners were importuned for relief. On this occasion the manufacturers urged a new method of levying the duty, upon the finished or squared plates. This request was eventually granted, in 1787.[118] Although the company's troubles with the excise were by no means over—the excise officers interpreted 'squared' to mean at right angles and broke every plate that was not so cast[119]—there were some signs of improvements in technique and of a greater volume of business. Between 1787 and 1792, for instance, the wastage was reduced from 200 per cent to 100 per cent; and in 1788 an attempt was made at long last to extend the hitherto extremely limited output of polished glass. A Boulton and Watt engine was installed at Ravenhead to drive the necessary machinery.[120] Almost as much saleable glass—405 tons— was produced in the five and a half years following June 1787, as had been made in the previous eleven.[121] But Ravenhead was still but a pale reflection of St Gobain. A mere eighty tons of glass a year would have looked almost insignificant beside St Gobain's comparatively huge annual output of more than 1,000 tons. It was not until Robert Sherbourne took over the management at Ravenhead, in 1792, that the manufacture of cast plate glass on the English side of the Channel really began in earnest,

Sherbourne inherited the results of many years of inefficiency and mismanagement when, as the proprietors later recalled, the records were full of 'the failure of expensive experiments' and 'the misconduct of managers'.[122] As we have seen, the company was deeply involved in debt. The original capital of £40,000 had been spent long before, and loans had been raised totalling a further £60,000. In 1794 the twenty-one year charter of incorporation expired and creditors were clamouring for payment. The company petitioned

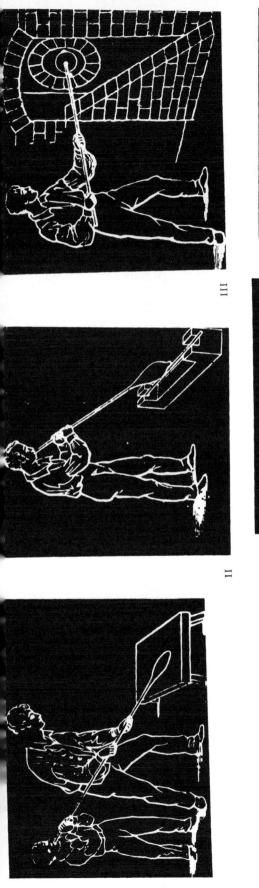

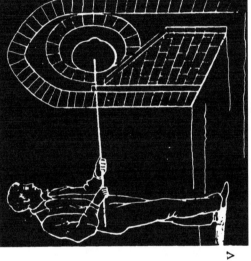

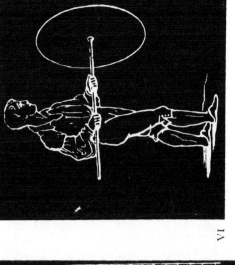

I

II

III

IV

V

VI

3   Stages in the manufacture of crown glass

The molten glass, cooled to working consistency, was formed into the shape of a small pear by blowing and rolling on a polished metal surface (a marver). A boy was required to blow down the pipe while a man rotated it (figure I), re-heating being necessary from time to time as the glass cooled and set. The pear-shaped glass was gradually worked into a globe to which an iron rod, known as a punty (an anglicization of the French *pontil*) was attached (figure IV). The blowpipe was then broken off and the piece re-heated at a flashing furnace (figure V). As the piece began to soften, it was rapidly twirled round on the punty. By the effect of centrifugal force, the glass was opened out—or flashed—into a flat, circular plate known as a table (figure VI). The punty was then removed and the table placed in a kiln for annealing.

4 Windle Hall, near St Helens, in 1824. (Sketch by William Latham in the possession of Manchester Public Libraries, by permission of the Libraries Committee)

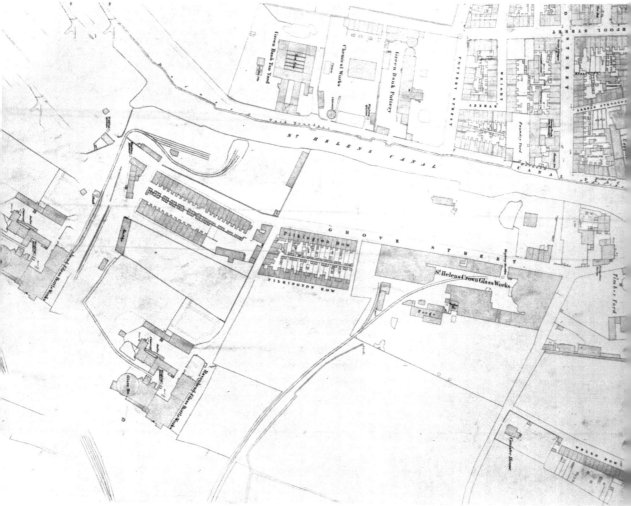

Site of the St Helens Crown Glassworks. (Ordnance Survey 1849, by which time the Bell's flint glassworks had become the Ravenhead Glass Bottle Works.) North is to the right of the map

Parliament for a new Act of Incorporation but, although this passed the Commons in May, 1794,[123] it failed to reach the Statute Book. The shareholders were at the mercy of their creditors and decided at a general meeting on August 9th to sell all their property at once before they lost their privilege of limited liability. But at this eleventh hour Thomas Oakes of Upper Wimpole Street, by arrangement with the proprietors, stepped in and bought the entire business for £105,000.[124] Oakes and the proprietors continued to run the concern as a private company until 1798 when a second attempt to secure reincorporation met with success. The new company included some of the old names: Philip Affleck, Thomas Dundas, Robert Sherbourne, John and Henry Grant and Alexander Aubert. Its title was changed by dropping the word 'cast'. It was hereafter known merely as the British Plate Glass Manufacturers.[125]

While these changes in the structure of the company were taking place in London, Sherbourne was busy transforming the works at Ravenhead. He was well fitted for the task for he had an intimate knowledge of the works and all its processes. He had helped to lay the foundations of the casting hall in 1773 and had, indeed, been brought up at Ravenhead.[126] Moreover, he was, as a grateful committee later observed, 'on a different footing from a common manager',[127] for he possessed three £500 shares.

His first action was to install a cuvette furnace which produced results 'so flattering as to encourage the Committee to go to the expense of additional Buildings etc. for the purpose of completing the plan he had recommended, the object of which was to double the then produce of glass'.[128] The depressed economic condition of the country and the financial troubles of the company prevented this target being reached before 1801; the average weight of glass squared annually between 1794 and 1801[129] was 130 tons, an increase in production of five-eighths. But, most striking, was the reduction of waste from 100 per cent. to less than 25 per cent. The company persuaded the Excise Commissioners to change the method of levying duty back again to the weight of metal in the pot and on this measure had been granted an allowance for wastage of $33\frac{1}{3}$ per cent.[130] They were therefore recouping some of their previous losses at the expense of the Excise. At the same time, Sherbourne found ways of saving money in other directions: for example, emery was bought as stone and prepared at the works instead of being purchased in a prepared state; and some local sand was used in place of that from Lynn.[131] In 1809 the committee recorded thankfully in the Minutes: 'the business of the manufactory being now brought to such a state of perfection . . . goes on like clock-work.'[132]

All these improvements and economies turned the Ravenhead Works from a heavy liability into a valuable asset. Output soared. Profits rose from £15,000 on sales totalling £46,000 in 1801, to £20,000 on £52,000 in the following year, and £30,000 on £85,000 in 1811. Five per cent. dividends reached shareholders with regularity: four of them in each of the two years 1807 and 1808 and five in 1809, a rate that was still being paid in the three years 1812–15. Nor did these large distributions prevent capital from being ploughed back on extensions and improvements to plant and the purchase of land in the vicinity of the factory. The minutes abound with eulogies of the energetic manager at Ravenhead to whose efforts all this prosperity was due. His salary was raised from £500 a year to £700 in 1809 and to £1,000 in 1815. When he retired in 1829, he was voted an annuity of £500.[133]

The Ravenhead Works were added to the list of those industrial wonders which so attracted eighteenth century Englishmen. It was a sight not to be missed and was prominently featured in the itineraries of any traveller who visited south-west Lancashire, though few of these sightseers could get permission to go round the works themselves: even proprietors had to obtain a special order from the committee in London before they could pass through the gates.[134] Most visitors had to be content to look down on the vast building from higher ground outside the walls.

The Ravenhead Works are now so much part of a wider organization that it is difficult to realize that the reputation of glassmaking in the St Helens district originally depended upon this one factory alone. The huge polished plates—surely a rival to delicately designed tableware as the best advertisement for glass—made Ravenhead famous throughout the country, drew attention to the local advantages of the neighbourhood as a glassmaking centre, and associated the district with glassmaking in the public mind.

Many years were to pass, however, before St Helens became as well-known for its ordinary window panes as it was for its expensive plates of glass. The real origin of the window branch of the industry was in a sense an offshoot of Ravenhead: three members of the first partnership to make window glass in the neighbourhood were members of the Mackay family.

John Mackay died in 1783, leaving his entire fortune to his daughter, Millicent, as his only son, John, had died before him. As we have seen, Mackay was particularly concerned in the formation of the British Cast Plate Glass Manufacturers and his interest in the factory, close to his home at Ravenhead House, did not flag: indeed, it seems to have been considerably greater than that of a mere shareholder or fuel supplier. He provided cottages for the employees at the new works[135] and a collector of land tax went so far as to describe the works in his return in 1781 as belonging to 'John Mackay and Co.'[136] George Mackay, of unknown relationship to John Mackay, though certainly a brother of Angus Mackay, another proprietor of 1773, was book-keeper at Ravenhead in 1785 and was still there five years later.[137] Clearly, the name of Mackay seems to have been particularly connected with the early period of inefficient administration at the works. We may perhaps be justified in surmising, therefore, that the appointment of Sherbourne in 1792 bore some relation to the eclipse of George Mackay as book-keeper. If this was the case, it may go far to explain why, in April of that year, a new firm called Mackay West and Company made its appearance in the district as manufacturers of window glass.[138] The original partners in this concern, besides the brothers George and Angus Mackay, were Alexander Mackay—another brother who was a Major-General in the army—James Campbell, and Thomas and William West. (Thomas West was the leading proprietor of the Thatto Heath Bottle-works which, since 1785, had been trading as Thomas West and Company.)[139] Mackay West and Company's factory, newly-opened in April, 1792, was situated in Eccleston, to the west of St Helens, though soon to become part of the town at what is now the corner of Boundary Road and Eccleston Street. This was within half a mile or so of the Ravenhead plate glassworks.

By the end of the eighteenth century window glass made on the cylinder principle, the method particularly associated with the Lorraine glassmakers, had gone out of favour in Britain and had been largely replaced for domestic glazing by glass made in a completely different way. This was known as crown glass, and sometimes as Normandy glass. Instead of the metal being blown into a cylinder, it was formed into the shape of a small pear by blowing, heating and rolling on a polished metal surface (known as a marver).[140] The end of the pear-shaped mass, remote from the blowpipe, was then flattened, and an iron rod, called a punty,[141] was sealed to the centre of this flattened surface. The blowpipe was broken off and the piece (as the mass of glass was now called) was re-heated at a flashing furnace. As the piece began to soften, it was rapidly twirled round on the punty. By the effect of centrifugal force, the glass was gradually opened out—or flashed[142]—into a flat, circular plate which could extend up to sixty inches in diameter, according to the extent of rotation and amount of metal which the gatherer had originally collected on the end of the blowpipe. This was known as a table of crown glass. The great advantage of this method of manufacture was that the glass never came into contact with any surface while it was still in a malleable state. As a result, it was remarkable for its polish and lustrous appearance. On the other hand, only small panes could be cut from the circular table, and the central 'bull's eye' (where the punty was attached) and the selvage at the rim were wasted.

No doubt it was the superior quality of crown glass which accounted for its growing popularity during the eighteenth century. Cylinder glass—usually called broad glass or (more descriptively) green glass—was a much cheaper article in all senses of the word. Yet crown glass had been made in England in the sixteenth century[143] but did not become established then and had to be reintroduced towards the end of the seventeenth century. In 1679 a certain Henry Richards went to Normandy 'solely to learn the art . . . of making Normandy or crown glass', and, so he claimed, 'brought that invention into

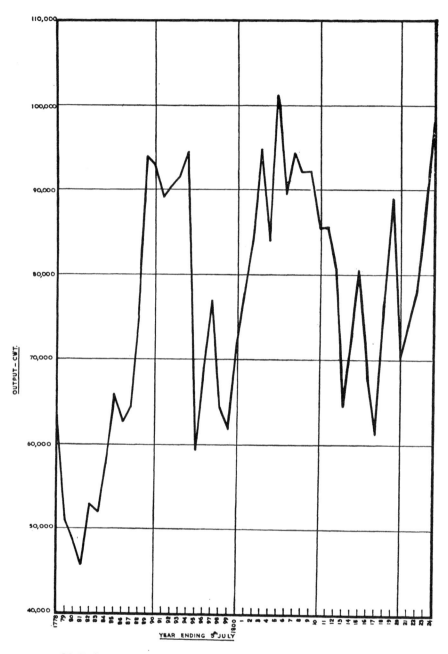

OUTPUT-CWT.

YEAR ENDING 5ᵗʰ JULY

OUTPUT OF CROWN GLASS ENGLAND AND WALES
1777/8—1823/4

Graph 1. Source: Excise Returns

52

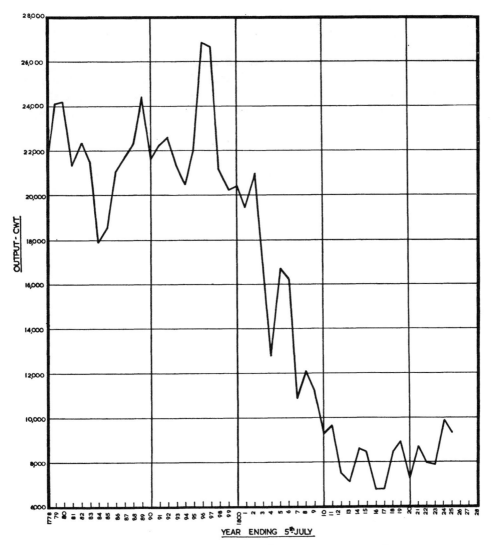

OUTPUT OF BROAD GLASS (ENGLAND & WALES).

1777/8—1824/5

Graph 2. Source: Excise Returns

53

England'.[144] According to Houghton's list of 1696, five houses in and around London were making this type of glass[145] and during the eighteenth century the process spread to the provinces. On the eve and at the beginning of the Revolutionary War, as may be seen from graph 1, output exceeded 90,000 cwt. a year. By the end of that century, as shown in graph 2, the days of broad glass were definitely numbered. In 1833 only one firm still made it.[146]

It was crown glass, therefore, that Mackay West and Company began to manufacture in 1792, and their factory was known as the Eccleston Crown Glassworks. It remained the only factory in the St Helens district making window glass until the 1820s.

In 1822, John William Bell, whose origins are not known, took over a disused iron foundry situated a little way to the east of the Ravenhead terminus of the Sankey Canal, and began to make flint glass there.[147] He was also conversant with the manufacture of crown glass and in 1826 he became the technical expert among a group of men who formed a partnership to set up the second window glass factory in the district. This was the partnership which, as we noticed at the end of the last chapter, William Pilkington joined.

CHAPTER 3

AN UNPROMISING START

THE middle of the 1820s was a most appropriate time to enter window glass manufacture. The building boom of 1822–5, the extent of which is seen on graph 3 (page 56) which shows brick output, called for a great increase in supplies of window glass. Demand was further stimulated by the halving of the tax on windows in 1823 and the increase in the number of tax-free windows from six to seven two years later.[1] Production of crown glass in England and Wales reached a peak 50 per cent. above the previous average, as may be seen from graph 4. There was obviously an opening for newcomers to share in this greatly-expanded market.

Moreover, the market for window glass was growing at an unusually rapid rate in that part of England which could be easily supplied from St Helens. The increase of population was particularly marked in the industrial north and, although most of the houses built there—as in other parts of the country—had fewer than seven or eight windows, Lancashire and Yorkshire could boast considerable numbers of larger residences which exceeded the tax-free quota. In 1829, for instance, over 19,000 houses were taxed in Lancashire and some 20,000 in Yorkshire, each considerably more than in any other county with the exception of Middlesex and Surrey.[2] Business premises, which were being put up in large numbers in the industrial areas, were exempt from window tax altogether and usually went in for glazing on quite an extensive scale. Clearly, close proximity to a rapidly growing market was an important factor in locating this branch of the glass industry at St Helens, as well as access to cheap coal and plentiful supplies of raw materials.

While the building boom of 1822–5 lasted, the cost of putting up new glassworks was excessive. By waiting until 1826, when the boom had broken and prices had fallen, the would-be manufacturer employed his capital to better advantage. This was particularly true in the neighbourhood of St Helens, where the recession in trade was especially marked; in May, 1826, the very month that the St Helens Crown Glass Company came into being, the proprietors of the British Plate Glass Company decided to vote a hundred guineas to a relief fund, 'their works at Ravenhead being in the distressed district'.[3] We

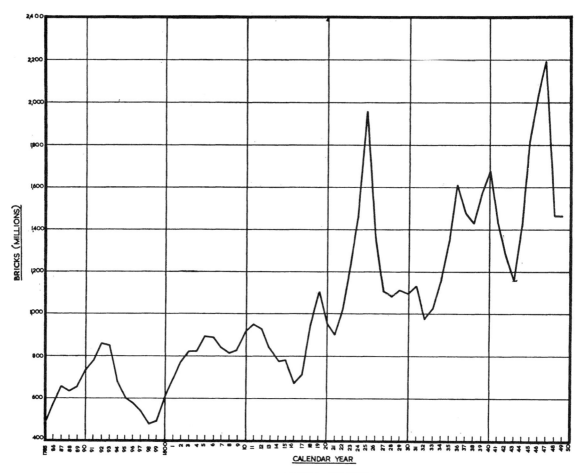

BRICK OUTPUT
1785–1849

Graph 3. Source: H. A. Shannon, 'Bricks—A Trade Index, 1785–1849,'
Economica, 1934

5   Exterior of the first glasshouse

6   Peter Greenall, brother-in-law of Richard
and William Pilkington. Portrait by
Spindler at the St Helens Town Hall

7   Richard Pilkington

8   William Pilkington

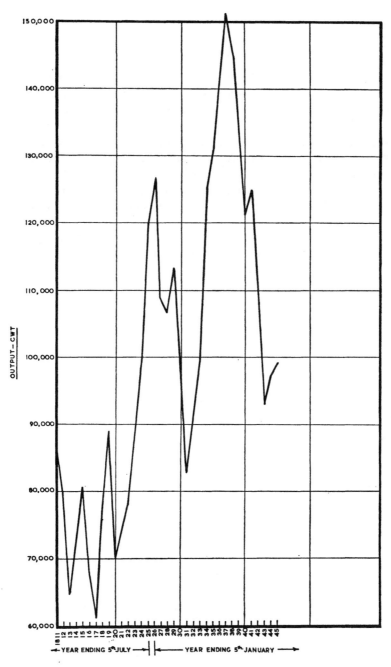

OUTPUT OF CROWN GLASS ENGLAND AND WALES

1810/11—1844

[Entries from 1826 refer to previous years. E.g. year ending 5 January 1827=1826]

Graph 4. Source: Excise Returns

57

do not know to what extent the founders of the firm took these economic circumstances into consideration—to what extent they seized the opportunity to erect a glasshouse during a lull in business when costs were low, in anticipation of sharing in the greatly-enlarged market when trade again revived. If they chose their moment by accident, it was an unusually fortunate one.

In its origin the St Helens Crown Glass Company was intended to be the combined product of the technical knowledge and ability of John William Bell and capital from three of the richest and most influential local families: the Bromilows, the Greenalls and the Pilkingtons. There were six proprietors altogether and the company's stock was divided into eleven shares. Two shares were held by Bell himself and one by a Thomas Bell whose relationship to J. W. Bell is not known. Thomas Bell was also described as a glassmaker, though he was not conversant with the manufacture of crown glass. The remaining eight shares were divided equally between four local men who knew nothing whatsoever of glassmaking. Of these, John Barnes was the only solicitor in the town, and James Bromilow was the second son of William Bromilow of Merton Bank, the foremost local coal proprietor.[4] The remaining two partners interest us most of all. They were Peter Greenall and William Pilkington.

Peter Greenall, born in 1796, a younger son of Edward Greenall of Wilderspool, came to St Helens in 1818 to take charge of their St Helens Brewery. Three years later, on March 6, 1821, he married Dr Pilkington's second daughter, Eleanor.

Their marriage testifies to the position and prestige of the Pilkington family in St Helens even before its members went into glassmaking. The Greenalls, who had been in a most lucrative line of business for more than sixty years, had already amassed a sizeable fortune. They had wisely invested much of their wealth in land and property which appreciated in value as the town grew. By the 1820s they possessed many acres of land in Eccleston and Windle townships and were by far the largest owners of house and cottage property in St Helens itself. Rent day at their Fleece Inn was a major collecting operation. They were undoubtedly of the class that contemporaries liked to describe as 'great people'. That Peter Greenall should have married Eleanor Pilkington shows very clearly that by this time the Pilkingtons could also be similarly described. Eleanor Pilkington had a marriage dowry of £1,000.[5] Five years later, in 1826, when her father, then aged 61, decided to retire, he went to live at Windle Hall which, with its large surrounding estate, he rented from Sir John Gerard for £300 a year.[6] He died in 1831 leaving a fortune of £20,000.[7] Like the Greenalls, the Pilkingtons, too, had risen rapidly in the world in the space of two generations.

Peter Greenall was a man of great resource and capability. In the course of a very active life he engaged in many industrial ventures besides managing the St Helens Brewery, and in 1841 he was elected one of the Members of Parliament for Wigan.[8] Already, by the early 'twenties, he showed the first distinct signs of speculative acumen outside the routine round of brewery affairs. In 1824 he started to supply the town with water—an unusual service for a brewer —and in the same year he became leading promoter of the first St Helens Building Society. This was formed to run up cottages, mainly on Greenall land. The success of this excursion into building, with which Barnes was also prominently connected and all the other partners in the glass concern were associated in a smaller way, may have led on to their advancing capital for glassworks on land nearby in the hope of even greater returns. Certain it is that during 1827 the Building Society was to advance £400 to each of the six partners on the security of their interest in the glassworks.[9] £2,400 was just over one-fifth of the total capital of the firm at that time, a considerable proportion of the initial outlay.

We do not know whose idea the glassworks was in the first place, though, presumably, J. W. Bell, being the technical expert and in the trade, must have been in the best position to be its originator. He certainly bought the necessary land on behalf of the others at the end of March, 1826,[10] a plot very close to his own flint glassworks. It was a quite narrow rectangular strip of freehold land about two and a half statute acres in extent, stretching from the corner of present-day Watson Street and Grove Street southwards. Grove Street, which then ran on to the Ravenhead Copper Works, formed the larger, western side of the rectangle and a road which cut across from Grove Street eastwards to the Bells' Ravenhead Flint Glassworks, formed its southern boundary. For this valuable industrial site, advantageously placed near to the Canal, the turnpike road to Liverpool and the Ravenhead Colliery, Bell paid £764 15s od. Seven weeks later, in the middle of May, the other partners confirmed that he had acquired the land on behalf of the company[11] and articles of co-partnership were drafted.[12] This draft would appear to confirm the view, already suggested by his purchase of the land, that Bell was the person most interested in the formation of the new company. At all events, he emerges as the man around whom the whole works were to revolve.

Although Bromilow was named as the general book-keeper and cash-keeper (for which he was to receive £250 a year) John William Bell, the manager (also to be paid £250 a year) was responsible for

'attending to the Workman, the manufacturing of the Crown Glass and all things incident thereto. And also in the travelling department to effect Sales of Crown Glass when manufactured and purchasing Articles used in the Manufacturing of Crown Glass on the best possible terms. . . .'

Moreover, he was not supposed to give these new works his whole attention for he was 'allowed to devote a reasonable part of his time to superintend his

Flint Glass Works'. While acting as works manager and chief salesman and at the same time keeping an eye on his other concern, he was also to

> 'teach and instruct . . . the said Peter Greenall, James Bromilow, Thomas Bell and John Barnes in the different operations respecting the mixing of metal, manufacturing of crown glass and all other things incident thereto',

it being understood that Greenall, Bell and Barnes were not 'to attend to . . . the management . . . further than . . . from time to time shall be convenient or agreeable to themselves.'

Two points emerge quite clearly from this allocation of responsibilities. The first is that Bell was charged with a whole host of duties which, even granted that the works were to start on a small scale, would tax the strength and ability of any one man. No doubt he hoped to delegate some of these jobs to others, but there was a limit to the extent of such delegation, particularly in the early stages of a new concern. The partners were expecting too much from one person.

Secondly, the draft articles do not mention William Pilkington at all. This may, of course, only have been an oversight which was eventually corrected in the final copy. In support of this view is the fact that his name appears in the purchase deed of May 16th, two days *before* the date on the draft articles. Yet the complete omission of one of the partners' names is curious, suggesting that William Pilkington was, in fact, brought into the company some time after the others. There is a later hint of this; it appears in William Pilkington's obituary notice which, published in identical words in the *St Helens Newspaper* and the *St Helens Standard*, bears all the marks of being both well-informed and accurate. According to this source, the works were promoted by Greenall, Bell, Bromilow and Barnes and 'to these names that of Mr Pilkington was added'.[13] It would seem that the possibility of William Pilkington's being brought into the company at a late stage in its formation ought not to be discounted. If this was the case, it seems reasonable to suggest that it was his brother-in-law, Peter Greenall, whose name appears first in the draft deed of co-partnership, who introduced him to strengthen the family interest.

The glasshouse, a single cone 120 feet high with an internal diameter of 66 feet, possibly modelled upon one of the cones at Dumbarton,[14] was built during the summer, autumn and winter of 1826 at a cost of about £8,500.[15] Tables of crown glass were blown and flashed[16] there for the first time on February 14, 1827.[17] It was later claimed that James Kenmore, a native of Northumberland, who came to St Helens from Scotland, made the first piece of glass at the works,[18] but we do not know the names of any of the other workmen concerned, forty to forty-five in number.[19] The earliest surviving list of employees refers only to the year 1849 and the first list of occupants of the company's cottages is dated 1835.

The partners were no sooner in a position to embark upon full-scale production than they ran into serious difficulties. John William Bell was never given a chance to show whether he was equal to the multitude of responsibilities he had assumed. In the spring of 1827 yet another worry was loaded upon his already grossly overburdened shoulders: he became involved in a tedious battle with the Commissioners of Excise in connection with his flint glassworks.[20]

Bell had been in the habit of removing some coloured metal from the bottom of one of his pots after working. This he did in the presence of an excise officer who made allowance for this glass, charging for it only when it became part of the new metal. This practice had been permitted up to April, 1827, but in that month the officers suddenly insisted that the metal was dutiable as soon as it was removed, on the grounds that it might be slipped into the pots again after gauging, unknown to the officer. Moreover they accused Bell of 'contriving and fraudulently intending craftily to deceive and defraud' them since July 5, 1825, when a new set of regulations had come into effect and they required that he should pay duty on all the cullet he had removed since that date. This involved the payment of some £243. Bell resisted the claim and took the matter to law. After lengthy (and, no doubt, costly) preliminaries, the case came on for trial in the Exchequer Court in London on February 16, 1828, with Bell and Barnes, his solicitor, in attendance. The jury gave a verdict for Bell being eleven to one in his favour. They did not believe that he had been guilty of any attempt to defraud. But the Commissioners, with a principle at stake, were unwilling to let the matter drop. They demanded a re-trial and this was heard at the end of November in the same year, 1828. Again Bell secured a verdict in his favour and again the Commissioners refused to dismiss the matter. Discussions concerning a third trial were still taking place in May, 1830.

These proceedings must have taken up much of Bell's time from early in 1827, precisely when the new crown glassworks required his wholehearted attention. The two trials and the legal business associated with them could not have been undertaken without incurring considerable expense. It is not surprising to discover, therefore, that both J. W. and Thomas Bell had to sell their shares in the crown glass company. At the end of December, 1827, when the first case was pending, J. W. Bell parted with a half of his two-elevenths' share for £1,000 to Greenall, Bromilow and Pilkington, who divided it equally among them.[21] Five months later, the first trial over and the second in prospect, he was obliged to sell his remaining eleventh share and Thomas Bell also sold his eleventh. Peter Greenall and William Pilkington each acquired one-third of these two-elevenths and James Bromilow and John Barnes each took up one-sixth.[22] The Bells withdrew from the partnership as from April 15, 1828.[23] J. W. Bell continued to manage his flint glassworks until 1838 when he was killed in an accident.[24]

The loss of Bell, to whom so much responsbility for the success of the works had been entrusted, was a most severe blow to the young firm; to some observers, it must have looked like a knock-out. But the partners were too far committed to the enterprise to accept elimination lightly. Already a large sum of money had been invested and more had to be put into the company every day. An eleventh share in December, 1827, was worth £1,000 and the two-elevenths which the Bells transferred at the beginning of May, 1828, fetched £2,485. This suggests that, within the space of five months, the partners had increased their total investment in the firm from £11,000 to more than £13,500. By the beginning of 1829 it exceeded £18,000. (An eleventh share was then worth £1,640.) This was a vast sum to have put into a firm which now lacked an expert manager. The four remaining proprietors, Peter Greenall, William Pilkington, James Bromilow and John Barnes, must have known some restless nights during this vital, formative, but headless period.

In this crisis William Pilkington was prevailed upon to take an active part in the firm's affairs.[25] No doubt he had already been schooled in the techniques of glassmaking (as the draft articles of co-partnership had laid down) and had the opportunity to get to know some of the details of its day-to-day affairs before the Bells retired from the partnership in April, 1828. His readiness to assimilate these details and his previous business training fitted him well for his new task. All his energies were to be needed.

To be masterly one had also to be masterful; William Pilkington soon came into collision with James Bromilow, the partner who had charge of the books. He later accused Bromilow of failing to keep accurate accounts, failing to credit the firm with a sum of £500 which was received, and failing to make allowance for trade discounts totalling more than £1,200.[26] Such a state of affairs could not be tolerated and, as James Bromilow's brother put it, with a lawyer's tact, 'differences' arose between the two men.[27] James Bromilow left the partnership in February, 1829, and John Barnes went with him.[28] William Pilkington, acting on behalf of himself and his elder brother Richard,[29] bought their five shares for £8,200. He now held eight of the eleven shares in the company, his brother-in-law, Peter Greenall, possessing the other three.

£8,200 was a considerable sum of money to advance in addition to previous investments in the firm. It can hardly have been a coincidence that this money was put into the glass concern at a time when the family wine and spirit business was yielding particularly handsome dividends. A general cash book of William Pilkington and Sons has survived which gives details of their income and expenditure from October, 1828. It shows that in the last three months of 1828, expenditure totalled £7,098 and income £8,251. In the following year £24,162 was expended as against £31,951 received. Even if we make due allowance for sundries—discounts and the like—the wine and spirit business was still making a clear annual profit of around £5,000. We do not know what Richard and William Pilkington's share in this happened to be, but there can be little doubt that these profits encouraged William Pilkington, backed by his brother, to take greater financial risks in the glassworks at this critical period than he would otherwise have been in a position to do. No doubt, too, the prospect of further profits from William Pilkington and Sons influenced his decision to borrow £500 at 4½ per cent interest from Thomas Astbury in January, 1829, and £4,000 from the executors of Sir William Gerard in the following April. It may also be said with some justification that the reduction of the spirit duty played its part, if not in the Pilkingtons' initial venture into glassmaking, then in enabling them to secure control of the company in order to save it from total collapse and failure.

Although Peter Greenall did not join his brothers-in-law in buying out Bromilow and Barnes, and although he never, so far as we know, took an active part in the conduct of the works, it would be a mistake to dismiss him merely as a sleeping partner. His name lent further respectability to the concern and, even though he held only a minority of the shares, the firm was known as Greenall and Pilkingtons and not vice versa. An excise officer in 1833 even returned 'Peter Greenall and Co.' as the title of the company. Moreover, the Greenall family had an interest in the leading bank in the neighbourhood, Parr's at Warrington, then known as Parr, Lyon and Greenall. Peter Greenall's brother, John, was a partner in this banking house and Peter Greenall himself may have been intimately connected with its affairs.[30] He certainly had considerable influence there and this probably made it easier for the glass firm to be granted and, what is more, to retain during a bad depression, a very large overdraft. Clearly, Peter Greenall was a considerable source of strength to the glass firm even though its management was not his particular province. But from February, 1829, so far as the day-to-day control of the company's business affairs was concerned, the St Helens Crown Glass Company was already Pilkingtons in fact, if not yet in name.

The years which immediately followed the retirement of the Bells must have been a period of uninterrupted anxiety for William Pilkington and his brother Richard. By purchasing Bromilow's and Barnes' shares, they were taking an enormous personal risk. This meant that, with his earlier investments, William Pilkington, acting on behalf of himself and his elder brother, had paid into the concern more than £13,000 in the space of three years. And there was no limit to the extent of their liability for losses were they to fail: they and Greenall would be called upon to meet the whole of the company's debts and not merely the amount that they had invested.

Greenall and Pilkingtons had considerable financial resources behind them and an able managing partner; but they lacked the experience of their competitors. In the north-east were men who controlled long-established businesses, the goliaths of the trade. In Lancashire itself, within a radius of less than twenty miles from St Helens and competing in the same markets, were the crown glassworks in Warrington and Liverpool, also long-established. And from

Greenall and Pilkingtons itself, smoke was to be seen pouring out menacingly from the cones up the hill, a quarter of a mile away, belonging to Mackay West and Company's Eccleston Crown Glassworks, almost forty years old.

Or, compare the Pilkingtons' background with that of the Chances, who were to be their chief business rivals for so many years.[31] Robert Lucas Chance, who bought the single-cone factory at Spon Lane, Smethwick, in 1824, had already spent much of his life in the glass trade. His father, William Chance, a Birmingham hardware merchant, and his uncle, John Robert Lucas, were both partners in glassworks at Nailsea,[32] and young Robert Lucas Chance had been sent there to gain experience before setting up as a glass merchant on his own account in London. By the time he acquired the Smethwick works, he had a thorough knowledge of the trade and knew everyone who mattered in it. In 1828, the year in which Greenall and Pilkingtons lost Bell, their only technical expert, John Hartley, one of the great authorities on crown glass in his day, was brought up from Nailsea to act as managing partner at Smethwick, by then a three-furnace concern. Robert Lucas Chance continued to superintend his glass merchant's business in London.

As William Pilkington surveyed the scene—one in which production had not diminished in proportion to the fall in demand—he could have found little to encourage him. He could only hold fast and lay his plans so that, when the building cycle took its next upward swing, he would be well placed to secure an increasing share of a rapidly expanding market. But, as so often happens when a dominating personality is concerned, fortune took his side even before the next building boom arrived. The workings of the excise, which had caused the departure of the Bells, now led to the elimination of Pilkingtons' most immediate competitor. It was the turn of the proprietors of the Eccleston Crown Glassworks to become caught up in the tax collector's toils.

CHAPTER 4

THE COLLAPSE OF A COMPETITOR
AND THE STRUGGLE FOR SURVIVAL

———————————

A T a time when the duty on crown glass was twice as great as the prime
cost of production,[1] there was a grave temptation for manufacturers to
add to their incomes by defrauding the excise authorities. We have the
informed testimony of Robert Lucas Chance that when the duty was paid on
metal gauged in the pots prior to 1815, frauds were 'enormous'.[2] Later, when
the tax was charged upon the panes of glass in the kiln, there was a considerable
tightening up of the regulations and few manufacturers thought it worth their
while to cheat the Government in order to gain an advantage over their competitors. But William West, the managing partner of Mackay West and Company, was a notorious exception.

His misdeeds were discovered towards the end of 1828 when an observant
Acting Examiner of Excise, named Thomas Priddis, visited the Eccleston
Crown Glassworks and noticed various irregularities which aroused his sus-
picions.[3] He kept a close watch for several weeks and discovered that it was
West's custom to bribe the excise officer on duty—a practice which West even
tried to adopt in the case of Priddis himself when he knew that his offence had
been detected. It was estimated that six hundred pieces of glass were fraudulently removed from the kiln every week. Sometimes John Garthwaite, the
officer, connived with West by lending him the keys of the excise lock which
fastened the door of the kiln. On other occasions (as the excise solicitor later
asserted) when 'Garthwaite for fear of a discovery could not conveniently
leave the keys', they used a secret way into the kiln.

'The entrance front of the lear underneath the grated doors was . . . so constructed
that defendants could, by the removal of a few bricks, take any quantity of glass
privately from the lear at their pleasure.'

West was brought before the Collector at Prescot and charged with these
offences. He wriggled and squirmed and did his utmost to explain away the
accusations, admitting only to giving £5 to the officer not, he was careful to

E   65

point out, as a bribe, 'but as an act of charity as he had been informed that he was in distress'. His explanations were not accepted: Mr Carr, the Solicitor of Excise, proceeded to file an information in the Exchequer for the recovery of penalties for breach of the excise laws amounting to nearly £20,000.

This news caused consternation among the three other partners in the firm— James Underhill West, brother of the culprit, and Thomas Holt and George Mackay. They sent the offending partner post-haste to London to see Mr Carr, in a last-minute attempt to compromise the information. But West, though well versed in the ways of influencing lesser officials in the excise service, made the very worst impression upon the department's solicitor who, we learn, 'expressed a determination never again to have any intercourse with him'. Thereupon the partners, after having taken advice from William Huskisson, M.P. for Liverpool and a member of the Government, optimistically offered to pay £100 as a compromise and, when this act of somewhat limited generosity was rejected by Their Lordships, they raised the figure to £1,000. When this more substantial gesture also proved of no avail, it was decided, in March, 1829, to send the firm's books for the Commissioner's inspection, this being the only condition under which there was any hope of compromising the case and thereby avoiding a public trial.

At this juncture there occurred a split among the partners, a result of the fraud, which was eventually to prove more disastrous to the firm than the detection of the fraud itself. West was resolutely opposed to permitting the books to be sent to London, for he knew that by doing this the full enormity of the offence (to which he alone among the partners was privy) would become known. This time it was his turn to take alarm. He hurried down to London to put his own case and by doing so jeopardized the chances of reaching a private settlement out of court. The other partners were most indignant at this display of independence on West's part and a definite schism appeared between West and his fellow proprietors.

The other partners continued to seek a compromise. They sent a memorial to the Commissioners of the Treasury on November 13, 1829, admitting the frauds, but pointing out that none of them had been in the habit of attending the works, 'which have been wholly under the care of the Superintendent', West. They offered to settle for £2,000 and there is good reason to believe that this offer would have been rejected outright had Carr still been in charge of the case for the Crown.[4] According to the firm's books, the defalcation even for the four years immediately prior to the detection of the fraud amounted to £4,500. The illegal removals of glass had been occurring before that, but West had been careful to mutilate the books so that the exact amount was a matter for conjecture. Carr favoured payment in full; but he died while the negotiations were proceeding and his successor, Dehany, was more lenient. The Commissioners of Excise agreed to settle for £5,000 and this was paid in January, 1830.[5]

66

The forfeiture of this large sum of money and the apparent lack of confidence among the proprietors completely disrupted the partnership. In January, 1830, the works were advertised for sale by private treaty[6] but did not find a purchaser. Shortly afterwards they were leased by Mackay, West and Company to a new firm, West and Bromilow, James Bromilow, fresh from two years bookkeeping at the St Helens Crown Glassworks, having gone into partnership with the tax evader, William West. Although up to this time Mackay, West and Company appear to have had some degree of success in hushing up their previous misdoings, West and the other partners in Mackay West and Company do not seem to have straightened out their differences, and in 1831 West's brother, James Underhill West, sent a circular to the old customers of Mackay West and Company which, though concerned with old debts owing to them, presented their new tenants, West and Bromilow, in a most unfavourable light. Although we no longer possess a copy of this circular, we know that it was directly responsible for causing many customers to switch their orders from the Eccleston concern to Greenall and Pilkingtons. This is made abundantly clear from a letter which William West wrote to his brother on May 19, 1831:

'Whatever hostility you have shewn towards me I have said little of it, but when I contemplate the hasty steps you took in sending off the Circulars, I must, as I said in a former letter, charitably suppose that you could not be aware of the consequences to the Firm of West and Bromilow; indeed, I little calculated on the issue, nor can I now tell myself where the mischief will end; to give you some idea, however, I will just tell you what occurred to me in Manchester. I went round as usual. The first I called on was Mr Occleshaw. He had given an order for fifty crates and several thousand feet of glass were cutting here for him. The whole was countermanded and transferred to [the] St Helens [Crown Glass Company]. Next Jos. Elleray who not only countermanded his order for 20 crates but returned four crates and insisted on a receipt in full of all demands. Thence I went to Mr Winder, on whom Elleray had waited to know whether he has a letter similar to the one he held in his hand. Mr Winder replied No, but the consequence was that when I asked Mr Winder for the confirmation of the order for 50 crates, he said he had given it to another house for that under the circumstances he knew not how to act. . . . I thence crossed over into Salford where our best customer William Harrison recalled his order and gave it to the St Helens house; his next door neighbour did the same, Mr Livingstone the same. . . . In a word here is a sample of what we may expect throughout the country. An alarm is given which will take months to quiet and such is the distress caused by it, what with glass being returned and orders countermanded, I am almost distracted. . . .'[7]

For the Eccleston works the situation went from bad to worse and West must have become even more harassed as the months passed. He tried to recoup his losses by again attempting to defraud the excise, but was again detected.[8] The differences between Mackay West and Company and West and Bromilow soon ripened into open dispute, and the whole matter was sent for arbitration in June, 1833.[9] The firm of West and Bromilow was tottering. In 1834 it fell. The works were advertised for sale by auction on June 24, 1834, on which day West signed a promise to vacate the premises by December 24th[10]. There were no satisfactory bids, however, and West appears to have contrived to remain in possession for another two years. It was not until October, 1836, that he finally left the works. At a dinner on that occasion his workmen presented him with a silver cup which (in the words of the inscription on it) was 'to mark their respect and gratitude towards him for the uniform kindness evinced and practised by him towards them'.[11] In January, 1837, he sold his share in Mackay West and Company[12] and a few months later filed his petition of bankruptcy.[13] Thereafter the Eccleston Crown Glassworks appear to have been idle until 1846 when they found a new owner.[14]

The decline and fall of the Eccleston Crown Glassworks removed Greenall and Pilkingtons' nearest competitor just at the time when William Pilkington was making the utmost effort to secure new outlets for his firm's glass. It is not unreasonable to suppose that the fateful circular of 1831 caused merchants to withdraw their custom from West and Bromilows in other towns besides Manchester.

While Mackay West's misfortunes were of most direct assistance to Greenall and Pilkingtons, troubles at other glass factories elsewhere probably also helped William Pilkington to secure orders. Chance and Hartleys went through a crisis in 1831, possibly because of a heavy loss in a patent speculation which had nothing at all to do with the glass industry. William Chance, Robert Lucas Chance's brother who had inherited the family hardware business, came to the rescue. The crisis was surmounted, but Robert Lucas Chance was obliged to remove from London to Handsworth to be able to give his Smethwick works proper supervision.[15]

The crisis at Smethwick was short and temporary; that at the large and important glassworks at Dumbarton was longer drawn out and ended in the total collapse of the concern. This factory, which had been started by members of the Dixon family from Sunderland late in the eighteenth century, had begun to produce crown glass in 1781. By the early nineteenth century the Dumbarton works were among the most important in the country and the managing partner, Jacob Dixon, was one of the most prominent manufacturers in the trade. As will be seen from the graphs 4 (p. 57) and 5, crown glass output in Scotland, between 1811 and the great building boom of the mid-1820s, ran at about one-third of the production of that type of glass in England.

Scottish window glass manufacture did not share to the same extent as the English in the building boom, however, and after 1828 production in Scotland fell off steeply. In 1827 nearly 32,000 cwt. of glass had been produced there. By

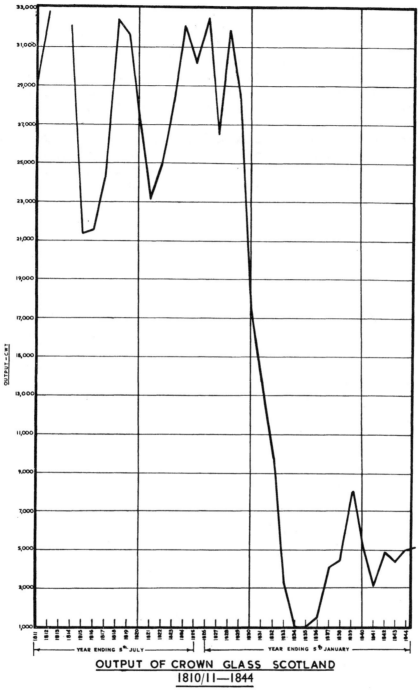

OUTPUT OF CROWN GLASS SCOTLAND
1810/11—1844

[Entries from 1826 refer to previous years. E.g. year ending 5 January 1827 = 1826]

Graph 5. Source: Excise Returns

1830 output had fallen to 14,000 cwt. and in 1831 to under 10,000 cwt. In that year Jacob Dixon died and the management became divided. Production ceased during 1832 and, although the works were started again by other proprietors at the close of the 1830s, they did not enjoy any real success and were closed for good in 1850.[16]

The collapse of Dumbarton at the beginning of the 1830s must have been of considerable assistance to the English factories with whom they had competed. The quite dramatic downfall of Scottish window glass manufacture was no doubt watched with interest at Greenall and Pilkingtons.

It is helpful at this juncture to examine the extent of competition within the glass industry at this period. It was, in fact, competition within carefully prescribed limits. Rivalry between manufacturers was curbed by price agreements and competition was confined to the quality of the glass which each firm produced.

Glassmaking was a trade in which there had long been 'understandings'. There were relatively few units of production and it was, therefore, easy for the handful of manufacturers to join together to prevent cut-throat competition by fixing the selling prices of their goods. They could also, if they so wished, unite to prevent any interloper from breaking into their circle.

Restrictive practices in the industry can be traced back to the beginning of the seventeenth century when the London glaziers complained that two manufacturers, named Bungar and Bennett, had secured control of all the Sussex glasshouses. Prices were kept high and, added the irate glaziers,

> 'if at any time we paid less, it was when another man set up a furnace. And then they would advance their size and fall their price . . . though it were (by their own protestation) to their loss £200, of purpose to overthrow the party, which in short time they effected. By which their policy they brought the market to their own desires and so sunk their size and raised their price as before they had done . . .'[17]

Not long afterwards the industry fell into Mansell's monopolistic grip and there is evidence in later years of further attempts to restrict competition: in 1684 makers of green glass in London fixed the prices at which they were to sell to merchants between London Bridge and Ratcliffe;[18] in 1703 Benjamin Perrott of Bristol and his son signed a very detailed agreement with several Stourbridge broad glassmakers whereby their markets were to be carefully partitioned during the following eleven years;[19] half a century later, as we have seen[20] one of the Stourbridge firms acquired the Prescot glasshouse in order to close it down. In London, the glass sellers, in their turn, were operating a price ring by the 1780s.[21] The excise duty on glass, levied as a temporary wartime measure between 1695 and 1699 and imposed continuously from 1746, made such agreements and associations all the more necessary; it was essential for manufacturers to be able to utter their protests and advance their suggestions with one voice and thus bring to bear the maximum possible pressure upon those who levied the duty.

The St Helens Crown Glass Company was a member of such a manufacturers' association from the outset.[22] Bell attended one of the meetings of this Crown Glass Manufacturers' Association at Harrogate on July 9 and 10, 1827, and Bromilow represented the company at meetings in Liverpool on September 28, 1827, and in Harrogate on March 28 and September 19, 1828. William Pilkington was present for the first time at such a meeting held at the Swan Inn, Ferrybridge, near Pontefract, on June 24 and 25, 1829. It was usual at this period for Jacob Dixon, of the Dumbarton Works, to preside and for a Mr Lamb, of the Northumberland Glass Company, to act as secretary. There is no indication how long this alliance of crown glass manufacturers had been holding regular deliberations, for the earliest surviving minutes relate to the Harrogate meeting of July, 1827. These do contain references, however, to a tariff which was drawn up in April, 1825, and make it clear that the Association was already in being at least two years before the new works at St Helens came into production.

The Association was chiefly concerned with regulating the prices at which manufacturers sold their glass to merchants and dealers. The tariff took account of regional differences and this respect for the traditional channels of trade gives the lists of prices a realistic appearance and suggests that many years of trial and error may possibly have lain behind this particular arrangement. There were three separate English price lists: for London; for Liverpool, Manchester, Leeds, Sheffield, and Birmingham; and for Newcastle glass sold to 'country dealers'. Ireland had its own list and so had Scotland. There were five qualities of glass: firsts (an ideal which was never realized at either the St Helens or Spon Lane works), seconds, thirds, fourths and CC, the last being described as 'the worst glass ever made'.[23] The chief difference between the three English lists was not in the basic price of the glass but in the size of the crates and the amount of discount which was allowed. For the London market, for Scotland and for 'glaziers on the West' supplied by Newcastle, the imaginary firsts were quoted in crates of twelve tables, seconds in crates of fifteen, and thirds, fourths and CC in crates of sixteen. Elsewhere, however, all qualities were packed in twelve–table crates, though the inferior qualities could be obtained in crates of fifteen or eighteen, if so preferred. The basic price of the glass sold to English dealers ranged from about 15s a table of 4 to 5 feet diameter for firsts to about 10s a table for fourths and 9s 6d a table for CC. But the actual price quoted varied according to the size of crate and the amount of discount. In London, where a discount of only 5 per cent. was allowed for payment within three months and forty-five days, 12 tables of firsts were listed at £9 10s 0d and 18 tables of fourths fetched £9 9s od. The Newcastle rates were almost identical (as might be expected, the Newcastle factories being the traditional suppliers of the London market) but 7½ per cent. was allowed for prompt payment or 5 per cent. within six months. A larger discount was allowed in the other English price zone (Liverpool, Manchester, Leeds, Sheffield and Birmingham): 15 per cent. for payment within three months and 10 per cent. for payment within six months. Prices were correspondingly higher: a 12-table crate of firsts cost £10 15s od (25s more than in London) and fourths in a crate of the same size cost £7 8s od. The inferior quality of glass which was disposed of in Ireland was sold much more cheaply. For that market there were only four categories: A, B, C and CC. A crate of the first cost only £4 10s od and of the last £2 10s od, 5 per cent. discount being allowed upon bills paid within six months. The following is an indication of the prices in force during the St Helens Crown Glass Company's first years:

London	1st	12 tables	£9 10s od	
	2nd	15 tables	£9 18s od	Discount 5% if bill
	3rd	18 tables	£10 2s od	paid within 3 months
	4th	18 tables	£9 9s od	and 45 days
	CC	18 tables	£8 12s 6d	

Liverpool, Manchester, Leeds, Sheffield, Birmingham

	1st	12 tables	£10 15s od	
	2nd	12 tables	£8 15s od	Discount 15% if bill
	3rd	12 tables	£7 17s od	paid within 3 months
	4th	12 tables	£7 8s od	and 10% within 6 months.
	CC	12 tables	£6 18s od	

Newcastle	1st	12 tables	£9 10s od	
	2nd	12 tables	£8 0s od	Discount 7½% for immediate
	3rd	12 tables	£6 18s od	payment or 5% if bill
	4th	12 tables	£6 9s od	paid within 6 months.
	CC	12 tables	£5 18s od	

Scotland and 'Glaziers on the West from Newcastle'

	1st	12 tables	£9 15s od	
	2nd	15 tables	£10 5s od	Discount 7½% for immediate
	3rd	18 tables	£10 11s od	payment or 5% if bill
	4th	18 tables	£9 18s od	paid within 6 months.
	CC	18 tables	£9 3s od	

Ireland	A	12 tables	£4 10s od	
	B	12 tables	£3 10s od	Discount 5% if bill
	C	12 tables	£2 15s od	paid within 3 months.
	CC	12 tables	£2 10s od	

The formal minutes of these manufacturers' meetings, handwritten at first, lithographed from 1836 and printed from 1841, contain only the results of each conference and are concerned almost entirely with variations in prices. Although the contents of the minutes were not to be divulged, as each manufacturer sent out his price list they soon became common knowledge within the trade. The minutes, therefore, contained very little of what we might call secret information. That is not to say, however, that the manufacturers did not discuss matters not mentioned in the minutes. It would be surprising if their conversations did not cover most of the topics of interest and range over the current trends in their industry. We have evidence that in later years most of the real business was transacted privately over dinner on the night before the formal, minuted meeting and this practice may have had a long history.

It is difficult to say with certainty what degree of success was achieved by the Association. We cannot discover whether the manufacturers honoured the resolutions which they passed or whether they were tempted to steal a march on one another by allowing higher discounts, selling thirds for the price of fourths or employing some other stratagem to evade the list prices. It is difficult to imagine complete harmony among rival manufacturers competing in a limited market. Disobedience to the rules could always be excused on the grounds that one was only repaying a rival in his own coin. Thus, despite several resolutions of the Association not to employ workmen who could not produce a note of discharge from their previous master, William Pilkington had no qualms in writing to his brother, Richard:

> 'As the Bristol house has a good name for well-annealed glass, it would be desirable to engage Grimes, and as you are perhaps not aware that they made overtures to Kenmore, we need not have any scruples on that head.'[24]

Nevertheless, so far as the tariff was concerned, the league of manufacturers possessed machinery which encouraged the reporting of low prices. On the complaint of two constituent firms, the secretary was obliged to summon within six weeks a full meeting of manufacturers to consider the charges and to seek redress. During the interval between the protest and the meeting, the other houses were permitted to sell at prices even lower than those charged by the allegedly offending party. Despite these strong incentives to report those who deviated from the agreed lists, the minutes of the Association contain no hint of any such complaints until 1836.[25] But the evidence is somewhat inconclusive, for there is a large gap in the minutes: at neither Pilkingtons nor Chances is there any record of a general meeting of manufacturers being held between September 16, 1830, when they met in Buxton, and October 26, 1835, when they met in Newcastle.[26] This may mean either that prices were maintained without consultation during these five years, or that meetings were held and the minutes have not survived, or that the Association had ceased to exist. On the one hand, William Pilkington reported from London in 1831 that 'the price . . . is low and squares shockingly so',[27] which suggests that price-fixing had been suspended; yet, on the other, when the minutes are resumed in 1835, they reveal every sign of continuity, which suggests that price-fixing had never been abandoned. On the whole, the slender evidence that we have during this period when demand was rising rapidly seems to point to an unbroken tradition of agreement and organization rather than to an interregnum of what contemporaries chose to call 'fighting trade'.

If this was, in fact, the case, it follows that competition within the trade was confined to the quality rather than to the price of the glass which each house produced. The more manufacturers were precluded from seeking orders by promising lower prices, the more they were obliged instead to prove to their customers that the goods which they offered were of better quality—for which the agreement permitted higher prices to be charged. In order to manufacture the necessary high-grade glass, each house sought to collect together the most skilled body of glassmakers that could be found, and each manufacturer was constantly badgering his managers and men to provide him with glass of a higher quality than that of his rivals.

This emphasis on quality was the recurring theme in the letters which William Pilkington wrote home to his brother as he travelled round the country for orders. In April, 1831, he was in London seeking to establish personal contacts in the capital, particularly with the wealthy, glass-selling house of Hayward and Chater to whom the St Helens Company's glass had been sent since the beginning of 1828.[28] He bewailed the fact that the glass which the firm had sent to London previously was 'very indifferent' and went on:

'the flashing of it is downright bad, and tell both Charles and Spanton that if we cannot have our work flashed as well as other houses, I will discharge both, if you have not done it by one already, and if James Wood does not give it us less bent out of the kiln, I will serve him the same. I am surprised, too, that Roger should say such glass was good. If he does not inform us when the work is bad and be more decided I shall be very angry with him. In consequence of the flashing being so bad and the tables so bent, there is not a crate but what has four, five, or six tables broken. Tell Robert Morgan to make his crates wider at the bottom so that they be not pinched and broken.'[29]

A week later, still in London, he returned to the charge:

'I should wish you to tell Robt. Morgan to get as many 18 table crates made as possible. Let them be a little wider at the bottom—four slips on each side—and made as strong as possible. Let Roger re-assort all glass of bad or poor colour as well as bad make, pack the worse into tables with no mark but simply 18 on the end of the crate; the better qualities of the same, as also better colour, pack into 18 table crates and mark them 18 CC. He must also pack the best glass of our present make into 18 for the London market. I hope that every exertion will be used at present to send good work, it makes glass appear 10 p. cent better. Tell Blanshard that I have seen glass from Richardsons[30] without any rim or selvage *at all*—and some Birmingham glass with very little indeed. I am not overstating facts. I could not have believed it had I not seen it. As therefore it is possible to be done, *we must if possible do the same*—and without it we need not attempt to send glass here. There will be one advantage in selling here (if we can sell it in safe hands and which I trust we shall) that as credit is shorter, we may curtail our accounts in other quarters. I have done better than I expected in getting orders but I repeat that they are all given as trial orders and our future will depend on our present execution; in fact, if the glass is good I believe I could here sell all our make.'[31]

This persistent chevying is a constant feature of William Pilkington's correspondence at this time and we may assume that, when he was present at the works, his observations were no less frank and to the point. But his criticisms were always more than mere reprimands. He always followed caustic comments by detailed remedies. On one occasion, for instance, when he learnt that there had been trouble with the furnace, he was most indignant:

'I find that the furnace broke out on Monday. Now what childish nonsense that is! They have scarcely a circumstance of that sort ever happening at Spon Lane. Then why with us? Our founders and teasers are surely old enough and have had experience enough. Then why should it happen? Let Peter take the charge of it to one period—and then the skimmer. But first ask Roger as to the right division of the time and then let a penalty be the consequence of such results in future. But if the manager says that the furnace is good when the founder leaves it, the teaser must be punished—or why give them plus at all? I was quite out of patience to hear the *cool, quiet, amiable* proposition of going four rounds this week, thereby (with number four *slightly* running) incur the risk of breaking a pot, hurry the furnace, change the mixture and waste material—all forsooth rather than a penalty should be inflicted.'[32]

If William Pilkington was insistent that the firm's glass was to be of good quality and that the works were to be conducted as efficiently as possible, he was no less concerned that proper attention should be given to salesmanship. Here he was able to draw upon his earlier training and experience in the wine and spirit business. He realized that direct contact with his customers was the key to success. As he remarked to his brother:

'I feel . . . assured of the necessity of personal interviews and regular visits to our connexions. It not only pleases them but affords them an opportunity of stating their views and wishes *in a conference*, which cannot be communicated in a letter. It also—which is an important matter—keeps that tie stronger and closer between you and them than either could or would be prudent to entrust to a traveller—"ecce signum"'—and none but who would rather do business with a principal than a clerk.'[33]

He put these principles into practice and during the early years did all the travelling for the firm himself. These journeys often involved considerable discomfort and sometimes even danger. In 1834 when he was on his way in a small 100-ton steamer from Liverpool to Holyhead *en route* to Ireland, a violent storm sprang up, prolonging the rough passage by ten hours. Another vessel which had made the same voyage at the same time sank after she had been towed into Holyhead harbour.[34] The overland journeys in these early days were made by stage coach, often in the open. During the 'thirties and 'forties the new railways made travel easier but at the outset the companies were primarily interested in goods traffic and paid little attention to the comfort of passengers. In 1838, for instance, when William Pilkington caught the train home from Birmingham, he had to be at the station by six in the morning. 'The trains from Birmingham', he grumbled—not without justification—'are at such untimely hours.'[35]

Messages to his brother give us occasional glimpses of his travels about the country making new openings, gaining customers' confidence and securing regular orders. His first visit to London, in 1831, was followed by many others. He became friendly with the Chater family and was able to write home on September 15, 1834:

> 'Mr Chater is still all kindness. He wants us to dine today in a quiet way and he has made a party of his friends and his family and friends to meet us tomorrow. He kept the last brace of birds until they were spoiled in the hope that we should return in time to eat them. To give you some idea of the extent of their, or rather his business—he received £10,000 in part payment of one contract last week.'[36]

Also in 1834 he referred to export orders, wrote about his visit to glass merchants in the West Country and described the pleading antics of hordes of beggars which he witnessed as he journeyed from place to place in search of customers in Ireland. Later, he wrote from Birmingham, Glasgow and Edinburgh. These long journeys, regularly undertaken, must have been a very severe strain. He was not a man to reveal his feelings but on one occasion, having read a depressing letter from home, he confessed that it had vexed him considerably. He confided to his brother:

> 'After having had a solitary long day's ride with my thoughts continually bent on home and its concerns, a letter ought to be a relief and a pleasure, but I really felt inclined to put off opening yours, feeling low and fatigued. . . . Mr Chance carries a book on his journeys to rest his mind from thinking about matters at home when he cannot do any good by thinking only .. .'[37]

But these long journeys were enormously successful, and the growing volume of orders which resulted from them must have gone far to cheer the lonely traveller and buoy up his sinking spirits when he was inclined to be disheartened by depressing news. The rapid expansion of output at the works bears testimony to the success of William Pilkington's salesmanship as well as to the quality of the glass which he sold.[38] In 1828 an average of 742 tables were manufactured every week. In the following year, when William Pilkington first assumed control, output fell slightly to 722 tables a week but in 1830 it rose again to 758. Then followed five years of steady, uninterrupted progress. In 1831, the year of the Mackay West circulars and the year of William Pilkington's first visit to London, glass was produced at the rate of 945 tables a week. This rapid increase was sustained in the following two years when the rate rose to 1,215 and 1,483 tables a week respectively. The building cycle was swinging upwards again, particularly in the textile districts.[39] Business was so brisk that the partners decided, in 1834, to erect a second glasshouse, which came into use in October of that year.[40] With the aid of this new furnace, output during the whole year averaged almost 2,000 tables a week and in 1835, when both houses were in operation throughout the twelve months, it exceeded 3,000. Demand was reaching a climax and the output of window glass from English factories was one-third greater than during the boom of the mid-1820's, though if Scottish production is also taken into account, the two peaks were roughly of the same magnitude. In these circumstances Greenall and Pilkingtons decided to build a third furnace. Production in 1836 exceeded 5,000 tables per week.[41] Many of the skilled glassmakers for the second and third furnaces appear to have been recruited from those who found themselves unemployed when the Dumbarton works were closed.

PRODUCTION 1828–1835

Year	Total	No. of tables per week	Annual Weight (cwt.)
1828	38,566	742	3,419
1829	37,560	722	3,229
1830	39,399	758	3,322
1831	49,152	945	4,193
1832	63,161	1,215	5,226
1833	77,136	1,483	6,350
1834	100,813	1,939	8,328
1835	160,804	3,092	13,662
1836	264,921	5,095	21,525

These extensions to the works involved additional capital outlay. By 1834 the partners had advanced £24,300 and there was an overdraft from the bank amounting to a further £9,661. When the annual turnover continued to grow and more than £5,500 had to be spent on the third house, the Pilkington brothers decided that the time had arrived to part with the family wine and spirit business and to concentrate their entire time and wealth upon the glass company.

The profits of William Pilkington and Sons were never so great after 1830 as they had been before, for in that year the duty on beer was repealed and this exercised as decisive an effect upon the sales of wine and spirits as the reduction of the spirit duty had done four years before. In 1826 the scales had been tipped in favour of the distiller and rectifier. Now they were redressed in favour of the brewer. After 1830 the margin between expenditure and receipts in the account book of William Pilkington and Sons grew ever closer. In 1830 the difference was £7,107. In 1831 it had dropped to £5,160, in 1832 to £4,872, in 1833 to £3,496, in 1834 to £3,131, and in 1835 to £2,210. As the sales of the glassworks had grown, those of the wine and spirit business had dwindled. In 1836, Richard and William Pilkington's younger brother, Thomas, who was a partner in William Pilkington and Sons, grew restive and decided on retirement.[42] (Thomas—not to be confused with William Pilkington's son of the same name, who was a partner in Pilkington Brothers from the mid-nineteenth century—turned out to be the black sheep of the family. He was a source of embarrassment to his brothers and, when he died at Leyland in 1880, their sons were concerned about the welfare of 'the two children' who 'in the natural course . . . would go to the workhouse'.[43]) It was Thomas's withdrawal from William Pilkington and Sons rather than the fall in profits that seems to have caused his elder brothers to sell the business, for the glassworks were now taking up all their time. William Pilkington confessed that they would have continued to manage the wine and spirit business, which brought in 'from 14 to 17 hundred p. annum besides keeping our two families', had the glass business not grown to such immense proportions:

> 'If we could have given up the Glass Works [he wrote] we should, but from the great outlay of Capital, in Building, etc., we should find it next to impossible. You are also aware that this is a step we at one time never contemplated but from the circumstances of our Brother Thomas giving up active business and the glass trade growing too heavy for one person to manage to advantage, we thought it better to give up one than verify the old adage of having too many irons in the fire and letting some burn.'[44]

Accordingly, the rectifying plant was sold and the premises rented as a shop from the beginning of 1837 for £250 a year.[45] This meant that William Pilkington, his wife Eliza Charlotte (whom he had married in 1824)[46] and his already large family had to find a new home. They removed to Millbrook House in Eccleston, then in the country outside St Helens, once the residence of Dr Adam Clarke, the Methodist biblical scholar, and at that time unoccupied. William Pilkington leased this property from his brothers-in-law, the Greenalls, for a term of fourteen years, at an annual rent of £30.[47]

The year 1836 marked a turning point both for Greenall and Pilkingtons and for the glass trade in general. For the Pilkington brothers, it ended the first phase in the struggle to secure a foothold in the industry. Their works were not yet fully developed and their overdraft at the bank was still increasing. But they were gradually seizing more and more of the trade. They had, indeed, done well to establish themselves firmly while trade was good; after 1836 it entered a period of depression and the Manufacturers' Association decided to set limits upon output as well as upon prices. Had Greenall and Pilkingtons not been so successful in their quest for orders while business was brisk, their quota would have been smaller and their lot would have been all the harder in the following years of depression and restriction.

The later 1830s were also a critical time for the glass industry from a technical point of view. These years saw the beginnings of the mechanization of an industry which had depended for so long upon human skill alone. The introduction of machinery into first one and then another department of glassmaking confronted manufacturers with a new challenge. It was a challenge that was taken up by the newer firms rather than by the older goliaths. It was one of those pebbles in the hands of the younger firms which were, within the space of twenty years, to prove the giants' undoing.

CHAPTER 5

THE INTRODUCTION OF A NEW TECHNIQUE

DURING the eighteenth and early nineteenth centuries, as has been noticed, crown glass slowly drove off the British market the crude form of cylinder glass, known as broad, or green, glass. Unlike broad glass, crown glass never came into contact with any surface while it was still in a malleable state. The resultant polished, lustrous appearance gave it an obvious advantage even though, since it had to be cut out of large circles, it could only be obtained in quite small-sized panes.[1] On the continent of Europe, however, crown glass went out of fashion during the eighteenth century because manufacturers there began to employ a much improved method of making cylinder glass, from which much larger panes could be cut.[2] Under the old method, the cylinder had been slit, when still hot, by means of a cold iron and clumsily opened out (or spread) on an iron plate at the mouth of the furnace.[3] By the improved method, the cylinder was allowed to cool down before being slit from end to end with an iron or a diamond.[4] It was then re-heated in a special kiln—known as a flattening kiln—to a temperature at which it could be opened out upon a piece of polished glass, called a lagre, with little damage to its surface.

There were various attempts to introduce this improved form of cylinder glass on to the British market before it was successfully launched in the 1830s. So early as 1758 the Excise Commissioners were aware of the manufacture in England of an improved form of broad glass 'appearing to be of a quality and colour greatly superior to common Green Glass and of as good colour as some Crown Glass and being judged to be Crown Glass by several Glass-makers and Glaziers'.[5] In 1777 when the excise duty on glass was doubled, special provision was made for 'Glass now called German Sheet Glass': it was taxed at twice the rate levied on broad, and at the same rate as crown.[6] At the beginning of the following year, the Society for the Encouragement of Arts, Manufactures and Commerce awarded a prize to George Ensell of Amblecote, near Stourbridge, for some sheet glass which he had manufactured, all of it in panes over 30 inches by 26 inches.[7] Shortly afterwards, in July, 1780, the firm of Honeyborne and Ensell advertised in the *Birmingham Gazette* that they were making sheet, as

80

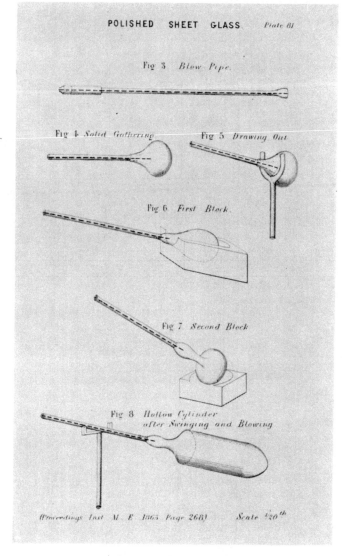

9 *Stages in the manufacture of sheet glass.*

The molten glass, cooled to working consistency and kept at this consistency by re-heating when required, was blown into a globe and, by 'blocking', formed into a shape which, when swung from side to side in a trench and further blown, became a cylinder. The ends of the cylinder were removed and it was allowed to cool before being split along its length with a diamond. It was then re-heated in a flattening kiln and opened out on a piece of polished glass, known as a *lagre*. After this the flattened sheet was taken to another kiln for annealing.

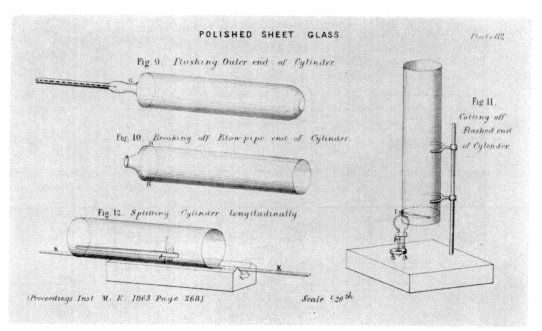

Millbrook House

10   The Residences of William Pilkington

Eccleston Hall

well as crown, glass at their factory near Stourbridge.[8] This venture appears to have been short-lived; but there are various scraps of later evidence to show that manufacturers continued to be interested in the possibility of launching sheet glass on the British market. Robert Lucas Chance's uncle, John Robert Lucas, for instance, who was a proprietor of Nailsea glassworks, took out a patent in 1805 for 'An Improvement in the Art or Method of Making, Spreading or Flattening Sheet Glass, Plate Glass or any other Spread Glass requiring a polished surface'.[9] The Tyneside glassmakers attempted to develop a market for sheet glass some time after this but did not succeed.[10]

Two explanations are usually advanced for Britain's clinging to crown glass manufacture when a better process was available. The first is that, by the later eighteenth century, crown glass with its lustrous finish had become so firmly established and so highly esteemed that no alternative which lacked such a finish could be made to appeal to the customer. The second is that, since the production of sheet glass involved a new type of skill, it could only be introduced if workmen, trained abroad, were brought over here at great expense to start the new process and if new kilns were built. It is hard to believe in either of these explanations as the main reason for the tardy arrival of sheet glass, though they may have been quite important secondary ones. One would expect, rather, to trace Britain's slowness in adopting this innovation in some way to the workings of the excise duty on glass, for this was the only fundamental point of difference between the industry in Britain and that on the continent of Europe.

Here there is, in fact, a much more plausible explanation to be found. The duty on window glass was levied by weight, but the glass was sold by size and quality. With the duty so high—twice the prime cost of production—the manufacturer had every incentive to make his panes as thin, and therefore as light, as he could. He then paid the least possible amount of duty and yet received roughly the same market price for his product since the size would not be affected at all and the quality very little. Because it was made by a centrifugal process, crown glass could more easily be made thinner than could sheet glass. It was easier to spin out a thin table than to blow a thin cylinder. The higher rates of duty imposed during the Napoleonic Wars and not subsequently reduced did, in fact, cause crown glass to be made very much thinner than it had previously been. The window glass manufacturers who, in 1830, urged a revision of the excise duties and cited the very small increase in the total output of window glass by weight since the early 1790s, had to agree that this was attributable in part to 'the skill of the manufacturer having diminished the weight of glass relative to the surface'.[11] It was suggested in 1835 that sheet glass was usually about 40 per cent. thicker than crown.[12] Even if this were a slight overestimate, and if we make due allowance for the greater wastage in crown glass manufacture, the balance would still be tipped strongly against sheet glass, particularly in the early days of its manufacture, so long as the rate of duty remained high. When the considerable initial capital expenditure (in securing labour and building plant) and the public prejudice against any window glass without a bright surface are also taken into account, it is hardly surprising that would-be pioneers became discouraged. The initial obstacles were great and the ultimate success far from certain.

We have already seen, however, that the operation of the glass excise duty was quite unpredictable in its effects. Here again it sprang one of its surprises. Paradoxically, the workings of the duty, which had done so much to discourage the introduction of sheet glass manufacture, eventually made its introduction possible.

Since 1813 an additional drawback (or rebate of duty) of one-third had been granted on squares of window glass when exported. For every hundredweight of glass on which £3 13s 6d was paid in duty, the manufacturer was entitled to draw back £4 18s od from the Excise Commissioners for glass exported in the form of panes.[13] The intention of this rebate was to compensate crown glass manufacturers—that being the only kind of window glass then exported—for the wastage in cutting the square panes out of the circular tables. The excise authorities, however, put sheet glass in just the same category as crown and any sheet glass which was exported could also claim the rebate, even though there was no wastage in cutting panes out of the flattened cylinders. What was a compensation to the exporter of crown glass became a bounty for anyone who chose to send abroad panes of sheet glass.

This, William Chance (R. L. Chance's brother), who was a prominent Birmingham merchant with important American connections, decided to do. Having come to the rescue of the Spon Lane business in 1831, he was determined to inject new life into it by introducing the manufacture of sheet glass chiefly for export, counting on a welcome little subsidy from public funds to assist him in this praiseworthy and patriotic venture. As the firm frankly confessed when the Excise Commissioners asked how, in sixteen months, Chances had paid £24,451 in duty and drawn back £25,061—an estimated gain of some £1,250, allowing for home sales:[14]

'This [bounty] was taken into consideration by them as a set-off against the overwhelming expense that was necessarily attendant on the establishment of a new branch of the manufacture; and it was not to be supposed that a Law of Twenty Years standing would be abrogated for the simple purpose of suspending a new manufacture until the duty should be taken off and this under an enlightened Government which would be naturally anxious that a source of National Wealth, so scientific and so important, should meet with all the fostering encouragement it deserved.'[15]

The Excise Collector at Stourbridge reported in May, 1832, that William Chance had sent James Hartley to a factory near Paris where he gained 'such a competent knowledge of the manufacture he has no fear but he can superintend and carry on a similar one in this country with the assistance of workmen from the Continent'. Accordingly, William Chance had ordered that one of the crown houses be converted for the purpose and these alterations were then proceeding under the direction of John Hartley and James, his son.[16] In gaining knowledge of the sheet glass process and in recruiting workmen, Chance and Hartleys were greatly assisted by Georges Bontemps, whose factory at Choisy-le-Roi was almost certainly that referred to by the Excise Collector. Bontemps had visited England in 1828 and R. L. Chance, together with John Hartley, had gone to see Bontemps' factory in 1830.[17]

Sheet glass was first blown at Spon Lane in August, 1832.[18] North America was its principal destination. The firm had a depot in New York, with George Chance (R. L. Chance's brother) in charge. By October, 1835, this market was described in the Board's minutes as 'one of the greatest importance to our manufacture'.[19] In 1835 the Excise authorities, at last alive to the bounty which they were unwittingly giving to the exporter of sheet glass, reduced the drawback from £4 18s od to £4 4s od per cwt., and in 1838 this was further reduced to £4.[20] By then, however, the new process was firmly established and some of the glass was beginning to be sold on the home market. The great demand for window glass during the building boom of the mid-1830s had enabled Chances to sell over 4,000 cwt. at home in 1835, though for some reason—possibly the boom in America—all their output was shipped abroad in the following year, despite an even greater strengthening of demand. Home sales did not really begin until after 1837. This may be seen from the following table:

BRITISH SHEET GLASS EXPORTED AND RETAINED FOR
HOME CONSUMPTION, 1832–1844

Calendar year	Exports cwt.	Home consumption cwt.	For comparison: Total production of Crown Glass cwt.
1832	692	179	103,030
1833	4,422	Nil	125,562
1834	5,343	Nil	131,365
1835	6,135	4,248	144,210
1836	8,498	Nil	155,431
1837	5,449	707	150,399
1838	4,412	2,262	140,879
1839	4,787	5,170	126,755
1840	8,156	7,914	128,113
1841	8,766	11,298	116,895
1842	7,662	17,117	97,495
1843	7,520	21,634	102,222
1844	7,703	23,857	104,340

Sources: Parliamentary Returns, 1839 [419] XLVI; 1844 [414] XXXII; 1845 [169] XLVI; statistics at Library of H.M. Customs and Excise.

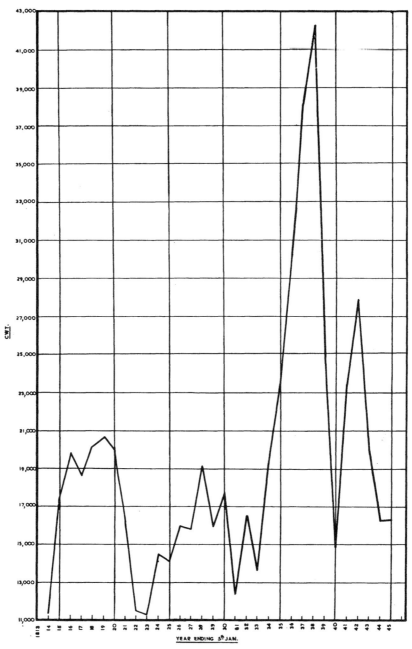

CWT.

YEAR ENDING 5ᵗ JAN.

EXPORTS OF CROWN & SHEET GLASS (ENGLAND & SCOTLAND)

1813 – 1844

[Entries refer to previous years. E.g. year ending 5 January 1814 = 1813]

Graph 6. Source: Excise Returns

84

The increase in home sales of sheet glass at the beginning of the 1840s, during one of the worst depression periods in British history, was chiefly due to the resourcefulness of James Timmins Chance, R. L. Chance's nephew. He entered the business in 1838, straight from Cambridge where he had read mathematics and had been seventh wrangler in his year.[21] He is an interesting early example of the graduate entering British industry. Without any previous technical training, he proceeded to add a refinement to the sheet glass process which improved the finished product considerably and made it a much more attractive selling line.

Glassmakers in France had already tried to remove the dull appearance of sheet glass by smoothing and polishing it, using techniques similar to those employed in the manufacture of plate glass, but these experiments had been unsuccessful. In 1836 two Birmingham men, Robert Griffiths, a machine maker, and John Gold, a glass cutter, took out a patent for improvements in machinery 'for grinding, smoothing and polishing plate glass, window glass, marble, slate and stone and also glass vessels, glass spangles and drops'.[22] R. L. Chance bought a half interest in this somewhat all-embracing patent[23] and used it as a prototype to be adapted to his own particular needs. It was at this juncture that J. T. Chance entered the business. Within the space of a few months he felt justified in taking out a patent of his own.

The patent specification, dated October, 1838,[24] sets out quite clearly the difficulties associated with the polishing of sheet glass as well as the manner in which they were overcome. The excise duty on the thicker plate glass was levied at a higher rate than that upon window glass. A maximum thickness had therefore to be fixed for window glass to prevent its being ground and polished and exported as plate glass at a higher rate of drawback. One-ninth of an inch was the stipulated maximum.[25] Smoothing and polishing at this thickness was an extremely tricky operation, only possible if the flexible characteristic of this glass could be turned to good account. Chance's patent depended on bedding the glass to be polished, not upon plaster of Paris as was the prevailing practice for plate glass, but upon a foundation of damp leather. As the patent specification put it:

'The glass, when laid on this level or plane surface, will seldom, if ever, lie flatly, so as to touch at all parts upon the table, but as the glass is flexible to a considerable extent, and may be readily bended, it is capable of being pressed down close to the damp bed or table by commencing pressure at the one edge, and passing over the other, in a somewhat similar manner to the action used in pasting a sheet of paper on to a level surface.'

Two sheets of glass, each bedded upon this impressionable leather base, were rubbed one upon the other with emery powder or burnt copperas (rouge)—the smoothing and polishing materials—placed between them.

The newly-patented idea took time to develop. 'My new process,' wrote J. T. Chance on July 2, 1839, 'as far as it extends at present answers perfectly: but we have determined not to make any regular sales until we can ensure a large supply.'[26] Among his earliest customers was Joseph Paxton who, in 1839, glazed the conservatory at Chatsworth with what a rather bewildered newspaper reporter described as 'patent flattened crown glass'. This, it was observed, was 'much thicker than the common crown glass . . . and the panes may be made 40 inches long at the same cost per foot as ordinary sized panes'.[27] In the following year, 1840, J. T. Chance was able to tell the makers about the successful trial of the first seven smoothing machines. He went on to ask when he was to receive 'the last pair of eight polishing machines so as to finish the first division'.[28] In making these preparations, the pioneer of the Midlands depended to a large extent on the skill and resources of Lancashire. Wren and Bennett of Manchester built all his machinery. A. B. Goss of Ormskirk, was approached for a supply of felt[29] and enquiries were made at a St Helens chemical works to see if the proprietors would provide the necessary polishing powder. Chances appear to have begun at last to market their new product towards the end of 1840.[30] In January, 1841, its creator was able to write jubilantly that 'our sheet plate [sic] is carrying all before it', though he had to admit that initial sales were hampered by the high retail price.[31] Although J. T. Chance himself called the product sheet plate, it came to be generally known as patent plate.

Once a growing home demand for cylinder glass began to emerge, other concerns started to take an interest in its manufacture. Among them was the new firm of James and John Hartley. Although they had gone into partnership with the Chances after their father's death in December, 1833, they soon became restive and in November, 1836, the partnership was dissolved.[32] They moved to the north-east and established the Wear Glassworks at Sunderland in 1837. There they began to experiment with cylinder glass in the following year.[33] Cooksons, the old-established Tyneside firm, also began to take an interest in the new sheet glass, as did Greenall and Pilkingtons. At a manufacturers' meeting in August, 1841, it was decided that Greenall and Pilkingtons, Cooksons, and Hartleys should all be given a sheet glass quota, but the production of none of these firms was to exceed half that of Spon Lane.

Greenall and Pilkingtons chose a good time to enter this promising field. A market had been created without any trouble or expense on their part and glassmakers skilled in this particular type of manufacture were by then to be found in England. It was an extremely wise move to begin the manufacture of sheet glass during a period of depression when capital expenditure was at a minimum and when there was the prospect of a few years of moderate, or slack, demand in which to overcome teething troubles before the next building boom arrived.

Abraham Hartley—a distant relative of James and John—who came to St Helens from Spon Lane to work for Greenall and Pilkingtons in 1835, later recalled that the first sheet glassmakers to be employed at St Helens were some Belgians who had previously worked at Spon Lane and then in Sunderland. He went on to describe how they came to St Helens and how others learned the tricks of their trade:

'One day a Belgian whom I had known at Chances, named Legget—nay, I don't know how the name is spelt—called on me and asked what sort of masters I had. I told him and he came to terms, I suppose, with them for he started blowing sheets soon after. Then others came along and they worked away amongst us. Certainly they tried to keep their operations as secret as they could, but they each had to have a gatherer and the gatherers saw how the thing was done. It was all a question of knack. . . . Gradually our men picked it up and they and the Belgians used to work side by side at the blowing. . . . One or two of them were big, powerful chaps; and they were rather objects of curiosity when they walked the streets. They only spoke English indifferently well; most of their leisure time they spent playing bagatelle at the Peel Arms in Westfield Street. . . . They gradually got scattered; one went to Liverpool where he started business in the public line; two of them died and are buried in Windleshaw.'[34]

The census of June, 1841, shows that a glassmaker named Jean Baptiste Leguay, aged 33, was then living in St Helens. Two other foreign glassmakers, Daniel Schmidt and Louis Dartes, lived close by.[35] Alphonse Demanet, described on the tombstone as 'Directeur de la Verrerie Francaise' at Pilkingtons, who was born in Namur on February 19, 1812, died in St Helens on April 7, 1845, and was buried at the old Roman Catholic cemetery at Windleshaw as Hartley stated.[36]

Early in 1842, Greenall and Pilkingtons acquired a vacant two-storey cotton mill, not far from their factory, in which to erect their smoothing and polishing equipment. (The site was not far from present-day Kirkland Street.) There was no difficulty in securing a lease, for the owner was Peter Greenall himself. On March 4, 1842, the three partners (now described as crown and sheet glass manufacturers) agreed to rent the building for £131 10s 0d a year, the first payment to be made six months after the firm should 'commence polishing German Sheet Glass at or upon the aforesaid premises'. Exactly how sheet glass was polished there must remain something of a mystery, for Greenall and Pilkingtons never took out a licence from J. T. Chance to use his patented process. On September 14, 1842, the holder of the patent wrote to Wren and Bennett:

'You are probably aware that two glass manufacturers, Cooksons and Pilkingtons, are now grinding and polishing German Sheet glass, *in what manner* I am quite in the dark.'[37]

By March of the following year, he seems to have made up his mind on the matter. The Board of Chances resolved:

'That J. T. Chance write to Mr Pilkington to inform him that we are satisfied that he is invading our patent in his mode of grinding and polishing glass.'[38]

Greenall and Pilkingtons appear to have started off by trying to adapt to their needs the unpatented smoothing and polishing methods then used in the manufacture of plate glass. This used plaster of Paris as a bed for the glass. J. T. Chance himself thought that plaster of Paris might be able to serve the purpose and, in September, 1842, he wrote to Wren and Bennett, telling them to hold up any further work on the machinery he had ordered from them until it was known whether these experiments were a success.[39] Two months earlier Hartleys had written from Sunderland to the British Plate Glass Company to enquire whether their sheet glass could be finished at Ravenhead; but this request was refused.[40] These experiments with plaster of Paris do not appear to have met with any success; a few years later J. T. Chance could say dogmatically that 'People may grind [sic] this glass upon the principle of cast plate glass as much as they please, for it will prove a failure'.[41] This being the case, Greenall and Pilkingtons had to devise another method in order to avoid having to pay royalties to their greatest rival.

They called in Henry Deacon, a young man in his early twenties, who was later to achieve a considerable reputation as a manufacturing chemist at Widnes. Deacon had been apprenticed to the London engineering firm of Galloway and Son. When they went out of business, his indentures had been transferred to Nasmyth and Gaskells, at whose Bridgewater Foundry at Patricroft he is said to have been intimately concerned with designing the famous Steam Hammer.[42] We do not know the date of his arrival in St Helens, but it is unlikely to have been before 1843, when he reached his majority and, assuming his apprenticeship was of seven years, when he had served his time. Perhaps he first came to Greenall and Pilkingtons as one of Nasmyth and Gaskell's employees. It is possible that this firm may have had the contract to install the polishing benches and that young Deacon was sent to assist. In this case he may have agreed to stay on with Greenall and Pilkingtons when the work was completed.

The first definite evidence that Deacon was engaged in this work is contained in a statutory declaration that he had 'invented Improvements in Apparatus for Grinding and Smoothing Plate Glass, Crown Glass and Sheet Glass'.[43] The declaration itself was undated, but it was written on a piece of paper bearing a legal stamp dated December 17, 1844. Having reserved the right to this invention, he described it in greater detail in the specification of a patent taken out in May of the following year.[44] He continued to lay the sheets of glass either on plaster of Paris 'in the usual mode . . . or, when sufficiently true . . . on a wet cloth supported on a piece of felt of about half an inch thick'. In essence this was the same as Chance's patent, the only difference being the substitution of wet cloth upon felt for wet leather as the all-important impressionable surface. (Pilkingtons were still using wet cloth for this purpose twenty years later.)[45] The detailed enumeration of the speeds at which the machinery was to run with different grades of emery and a device for allowing 'the more perfect spreading of the raw emery or other abrading material' did not disguise the fact that Deacon may have succeeded in getting round Chance's patent by a comparatively minor change. In this respect James Hartley kept him company: in July, 1843, Hartley had taken out a patent for polishing sheet glass in which he employed india-rubber in place of leather.[46]

From polishing sheet glass, Deacon turned his attention to designing flattening kilns.[47] Here again he was concerned with only minor improvements, scarcely comparable with those continental developments in kiln construction which J. T. Chance introduced into England in 1842.[48] Deacon realized the importance of preserving a good surface to the lagre, the piece of glass that was placed over the stone in the flattening kiln to give the flattened cylinder an even surface. By the method then in use, the lagre and sheet, still hot from flattening, were both loaded on to a small carriage and pushed from the flattening kiln into the annealing kiln, where the sheet was unloaded by means of a fourchette and piled by the side of other sheets to be slowly cooled. While the lagre was removed from the flattening kiln, dust fell on to the flattening stone which, on the return of the lagre, raised (in Deacon's own words) 'bumps and cockles, only too faithfully copied by the sheets afterwards flattened upon it'. By Deacon's patent, the flattening stone was no longer left exposed to the dust. He placed a series of wheels in the floor itself, each wheel protruding very slightly, so that the flattening stone *and* the lagre with the flattened sheet upon it could all be pushed through into the annealing kiln. He also devised a method, using counterbalancing weights, by which the door between the two kilns could be opened with the least exertion. At the end of 1845 William Pilkington was able to describe the firm's flattening kilns as 'the best kilns of the day'; they were sufficiently unusual to cause an employee to abscond with a model of them which he tried to sell to a rival.[49]

The successful introduction of cylinder glass to the British market in the late 'thirties and early 'forties was a development of great importance to the glass industry. Crown glass had survived so long unchallenged in Britain chiefly because of the excise laws. In 1845, when the excise duty was removed, those firms which had already managed to establish cylinder glass departments, had an enormous advantage over their competitors who had clung to crown glass alone. The technical changes which had taken place were to have profound economic consequences. We must now retrace our steps, therefore, and look at the late 'thirties and the 'forties from the window of the counting house rather than from the heat of the furnace or the dust of the polishing bench.

CHAPTER 6

YEARS OF CONTRAST

THE building boom of the mid-1830s, which had been particularly marked in the Lancashire textile districts, reached its peak in 1836. In 1837 and 1838 building activity slackened. It rose again in 1839 and 1840, only to fall more sharply in 1841 and 1842 to a trough in 1843. From then onwards there was a renewal of activity and the boom which developed in the middle of the 1840s reached a higher level than that of ten years earlier and was higher even than that of 1825.

Output of window glass reflected the movement of the building cycle, though the recovery of 1839 and 1840—attributed chiefly to railway building[1]—found no echo in home demand for glass. Output of crown glass continued to be reduced until, at the depth of the depression, it was 30 per cent. lower than it had been at the height of the boom:

BUILDING ACTIVITY AND WINDOW GLASS OUTPUT, 1836–1846

Calendar Year	Brick Output (million bricks)	Crown Glass		Sheet Glass	
		retained at home (cwt.)	exported (cwt.)	retained at home (cwt.)	exported (cwt.)
1836	1,606	125,779	29,652	nil	8,498
1837	1,478	113,562	36,837	707	5,449
1838	1,427	120,465	20,414	2,262	4,412
1839	1,569	116,671	10,084	5,170	4,787
1840	1,678	112,797	15,316	7,914	8,156
1841	1,424	97,793	19,102	11,298	8,766
1842	1,272	85,126	12,369	17,117	7,662
1843	1,159	93,481	8,741	21,634	7,520
1844	1,421	95,709	8,631	23,857	7,703
1845	1,821	Excise duty removed			
1846	2,040				

Sources: H. A. Shannon, 'Bricks—a Trade Index, 1785–1849', *Economica*, 1934; Parliamentary Returns, 1839 [419], XLVI; 1844 [414], XXXII; 1845 [169] XLVI; statistics at Library of H.M. Customs and Excise.

By contrast, output of sheet glass showed steady growth throughout these years. Home sales exceeded exports regularly after 1841, and by 1844 about 25 per cent. as much sheet glvss as crown glass was being made in Britain. This was despite the operation of the excise laws which had tipped the scales in favour of the thinner crown glass. The repeal of the glass duties in 1845 removed this handicap and at last gave manufacturers of sheet glass an advantage. The firms which clung to crown glass manufacture alone were not able to withstand for long the unfettered competition from the new technique.

Greenall and Pilkingtons, having greatly increased the capacity of their works to meet the heavy demands of the mid-1830s, were soon obliged to retrench. They could have had very little return on the new furnaces they had installed for the shrinking market soon left them with surplus capacity. On November 30, 1838, William Pilkington wrote home:

'. . . As the demand for glass, both in Ireland and England, will fall off, we must immediately give notice to more hands to go, which as we have already commenced, must be followed up—and notice must be given too, to the customers to reduce their accounts as much as possible.'

Again on December 8th:

'I am glad that you go on discharging hands. I told Peter Benson that his wages should remain as they were but I did not say that we would never give him notice. Of course he must have notice, and can if he chooses. . . . If you think proper to give him 22/- I have no objections, but it is come to something if we cannot discharge a workman who is of value only in his own estimation.'

Meanwhile the manufacturers were making their own plans to meet the coming depression through their Association. Richard and William Pilkington were present at a well-attended meeting held at the Adelphi Hotel in Liverpool on October 10, 11 and 12, 1838, at which a proposal was made to restrict the total British output of crown glass to 1,500,000 tables a year. Each firm's quota was to be based upon the proportion that its output had borne to the total production of the country during the four years 1834-7. Thus, for example, a company that produced one-thirtieth of the total product of British factories during those four years would be permitted to make one-thirtieth of 1,500,000 tables of crown glass during the first year in which the restriction was in force. The necessary details of each firm's output were to be ascertained from the returns of excise duty, and Richard Shortridge, a member of the Association, was delegated to inspect these returns. Provision was made for a system of fines in order to penalize those concerns which exceeded their quota. At the outset, each firm was to pay into a central fund the same number of shillings as its allotted weekly quota of tables of glass. From these payments each stood to lose one shilling for every table it produced in excess of its quota. There were, however, arrangements to wipe out such fines if output subsequently fell below the allocation to such an extent that the prescribed limit was not exceeded over three consecutive quota periods.

This stinting of output was a scheme which favoured the larger, well-established house at the expense of the smaller, growing firm. The latter's production was bound to be more heavily curtailed by a quota based on a four-yearly average than was the output of the older firms, whose rate of growth had not been so rapid. The policy of restriction guaranteed to the older firms a larger proportion of the total British output than they were making at the time the quota was mooted. It is not surprising, therefore, to discover that the whole plan of limiting output was devised by the men of the north-east. Nichol, of the Newcastle Broad and Crown Glass Company, originated it. Shortridge, a proprietor of the firm in South Shields which bore his name, supervised it, and a bank in South Shields held the forfeit fund.

The conception of restricting output along the lines suggested aroused strong opposition; so much so that the men of the north-east had to agree to delay its introduction. Two months after the Liverpool meeting William Pilkington still believed that restriction would not be applied. On December 8th, for instance, he wrote to his brother:

‘ I would take no notice of the restriction if it be carried. It will soon be broken up before any penalty can be required.’

Ten days later, having seen three of the manufacturers of the north-east, Shortridge, Ridley and Nichol, two of whom were prime movers in the scheme, he wrote again:

‘The restriction is their sole panacea and their object is to keep us out of the market and prevent us upstarts from growing greater. I contend that if the restriction is not carried, the prices may remain as at present. . . . I am convinced that we must discharge more hands and just make for our demand which the present rate of plus [3] enables us to do at less cost, for again, if the restriction were carried it would not long exist. . . . I think that there is very little hope of the Gentn. in the North either agreeing among themselves or with us. Therefore we must cultivate as good an acquaintance as possible with our neighbours, Messrs Chance and the Bristol house. In that case, too, restricted make is at an end.’

But at the beginning of the new year there was a complete change in William Pilkington's attitude to the restriction policy, probably occasioned in part by a worsening of the economic situation and in part by concessions he gained as a result of hard bargaining with the promoters of the policy. Although the four-year quota was retained, there were two changes in the scheme as it had been originally proposed at Liverpool. The quota was no longer related to a national total; each house was to make ten per cent. less than it had *itself* made during the four-year period. This was a definite gain to the rising concerns. It was also decided that any house could by arrangement transfer part of its allotted make to another firm. Further flexibility was gained when three of the north-eastern companies—the Newcastle Broad and Crown Glass Company, the North Tyne Glass Company and Isaac Cookson and Company—agreed to amalgamate their quantities with the Bristol house (Lucas Coathupes and Company) and Greenall and Pilkingtons. Thus, three months after William Pilkington had declared himself irreconcilably opposed to the schemers of the north-east, we find him supporting them, having obviously struck a bargain which was to his firm's advantage.

Nevertheless, his forecast that this attempt at regulating output would fail was soon realized. The refusal of one of the Association's members to agree to a further ten per cent. reduction in output, which was decided by the Association in August, 1839, caused the whole scheme of regulation to be dropped from the following November 20th. When market conditions deteriorated still further, however, the Association was driven to attempt another quota—this time successfully—in August, 1841. Again, the quota involved a ten per cent. reduction, but on this occasion it was upon the output of each firm in 1839 and 1840. There was also a most significant arrangement relating to sheet glass. Chances were to make ten per cent. less than they had made in the previous year. Cooksons, Hartleys, and Greenall and Pilkingtons were also given an allowance; they could each make half as much sheet glass as Chances. This was a generous quota when Chances' lead in this field is taken into account. The other concerns appear to have been quite content to forgo this opportunity of making sheet glass themselves. Indeed, it was agreed that they should not start to make it during the term the quota was in force, it being understood that the four firms who had an allowance would supply them at a discount. This interesting—and for all the abstaining firms, suicidal—clause deserves quotation:

> 'In consideration that such Crown Glass Manufacturers as are not now Manufacturers of German Sheet agree not to commence the manufacture of it, Messrs Chance, Cookson, the St Helens Compy. and Hartley, agree to allow the other Crown Glass Manufacturers not less than five per cent. on the net price charged to London first-class dealers for the Sheet Glass they may purchase by way of Commission and Guarantee; and they also undertake to supply them with whatever quantity of Sheet Glass they may require in the ordinary way of trade so long as the regulations are in force.'

Cooksons never took enthusiastically to sheet glass. In April, 1842, they even went so far as to sacrifice one-third of their total allocation to Chances in exchange for an addition to their own crown glass quota. (The amounts involved

—2,000 cwt. of sheet glass for 1,250 cwt. of crown glass—are a further indication of the greater weight of sheet glass in proportion to surface area.) It was clearly not the men of the north-east but Chances, Hartleys, and Greenall and Pilkingtons who were taking full advantage of the new technical developments in the industry. By 1841, therefore, the restriction policy, at first so carefully devised to prevent the 'upstarts from growing greater', was having precisely the opposite effect.

Greenall and Pilkingtons' production figures during these years reveal to what extent William Pilkington had succeeded in turning the restriction policy to his firm's advantage. The amount allocated under the first short-lived quota is not known. As it was in force only for a few months, it could have had little effect. In fact, during the whole of that year, 1839, Greenall and Pilkingtons' production was at the same level as it had been in 1835, when demand was strong. The firm's second quota was in the region of 11,250 cwt. of crown glass and 6,450 cwt. of sheet glass. The allocation of crown glass was not quite taken up in 1841 and 1842, but it was reached in 1843 and exceeded in 1844. The firm's share of the total national output of crown glass rose during these years from one-twelfth to one-tenth. The production of sheet glass, in its infancy so far as Greenall and Pilkingtons were concerned, fell short of the quota by one-third in 1842 and by one-seventh in 1843, but in 1844 it came much closer to the permitted amount. Taking crown and sheet glass together, the firm's total production of window glass steadily increased from 1840, right through the trough of the depression.

GREENALL AND PILKINGTON'S OUTPUT OF GLASS, 1838–44

Calendar Year	Tables	Crown Glass Weight cwt.	Quota cwt.	Sheet Glass Weight cwt.	Quota cwt.
1838	145,132	11,662	No quota		
1839	167,286	13,681	Not known		
1840	140,872	10,237	No quota		
1841	68,680*	5,241*	5,609*	1,970*	3,214*
1842	135,536	10,350	11,249	4,380	6,445
1843	141,419	11,250	11,249	5,590	6,445
1844	144,625	11,385	11,249	6,655	7,070

*Half year only.

Source: Two lists of production figures drawn up by William Pilkington about 1840 and about 1844.

Greenall and Pilkingtons' policy of taking calculated risks, which led them to build two additional glasshouses in the mid-30s when trade was brisk and to embark upon a new technique of manufacture in 1841 when it was slack, yielded encouraging results even before the building cycle started to swing upwards once more. But heavy expenditure of capital was involved, and, as the years passed, the firm's overdraft at the bank grew larger. As early as September,

1834, when William Pilkington had just returned from a visit to the continent, he admitted that this debt was his major worry. 'My principal uneasiness at being absent', he wrote, 'is that the world may say that I am spending time and money abroad that ought to be spent elsewhere. If we were out of debt, I would not mind'. At that time the overdraft at Parr's Bank in Warrington was just under £10,000. By the end of 1835 it had reached £13,410 and a year later it had risen to £17,292. When trade deteriorated towards the end of 1838, there are signs that the bank began to grow restive about the size of this overdraft and William Pilkington for a time gave Warrington a wide berth in order to avoid his bankers. On one occasion, in November 1838, he told them that he had no time to call and, relating this to his brother, he added: 'any excuse, you will say, is better than none'. He did not wish anything to be mentioned 'about our account as we will endeavour to reduce it by changing our system as much as we are able and will try afterwards not to increase it but to decrease it as much as possible after the latter end of March [1839]'. In May 1840, £6,000 was raised on mortgage at 5 per cent. from Thomas Brooke of Norton Priory in Cheshire, and some of this may have been used to reduce the debt at the bank. The beginnings of sheet glass manufacture in the following year, however, certainly caused the overdraft to be increased and in 1842 it stood at £20,000. In that year a three-elevenths share in the partnership was valued at £7,000, making the entire partnership capital worth a little more than £25,660. When the £6,000 mortgage is taken into account, the overdraft at the bank was not quite covered by the estimated value of the shares. That the bank permitted the overdraft to be increased under these circumstances at a time when trade was depressed, makes it quite clear that Greenall and Pilkingtons were able to take advantage of the Greenall interest in Parr's Bank.[4] Without this private influence, it seems highly unlikely that the additional capital would have been forthcoming for the all-important venture into sheet glass manufacture. Greenall support at this critical juncture was of crucial importance to the firm's later success.

It is difficult to explain why Peter Greenall, having exercised his decisive influence on the firm's behalf, should have chosen to withdraw from the partnership shortly afterwards. Perhaps his election, in 1841, as one of the Members of Parliament for the Borough of Wigan, may have had some bearing on the matter. Certainly Greenall withdrew from the firm on the best of terms with his brothers-in-law, and the conditions under which the partnership was dissolved make it quite clear that Greenall did not need the money and had no intention of embarrassing the firm by demanding its immediate repayment. According to the agreement, signed on February 1, 1842, Richard and William Pilkington were to repay him his share, then worth £7,000, over seven years in twenty-eight quarterly instalments of £250. The partnership of Greenall and Pilkingtons was not formally dissolved, therefore, until 1849. By that time, however,

Peter Greenall was but a legal fiction. He died from a stroke while on a visit to William Pilkington at Millbrook House on September 18, 1845.[5] The official notice announcing the dissolution of the partnership, which eventually appeared in the *London Gazette* in 1849, stated that it was dissolved as from the date of Peter Greenall's death.

The mid-1840s saw a big increase in demand for window glass. Subsequent writers have tended to explain this remarkable development solely in terms of the removal of the excise duty, without reference either to the growth in building activity or to the effects of the window tax. A discussion of the effects upon the glass industry of both the excise duty and the window tax is therefore necessary at this point.

Until the nineteenth century windows were considered a luxury. It was not until the pioneers of sanitary reform began to campaign for light and airy houses that the inhabitants of the British Isles came to realize that the provision of more windows would help to reduce the death-rate. Until it was appreciated that windows were a necessity and not a luxury, they were considered suitable objects of taxation. They were, in fact, taxed twice—by a duty on the glass and by a further duty on the house windows themselves. Both duties had been first imposed during the 1690s as a means of raising supplies for the wars of William III. The tax on glass was dropped in 1699 and not levied again until 1746, but that on windows was retained. From the middle of the eighteenth century both were greatly increased, as the public expenditure of the day dictated.[6]

Glass manufacturers showed more opposition to the window tax than they did to the excise duty. According to them, the excise duty might be a cause of irritation—the activities of the excisemen in the factories and the rules and regulations for levying the duty were constant causes of complaint—but it did not limit demand as did the window tax. This was the theme on which manufacturers constantly harped. R. L. Chance, for instance, was asked by the Commissioners of Excise Enquiry:

'You are of the opinion that the tax on windows is much more injurious to consumption than the duty on window glass?'

He replied:

'Most assuredly. I think that is obvious from the style of building here and on the Continent. If you go to Hamburg and the northern, or to France and the southern, parts of Europe, the windows are double to what they are here.'[7]

It seems unlikely that the excise duty, heavy though it was, had much effect upon demand. Just after its repeal, in 1845, *The Economist* noted that the tax

96

on glass had raised the selling price to as much as three times its untaxed cost; but even at that price the cost of putting windows in a building was not greater than that of the same quantity of plain brickwork.[8] This branch of the industry had not much to gain from repeal. On the other hand, it had much to lose. Manufacturers held large stocks of glass on which duty had been paid and were afraid lest they should have to bear the loss involved when the duties were removed. More important, they realized that the repeal would lead to loss of protection against glass imported from abroad. While the excise duties were high, hardly any foreign glass came into the country;[10] but once these duties were removed, the selling prices of both British and foreign glass would grow closer to one another. As Chances noticed in 1833:

> 'one of the effects of the repeal of the glass duties would be that the cheap Green Glass of Belgium would come into Great Britain in large quanties unless a considerable duty by weight was laid upon it, and as the best quality of sheet glass would also come in, it would behove us in case of such repeal to do all we can with [the] Government to lay on not only a duty by weight but by value also.'[11]

Chances were then beginning to profit from the excise drawback, as we have seen. It is significant that, once their sheet glass was well launched on the market and the advantage of the drawback had been removed, they began to change their tune. (As we have also noticed, the crown glass manufacturers had a vested interest in the tax, for it favoured those who could make the thinnest panes.) Chances were soon wholehearted advocates of repeal. 'Take off the Excise Duty,' they begged the authorities in 1842, 'and give us three or four years to shake off the effects of having been trammell'd by it for half a century [sic] and we shall be able to meet all the manufacturers in the world.'[12]

How important was the window tax in limiting demand? It was levied only on inhabited houses. Factories, warehouses and offices, rapidly increasing in number, were exempt. The window tax did not, therefore, have any effect at all upon the very considerable industrial and commercial demand for window glass. As early as 1780 we hear of a factory with three hundred windows and upwards,[13] and when Peter Drinkwater was building his factory in Manchester in 1789, he wrote to Boulton and Watt:

> 'I wish you to block up no more of my intended windows than you can help by either the width or the height of your brickwork or roof, for to give the building (I mean the factory part) its greatest possible convenience, it should have a continuous series of windows—one and a pier introduced in the distance of every 8 or 9 foot or thereabouts.'[14]

Glass manufacturers, particularly those in the north, must have sent a considerable proportion of their output to glaze business premises such as these.

Inhabited houses, however, were subjected to an increasingly heavy window

G   97

tax. From the middle of the eighteenth century they had been taxed on a sliding scale, at first starting with ten windows (1747), then with eight (1762) and finally with seven (1766). This tax was paid by the occupier, not the landlord. In subsequent years the rate per window was greatly increased, as may be seen from the following figures:

INCREASES IN WINDOW TAX, 1766–1808

	1766	1784	1802	1803	1808
House with 7 windows	1s 2d	7s 2d	14s 6d	18s 6d	20s 0d
House with 8 windows	4s 0d	12s 0d	21s 0d	30s 0d	33s 0d
House with 9 windows	6s 0d	16s 6d	27s 0d	38s 0d	42s 0d
House with 10 windows and rising scale up to	8s 4d	21s 4d	34s 0d	50s 0d	56s 0d
House with 180 windows	£18	£20	£61	£83	£93

The high level of taxation continued until 1823 when the rates were halved. In 1825 the seventh window was exempted. This was still the position in the 1840s.

We know, from the window tax returns, that the overwhelming majority of houses in Britain in the later years of the tax possessed fewer than eight windows and therefore paid no duty. Out of 2,750,000 houses in England, Wales and Scotland in 1830, only 380,000 had eight windows or more.[15] By the middle of the 1840s, this figure had only increased to around 450,000[16] out of a total of over 3,000,000. But how many of these homes would have had more than seven windows but for the tax? Unfortunately very little is known about housing before the mid-nineteenth century. We cannot answer this question with any certainty. It is arguable that most of the cottage property in which the majority of the population lived consisted of one room upstairs and one down. If these dwellings had a window at each end on each floor, they would have had only four windows altogether. It would be a mistake, therefore, to run away with the idea that, but for the window tax, demand would automatically have been far greater. Obviously the better-off section of the population who lived in bigger houses made do with fewer windows than they would otherwise have had; it was in the bigger houses that windows were blocked up. To this extent the window tax undoubtedly did limit the total demand for glass. But it can be argued that in the majority of cases housing standards exercised an even greater influence by keeping the number of windows below even the tax-free maximum.[17]

The excise duty on glass was repealed on April 5, 1845, a sacrifice to the Treasury of £650,000 a year. To this total the manufacturers of window glass had contributed £450,000. This was less than a quarter of the revenue from the window tax.[18] It is not surprising, therefore, that, despite the industry's views, and despite the growing public outcry on health grounds, the window tax survived for several years longer. The repeal of the excise duty was carried through with considerable regard to the manufacturers' interests; their fears of being left with duty-paid glass on their hands were not realized. Any glass made after February 15, 1845, was not dutiable, provided it was stored until the date of repeal, and duty could still be drawn back on glass exported up to June 15th. On all other glass which had not been disposed of by that time, manufacturers could recover three-quarters of the duty they had originally paid.[19]

The immediate effect of repealing the duty was to cut the manufacturer's prices by more than half. The following list of one 'extensive' firm (not identified) indicates the fall in crown glass prices:

Per 12 tables	PRICES BEFORE REPEAL			PRICES AFTER REPEAL		
	Gross	Discount	Nett	Gross	Discount	Nett
Best	£9 4s 0d	36s 5d	£7 7s 7d	£4 0s 0d	4s 0d	£3 16s 0d
Seconds	£8 4s 0d	32s 5d	£6 11s 7d	£3 0s 0d	3s 0d	£2 17s 0d
Thirds	£7 14s 0d	30s 5d	£6 3s 7d	£2 14s 0d	2s 8d	£2 11s 4d
Fourths	£7 10s 0d	30s 0d	£6 0s 0d	£2 10s 0d	2s 6d	£2 7s 6d

Source: *The Economist*, July 19, 1845.

Manufacturers were clearly not reducing the gross price by the full amount of the duty and, by reducing the rate of discount from four shillings to one shilling in the pound, they were pocketing even more of the balance. This they were able to do because of the insistent demand for glass at that time. The building cycle was moving sharply upwards as a new boom developed. Moreover, orders, which had been held up for weeks so that glass could be had at the new price, poured in from all parts of the country, particularly from Lancashire and Yorkshire.[20] Very heavy orders also arrived from London. This was attributed to the Building Act which imposed more stringent regulations upon houses begun in the London area after January 1, 1845.[21] There had been a rush to start building before that date so as to avoid conforming to the new regulations.[22] As a result, an unduly large number of houses was ready for glazing about the time when the excise duty was removed. There arose what one window glass manufacturer described as 'a famine of sheet and sheet plate in London.'[23]

The extent of this sudden huge demand took even the manufacturers themselves by surprise. 'None in our branch', wrote a window glass manufacturer at the beginning of 1846, 'had any notion that the demand would have been so extraordinary as it has proved. . . . The extra make, since the repeal, could not be less than fifty per cent'. This great boom caused speculators to venture their capital in what appeared to be a most promising industry. The manufacturer just quoted went on to report the starting of no fewer than five new factories and five more 'under way.'[24]

Growth at such a rate brought about an acute shortage of skilled labour. For Pilkingtons, a very serious crisis arose because of an attempt to challenge the validity of the firm's contracts with its employees when the labour shortage made it extremely difficult to secure new men. Months of legal haggling ensued before these contracts were finally declared to be binding and during these months some employees, assuming that they were free to leave the firm's employment at their pleasure, left the works when their services were most urgently required. Before considering the rationalization which took place in the industry in the wake of the excise duty's repeal, it is necessary, therefore, to interrupt the story in order to see how the labour crisis arose at Pilkingtons and, at the same time, to learn something about the wages and working conditions there at that time.

CHAPTER 7

A LABOUR CRISIS

B Y the middle of the nineteenth century each window glass factory employed
several hundred people. Remarkably few of these were themselves skilled
glassmakers or even assistants to glassmakers. Numbers of employees
worked at a wide variety of tasks outside the glasshouses. Many hands were
needed in the cutting rooms and warehouses, for instance, sorting, cutting,
packing and loading the finished product; in the polishing rooms transforming
sheet into patent plate glass; in the joiners' shop putting the crates together and
in the pot rooms making pots. Of those who actually did work at the furnaces,
many were juveniles serving their apprenticeship. They were assistants to the
fully-trained glassmakers, and performed such menial tasks as wiping blowpipes
before the metal was gathered from the pots, holding a shovel to shield the
gatherer's face from the intense heat, or carrying the cooled cylinders from the
splitters to the flatteners. Eventually these boys, if employed in crown glass
manufacture, graduated to punty sticking—the process of sealing the piece to
the pontil or punty on which the piece was twirled into a circular table—and to
gathering the metal.[1] Some became skilled blowers, flashers of crown glass, or
flatteners of sheet, while others piled the glass into kilns to be annealed.

Very few of those who worked at a glass factory, therefore, had the right to
call themselves glassmakers. At Pilkingtons, where about five hundred were
employed in 1845, there were only four blowers and four gatherers to each of
the three houses.[2] If we add the flashers, flatteners and pilers, the firm probably
employed altogether about fifty fully-skilled glassmakers, ten per cent. of the
total number in its service.

In 1845, just before the repeal of the excise duty, there were fourteen factories
in Britain engaged in the manufacture of window glass.[3] Some of them were
larger and some smaller than the St Helens works. If we may assume that
Greenall and Pilkingtons represented the average size of concern (an assump-
tion that will certainly not lead to any underestimation of the total) there were
at that time probably about 700 skilled glassmakers in the whole of Britain; of
these fewer than 200 were blowers, the key men upon whom the whole industry
depended. Moreover, only a minority could blow the long cylinders needed for

the manufacture of sheet glass; there were perhaps fewer than 50 sheet glass blowers in the country when the excise duty was repealed.

It was always the policy of the few skilled workmen to keep their practical knowledge of the various glassmaking processes within their own families, fathers passing on the closely-guarded secrets of the trade to their sons. They sought to maintain an aristocracy of skill by barring all strangers from entering their ranks. Immediately after the repeal of the excise duty, for instance, when they joined together to form the Crown Glass Makers' Society—the first trade union in the industry of which we have any evidence—one of the rules laid down that

> 'any Glass Makers not becoming members of this Society, his or their sons shall not go forward in our business.'

A special allowance of one pound a week was to be paid to any member who was discharged from his employment 'because he will not teach any person who is not a Glass Maker's son'.[4] Such an exclusion policy, which harked back to the days when the industry was more static and when glassmaking was the jealously-guarded preserve of but a few families, could still be enforced to some extent. In a list of Pilkington Brothers' employees, drawn up in 1849,[5] the same names recur frequently, particularly among the higher-paid workmen of the glass-houses; in several cases fathers and sons still worked together. But as the firm grew in size and importance, the existing glassmaking families could no longer provide all the skilled labour required; new blood had to be introduced from outside. Often the partners selected recruits from families already known to them. Frederick Vose, for instance, the son of William Pilkington's cook, was trained as a glassmaker.[6] In 1836, Thomas Gerard, a son of the Greenall's head brewer, began to serve his time[7] and when the national census was taken in 1841, James Oldfield and James Appleton, who were living on brewery property in Hall Street, were also described as apprentice glassmakers.

Local recruitment was a satisfactory method of obtaining a gradual supply of skilled labour over a period of time by way of seven-year apprenticeships; but it was quite useless as a means of meeting a sudden emergency, such as arose in 1845, when fully-trained men were required immediately. The supply of sheet glass blowers and flatteners was so strictly limited in Britain that every firm had to send scouts to the continent in search of additional hands. Pilkingtons sent on this errand William Pilkington's eldest son, William, who had only just entered the business in the previous year at the age of seventeen.[8] In July 1845, he was reported to be trying to recruit men from St Gobain.[9] These foreign workmen could only be persuaded to leave home and come to England by the offer of fantastically high wages and special concessions. Charles Singré, for instance, a sheet glass blower from Choisy-le-Roi near Paris, one of the men who signed a two-year contract with Pilkingtons, was to receive £6 10s 0d per week and to be provided with a house and all the fuel he should require without any payment. Moreover, £240 was advanced to him as a loan (to be stopped out of his wages) and his fare was paid not only from Paris to St Helens but also back again to Paris after two years when he had fulfilled his contract.[10]

Such huge earnings had an unsettling effect upon the British glassmakers who worked alongside these fortunate newcomers. They found themselves contracted to perform the same skilled tasks for about a quarter of the foreigners' wages, and it was not long before they started to exploit their scarcity value by demanding more pay and additional concessions. 'We have exchanged the excise for a much severer taskmaster . . . our own men', wrote the proprietor of one English house early in 1846.[11]

The terms of service, moreover, gave the continental glassmakers an advantage over their British counterpart. In France and Belgium glassmakers served their masters for the life of a furnace, a period which they called a campaign.[12] They were thus obliged to serve only for short periods at a time and were, in consequence, freer to change masters than were the British glassmakers who usually contracted to serve their employers for seven years at a time. The Englishmen could not go away to another firm in search of higher wages unless their contracts happened to run out. In 1845 this was an unlikely eventuality, for most manufacturers had taken the wise precaution of binding their men anew just before the excise duty was removed. Some of the more adventurous spirits, however, were tempted to defy their masters and run the risk of imprisonment in order to better themselves financially. The sudden departure of one of their men, Richard Pemberton, led Pilkingtons into a series of legal actions which sharpened still further a labour crisis that was already dangerously acute.

Pemberton came of a Scottish glassmaking family. His father, John Pemberton, who had blown glass for Greenall and Pilkingtons for at least twelve years, was manager of one of the glasshouses in which his son worked.[13] Soon after the repeal of the excise duty, James Christie, who had re-started the Dumbarton Crown Glassworks some years previously,[14] offered Richard Pemberton the position of manager in one of his glasshouses. Pilkingtons agreed to release him from a contract he had signed on March 4, 1845, on condition that he provided a proficient substitute. This he was unable to do; but, rather than lose an opportunity of promotion, he decided to risk leaving St Helens without providing a substitute and in defiance of his contract. He set off for Dumbarton on June 18, 1845.

Pilkingtons demanded £100 compensation from Christie. When, after two months, there were no signs either of this compensation or of the runaway's returning, they exercised their legal right under the Master and Servant Law of obtaining a magistrate's warrant for his arrest.[15] A police officer brought Pemberton back from Dumbarton at the beginning of September and placed him in prison pending his appearance before the justices, who had the power to mete out a sentence of up to three months' imprisonment with hard labour should the case be proved. The prisoner, however, obtained the legal services of that remarkably able and wily lawyer, William Prouting Roberts, who was rapidly gaining notoriety for his agile defence of trade unionists, particularly in the mining industry. Perhaps one of Pemberton's fellow-glassmakers named Lyon, who was the first to visit him in prison when he arrived from Dumbarton, was responsible for suggesting that Roberts be called in. At any rate, this was the construction put on the course of events by William Pilkington, who made the significant observation that Lyon had been 'collier bred'.

When the case came before the justices at Prescot on September 6, 1845, Roberts was in characteristically aggressive form. He made a fierce onslaught upon the validity of the firm's contracts and this radical display was eagerly listened to by a crowd of Pilkingtons' employees who thronged the court room. Roberts's tirading defence failed to impress the magistrates, however, and Pemberton was sentenced to a month's imprisonment with hard labour. Here the matter might, and probably would, have rested had Roberts not been involved in the case. But 'the miners' attorney general' refused to admit defeat. On September 19th (when the prisoner had already served the greater part of his sentence) Roberts applied to Mr Baron Platt, the judge, in London, for a writ of *habeas corpus* to transfer Pemberton to the capital and for a writ of *certiorari* directed to Samuel Taylor, requiring Taylor, as the magistrate who had presided over the court at Prescot, to return the record of Pemberton's conviction. This application was successful, and on September 25th the learned judge, after two and a half hours' consideration of this record, reached the conclusion that Taylor had not shown sufficient cause for the detention of the prisoner. He therefore ordered Pemberton's discharge.

Although Roberts's success resulted solely from a legal technicality, Pilkingtons' employees, recalling Roberts's scathing remarks about the firm's contracts, immediately jumped to the conclusion that the release of the prisoner meant that all the contracts had been proved null and void in law. This, they thought, freed them to seek employment elsewhere, just as Pemberton had done, without fear of any legal action being taken against them. This interpretation of the judge's decision was vigorously fostered by Roberts himself who, true to his radical colours, kept on paying regular visits to St Helens to harangue the men. Other employers, taking advantage of Pilkington's difficulties, sent agents to lure workmen away by offers of higher wages. Despite a full explanation of the facts which Richard and William Pilkington issued in the form of a public address on October 7th,[16] the proprietors of other companies had some success in persuading a few of Pilkington's most valuable men to desert. The first of these enticers, somewhat fallen in the world but nevertheless morally unchanged by his descent, was none other than William West, the author of the gigantic excise frauds at the Eccleston Crown Glassworks some twenty years before. He subsequently became manager of the Birmingham Plate Glassworks. This factory had recently formed crown and sheet glass departments and was in need of men.[17] On October 14th William Pilkington reported upon the position to his solicitors:

'On Sunday Roberts held a large meeting on Green Bank as usual and yesterday and today several of our workmen have absconded and gone to that pattern of purity W. A. A. West, who is now ready and for want of them was obliged to lade his first found of metal because they were not there to blow it and this morning I have received a most Jesuitical letter from him. . . . It was hinted to me some time ago—say three or four months—that these men had formed an engagement with Mr West and that so soon as he was ready, they would leave us. As they were under contracts and some of our steadiest and, as I believed, best men I disbelieved it but of course could only await the results. . . Lyon, who has gone to Mr West with the others . . . no doubt encouraged him [Pemberton] to resist [imprisonment] and arranged the plan of employing Roberts not to get Pemberton off merely but to break through their agreements to enable them to go to Mr West. This they have now done. . . . We learn today that Richard Pemberton is [again] working for the Dumbarton Company along with two others of our men who have absconded. . . . Now I would rather fight the masters than the men who have no reason nor money but strong sympathies for each other. . . . In case we are obliged to stop a house, which at present we are on the verge of doing, this would not only be strong ground for damages but also strong proof of the necessity of making very stringent agreements as there is not a surplus of hands and if our men choose to leave and give us a month's or even three months' notice our capital is at a stand and our warehouse apprentices and others of no use whom we must under any circumstances pay; and what is worse we are obliged to keep up our fires to protect our pots and to preserve our furnaces.'

A few days later a further item of depressing news reached William Pilkington's desk. He had sought counsel's opinion on the best way of regaining the services of Richard Pemberton and was informed that the period of imprisonment purged the offence and no further action was likely to succeed. This news caused him to write in another letter to his solicitors:

'If a man enters into a contract for seven years and receives £15 binding money [[18]] he may the day after refuse to work and if we venture to take him before a magistrate and get him committed very much to our loss and inconvenience, it would appear that he not only purges himself from the crime but is absolved from his contract on his liberation . . . he receives £15 from us as the price of a month's incarceration.'

William Pilkington went on to observe that 'none of the truants' had returned from Birmingham. From another quarter, Christie's emissaries were at that moment 'regaling our workmen and sowing dissatisfaction as much as possible among them.'

The months of September and October, 1845, when the labour crisis reached its peak, must have been a period of great anxiety for the proprietors, comparable with some of the worst worries of earlier years. Several of their best men had absconded and there seemed to be no means of preventing others from following if they chose to do so. At a time when the demand for glass had reached unprecedented heights, the firm was faced with the prospect of closing one of its houses and was able to keep going only by maintaining three sets of men at work constantly at each furnace. (It was customary to employ a fourth set to relieve each of the others in turn to allow them a spell of rest.) And with new companies about to start, all of them clamouring for men, the labour shortage promised to grow worse rather than better.

On top of all this worry came the sudden, unexpected and premature death of Peter Greenall on September 18th, a very sad family loss which was felt particularly keenly by his brothers-in-law. It is but little wonder that by the end of October William Pilkington found himself under doctor's orders and was annoyed with himself for being 'so distracted and tired'.

But Pilkingtons still had one means of redress. As William Pilkington made clear in his letter of October 14th which has been quoted, they could always sue competing firms for damages arising from the loss of their hired servants. Had the other concerns refused to comply with the request to discharge Pilkingtons' bound employees, there would have been an inevitable time-lag before the matter could be settled in the courts and this delay might have had serious consequences for Pilkingtons. But as events turned out, the mere threat of such an action was quite sufficient to frighten both West and Christie into discharging the runaways. The truants then returned to St Helens, begged forgiveness and sought to be employed by their lawful masters once more.

William Pilkington seized the opportunity offered by the pardoning of the first group of runaways to enter into negotiations with the men's representatives in order to bring about more cordial labour relations and put an end to the reign of uncertainty and indiscipline. He proposed to introduce new contracts, to be valid for three and a half years. The men, however, insisted on the seven years then customary, and six years was eventually decided upon as a compromise. These would, of course, be accompanied by binding fees or premiums. In the past such premiums had amounted only to a few pounds but, owing to the dearth of skilled labour after the repeal of the excise duty, employers had been obliged to pay up to £15. It was the payment of this lump sum, the 'golden bait' as William Pilkington termed it, that sweetened the negotiations and brought the men to terms. They on their side agreed not to employ any longer the services of W. P. Roberts as their legal adviser and consented to a clause in the new contracts whereby their masters were empowered to suspend workmen for up to a week at a time in cases of disobedience or non-attendance without just cause. These new contracts were signed on November 19th.

On the whole, these agreements restored discipline and checked the rate at which glassmakers left St Helens in quest of more highly-paid work elsewhere. But there were still some men who refused to honour the new agreements and letters from the firm's solicitors continued to reach West and Christie, warning them that legal action would be taken if certain men were not discharged. After some prevarication on the part of the pirate employers, the men usually returned. The proprietor of Dumbarton, in particular, was a past master at holding out as long as he could: 'Christie's plausibility', William Pilkington thought, 'would overmatch W. A. A. West's Jesuitism'.

In November 1845, the plausible Christie even managed to obtain a model of Pilkingtons' improved flattening kilns from one of the runaways. William Pilkington explained to his solicitors how Frederick Vose, the son of his cook, who had been 'almost nursed' by the Pilkington family and had been trained as a glassmaker at their works, was involved in the theft:

'This scamp has been privately instructing one Garralty in the art of flattening sheet glass contrary to our expressed directions but it was done stealthily and during night. This Garralty was not a hired servant and therefore left us about a fortnight ago to go to Dumbarton and returned the latter end of last week and Mr F. Vose is now missing and has we believe absconded along with him. But this is not the worst—between them, we are informed, they have made and taken away with them a model of our flattening kilns which are the best kilns of the day and have thus obtained an engagement at Dumbarton.'

Ten days later, however, William Pilkington was able to report:

'Vose is back and has made peace with us, which I am sorry to say is too easily done nowadays. . . . Frederick Vose admits that Garralty has carried the model of our kilns to Dumbarton.'

The sequel to these events came in July 1846, when Pilkingtons appealed—successfully—against Mr Baron Platt's judgment in the Pemberton case. This meant that Christie was at last obliged to discharge Pemberton from his service. An abject and apologetic letter from this, the first of the runaways, dated July 20, 1846, ends the whole unfortunate chapter which had started with his release from prison almost ten months earlier:

'If I did wrong in entering an agreement with Mr Christie, it was from the advice I got from my lawyer [Roberts] who assured me that your agreement was not a binding one and that my being discharged from prison was sufficient to show that you had no further claim upon me. . . . I have no wish to have any expenses incurred on my account and I have no objection to return to your service, if you will allow me to work here a reasonable time to get arangements made so that I could leave with my wife and family. I have a large family and my wife has not yet recovered from her late confinement and in my present situation I have not the means to remove either myself or family; one of my sons is an apprentice to Mr Christie and he is too young to be left without a proper person in charge of him.

    If you favour me with a discharge upon paying a sum of money, I would be obliged by your naming the amount and if at all reasonable I think I would be able to raise the money: and if you would be kind enough to oblige me in this way, it might perhaps be best for both you and myself. In the event of your not being inclined to make an arrangement of this nature, I must throw myself on your generosity and request you to allow Mr Christie to employ me until I can make enough to remove with my family, which at present it is entirely out of my power to do, and I do not suppose that you would be inclined to advance me any money.'

William Pilkington's reply was kindly and lenient. He had, he said, 'no vindictive feelings in the matter' and would be willing to accept £50 for Pemberton's discharge payable over two years, or £40 to be paid at once. This was a most generous offer, for when Pemberton's own father had gone to work at St Helens, Greenall and Pilkingtons had been obliged to pay £150 to his master in lieu of the seven months that his contract was still due to run. To some extent, perhaps, William Pilkington's generosity may have been born of relief: relief that, after a year of worry, the matter of the disputed contracts was finally settled.

    These contracts, signed during the turbulent months of 1845, together with one or two others of earlier date and wages sheets for two weeks in 1849, provide us with details of glassmakers' pay at that time. To them may be added evidence from other sources about hours and conditions of work, home life and leisure occupations.

    So long as the materials used in glass manufacture were prepared in pots, there could be no continuous production. The pots, once emptied, had to be recharged and the contents heated up to the correct viscosity for working. The duration of this period of preparation determined the glassmaker's timetable. A complete charging, melting and cooling cycle usually took twenty-four hours. The working itself took rather less than half that time, usually about ten hours. This meant that even at the maximum rate of production the glassmakers were bound to have about twenty-four hours off at the end of each ten-hour shift. They started at 6 a.m. on Monday morning and worked a ten-hour shift until Monday afternoon, began the second shift about 4 p.m. on Tuesday, the third at

2 a.m. on Thursday, and the fourth about noon on Friday, finishing work for the week late on Friday night. This left them with Saturday and Sunday completely free.

These hours, of course, were very approximate, for the teazer (or furnace-man) could never guarantee that the metal would be ready precisely at any pre-arranged time, nor could the glassmakers be absolutely sure of emptying their pots within ten hours. The time-table could not be a rigid one: when the men left the works, they were on call. One of the apprentices, summoned before-hand by the furnaceman to sweep up and prepare for the next shift, was sent round to call the glassmakers when the metal was ready.[19] A twelve-year-old boy named Gaskell, one of Pilkingtons' apprentices, has left this brief account of how they, in their turn, were called by the furnaceman:

'We are about ten hours on and twenty-four off, that is the journey; but we boys always get called about three hours before we start with the men, for we have to sweep up and get ready for them before they come. We could do it all in an hour if we liked but we like to play in that time. We are called at all times night and day. The "teazer" or furnace man goes round the town and calls every boy in the house when the furnace in that house has heated the metal in the pots enough to start working in about three hours. He comes to the door at home and knocks and calls "Gaskell", and then, if it's night, my father looks out of the window and the teazer says, "Number —— called"; that is the number of the house. So I get out of bed and go off.'[20]

Four blowers and four gatherers made a set, as we have noticed. Only three pairs made glass at any one time, thus allowing the fourth an opportunity to rest. These rest periods were essential, for the work was extremely hot and exacting and the glasshouses themselves dark and ill-ventilated. In order to stimulate the draught through the furnaces via the underground flues, the actual cones were built to exclude draughts of air from other sources. Very little air was permitted to penetrate the glasshouse in the normal way except through such openings as were absolutely necessary to allow the men to move in and out of the building and to permit the raw materials and finished products to be carried in and out. This meant that there was very little light apart from the bright glare from the molten glass. The heat close to the openings into the fur-nace was unbearable for any length of time and the men only went near when they were actually engaged in one or other of the processes of manufacture. Each glassmaker was, therefore, constantly moving to and fro in the firelit gloom. Around him scurried his band of assistants, fetching and carrying. Heat, bustle and dexterity, as one observant visitor remarked, were the characteristic features of the old pot furnaces.[21]

The men were invariably paid by the set and at piece rates. In the manu-facture of crown glass, 1,200 'good and merchantable' tables were deemed to constitute a week's work for each set of four blowers and gatherers. According to William Pilkington, writing in April 1846, 'at a low average a set would and do make 1,600 [tables]'. These additional four hundred or so tables were paid for at a higher rate—'plus' as it was called. When John Pemberton, manager of one of the crown houses, contracted in 1833 to serve Greenall and Pilkingtons as a blower, the firm agreed to pay him 27s 6d for his contribution to the set's production of 1,200 tables 'with plus as usual'. From two later agreements of October 1839 and March 1845,[22] 'plus as usual' appears to have meant a rate of 30s 0d for a further 1,200 tables or 2s 6d per 100 tables. James Pye, signatory to the first of these two agreements, was to receive 27s 6d for the basic 1,200 tables if he served as a piler, 26s 0d if as a blower, piece warmer or flasher, 21s 0d if as a gatherer or kiln assistant or 18s 0d if as a punty sticker, 'plus' being 30s 0d as a piler, blower, piece warmer or flasher, 25s 0d as a gatherer or kiln assistant and 21s 0d as a punty sticker. James Oldfield who signed the agreement of March 1845, was only to receive 26s 0d for the first 1,200 tables if he worked as a piler and 15s 0d if as a punty sticker but otherwise the rates had not changed since 1839. The greatly increased demand for labour in subsequent months led to an advance in wages. By August 15, 1845, when Thomas Cutter contracted to serve Pilkingtons,[23] the basic rate had been raised by 4s 0d for all tasks except that of punty sticking which remained at 15s 0d. This advance brought the basic rate up to the 'plus' rate for all but the lowest ranks.

At these rates, and under the boom conditions of that time, the highest paid glassmaker could earn about 40s 0d a week if he was the member of a set which made 1,600 tables. Gatherers could make about 33s 0d and punty stickers about 22s. 0d. No doubt during the boom of 1845–7 glassmakers were, in fact, making that much 'plus'; but the wage lists for the weeks ending May 12 and 19, 1849[24] —the only ones which survive—show what earnings were like when trade was slack. In the first of these two weeks, for instance, two sets of blowers made £1 12s 0½d and £1 11s 3d and in the second they made £1 17s 8½d and £1 11s 10½d respectively. William Blanshard, superintendent of all the crown houses, earned more than this, £2 17s 9d per week, and the other glassmakers and their assistants earned proportionately less, the apprentices receiving only a few shillings.

The makers of sheet glass were paid at a much higher rate. Like Singré, whom we have already noticed, the other foreign workmen had to be given exceptionally high wages and these influenced the rates paid to the British sheet glassmakers. Henry Dodds, one of the runaways, had agreed in May 1845, to make, weekly, 425 cylinders 40 in. by 30 in., of a thickness thirteen ounces to the foot, or proportionately fewer cylinders of larger size and greater weight, for 53s 8d.[25] This, his basic weekly wage, is to be compared with the crown glassmaker's of 30s 0d. But it was only the actual blowers, in the sheet houses, who benefited in this way. The gatherers were given the same rate as if they had been working in a crown house, as another agreement of November 19th makes clear.[26] The wages lists for the two weeks of May 1849, confirm that although the few key men in the sheet houses were earning large sums of money, gatherers were no better off than their counterparts in the crown houses and there was a far larger proportion of low-paid juveniles fetching and carrying for the sheet than for the crown glassmakers. This meant not only that more menial labour was required but also that the sheet glasshouses had already become the main training centres at the works. M. Hypolite, who appears to have been Demanet's successor as the firm's superintendent of sheet glass manufacture, was paid £4 4s 0d a week and the other foreign workmen earned between £3 and £4. One of them, who had his son helping him, reached £4 3s 0d. The British sheet glass blowers earned between £2 and £3.

The highest paid employee of all was Henry Deacon who, in 1847, was described as the firm's Chemist and Engineer.[27] In 1849, when he was only in his twenty-seventh year, he was earning £5 18s 6d a week, considerably more than young William Pilkington who earned £4 4s 0d, and very much more than the £2 6s 0d received by James Varley, the firm's cashier who had eleven years' service behind him. Among others who were employed in departments away from the glasshouses, several were earning as much as the more highly paid glassmakers, particularly those in the joiners' shop where the departmental manager, Thomas Colquitt, received £3 5s 0d. At the other end of the scale were some of the boys in the cutting room (who sometimes earned so little as 3s 0d), and the smoothers and polishers: the women, girls and 'red lads'—so called because they worked with rouge.

These rates of pay placed the skilled glassmaker in the forefront of the artisan class. Estimates of earnings are hard to arrive at, but, for the sake of comparison, ironfounders, generally agreed to be among the highest paid work-people at that time, were then earning up to £2 per week and skilled engineers sometimes received a little more than that. The general run of skilled craftsmen, such as carpenters, builders and stonemasons, usually earned round about 30s 0d.

The glassmaker also received various concessions which were not enjoyed by other artisans. He received an allowance for house rent and firing. This was a legacy of former days before the growth of the towns, when the master had to house his own servants. In their early days, Greenall and Pilkingtons built a row of thirty-seven cottages adjoining their works, for there was a shortage of accommodation at that time. But with the growth of the town, alternative accommodation was available. £10 per year was, therefore, granted to each man as a 'living out' allowance.

The glassmaker's contract also contained a clause giving him a guaranteed minimum wage. In the event of work being interrupted because of furnace trouble, lack of fuel (owing to a coal strike) or other unforeseen cause, he was to receive half pay. He received no accident or sick pay but a large number of friendly societies existed in the district and the glassmakers themselves, as has been seen, had their own association, which also served as a friendly society.

Pilkingtons also made provision for leisure-time activities from the later 1840s. The recreation section dates from 1847.[28] Cricket appears to have been the main interest of members at the outset, and two of William Pilkington's sons were keen players.[29] In course of time, as membership grew, other activities were arranged. By the early 1860s there were a bowling green and skittle alley attached to Pilkingtons' cricket field close to the old cotton factory which they acquired (see page 87), and William Pilkington spoke of a new building in course of erection where members would have 'billiards and draughts and other games . . . conveniences for washing and a refreshment bar for tea and coffee and light drinks'.[30] The recreation section was probably responsible for organizing works outings during the summer, and dances in the winter. In July 1850, a party from the works went to Runcorn and Halton,[31] possibly the first of the annual one-day excursions. In January of the previous year the firm had held an all-night ball, also described as an annual event. This lasted from 8.30 at night until 7 o'clock the next morning.[32]

About this time Pilkingtons engaged a schoolmaster to teach the three Rs to the boys and lads in their employment up to the age of seventeen. All the apprentices had to attend classes for an hour or two in their own time after work. They paid no fees but were fined one penny for every absence without good reason. At first, it would seem, attendance was rather erratic. Fines sometimes reached 30s od per week. But a later teacher, Edward Johnson, achieved better results and was able to boast that

> 'They used to duck all who went to school but now they "rundle" any who don't; that, is put him in a ring of them, each of whom pulls his hair.'

He went on to tell how some of the boys were so tired after their day's work that they fell asleep and had to be sent home. The 'red lads', coming straight from the polishing benches, made everything they touched, the forms and the books, red too.[33] Perhaps some of these tell-tale marks were also to be found on books in the works library. This has been built up from the proceeds of some of the fines levied on the men as penalties for indiscipline.[34]

Glassmakers as a class are said to have been 'in general a very decent set of fellows but . . . given to drinking'.[35] To some extent the nature of their work obliged them to consume large amounts of liquid, and, in days before an unpolluted water supply was readily available, beer—untaxed and very cheap— was the usual beverage. While they were at work, glassmakers used to send their apprentices to fetch jugs of beer, and a commission which investigated the employment of children in the 1860s reported that 'running out for men's drink is a very common errand'.[36] Some employers paid their men a special beer allowance in addition to their wages. At the Eccleston Crown Glassworks, for instance, two glassmakers brought an action against their masters for failing to give them their 1s 9d a week beer money.[37] Pilkingtons' contracts contain no such clauses; but there is plenty of evidence to show that the men drank heavily. John Blundell, for instance, who started to work for the firm in 1857, later recalled that, in his early days there, a great deal of beer was carried into the works.[38] But as opinion hardened against drinking, particularly within working hours, the practice came to be forbidden. The men, therefore, stole away across the canal to the Navigation Tavern or to one or other of the numerous hostelries nearby in Liverpool Road and Greenbank. William Windle Pilkington, Richard Pilkington's eldest son, determined to put an end to drinking in working hours and waged a constant campaign against this long-established habit. His angry visits to the Navigation Tavern are often recalled by descendants of the glassmakers of his day. But drinking persisted. Deprived of their jugs of beer inside the factory and forbidden to go drinking outside during working hours, the men often preferred to take time off altogether. An employee of the firm from 1871 to 1926 spent much of his time during his last years as a sick visitor searching out men who had been neglecting their work, usually because of excessive drinking.[39]

The glassmaker of a century ago, then, whose labour was highly skilled and physically exacting and whose hours were irregular and unsettled, had several advantages over his fellow artisans. He inherited a tradition of privilege. He had a living-out allowance. His wages were high and were guaranteed in case of interruptions at the factory. He only worked about forty hours a week, and, though a certain amount of night work cut into such leisure time as he had during the week, he enjoyed a longer week-end than most other work-people who at that time only finished for the week late on Saturday afternoon or even on Saturday evening. These were the privileged minority on the pay-roll. Further down the list came other employees, such as carpenters and glass cutters, who were paid at skilled rates. At the bottom there was the residuum of poorly paid unskilled, and juveniles.

This is, perhaps, an appropriate point at which to discuss the growth of the Pilkington family and the entry of the second generation into the business.

In 1824 William Pilkington married Eliza Charlotte Boyes, who was then living with her widowed mother at Parr Hall, near St Helens.[40] The pedigree on page 115 gives details of their fourteen children, born between 1825 and 1849. Twelve of them survived infancy and six of the survivors were sons. Richard Pilkington, William's elder brother, did not marry until 1838. His bride was Ann Evans, a daughter of Richard Evans of Haydock, one of the most successful coal proprietors in Lancashire. All of their six children were boys.

CHART III

THE DESCENDANTS OF RICHARD PILKINGTON

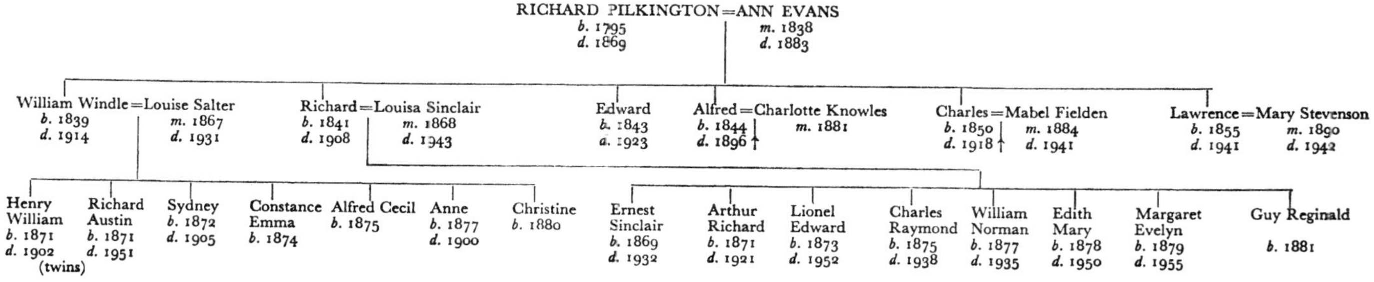

RICHARD PILKINGTON=ANN EVANS
b. 1795   *m.* 1838
d. 1869   *d.* 1883

William Windle=Louise Salter
b. 1839 *m.* 1867
d. 1914 *d.* 1931

Richard=Louisa Sinclair
b. 1841 *m.* 1868
d. 1908 *d.* 1943

Edward
b. 1843
d. 1923

Alfred=Charlotte Knowles
b. 1844 *m.* 1881
d. 1896

Charles=Mabel Fielden
b. 1850 *m.* 1884
d. 1918 *d.* 1941

Lawrence=Mary Stevenson
b. 1855 *m.* 1890
d. 1941 *d.* 1942

Henry William
b. 1871
d. 1902
(twins)

Richard Austin
b. 1871
d. 1951

Sydney
b. 1872
d. 1905

Constance Emma
b. 1874

Alfred Cecil
b. 1875

Anne
b. 1877
d. 1900

Christine
b. 1880

Ernest Sinclair
b. 1869
d. 1932

Arthur Richard
b. 1871
d. 1921

Lionel Edward
b. 1873
d. 1952

Charles Raymond
b. 1875
d. 1938

William Norman
b. 1877
d. 1935

Edith Mary
b. 1878
d. 1950

Margaret Evelyn
b. 1879
d. 1955

Guy Reginald
b. 1881

CHART IV
THE DESCENDANTS OF WILLIAM PILKINGTON

WILLIAM PILKINGTON = ELIZABETH CHARLOTTE BOYES
b. 1800, *d.* 1872 — *m.* 1824

- Mary = Henry Chater — *b.* 1825, *d.* 1895 — *m.* 1850
- William (Roby) = Elizabeth Lee Watson — *b.* 1827, *d.* 1903 — *m.* 1854
  - Alice — *b.* 1855, *d.* 1926
  - William Lee — *b.* 1857, *d.* 1919
  - George Herbert — *b.* 1858, *d.* 1931
  - Lionel Watson — *b.* 1859, *d.* 1859
  - Edith Eliza — *b.* 1860, *d.* 1884
  - Reginald Murray — *b.* 1862, *d.* 1931
  - Elizabeth Ethel — *b.* 1864, *d.* 1933
  - Annie May — *b.* 1866, *d.* 1932
  - Helena Gertrude — *b.* 1868, *d.* 1871
  - Francis Cecil — *b.* 1870, *d.* 1899
  - Albert Leonard — *b.* 1871, *d.* 1908
  - Evelyn Constance — *b.* 1874
- Richard — *b.* 1830, *d.* 1894
- Charles — *b.* 1831, *d.* 1832
- Eliza — *b.* 1833, *d.* 1913
- Lucy Todd[1] = Thomas = [2]Katherine Douglas — Thomas *b.* 1835, *d.* 1925 — (Lucy Todd) *m.* 1860, *d. s. p.* — (Katherine Douglas) *m.* 1866
  - Katherine Douglas — *b.* 1867, *d.* 1942
  - Margaret Douglas — *b.* 1869, *d.* 1954
  - Lilian Douglas — *b.* 1871, *d.* 1936
  - Millicent Douglas — *b.* 1872
  - Annie Douglas — *b.* 1874, *d.* 1944
  - Thomas Douglas — *b.* 1876, K. in S. Africa 1900
  - Sybil Douglas — *b.* 1877, *d.* 1931
  - Alan Douglas — *b.* 1879
- Peter — *b.* 1837, *d.* 1838
- Eleanor = Hadden William Todd — *b.* 1838, *d.* 1908 — *m.* 1861 ↑
- George = Frances Carlisle — *b.* 1840, *d.* 1923 ↑ — *m.* 1867
- Anne = Gavin T. Todd — *b.* 1842, *d.* 1863 ↑ — *m.* 1861
- Harold — *b.* 1844, *d.* 1879
- Matilda = Henry Deane — *b.* 1845, *d.* 1903 ↑ — *m.* 1871
- Leonard — *b.* 1847, *d.* 1925
- Jane = Henry Rigg — *b.* 1849, *d.* 1933 ↑ — *m.* 1874

That both partners had six sons from whom to choose their successors—in the event each chose two—relieved them of any worries about the future of the business as a family concern for at least the next generation. Indeed, the chief problem appears to have been not whom to choose to enter the firm but rather what to do with those for whom there was no partnership share.

As we have already noticed, William Pilkington's eldest son, William (later called Sutton or Roby after his places of residence to distinguish him from his cousin) entered the business in 1844 and subsequently became a partner. The second son, Richard, was trained as a mechanical engineer. He seems to have been associated with the firm for some time, but, certainly from 1864, and possibly from an earlier date, he severed his connection and took his skill elsewhere.[41] The third son, Thomas, went into the business in 1853 and later became a partner. The fourth son, George, who had been to the Royal College of Chemistry,[42] was works chemist for a time but later became a chemical manufacturer on his own account together with the sixth son, Leonard. The fifth son, Harold, was given a legal training and eventually became Town Clerk of St Helens.

Of Richard Pilkington's sons, the two eldest went into the business. William (who was always known as William Windle) was sent to Bruce Castle, Tottenham, a famous private school in its day.[43] He joined the firm in 1857 at the age of eighteen. His younger brother, Richard, arrived in 1858 or 1859. None of Richard Pilkington's other sons went into the works. Edward, Alfred and Lawrence joined their uncles, Joseph and Josiah Evans, in the Clifton and Kearsley Colliery Company near Manchester.[44]

All of Richard Pilkington's sons were baptised at the St Helens Congregational Church. William Pilkington, however, had his children baptised there only up to 1838. In that year a new Anglican place of worship, Christ Church, Eccleston, was opened quite close to Millbrook House, where he had recently gone to live. He started to attend service there and became one of the first churchwardens. It was left to Richard Pilkington to maintain the nonconformist traditions of the family. Throughout his life he was one of the Congregational Church's most active members. Up to the time of his marriage, in 1838, he was for many years superintendent of the boys' Sunday School.[45] In those days the classes met at 8.30 in the morning and Richard Pilkington used to make the journey on foot from his home at Windle Hall to the school in College Lane two miles away. After morning school, he went to church, had lunch in town and was at his desk again when the afternoon school began at 1.30.

Richard Pilkington's deep religious sense, and quiet, contemplative—almost retiring—nature mark him out as a man of a very different temperament from his more active younger brother. 'You underrate yourself and your abilities sadly too much', chided William Pilkington, brimful of justified self-confidence, in a letter he wrote in 1834. Richard Pilkington does not seem to have taken very kindly to the hurly-burly of business and it was left to his brother, more a man of the world, to rescue the infant glass concern from failure and nurse it to success. This success was chiefly the product of William Pilkington's flair for salesmanship. As the search for orders took him away from the works for long periods at a stretch, it was essential that the partner who stayed at home should be someone in whom he could have complete trust, a man who did not possess a fiery temper and was not likely to lose his head in a crisis. Richard Pilkington does not seem to have been the type of man who could himself have achieved great things in business; but he was the ideal business associate.

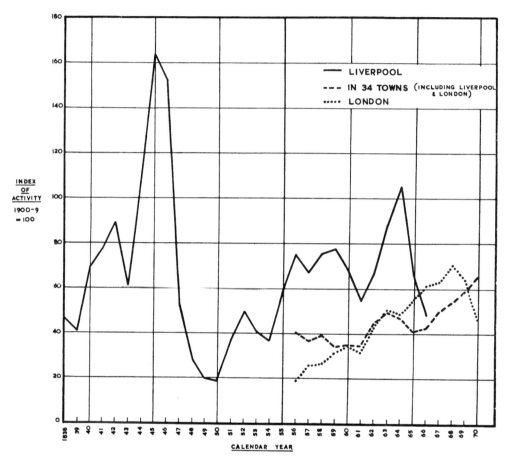

INDEX OF HOUSEBUILDING
1838-1870

Graph 7. Source: B. Weber, 'A New Index of Residential Construction, 1838–1950,'
Scottish Journal of Political Economy, June 1955

CHAPTER 8

THE REMOVAL OF BRITISH COMPETITORS

T HE repeal of the glass excise duty in 1845, by removing the fiscal advantages bestowed upon crown glass manufacturers, placed Chances, Pilkingtons, Hartleys and (to a smaller extent) Cooksons, who had already started to make sheet glass, in a stronger competitive position than those firms which made crown glass alone. During the great building boom of the mid-1840s, and, in particular, immediately after the repeal of the duty when there was a huge pent-up demand for glass at the lower price, glass manufacturers could sell all they made, whether it was crown or sheet. The prosperity of the industry at that time was such that many optimists were decoyed into entering it. According to James Hartley, the number of firms grew from 'thirteen or fourteen' immediately before the repeal to twenty-four in 1846–7.[1] Then prices fell. Many firms, particularly the newcomers, were driven out of business. From a total of twenty-four concerns, the number fell, by 1852, to ten, and, by 1856, to seven.[2] Thus, within ten years of the repeal, the number of firms making window glass had been halved.

The failure, before 1850, of two window glass factories within ten miles of St Helens removed much of Pilkingtons' local competition. Clare and Brownes at Warrington had apparently stopped production during the previous depression, in 1842, and do not appear to have reopened subsequently.[3] The Liverpool Union Crown Glass Company, which had belatedly added a sheet glass furnace to its two crown houses at Old Swan, ceased manufacture at the close of 1847 after having lost £3,743 on the year's working.[4] This concern, which had been formed in 1836, with 2,500 £20 shares, to take over the existing Liverpool Crown Glass Company and had, in the later 1840s, fifty-five shareholders, mostly local men,[5] was finally dissolved in December 1849. The premises were eventually sold in 1851. See plate facing page 128.

Crippling losses on the scale of those sustained by this Liverpool concern were also experienced by the old goliaths on the Tyne, which, one might say, almost had a vested interest in the excise duties. It was, perhaps, a sign of the times that Isaac Cookson, who had inherited the large glass business which his family had built up at South Shields and Newcastle over a period of more than a hundred

119

years,[6] took the opportunity to sell out in 1845, immediately after the duty had been removed. It was bought by a new firm trading under the name of Cookson's manager, R. W. Swinburne. The partners included George Hudson and George Stephenson.[7] Later in the same year Richard Shortridge, chief proprietor of the South Tyne Glass Company, also retired; he had been in the business for forty years.[8]

Those Tyne glass firms which continued to manufacture only crown glass found it impossible to compete when prices fell. The business with which Sir Matthew White Ridley had been particularly associated—still called the New-castle Broad and Crown Glass Company, even though broad glass had not been made there for many years—began to run into difficulties in 1847. £20 were raised on each of the thirty-six shares in the concern. At the end of 1848 the 'extremely unprofitable state of the glass trade and the failing health of the managing partners' caused the works to be put up for sale. The partners were paid off gradually between 1849 and 1855.[9] The works never again made window glass.

The other firms on the Tyne also stopped making window glass, though Swinburnes at South Shields,[10] who had inherited a sheet glass department from the days when the factory belonged to Cooksons, had a longer lease of life than the rest. *The Newcastle Guardian*, in April 1849, reported that the Tyne glass industry was 'reaching the climax of its decline';[11] and *The Builder* later noted, on May 11, 1850:

> 'The Crown Glass Trade on the Tyne is said to be now completely paralysed, only three out of twenty houses [furnaces] being in operation and even those not fully employed.'

By 1863 no window glass of any kind was being made on the Tyne; the South Shields works were then only making plate glass.[12]

A satisfactory explanation of the sudden collapse, within a decade, of an industry which had flourished on the Tyne and provided most of Britain's glass for nearly 250 years, must await a regional study of the north-east in the nineteenth century. It is necessary to know, for instance, whether capital previously invested in window glass manufacture was attracted away by other, more lucrative, avenues of investment. Or was it merely removed by elderly proprietors who, having stubbornly clung to outdated methods, were in a position to retire when these methods no longer brought in profits? Why were their businesses not purchased by men with more up-to-date ideas? Although, as we shall see, factories elsewhere, when they came on the market, were purchased by the surviving window glass manufacturers in order to close them down, there is no evidence of this having happened on the river Tyne. Were there, in fact, serious disadvantages in costs of raw materials and transport which made the north-east *suddenly* so unattractive? If so, why was window glass manufacture carried on so successfully on the Wear right to the last decade of the nineteenth century? In 1863 James Hartley and Co. were said to be making as much window glass as all the factories on the Tyne had previously produced.[13] Can Hartley's prosperity at Sunderland be explained, as an obituary suggested,[14] solely in terms of the one patent which is dealt with in the next section of this chapter? These are all questions to which a careful consideration of the local records may provide clear answers. For the present we can do no more than raise the questions and return to the story of the surviving concerns who profited very considerably from the collapse of the old giants of the northeast.

James Hartley's patent for rough (or rolled) plate glass, which he took out in 1847,[15] not only gave rise to a lucrative branch of window glass manufacture but also led to closer collaboration among the leading firms.

There was at that time a rapidly growing need, particularly from the railway companies, for a type of glass which would be suitable for skylights and for the roofing of railway stations, then being built in large numbers. Such glass needed to be strong and cheap. So long as it was translucent, it mattered little or not whether it was also transparent. Hartley devised a very simple means of meeting this need. His patent was remarkable for its brevity: it ran to only a small page of print. The patentee noted that rough plate glass was at that time made by ladling the metal from the pots into a cuvette, or cistern, re-heating it, pouring it on to a casting table and rolling it out flat. He proposed to dispense with the cuvette and ladle the metal direct from the furnace to the casting table where it was to be rolled out in the usual manner but into smaller plates. The roller could, if required, impress a pattern. He found that

> 'the several ladlesful do not require to be poured at the same time but may be added towards the end of the preceding quantity and that is the manner of producing long sheets which are comparatively narrow.'

Since the existing method of making plate glass was not subject to any patent, nobody could object to Hartley's patenting what appears to have been an identical process with the omission of only one stage.

Simple though it was, this patent apparently took time to develop. Hartleys were able to use it to tender for glazing the Great Exhibition building; but Chances put in a lower tender, using 16 oz. sheet glass, and this was accepted. (That Chances were able, within a few months, to produce nearly a million square feet of sheet glass in panes 49 in. by 10 in. in addition to their other orders,[16] is clear proof of Spon Lane's ascendancy at this time.) Hartley did not, however, consider his rolled plate glass was 'fairly on the market' until the beginning of 1852.[17] Besides making the glass himself, he also licensed Chances and Pilkingtons to make it for an annual fee of £500 per furnace. This he only did reluctantly for, as he was quick to point out to Pilkingtons:

'I have no desire to license the patent to any one, it is no advantage to me to receive £500 a year from a House, I am out of pocket by what you and Messrs Chance pay me, as compared to what I should be if you did not make rolled glass, but it is not good policy for a patentee to grasp too much, but to be satisfied with a fair amount of reasonable compensation, hence my satisfaction with our present agreement.'[18]

Hartley's patented process was so like the usual, unpatented method of making plate glass that some manufacturers—including Chances for a time[19]—were sorely tempted to make rolled plate glass without paying any royalties. Richard Hadland tried to do this, and his downfall brought about an even closer association between Chances, Pilkingtons and Hartleys.

During the boom of 1845-6, Hadland, who was previously connected with the Liverpool Union Crown Glass Company at Old Swan,[20] purchased for a little over £2,000 the Eccleston Crown Glassworks,[21] which had been at a stand-still since West had gone out of business. Much of the capital appears to have been advanced by William Stock, a Liverpool glass merchant, to whom the factory was mortgaged in February 1847 for £6,333.[22] In 1850-1 it was extended and its ratable value was increased from £291 to £445.[23] Hadland started to make rolled plate glass and Hartley brought an action against him for infringement. Hadland lost the case and this defeat led to his bankruptcy. In the spring of 1852, Chances toyed with the idea either of acquiring the Eccleston works by compounding with Hadland's creditors for five shillings in the pound or of purchasing them in concert with Pilkingtons; but, while Chances were hesitating, Pilkingtons stepped in and themselves bought the works—then equipped with four furnaces—for £13,500.[24] They continued to make rolled plate glass there under licence from Hartley.[25]

At the close of 1854, Hartley proposed to grant licences to other firms. This Chances and Pilkingtons vigorously opposed. They entered into negotiations with Hartley and the three finally agreed that no other firm should be licensed to use the patent without their joint consent, and that Chances, Pilkingtons and Hartleys should together be responsible for the defence of the patent. As J. F. Chance has observed,

'the alliance thus formed was strong enough to keep the process, during the term of the patent, in the hands of three firms.'[26]

The alliance led to further collaboration between the three firms, this time to bring other parts of the window glass industry more closely under their control. With the downfall of the factories in the north-east, they had already come to dominate the manufacturers' association, which continued to hold meetings.[27]

Independently, they had taken the opportunity, when competing firms ran into difficulties, of buying out these competitors lest their factories should, at some later date and under new ownership, become serious rivals. At the beginning of 1848, for instance, Chances bought a window glassworks at Baggot Street, Aston, Birmingham; R. L. Chance feared that 'they will be the means of keeping prices low for many a long year'.[28] A few years later, as we have seen, Pilkingtons acquired the Eccleston works. In 1855, Hartleys were considering buying the Tyne and Tees works at Stockton, if they had not already done so, and, in June of that year, William Pilkington, in a letter to Chances, makes it clear that Pilkingtons and Chances had between them acquired the Old Swan Glassworks after it had been put up for sale in 1851. 'Would you in such a case', he wrote, 'contribute in the same way as we do with the Old Swan Works already, that is *pro rata* so long as the remainder of the works continue silent?'[29] The particular case to which he referred in this letter was a factory at Newton-le-Willows, only a few miles from St Helens. In closing down this factory, the three firms acted for the first time in concert.

The Newton works, built in 1832, had started to make glass in the following year.[30] They eventually passed into the hands of William Stock, the Liverpool glass merchant whom we have already mentioned, and he appears to have been in partnership in this particular venture with one Robert Gardner, whom William Pilkington described as a 'thoroughly go-ahead Manchester man'.[31] The new proprietors extended the works which by the close of 1854 consisted of two crown houses and one sheet house capable of producing 7,000 tables of crown and 4,000 pieces of sheet glass per week.[32] This company was obviously a most serious rival to Chances, Pilkingtons and Hartleys, the more so as Gardner was reported by William Pilkington to have imbibed the sound economic doctrine that 'the more he makes, the cheaper he gets it'. William Pilkington also conveyed the sad news that Gardner had 'a strong antagonistic feeling against the Glass Trade and its members, which he says he will "purge" if he stays in it.'[33]

But although Gardner knew what he wanted to do, he was in no position to do it. As he himself admitted, he was 'as ignorant of the Glass trade as the pen I now write with',[34] and he therefore had to rely heavily on his partner, Stock. By 1855, however, the two proprietors were drifting apart. Stock was putting up another works at West Leigh, not far away, and Gardner confessed that he had lost all confidence in him. It was under these circumstances that William Pilkington urged his fellow manufacturers to buy out 'the most *formidable enemy* that we have ever encountered'.[35] On July 4, 1855, it was agreed between Pilkington and Gardner that £12,000 should be paid for the works plus an additional £2,500 for the furnaces, and it was understood that all the materials on the premises, apart from finished glass, were to be taken at a valuation.[36] A week later representatives of Chances, Pilkingtons and Hartleys met at the

Great Western Hotel in London and agreed to bear joint responsibility not only for the purchase of the Newton factory but also for the Tyne and Tees, Old Swan and Baggot Street works, the whole scheme depending upon the successful accomplishment of the Newton agreement of July 4. They invited three of the other window glass firms—Swinburnes at South Shields, the Wearmouth Glass Company and the Nailsea Glass Company (Bristol)—to join them. Each firm was to contribute in proportion to the number of glasshouses it possessed. Chances and Pilkingtons, which then had nine each, were to pay the most, then came Hartleys with six, Swinburnes with four, and the Wearmouth and Nailsea Companies each with two.[37]

Little time was lost. Two days after the London meeting, Swinburnes and Matteson (of the Wearmouth Company) agreed to collaborate in the plan[38] and on the following day James Varley, Pilkingtons' book-keeper, wired Chances with the news:

> 'Newton is shut up. We have possession. Our own manager has charge of the Furnaces six p.m.'

There were hitches in valuing the materials at the works and these caused James Hartley to complain bitterly against William Pilkington who, he believed, was temporizing for his own ends.[39] But when all the facts were explained to him, he agreed that

> 'The whole difficulty has arisen from a most unjustifiable interpolation by Mr Gardner's Solicitors.'[40]

Unfortunately our documents cease at this point and we have no evidence of when the whole matter was finally settled. But it is certain that the Newton factory, though it manufactured bottles, never made any more window glass and from this we may infer that the manufacturers' agreement was eventually carried through.

Chances, Pilkingtons and Hartleys again acted in concert in 1860, this time to close down the factory belonging to Joshua Bower and Co. of Hunslet, near Leeds.[41] Bowers agreed not to make any crown, sheet, rolled plate glass or other window glass anywhere in Lancashire, Yorkshire, Northumberland, Durham or the Midlands for fourteen years in consideration of a payment of £1,000 a year. They also received £3,204 for their stock and the three purchasers promised to honour all the agreements Bowers had made with their workmen and to fulfil all the contracts with their customers.[42]

The ending of window glass manufacture at Hunslet was soon followed by an attempt to launch another concern to start manufacture not far away, at Castleford. This venture, however, does not appear to have got beyond the issue of a prospectus. It claimed that window glass could, 'without doubt', be made at Castleford 20 per cent. more cheaply than at Birmingham, and 15 per cent. more cheaply than at St Helens. In addition to this alleged cost advantage, profits in that branch of the glass industry were, they asserted, 'unequalled by any other manufacture in the kingdom. . . . The present manufacturers, about five or six in number, have practically become "One Firm" and this established a great monopoly.'[43]

The road to success, however, was not so easy as the writers of this prospectus would imply; we hear no more of window glass manufacture at Castleford. It is true that by this time the three large firms were making 75 per cent. of all the window glass then made in the country;[44] but, as shall be seen in the next chapter, Belgian competition had become greater and was growing even more intense. There could be no question of a monopoly so long as cheap Belgian glass flooded the British market. Before proceeding to consider the effects of this growing competition from abroad, however, we must discuss the changes which took place at Pilkingtons' works at St Helens during the years following the repeal of the excise duty.

Two plans of the Grove Street factory (page 126), the first drawn in 1840 and the second in 1856, provide a useful commentary on the firm's development between those two dates. In 1840 the works, still confined to the original rectangle of freehold land on the eastern side of Grove Street, consisted of three glasshouses, two cutting rooms with pot rooms over them, a mixing room, a warehouse and joiners' shop (both in one building), a crate shop, a masons' shop, a clay mill, a clay room, brick kilns, a smithy and a timber yard. About one-third of the site was occupied by two parallel rows of cottages, thirty-seven in all, stretching from the timber yard southwards to the road leading from Grove Street to the Bells' Ravenhead Flint Glassworks. There were in the area of the works itself three more cottages and the manager's house. The lodge and office were both accommodated in a small space at the end of the mixing room building.

So many additions and alterations were made between 1840 and 1856 that within those sixteen years the whole appearance of the works was transformed almost beyond recognition. The first house had been turned over from crown to sheet glass manufacture and several blowing furnaces and flattening kilns had been added. The second and third houses were still used for making crown glass and a fourth, adjoining the third on ground previously occupied by the timber yard, was also devoted to this branch of the manufacture. Further ground had been acquired immediately to the east of these glasshouses (behind them if viewed from Grove Street), an area as extensive as the original purchase of 1826. On this site had been erected, in two compact groups of buildings, five melting furnaces, together with their attendant blowing and flattening furnaces and annealing kilns. The joiners' shop (with timber yard behind), smithy and

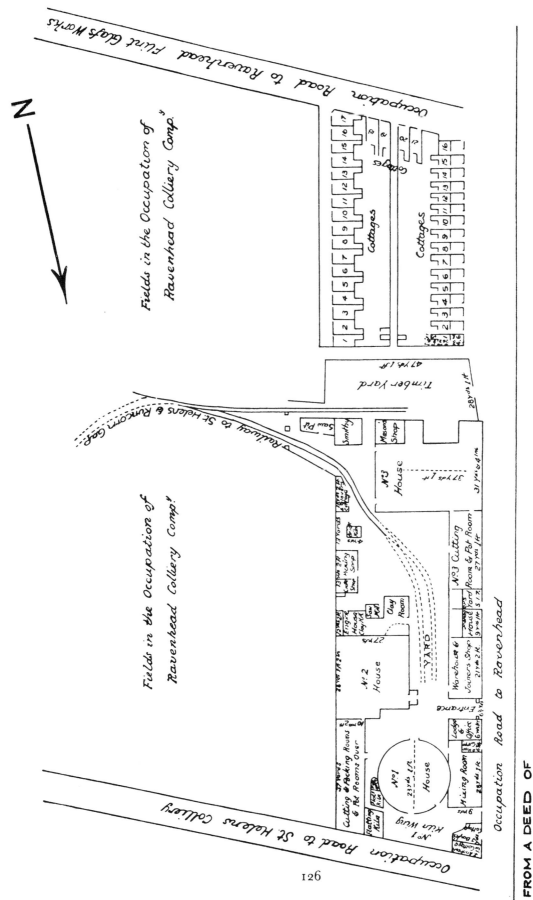

Plan 2. Greenall and Pilkingtons in 1840

FROM A DEED OF
1840

turning shop were all housed in a single U-shaped building to the east of the two rows of cottages. There was also a shed in this building where experimental work was undertaken. The original warehouse in Grove Street had been trebled in size and additional warehouse space had been provided in two buildings behind it. In place of the combined lodge and office, squeezed in at one end of the mixing room building, more spacious counting houses had been put up at one side of the main gates and a lodge built at the other. A few small plots of land between Grove Street and the Canal had been acquired in the 1830s and 1840s, presumably to provide loading facilities. A further large piece of ground bordering on the Canal was purchased in 1854.

Among the furnaces in the new group of buildings was one at which shades were blown. These pieces of glass, usually bell-shaped, were used to keep dust off articles which needed to be displayed, such as goods in shop windows or clocks in family drawing rooms. There is no record of when Pilkingtons entered this branch of trade, which was a development from sheet glass manufacture. It was certainly sometime between January 1845 (when one set of production figures ends without any reference to shades) and January 1848 (when the next set begins with the information that about 800 shades were then being made every week). Henry Deacon has left a description of how shades up to 16 inches diameter were made from cylinders,[45] while larger-sized and square- or oval-shaped shades were blown in moulds. The mould sheds adjoining the shade house are to be seen in the 1856 plan.

Several of the pots in the shade house were filled with coloured metal, used by the ornamental department.[46] This department seems to have come into existence about the same time as shade blowing. By 1850 the firm was in a position to issue a handsomely-produced *Trade Book of Patterns for Ornamental Window Glass with Designs for Church, Hall, Staircase and Memorial Windows*, the designs being by Frank Howard, described in the *Trade Book* as 'a well-known and celebrated artist'.[47] A window of his design, made by Pilkingtons, was installed in Liverpool Parish Church in January 1853.[48]

Much of the expansion during this period occurred after 1851. The removal of the tax on windows on April 1st of that year, the upswing of the building cycle, and that great advertisement for glass, the Crystal Palace, all helped to stimulate demand. By the early 1860s, warehouses had been opened in Birmingham, Leeds, Bristol and Sheffield.[49] And from this period comes the earliest definite evidence of exports of Pilkington glass. William Nash, who emigrated to Australia in 1853, became Pilkington's agent at Geelong and correspondence to him from St Helens in 1857–8 still remains.[50]

Growing orders, both from at home and abroad, led to the firm's output being increased from 80 tons a week in 1851 to 150 tons a week at the beginning of 1854. Pilkingtons were then employing 1,350 hands and paying out £1,050 in wages every week.[51] Despite the growing popularity and economic advantages of sheet glass, it is interesting to notice that, even at this date, total production of sheet glass had not yet overhauled that of crown at St Helens, as may be seen from the firm's weekly production figures:,

WEEKLY PRODUCTION AT PILKINGTON BROTHERS AT THE
BEGINNING OF 1854

Crown	12,400 tables	161,200 lb.
Sheet and Patent Plate	9,800 pieces	132,300 lb.
Rolled Plate	15,000 ft.	45,000 lb.
Shades and Miscellaneous	3,500 items	10,500 lb.

Source: Lecture by R. B. Edmundson, published in The Builder, April 8, 1854.

As there was much more waste with crown glass than with sheet, Pilkingtons were probably already making more *saleable* sheet glass than crown. There were then four crown and four sheet furnaces. A fifth sheet furnace, then under construction, must have tipped the balance much further when it came into use. By 1855, as we have noticed, Pilkingtons had nine furnaces, the same number as Chances and three more than Hartleys.

As Pilkingtons extended the scale of their operations, they required an increasing supply of coal and raw materials, particularly sand and alkali. Coal was needed in very large amounts, several tons being necessary to produce one ton of glass. In 1851, for instance, when Pilkingtons were making 80 tons of glass every week, the various furnaces at the works were devouring no less than 650 tons of coal, a ratio of more than eight tons of coal to one ton of glass. An uninterrupted supply of fuel was vital to the successful operation of the works. It was to safeguard their deliveries that Pilkingtons were obliged to go into coalmining in 1844.

During the later months of 1843 the colliers of the Lancashire coalfield had organized themselves into a powerful trade union, and in January 1844 the St Helens men—but not their fellow workers elsewhere on the coalfield—went on strike. For two or three weeks the factories in the St Helens neighbourhood were able to keep open by drawing on their accumulated stocks, but as the strike dragged on these stocks became depleted almost to the point of exhaustion. Some firms sent for coal to the collieries on the southern fringe of the Wigan coalfield: others began to prospect for coal themselves. F. Fincham, the resourceful and energetic manager of the Ravenhead Plate Glassworks, began to open out some old disused workings within his company's grounds.[52] Pilkingtons followed his example and began to look for their own source of coal. On February 19th they engaged Robert Whyte, a skilled mining engineer, to select a suitable site in the town and there sink a pit for the firm's use.[53]

After one or two trial bores for coal on land to the north of Duke Street,

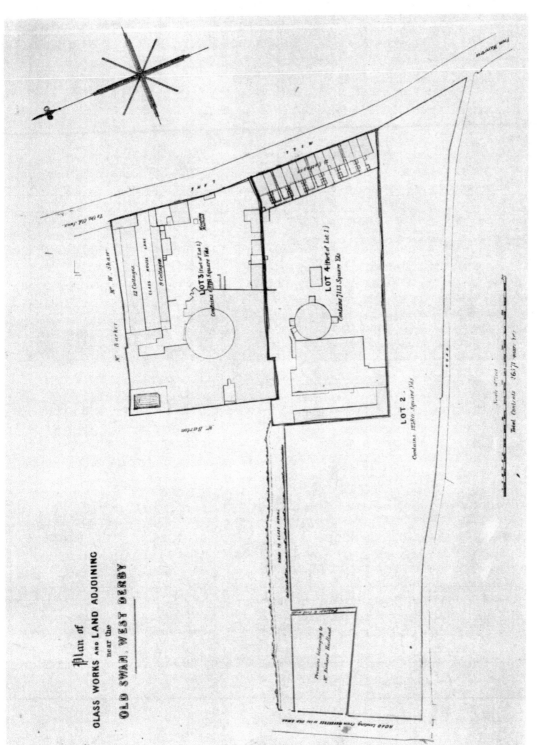

11 Plan of Old Swan glassworks which ceased to make window glass after it had been acquired by Chances and Pilkingtons in the early 1850s. An old glassmaking cone may still be seen on this site

12   A photograph and a portrait of William Pilkington in his later years

Whyte began, in June 1844, to prospect further along the Ormskirk road about two hundred yards beyond Four Lane Ends (later known as the Lingholme) on the north side of the road. This land had the added recommendation that it belonged to Peter Greenall.[54] Boring on this occasion was successful and, although the colliers had long since resumed work and the men showed no signs of a further turn-out, Pilkingtons decided that they ought to continue with plans for getting their own coal. In September 1844, Whyte began to sink an engine pit at the Green Lane Colliery (as it came to be called) and the winding of coal from the Little Delf mine, a seam just under three feet thick, started in February, 1845. The workings soon became extensive. During the six years between the colliery's opening and the end of 1850 the Little Delf measures were worked from under a total area of more than twelve statute acres of land. By that date all the coal that could be worked economically from the Green Lane pit had been dug and the colliery was closed. A second pit was sunk farther to the south, in Eccleston township, and 'Messrs Pilkingtons' new Colliery in Eccleston' was referred to in the *Liverpool Mercury* of September 8, 1854. Robert Whyte remained colliery agent to the company until 1856 when he emigrated to Australia.[55] In 1857 Pilkingtons purchased from John Clare and the executors of Thomas Haddock the remains of the extinct St Helens Colliery, close to their glassworks on the south-east side, which Clare, Haddock and Company had operated until 1844.[56] By this time Pilkington Brothers had become coal proprietors in their own right. Much of the coal wound from their pits was sold to other firms and to the public, and by no means all of it was used to stoke the furnaces at their glassworks. It was as Pilkington Brothers, coal proprietors, and not as Pilkington Brothers, glass manufacturers, that the firm made the St Helens Colliery one of the largest and most profitable concerns in the district.

Sand, relatively free from iron oxide and therefore suitable for window glass manufacture, was also available locally. In 1834 excise officers in various parts of the country were asked by the Treasury to send in information about glass manufacturers' sources of sand. The sand available in Eccleston, near St Helens, was singled out for particular mention. It was of a good quality, almost in the same category as that from Alum Bay (Isle of Wight) or Lynn, and could be had locally for 12s 6d a ton, delivered.[57] Although Pilkingtons did, in 1869, order a trial cargo of foreign sand, this did not produce any better window glass than the local variety. They therefore continued to draw all their supplies from deposits which lay just under the surface soil to the north and west of St Helens.[58] From 1869 they employed a chemist to ensure that impurities in the sand were reduced to a minimum.

Alkali was also obtainable from local sources. The rise of the firm coincided with the growth of the Leblanc process and there was never any shortage of soda or saltcake, particularly at St Helens where several new chemical works were sited. The local alkali manufacturers were able to supply soda or saltcake of good quality (relatively free from iron) in sufficient quantity and at a reasonable price. Pilkingtons, therefore, preferred to buy from the existing chemical firms rather than to go to the trouble and expense of erecting plant to manufacture these products on their own account. Moreover, glassmakers during the 1830s and 1840s were learning how to use more of the cheaper salt-cake (sodium sulphate) in place of the dearer soda ash (sodium carbonate). Already by 1837 Greenall and Pilkingtons were purchasing saltcake from the nearby works of S. and W. T. Clough. By the late 1840s the firm was using saltcake almost entirely.[59] The glassworks were being supplied by several alkali makers: Morley and Speakman in Parr, Gamble at Gerard's Bridge, and, especially, Muspratt at Earlestown. Their saltcake was of a satisfactory quality for glassmaking and it was only after J. C. Gamble had patented a new process, employing iron retorts in place of brick furnaces,[60] that William Pilkington had any reason to complain. When, early in 1845, he was asked to support the development of Longmaid's process, whereby saltcake was to be manufactured by calcining together salt and pyrites, he replied:

> 'Salt cake made by this Process being very and, indeed, altogether free from Iron, is so peculiarly adapted for Glass making that unless we can procure some made either upon this or the old plan in contradistinction to Mr Gamble's patent, we must, though very unwillingly, put up chambers and manufacture our own salt cake.'[61]

But Pilkingtons were not driven to become manufacturing chemists just yet. Saltcake sufficiently free from iron continued to reach the glassworks from the local alkali factories and by canal from Earlestown. At the beginning of the 1850s, however, just at the time when output of glass increased and the firm's saltcake requirements took a sharp upward turn, Muspratt was obliged to close his works at Earlestown, and Pilkingtons were, consequently, thrown into greater dependence upon other manufacturers. This caused William Pilkington once more to contemplate setting himself up as a manufacturing chemist and he actually entered into a partnership for the purpose. His associate in this venture was Henry Deacon, the young man whom we have already encountered as the firm's highly-paid Chemist and Engineer.

Deacon left Pilkingtons at the beginning of July 1851, when he was just twenty-nine years of age. Although he was then earning the remarkable salary of £7 a week—14s 0d more than William Pilkington's eldest son—he no doubt saw that he could advance himself little further as an employee. Partnerships in the firm were obviously reserved for members of the family. If he was to maintain his very rapid rate of progress, he had to become a manufacturer in his own right.

At this time the chemical industry held out one of the brightest prospects for the intending industrialist, especially for a man like Deacon who was well versed in the theory of soda-making, even though, as may have been the case, he lacked detailed knowledge of the practical working of the Leblanc process. By now Widnes offered the prospective manufacturer better opportunities than St Helens on account of recent increases in the cost of carriage on the Sankey Canal for all materials except coal.[62] After 1848 it paid the alkali maker to carry his coal down the Canal rather than to transport vast quantities of salt, limestone and pyrites at greater cost up to the coalfield. By removing to Widnes in 1851, therefore, Deacon became one of the pioneers in the industry at the southern terminus of the Canal and thereby established his claim to a place in John Fenwick Allen's later book on *Some Founders of the Chemical Industry*.[63] Fenwick Allen wrote fifteen years after Deacon's death and relied largely, it would seem, on information provided by his eldest son, Henry Wade Deacon. According to this source, Deacon spent his first two years in Widnes as manager of a small works which had been opened three or four years before[64] by John Hutchinson, a man three years younger than Deacon, who had previously been manager at Kurtz's alkali works in St Helens.[65] It is hard to believe that the amazingly successful Deacon served Hutchinson in such a humble capacity, though he may have been in partnership with him.

Alternatively, as has recently been suggested,[66] he may have gone to Widnes at Pilkingtons' instigation to find out about experiments on a new method of making soda ash which William Gossage was then carrying out there, the intention being that, having learnt what he could from Gossage, Deacon would set up an alkali factory himself, supported to some extent by Pilkington capital. In this way, Pilkingtons would safeguard their supplies of an essential raw material. Gossage's experiments did not succeed; but Deacon nevertheless persuaded William Pilkington to go into partnership with him, each partner advancing £3,000 to build a Leblanc alkali works on the north bank of the Canal almost opposite to Hutchinson's. Pilkington and Deacon signed a thousand-year lease for the land on October 1, 1853.[67]

In the following year the partners made arrangements to install equipment for the production on a commercial scale of soda ash [*sic*] suitable for glassmaking, employing newly-patented processes.[68] Although this step was almost certainly undertaken at Deacon's suggestion, William Pilkington advanced the capital to buy the necessary equipment, £580 in all. The experiments yielded no quick results, however, and William Pilkington, the business man, grew more and more impatient with Deacon, the chemist. By the middle of 1855 William Pilkington decided to withdraw altogether. Another of Deacon's former employers, Holbrook Gaskell, was persuaded to take his place and the deed for the dissolution of the partnership was signed on June 15, 1855. It was then agreed that Holbrook Gaskell should pay William Pilkington the £3,000 that he had invested in the partnership. The outstanding £580 was to be repaid over a number of years, either by providing Pilkingtons' glassworks with high grade soda ash suitable for glassmaking at 5 per cent. below the invoice price if the plant eventually yielded such a product, or, if it did not, in annual payments of £100. (We do not know which method was finally adopted.) Although the partnership was dissolved without any outward show of ill-feeling, William Pilkington was not sorry to escape from his business relationships with Deacon. As he confided to his solicitors:

'I cannot tell or express to you how much pleased and relieved I shall be to get rid of such an unsociable, selfish and arrogant fellow as he is.'[69]

Almost ten years were to elapse before William Pilkington again ventured into alkali manufacture at Widnes. On this occasion he chose as his partners his two younger sons, George (b. 1840) who was already chemist at the glass-works,[70] and Leonard (b. 1847). The Mersey Chemical Works of William Pilkington and Sons, a short distance up the Canal from Gaskell-Deacons, was in course of erection when the Alkali Inspector drew up his First Report for the year 1864[71], and on March 9, 1865, William (Roby) and William Windle Pilkington were expecting that the arrival of the first deliveries of saltcake from these works would effect a great improvement in the quality of the firm's glass, an expectation that was soon realized.[72] As with Pilkingtons' colliery, the Mersey Chemical Works, though originally built chiefly to serve the require-ments of the glassworks, were soon supplying other customers as well. By 1870 the alkali factory employed between 100 and 150 men and manufactured 2,000 tons of bleaching powder and 120 tons of nitrate of soda annually, in addition to producing soda and saltcake. It later became part of the United Alkali Co. Ltd., and, later still, of I.C.I. Ltd.[73]

The elimination of most of their British competitors, and their own ventures into coalmining and chemical manufacture, assisted Pilkingtons greatly when they came to be confronted by growing imports of cheap glass. This foreign, and chiefly Belgian, competition, was far more severe than anything previously ex-perienced by British manufacturers. The Belgians were outside the jurisdiction of the Manufacturers' Association.

CHAPTER 9

COMPETITION FROM BELGIUM
AND CONSOLIDATION AT ST HELENS

ELGIUM did not emerge as a major window glass producing country
until the second quarter of the nineteenth century. In 1823, only ten
small factories were engaged in this branch of manufacture in that part
of the kingdom of the Netherlands which was to become, after 1830, the independent state of Belgium, and they could only muster 66 pots among them.
By 1834 the number of factories had increased to 21 and their combined
capacity to 224 pots. By 1847, although the number of factories had not increased, their average size had grown; there were then 272 pots in use altogether.[1] Almost all of this glass was exported. Concentrated in the Charleroi
area in the south of the country, where the necessary raw materials were to
hand, the industry was able to take advantage of good communications to the
coast; from there the crates of window glass could be shipped cheaply to all
parts of the world. During the 1840s exports of Belgian window glass averaged
just over 8,000,000 kilograms per year[2]—just under 160,000 cwt. This was an
amount exceeding the whole output of British factories during the early 1840s
and not far below their output in the boom of the mid-1830s.

The Belgian manufacturers exploited to the full the natural cost advantages
which they enjoyed and so were able to undersell the home producers in other
countries, especially in the more common grades of glass for which there was
the largest market. Although coal was not particularly cheap in Belgium, and
was certainly more expensive than in England, other costs were lower. Most
contemporaries emphasized labour as the factor of production which gave the
Belgians a particular advantage. In 1841, for instance, R. L. Chance visited
Belgium and found that glass blowers there made 50 per cent. more glass in a
week than their British counterparts and received less than half a British
glassmaker's wage. Chance believed that the Belgians were 'such formidable
rivals from their economy and activity that unless we manufacture on the best
principles, we can never sell our extra quantities abroad to a profit . . .'[3] This
was written when sheet glass manufacture was still in its infancy in Britain; but,

133

twenty years later, a British consular report from Brussels, dealing with the progress of Belgian industry generally, had this to say about the cost of labour:

'The characteristics of the Belgian workmen are steadiness and perseverance, combined with great intelligence in working after models; their habits are not so expensive as those of English artificers; their diet is more humble—they consume less meat, and their bread is seldom purely wheaten or white in quality . . . beer and spirits are both lower in price than in England. They seldom use tea and the chicory root constitutes a very economical and wholesome substitute for coffee. Instead of coals and open grates, closed stoves and artificial fuel, made of mere dust of coal and clay worked into lumps, are universally in use. The system of schools for infants from two to seven years, and from seven to twelve years, is very general and affords great facilities—the children being cared for—to both their parents to occupy themselves in daily service and by combined industry to ameliorate the condition of the family.'[4]

Unfortunately no detailed estimates of costs of production in particular Belgian factories are available to enable us to verify whether cheaper labour did, in fact, give Belgian glass manufacturers their great advantage over manufacturers in other countries. The only relevant information, published by Bontemps in the later 1860s, would suggest that, while the Belgians certainly benefited from cheap labour, their success was really due to economies in all departments for which cheap labour may have been only partly responsible.

BONTEMPS' COMPARISON OF THE COST OF MANUFACTURING 1,000 kg. OF WINDOW GLASS IN BELGIUM AND ENGLAND

| | Belgium | | England | |
	Francs	Centimes	Francs	Centimes
Furnace and pots	–	76	–	98
Frit materials	4	82	5	90
Fuel	5	10	2	55
Labour (melting)	–	81	–	88
(blowing)	4	60	5	40
Flattening	2	40	2	60
Warehousing	–	74	–	90
'Emballage' [Packing]	2	46	2	59
Carpentry and forge work	–	37	–	40
Rents and taxes	–	73	–	89
Management: general expenses	1	50	2	00
	24	29	25	09

Source: Georges Bontemps, *Guide du Verrier* (Paris, 1868), 405, 408.

British glass manufacturers began to complain about Belgian competition even before reduction of the import duties permitted Belgian glass to obtain a market in Britain itself. Already, in 1837, they were complaining of being undersold in all parts of the world by French, Belgian and German firms.[5] In 1841 they returned to the charge, arguing that they were 'in fact nearly shut out from all except in our own Colonies where we have hitherto had protection [*sic*]'.[6] Chances pointed to the loss of the Indian market 'by the partial application there of the principles of free trade'.[7] The trade figures confirm that re-exports of Belgian glass from Britain grew rapidly in the 1840s and, by 1845, were running at the same level as the exports of British glass:

RE-EXPORTS OF WINDOW GLASS (ALMOST WHOLLY BELGIAN) AND
EXPORTS OF BRITISH WINDOW GLASS, 1842–9 (CWT.)

Year	Imports	Retained for Home Use	Re-exported	British Exports
1842	2,104	106	1,998	20,031
1843	3,349	137	3,166	16,261
1844	7,451	240	7,147	16,286
1845	22,455	8,374	12,790	14,788
1846	44,811	9,882	32,716	20,345
1847	35,117	4,693	30,831	29,084
1848	31,037	6,888	25,883	19,708
1849	25,576	7,712	17,916	17,255

Source: Parliamentary Papers, 1843 [173] XXX, 1844 [200] XLV, 1845 [169] XLVI, 1846 [214] XLIV, 1847 [361] LIX, 1847/8 [305] LVIII, 1849 [534] L; *Economist*, February 11, 1850.

From 1842 to 1844 most of these re-exports went to the territory of the East India Company, as Chances had indicated. In 1845, however, Belgian glass began to be exported to British North America (Canada) which was then the British manufacturers' best export market. In 1846 twice as much Belgian as British window glass crossed the North Atlantic to Canada; but in subsequent years re-exports to Canada resumed more modest proportions and the territories of the East India Company again became the chief destination for Belgian glass in transit through Britain.

These shipments of Belgian glass to Britain represented but a small fraction of Belgium's total exports. Her glass was sent to all parts of the world by other

BELGIAN EXPORTS OF WINDOW GLASS, 1850–2 ('000 KILOGRAMS)

	1850	1851	1852
Total	11,672	14,681	16,444
To Britain	1,813	1,980	1,866
United States	3,429	5,213	4,949
Holland	1,507	1,920	1,848
Hamburg	1,048	1,337	1,662
Turkish Empire	1,230	1,085	1,215

Source: Tableau Générale du Commerce avec les Pays Etrangers (Statistique de la Belgique) for the years concerned.

Details for subsequent years will be found in Appendix 5.

routes. Three times as much was exported to the United States as to Britain, and America was, throughout the 1850s, by far the largest of Belgium's customers. Holland took as much Belgian glass as did Britain (presumably for re-export) and Hamburg and the Turkish Empire were also markets of consequence.

By this time the progressive reduction of British import duties was enabling the Belgians to sell more and more of their glass in Britain itself, instead of re-exporting it. Before 1845, imported Belgian glass had had to bear a prohibitive customs duty of 30s 0d per cwt. in addition to the excise duty. With the removal of the excise duty, the customs duty was reduced to 14s 0d per cwt. It was further reduced in 1846 to 7s 0d, in 1848 to 3s 6d, in 1853 to 2s 6d and in 1855 to 1s 6d. From April 1857 all glass was allowed to enter the country duty-free.[8] The reduction of 1853 and the abolition of the duty in 1857, coinciding as they did with a period of rising prices on the British market, were both accompanied by large increases in the amount of Belgian glass sold to British customers. Retained imports were, in 1853–6, double what they had been in 1850–2, and, after 1857, they doubled again. Re-exports, having dwindled to negligible proportions in the middle of the decade, resumed their former scale after 1857.

WINDOW GLASS (ALMOST WHOLLY BELGIAN) RETAINED FOR HOME CONSUMPTION AND RE-EXPORTED, 1850–60 (CWT.)

	Retained in Britain	Re-exported	British Exports
1850	9,406	11,604	15,518
1851	10,696	2,059	16,460
1852	13,170	3,197	22,162
1853	23,350	5,485	39,159
1854	27,127	3,012	35,514
1855	25,816	1,126	21,473
1856	27,787	2,399	28,522
1857	39,631	16,429	32,000
1858	61,927	33,655	26,008
1859	67,591	51,715	27,697
1860	75,088	25,116	33,408

Source: British Trade and Navigation Returns.

Within a decade the sale of Belgian glass in Britain had grown to formidable proportions. Moreover, the capture of a large share of this market had been achieved without the diversion of exports from elsewhere: Belgian exports to Britain continued to run at about one-sixth of the total, still considerably below those to the United States. After the outbreak of the American Civil War in April 1861, however, Belgian shipments to the United States fell off while those to Britain continued to increase. Britain became, and remained, the chief market for Belgium's huge, and still growing, output.[9] Between the plateau of the mid-1850s and 1870 sales of Belgian window glass in Britain increased nearly fifteenfold, from some 25,000 cwt. to 370,000 cwt.

WINDOW GLASS (ALMOST WHOLLY BELGIAN) RETAINED FOR HOME
CONSUMPTION AND RE-EXPORTED, 1861–1870 (CWT.).

	Retained in Britain	Re-exported	British Exports
1861	90,244	11,959	35,732
1862	117,145	25,425	49,171
1863	135,762	46,223	62,674
1864	173,726	62,881	58,010
1865	226,214	37,842	50,608
1866	Total retained and re-exported 272,392		59,171
1867	237,737	47,957	64,431
1868	320,786	81,908	73,301
1869	328,156	71,381	92,111
1870	369,874	53,183	76,654

From the middle of the 1850s prices fell during most years, recovering slightly on occasion in response to building demand, but always losing any slight gain by a much greater fall. In 1858, when Belgian glass first reached the British market on a really large scale, the price was more than 20 per cent. higher than at the end of the 1860s. And this was just the beginning of a secular fall which was to continue until the eve of the First World War.

By the middle of the 1860s the three great glassmaking firms in Britain—Chances, Pilkingtons and Hartleys—were together making about 340,000 cwt. of glass per annum.[10] Before 1870 sales of Belgian glass had almost certainly exceeded British sales and there was no sign of imports ceasing to grow. The Manufacturers' Association, having succeeded in curbing competition at home, was now confronted with other, and much more powerful, competitors who were unwilling to come to terms. Attempts were indeed made to open negotiations with the Belgians. The Board Minutes at Pilkingtons for August 4, 1865, record that, on the previous day, George Gwilliam, the permanent secretary of the Association,[11] had called 'in reference to the Belgian houses being induced to accept a fixed minimum for the lowest qualities, say 1½d for 15 oz. we agreeing not to go below 1⅝d'. Gwilliam then intended 'to see the London representative of the Foreign houses and work through them'. Six weeks later he called again at St Helens to report on a visit to Charleroi where he had met the Belgian manufacturers. He believed that a price-fixing bargain could be struck with them and advised that a deputation of English manufacturers should 'meet the Belgian houses, interchange ideas and do much good mutually'.[12] We know that by the beginning of 1866 the British manufacturers were seriously entertaining the idea of visiting Belgium during the summer,[13] but there is no evidence to show whether they actually went or, if they did, what was the upshot of their negotiations. If any agreement was reached, it was certainly short-lived, and did not halt the downward trend of prices. Ten years later R. L. Chance could write to Richard Pilkington:

'There is unfortunately no Association of window glass manufacturers in Belgium and no understanding of any kind amongst them. . . . I fear that Gwilliam would do no good by going amongst them.'[14]

Powerless when confronted with foreign competition, the Association had to be content with continuing its policy of driving out of business the occasional new competitor at home. When glassworks at Stourbridge fell into Hartleys' hands in 1867, it was agreed that Chances and Pilkingtons should each bear two-fifths of the cost and Hartleys the remaining one-fifth.[15] The Nailsea works near Bristol ceased production soon after this. They had been leased in 1862 by Samuel Bowen of West Bromwich—who had already been a bankrupt —and John Powis of London. This firm began to sell rolled plate glass—a branch in which Belgian competition was not severe[16]—at prices below those of the Association. They gained a considerable number of large orders immediately, including one for 100,000 feet for glazing the roof of London Road Station in Manchester.[17] The Association's machinery went into action and the other manufacturers cut their prices so that they undersold even Bowen and Powis. Within a year of the Association's intervention, there were negotiations afoot for James Hartley to purchase the works, William (Roby) Pilkington and R. L. Chance acting as arbitrators.[18] Bowen failed again in 1869, this time for about £30,000,[19] and, the lease having been surrendered, Hartleys sought to dispose of the property. Chances bought it for £14,000, made glass there for a short time during the boom of the early 1870s, and then closed it down for good because the local coal supplies proved unsatisfactory.[20]

Against the real competitors, however, the only course was for each firm to improve its efficiency. The 1860s saw the beginning of a new phase of technical improvement.

By this time Pilkingtons were in a much better position to keep abreast of technical development than they had been twenty years earlier. The founders of the firm owed their success chiefly to expert salesmanship and constant vigilance at the factory. They laid no claim to being technicians and were certainly not of an inventive turn of mind in the same way as was J. T. Chance or James Hartley. In the 1840s Pilkingtons had been obliged to call in Henry Deacon to take charge of the technical side of their business and it was Deacon, and not either of the partners, who addressed learned societies on the various techniques of glassmaking. The position was different, however, with the second generation: among the sons of the founders were two very capable engineers. William Pilkington's second son, Richard (b. 1830), became a mechanical engineer and, though he did not go into the firm, he was certainly interested in the mechanical side of glassmaking for a time. He was, from 1854, a member of the Institution of Mechanical Engineers and, in 1863, delivered a paper to that body 'On the Processes and Mechanical Appliances in the Manufacture of Polished Sheet Glass'.[21] By then, however, he was living away from St Helens and does not seem subsequently to have taken an active interest in glass manufacture.[22] It was left to his younger cousin, Richard Pilkington's eldest son, William Windle (b. 1839), who soon showed an aptitude for technical matters, to take control of this side of the firm's activities. Windle Pilkington served a long apprenticeship during the 1860s. During the 1870s, as we shall see in the next chapter, his determined advocacy of the newly-patented tank furnaces, which allowed continuous working to take place for twenty-four hours a day, tipped the balance decisively in Pilkingtons' favour.

He took out his first patent in 1860 at the age of twenty-one. In this he proposed to improve melting furnaces by delivering jets of steam on to the under side of the grate bars with the two-fold object of keeping the bars cool and supplying steam to sustain the combustion of the fuel.[23] A few years later he was concerned with introducing to the works improved machinery for finishing sheet glass and turning it into patent plate. Richard Pilkington, junior, had told the Institution of Mechanical Engineers in 1863 that it took about nine hours to polish each side of a sheet of glass, largely because much of the initial work had to be done by hand. The new benches, made at the Haigh Foundry near Wigan in 1866, reduced this time by half with a saving of 1¼d on every foot of glass produced. And it was reported that the quality was 'superior to Chances'.[24]

The most important innovation of this period, however, and the one which, more than any other, pointed the way to future development, was undoubtedly the Siemens Regenerative Gas Furnace. During the 1850s Frederick Siemens had invented and his brother, William, had 'matured',[25] a coal-fired furnace which was constructed in such a way that the flames and resulting hot products of combustion were made to travel alternately in opposite directions, thereby producing a regenerative effect and extracting most of the heat before the air was eventually allowed to escape up the chimney. This resulted in a considerable saving of fuel which William Siemens optimistically claimed amounted to as much as 79 per cent. in the case of one of the early prototypes.[26] Serious practical difficulties arose, however, when an attempt was made to apply the regenerative principle to larger furnaces. It was found impossible to use solid fuel.[27] The brothers Siemens, therefore, started to experiment with gas-firing and in 1861 they took out a patent for a gas-fired regenerative furnace suitable for glassmaking.[28]

The gas-fired furnace possessed a two-fold attraction for the glass manufacturer. It saved fuel and it prevented impurities from the coal from coming into contact with and discolouring the glass. In 1861 Siemens furnaces were erected at the flint glassworks belonging to Lloyd and Summerfield at Birmingham, and at Chances. The following year one of the new furnaces was being built at the Ravenhead Plate Glassworks.[29] Once again Chances had succeeded in forestalling Pilkingtons. It was not until January 1863, almost two years after the pots had first been set in the Siemens gas-fired furnace at Smethwick, that Pilkingtons even began to consider taking out a licence.[30] William (Roby) Pilkington consulted John Crossley, then one of the managing partners of the British Plate Glassworks who had already had some experience of the new furnaces at Ravenhead. Crossley agreed to superintend the erection of a Siemens furnace at Pilkingtons, and on March 26, 1863, Pilkingtons decided to write to Siemens for terms. Siemens' offer of £100 for the drawings and a levy of 5s 0d on each ton of glass produced was accepted by the firm and one of the Siemens brothers came to St Helens in May to talk the matter over. The furnace was lit for the first time on November 2nd. Three weeks later the quality of glass from the gas furnace was declared to be 'decidedly the best' and after a month's operation Windle Pilkington considered that 'the saving upon coal alone will almost pay Siemens' royalty ... of 5s 0d per ton on thirty tons per week'. On April 11, 1864, the new furnace was declared to be 'a decided success commercially' and on May 5th the Board discussed the possibility of installing a gas furnace in the first house

'instead of the present one which makes wretched metal. The house is the only one where the furnace could be put in without altering it. On the other hand the blowing house, etc., would cause great alteration, taking up the present warehouse and rebuilding one upon the site of the late No. 2 house—altogether involving a great outlay.'

The following week it was decided to build this second furnace 'with all speed in order to meet the demand in Autumn . . . but not to enlarge the blowing place or build the new warehouse till the new furnace has been fully tried'. Pots were set in this furnace on August 14th, the flattening kilns were then put in hand, and the warehouse was erected subsequently.

On the whole, although there were certainly the usual teething troubles, Pilkingtons appear to have found the new Siemens furnaces very satisfactory, particularly after they had substituted slack for coal in the gas producers. William (Roby) Pilkington reported to the Board on June 8, 1865, that

'a producer with slack burns ½ less fuel than if worked with coal but does a third less work. There is no doubt that the gas furnace to be used to any advantage should be worked with slack and not coal.'

Chances, on the other hand, do not appear to have found the new furnaces so economical. J. H. Chance confided to William (Roby) Pilkington on July 28, 1864:

'How does your gas furnace answer? We don't find any saving—fuel is more.'

And on October 24, 1865:

'How do your gas furnaces go on? Ours remain much the same.'[31]

Although Chances were first in the field, they were not so successful in developing this new type of furnace and—most important—in making it pay.

The emphasis at this time was wholly upon improvement rather than upon expansion, which had been the chief feature in the years before the mid-1850s. In 1865 Pilkingtons operated the same number of furnaces as they had done ten years before,[32] and Henry Chance's statement that his own firm, together with Pilkingtons and Hartleys, were making only 340,000 cwt. of glass confirms that Pilkingtons could not themselves have been making more than the 150 tons per week—or 156,000 cwt. per year—which was their reported production in 1854.[33] The additional demand was obviously being satisfied by Belgian imports. The most the British firms could do, apparently, was to consolidate their position in order to prevent their market from actually shrinking.

With technical changes and economy went the final extinction of crown glass. In 1865 Pilkingtons were still making crown glass at three of their nine furnaces.[34] Two years later the number had been reduced to two. Chances were then making 4,000 tables per week and Pilkingtons 3,600.[35] Soon after this Pilkingtons re-equipped these two furnaces, the last crown house being closed in July 1872.[36]

At a time when economy was the universal watchword, a reduction of a sixth in transport charges to and from the Mersey—and, moreover, the fixing of this reduced rate by Act of Parliament—was a concession of considerable value to Pilkingtons. The amalgamation of the St Helens Canal and Railway in 1845 had created a transport monopoly and rates had been advanced, since 1845, from 8d to 1/- per ton on the canal and from 1/- to 2/- per ton on the railway. When, in 1864, the London and North Western Railway presented a Bill to Parliament to take over the St Helens Canal and Railway, all the transport users brought pressure to bear to secure a reduction in the rates. By their persistence in committee, they obliged the London and North Western to insert into the Bill a clause fixing the rate to Widnes at 10d per ton on the canal and 1/8 on the railway.[37] The St Helens and Widnes Traders Association, created in 1864, has successfully defended these concessions ever since.[38]

We do not know when the founders' four sons actually became partners in the firm. As we have seen, William Pilkington's two sons, William (Roby) and

Thomas, went into the business first; the former acted as superintendent in the factory and the latter went on to the commercial side. They were joined, nearly ten years later, by two of Richard Pilkington's sons; William Windle went into the works and Richard joined his cousin Thomas to deal with sales. Richard, the youngest of the four, came of age in January 1862. A year later, they were certainly all partners in the concern, for they all attended the first meeting of the newly-formed Board on January 8 of that year. The fact that it was then considered advisable to have such formal meetings to decide matters of policy, suggests that the younger sons may only then have joined the partnership. Informality, possible where only two or three persons are concerned, becomes impracticable with six.

Board meetings were held at first on each alternate Thursday but after three meetings it was decided to meet weekly instead. A regular routine was soon worked out, each department being considered in turn. Symptomatic of the new and more methodical régime was the decision to fix the partners' holidays. On January 4, 1866,

> 'Some system being thought expedient for regulating the absence of partners, it was resolved that each be allowed a full month (31 days) of absence during the year; that exceptional days be unnoticed, but that if anyone be absent for a continuous number of days such as a week, it shall be taken into consideration against the yearly holiday. . . .'

The early minutes of the Board show that the two senior partners, both in their sixties, were content to exercise a general surveillance over the firm's affairs and leave all the active management to their sons, particularly to William (Roby), who had such an advantage over the others both in age and experience. Richard Pilkington, who reached the age of seventy in 1865, continued to live at the family home, Windle Hall, but his brother, William, removed from Eccleston Hall in 1869 and went to live at Downing Hall, near Holywell in Flintshire. At the age of sixty-nine he had finally retired from business: his removal away from St Helens was an admission of the fact. In February 1869, he told the firm's employees at a social gathering:

> 'My best wishes to you are that at our ages you may be as hale and strong as I am.'[39]

On September 10th he was able to report to his brother from Downing that he had enjoyed an excellent day's shooting and could not remember ever having shot better, but was obliged to confess:

> 'I can no longer do what I once could and am painfully reminded of the infirmities of old age, by over-exertion'.

This was one of the last letters in the long correspondence that had passed between the two brothers over a period of fifty years or more. Richard Pilkington died at Windle Hall at the end of December 1869. William Pilkington lived on in Flintshire for almost three years longer. He died on September 12, 1872.[40] Neither of them left a very large personal fortune. Richard Pilkington's will was proved at under £50,000 and his brother's at under £100,000.

The founders of the firm, without any specialised knowledge of glassmaking but with a thorough training in business methods, had saved a small glassworks from bankruptcy and guided it successfully through a period of concentration in the industry. Their sons, recapturing some of the boldness and persistence of earlier years, were soon to turn it into by far the largest glassmaking concern in the country.

CHAPTER 10

EXPANSION ONCE MORE

THE four partners of the second generation were men of purpose and determination. They are reputed to have possessed to a marked degree all the sternness and strictness which are particularly associated with Victorian industrialists, and there is clear evidence of these characteristics throughout the Board's minute books. They ruled their business like autocrats, though there are indications that the despotism was of a benevolent sort. Efficiency was their watchword: little escaped their hawk-eyed vigilance. Yet it was not efficiency of a penny-pinching kind. Their aim was to run existing plant as efficiently as possible so that the money which was saved should be available to finance further development. In this way the firm could be built up without having to turn to outside sources for capital. The partners were always willing to spend money—often very large sums of money—on innovations which would help to expand their business. They were very quick to try out anything which seemed at all promising. They experimented with electric lighting so early as 1880, for instance, and installed a telephone to their colliery in the same year. Windle Pilkington, the technical expert among the partners, was tireless in his advocacy of new and more up-to-date plant. His zeal for spending had often to be restrained by the other partners. Tradition has it that the four were often not of one mind and decisions were frequently reached only after periods of considerable tension. This interplay of strong personalities does not appear openly in the minutes; but they do contain hints of what passed orally before pen was put to paper. In June 1868, for instance:

> 'Building operations. T[homas] P. alluded to the great outlay going on. W. W[indle] P. stated that Rolled Plate kilns built by G. Harris were ab^t finished at a cost of ab^t £50 a piece. That the 1st House job will be ended in another three weeks after which the only things in prospect are our new flatt^g kilns and the mixing room job also Tank furnaces.'

And in April 1869:

> 'Resolved that it is essential that W. W. P. get a young fellow to act as draughtsman and lieutenant in concentrating the work and bringing it in such form to him,

13   William (Roby) Pilkington

14   Thomas Pilkington

leaving him more free to direct his attention to particular points without being required here, there and everywhere as at present. W. W. P. will look out for such a man accordingly.'

Despite—or perhaps because of—internal differences of opinion, the four partners formed an effective team. They all appear to have been men of considerable ability, and were unquestionably strenuous workers. They lived for their business and invested heavily in it. The last quarter of the nineteenth century was a period of generally falling prices and profits, and glass manufacturers suffered particularly because of the growing intensity of Belgian competition. Business men as a class were loud in their complaints about the difficulties of these years. It is a measure of Pilkingtons' success that they were able to thrive and grow rapidly amid these difficulties. As we shall see presently, between 1873 and 1894 the partners' investment increased sevenfold.

The Board ruled their domain through a number of picked men, known as managers. Each glasshouse had its own manager and there were also head managers who supervised departments. Soon after the second generation assumed complete control they became preoccupied with the poor quality of much of the glass that was then being produced. This caused them to look into the efficiency of their labour force—with results which will be discussed in the next chapter which deals with labour relations. They also brought in two men from outside who were to be of considerable service to them.

John J. Wenham was engaged in 1869 to take charge of the two outposts, the rolled plate department, which was located in the buildings of the former Eccleston Crown Glassworks, and the patent plate department, situated in the old cotton mill. He came from Richard Evans and Company, the Haydock coal proprietors, where he was then earning £2 per week. Pilkingtons came to rely heavily upon him, his salary was steadily increased, and, at the beginning of 1883, he reached a rate of £800 a year with the promise of £1,000 twelve months later. Douglas Herman, the other new recruit, became the firm's chemist. George Pilkington had left in the middle of the 1860s, when he set up in business on his own, and the firm had not been able to find a satisfactory replacement for him. In 1870, however, it was decided to enquire at the Royal College of Chemistry, where George Pilkington had been trained, for 'a German if possible'. Herman was strongly recommended by the College as 'a young Englishman though of German extraction . . . a clever young fellow of original thought'. He started at £150 a year and reached £1,000 at the end of 1892, having proved his worth to the firm not only in locating and supervising the supply of sand and dealing with all kinds of chemical problems but also in introducing Pilkingtons into business activity on the continent.[1]

Wenham's influence was soon felt. Within a few months of his arrival he was recommending the transfer of manufacture from the two outposts to the main works which, he estimated, would save £700 a year. No action was taken at the time but, two years later, in 1871, the Board were obliged to consider removing rolled plate from Eccleston because they wanted to expand this branch, the demand for this style of glass having become 'excessive'. The Eccleston factory, however, was 'a tumble down place', quite unsuitable for extension and, on the other hand, there were obvious advantages in building anew at Grove Street on vacant land immediately to the east of the existing sheet glass factory. The estimated cost of putting up two houses on this site was, however, on Wenham's estimate, about £10,000 and the Board 'discussed at length the policy of such an outlay, T. P. laying stress upon its so much exceeding what was first contemplated'. The expenditure was sanctioned, however, and the first new rolled plate house at Grove Street was in production in May 1872. A second house was put in hand almost at once, together with a warehouse. Some of the bricks from the dismantled Eccleston cone were used in this extension.[2]

In 1872, when rolled plate glass began to be made at Grove Street, the main sheet works there were benefiting from two recent innovations and were on the eve of a major technical advance. The first innovation, the Bievez lehr*, enabled sheets, rapidly cooled by being raised successively on iron bars and so kept apart, to be annealed in twenty-five to thirty minutes as against seven or eight hours in the piling kilns. A promising pilot model of the lehr was working at Pilkingtons in May 1869, and, after a visit to see other prototypes in action at Valenciennes in the following month, Windle Pilkington made certain improvements to this model. In its improved form the lehr was a great success and, in March 1870, Pilkingtons secured the exclusive British rights to the patent for £200 a year.[3] The other innovation was an appliance to assist glassmakers in blowing the heaviest of cylinders. It had been invented by Windle Pilkington, assisted by Wenham, and was patented in 1871. Four such machines were in use by the beginning of the following year.[4]

The major advance was the coming of tank furnaces. The advantages of tanks over pots had long been obvious. To feed in raw materials at one end of a tank, melt them as they passed along, and then cool the molten glass to the correct consistency for working by the time it reached the other end, would allow window glass manufacture to become a continuous process. The twenty-four hour interval while the metal was prepared, inevitable with the existing pot furnaces, could then be avoided and time, fuel and labour saved. The economic benefits were such that a number of inventors on the continent of

---

* Professor Turner has shown that the word 'lehr', certainly *not* of German origin, was first used in the United States between 1890 and 1900 and later came to replace the older spellings of the word: leer, lier and lear. (W. E. S. Turner, 'That Curious Word "Lehr"', *J.S.G.T.*, XXXIII, No. 154, October, 1949.) The first reference to a 'lehr' in the Pilkington Board Minutes does not occur until after 1900 but since the word is now universally used in this form, it has been decided to use it throughout this book.

Europe had already tried to develop a satisfactory type of glassmaking tank. They had all failed, however, because they were unable, using coal as a fuel, to obtain the necessary constant temperature. Pilkingtons had themselves made two unsuccessful attempts to produce glass from a tank. In 1868 they had tried to build a 'cistern furnace' based on a patent taken out by John Cannington, who had recently become partner in a local bottlemaking factory. In the following year another attempt was made, this time at Eccleston, but very poor glass was produced and the experiment had again to be abandoned.[5] It was left to the brothers Siemens, who, as we have seen, had already developed gas-firing for pot furnaces, to go on to apply gas-firing successfully to tanks. Their experiments at glassworks in Dresden soon reached a stage at which they felt justified in taking out patents. These were dated 1870 and 1872.[6]

Siemens' patent of 1870 reveals that they only took slowly to the unqualified use of tanks. They were then still considering the possibility of rather fancifully-designed pots as alternatives. In both pots and tanks, according to this first patent, the melting vessels were to be divided into three compartments, for preliminary melting, for further melting, and for working. The materials, when melted, were to pass *over* a barrier erected in the pot or tank, into the second compartment, where they were raised to a higher temperature. The hotter metal was then passed *underneath* the next partition into the working section.[7] In the 1872 patents, however, the use of pots had been forgotten. So, too, had the idea of fixed clay barriers, for it had been found in the interval that these soon became unserviceable. In a provisional specification, dated July 18, 1872, the stationary partitions in the tank were to be

> 'replaced by a number of movable rings made of fire-clay or other suitable refractory material which are introduced, by preference, at the working end of the tank and which, floating on the molten glass metal cover the whole of its surface, or nearly so, up to the point where the solid material is introduced. As these rings are gradually dissolved or worn away, they are replaced by fresh rings . . .'

The floor and sides of the tank were to be provided with special cooling flues. In the final patent, taken out a few months later, floating bridges made of fire-clay were to be placed transversely across the tank to prevent any imperfectly melted or impure material from reaching the working section.

Pilkingtons were quick to employ Siemens' important new discovery. From the end of May until the beginning of July 1872, Windle Pilkington missed five successive Board meetings. The minutes record that he was in Switzerland. He had, in fact, also gone farther afield. On his return, at a Board meeting held on July 10, it was decided 'to put a Continuous Tank in the cylinder place next to the flattening kilns upon the principles of the one that W.W.P. has seen working at Dresden'. At the following week's meeting—on the very day that Siemens registered the provisional specification of the patent in London—it was agreed that Windle Pilkington and William (Roby) Pilkington should 'meet Siemens in London on Monday next to discuss suggestions made to W.P. as to rings and divisions in furnace.'

Nine months elapsed before the tank was ready to be worked. Blowing began on April 14, 1873, and an enthusiastic entry in the minutes on the 17th records that 'the metal at first was slightly seedy from the cullet but has continued to improve and at the present moment is beating any pot furnace on the ground. . . . Consider that we ought to seriously discuss the advisability of getting the patent secured to us by Siemens for our especial use and will see Siemens if all be well next week'. This is followed by three months' silence, without a word about the tank or about negotiations with Siemens. It is not until July 21st that the next reference occurs and not until August 14th that the tank began to make glass 'for the second time'. Evidently, soon after April 17th, something happened to the first attempt which suddenly quenched the partners' initial enthusiasm. They were obviously still not very happy about the tank's prospects even after it had been re-lit and had performed successfully for over a month. On September 18th they noted: 'Working so far very satisfactory', but ordered that plans for making further tanks should be so made 'that if tanks failed, pot furnaces (to blow over) could be put up instead.'

What went wrong at the first attempt? James Taylor, then a young man working in the laboratory, has given us the answer. He later recalled that the tank

'only worked one week before the bottom was eaten through; the metal leaked and set the place on fire. Nothing further was heard of this experiment for several months . . .'

That a second attempt was made was due to the persistence of Windle Pilkington alone. The circumstances were indicated only two and a half years after the event by one of Pilkingtons' men:

'The first tank failing at the end of the first week, Messrs Pilkington decided to abandon them but after several Board Meetings and Mr Windle Pilkington stating that if they would not make another attempt, he would secure a piece of ground himself and erect one on his own account, they then gave way and agreed to another trial when he succeeded. . . .'[9]

In fact, at the second attempt, the tank ran non-stop for ninety-seven days.

Having built one successful tank, Pilkingtons began to substitute tanks for pots at a rapid rate. A second tank was in use by February 1874. By the end of August 1876, there were nine tank furnaces in operation and the ground was being cleared for a tenth.[10] By February 1877, there were ten such furnaces, an eleventh was being built and two others were described as 'in hand'.[11] In May 1877, twelve tanks were at work and more were being built.[12] The scale on which the patent was being operated was so considerable that the Siemens brothers agreed to receive royalties at a lower rate than the four shillings per ton of finished glass which they usually charged, itself considerably lower than the five shillings royalty on their pot furnaces.[13] In February 1877 William Siemens admitted to Henry Chance that 'with regard to royalty . . . Pilkingtons had a preferential arrangement', but he refused to divulge its nature.[14]

The earliest tanks were built with one wide bridge and rings on both sides of it[15] but in 1878 Windle Pilkington ordered that the rings be placed in the gathering end only, for they were thought to do 'a great deal of harm in the form of Knots and String'.[16] There is very little detail about these tanks among Pilkingtons' papers, but Chances, anxious to find out all they could about their rival's progress, kept a record of statements made by anyone who came to them from St Helens. Early in 1877, Thomas May, a furnace builder at Canningtons, the bottlemakers, who appears to have had an intimate knowledge of the Pilkington furnaces, gave them the information that Pilkingtons were building their tanks longer and less wide than they had done at first. They were at that time using tanks nine feet wide and thirty-six feet long whereas formerly their tanks had been twelve feet wide and rather shorter in length. These held,

'2'6" of melted glass when the tank is new. When the sides are worn thin, less glass is put in lest the sides should burst. The sides require renewal every 3 or 4 months. If they last 4 months it is good working.'

The bottom of the tank needed renewing every ten or eleven months. In each case these renewals took about three weeks. May therefore calculated that the furnace could work for forty-two weeks in the year.[17] Another informant, who had been a furnaceman at Pilkingtons, told Chances that Pilkingtons' tanks were fed by four producers which consumed about six tons of slack in twelve hours. At first one large flue was used 'for all the tanks and producers and one chimney', but they found the tanks overrunning each other and went back to separate producers and a chimney to each tank.[18] Yet another informant, who signed himself E. J. F., provided a plan of a Pilkington tank, revealing its main details.[19] There were two gathering and four blowing holes. The men worked in three eight-hour shifts, each blower making between seventy-five and ninety cylinders per shift.[20] Two men looked after the furnace during the day and two during the night.[21]

The lack of details about these early tanks among Pilkingtons' archives is partly explained by the manner in which they were built. Having obtained the original drawings from Siemens, Windle Pilkington made his own modifications and improvements as he went on. These he carried in his own head and did not commit to paper in the first instance. In 1890 S. E. Baddeley, who had just started to work in the drawing office—which then included only one other person—was told to measure up a small melting tank, newly repaired, and to make a drawing of it. He was struck by the unusual procedure of drawing the tank after, and not before, its erection. He made a search of the office for drawings but could find none. He then tackled the foreman bricklayer who informed him that he merely cleared the ground on which the tank was to be built. Windle Pilkington would then come round and trace the outlines with the side of his foot. Informal meetings took place between them afterwards as the work progressed. As the foreman bricklayer put it: 'Mr Windle can do owt'.

The tendency all the time was towards increase in the size of tanks. In 1880 a tank was built with four gathering and eight blowing holes, twice the capacity of the type of furnace which was being used in 1876, at which only four blowers could be employed. After the firm acquired land to the north of Watson Street in 1884 and 1885,[22] three larger tank furnaces were erected there with twelve blowing holes. By that date there were in all thirteen smaller tanks for making sheet glass and three larger ones.

The installation of continuous tank furnaces on this scale resulted in a considerable increase in sheet glass production. The largest recorded weekly output before the introduction of tanks was 350,000 ft. The weekly average throughout the year 1877 was just over 500,000 ft. and throughout 1887 was just over 900,000 ft. The 1,250,000 mark was passed in the early 1890s and, by the end of the century, production exceeded 1,600,000 ft. per week.

Tanks were also used for making rolled plate glass. The first one was being worked successfully in June 1878[23] and this led to further tanks in the rolled plate factory. In 1889 Windle Pilkington began to experiment there with tunnel type lehrs, presumably along the lines of the Tondeur and rod lehrs which had been used in America since earlier in the decade.[24] While the pilot model was being built at St Helens, he worked every day (according to an eye-witness) 'with just his trousers on'. Like the first tank furnace, the lehr was a failure: it blew up. The original aim was to develop a lehr suitable for annealing *cast* plate glass. This was not then achieved but, in 1891, a lehr was being used successfully for *rolled* plate manufacture and others followed.[25]

Output of rolled plate glass grew at a pace comparable with that of sheet, although the increase was not so regular year by year. The annual make rose from 2,750,000 ft. to more than 6,000,000 ft. in 1884, and then, after some ten years of arrested development, the upward course was continued, output reaching 10,000,000 ft. in 1898. In this field Chances maintained a technical ascendancy and this may explain to some extent the interruption in the growth of output at St Helens. In the late 'eighties George and Edward Chance successfully developed a machine, patented in 1884 by Frederick Mason and John Conqueror, whereby the molten glass was poured down an inclined plane and passed between a pair of iron rollers. In 1890 Edward Chance perfected the machine by adding a second pair of rollers, one of this second pair impressing a pattern where required. The manufacture of rolled plate glass became 'of the very first importance' to Chances[26] and the royalties from other companies—including St Gobain—which operated it under licence were considerable. That Windle Pilkington was actively engaged in developing a rolled plate machine at St Helens is evident from the patents he took out in 1891 and in 1894. Pilkingtons also began, in 1895, to make wired glass, using an American patent,[27] and developed this product to great advantage, though Chances were particularly successful with their figured rolled and cathedral.

Coloured glass continued to be produced in the ornamental department and the manufacture of shades was still carried on in a separate shade house. Another building was shared by the smoothers (who were making specially thin glass for the growing photographic trade) and the miscellaneous department. Among the products of the latter were glass cells, required by the infant electrical industry. The first cells were moulded by Pilkingtons in the early 1890s. Corrugated sheet glass was also made by moulding.[28]

All these developments, and particularly the increase in capacity for making sheet and rolled plate glass, called for more ground on which to build additional plant and warehouses. Fortunately Pilkingtons were able to acquire land in the immediate vicinity of their existing works. In the 1870s they bought a number of small factories which lay to the south and east of their own, including the property which had formerly been the Bells' flint glassworks. By the end of the decade they owned the whole of the large triangle bounded by the canal on the west, Watson Street on the north and the Ravenhead branch railway on the south. To this was added land to the north of Watson Street in the mid-1880s—the Jubilee Side as it came to be called.[29] Apart from the Greenbank site, which was acquired later, these have remained the limits of Sheet Works to the present day. The plan over the page shows the extent of the works in 1892.

This impressive phase of growth had been started off during the boom of the early 1870s when, for a few years, British manufacturers were able to obtain better prices for their glass because their Belgian rivals were temporarily handicapped by a coal shortage and high fuel costs.[30] The rising wave of Belgian glass, which had been so marked in the period before 1870, was temporarily stemmed for a few years: the official British returns show that total imports remained at around 420,000 cwt. from 1870-2, rising to just over 450,000 cwt. in 1873. Retained imports stayed at about 370,000 cwt. during these four years.[31] The price of imported glass rose, and in 1873 it was more than 30 per cent. higher than it had been in 1870. At the same time Pilkingtons, as colliery proprietors, also shared in the quite phenomenal demand for coal which was a feature of these years.

Siemens' tank furnace was developed just when the economic climate was

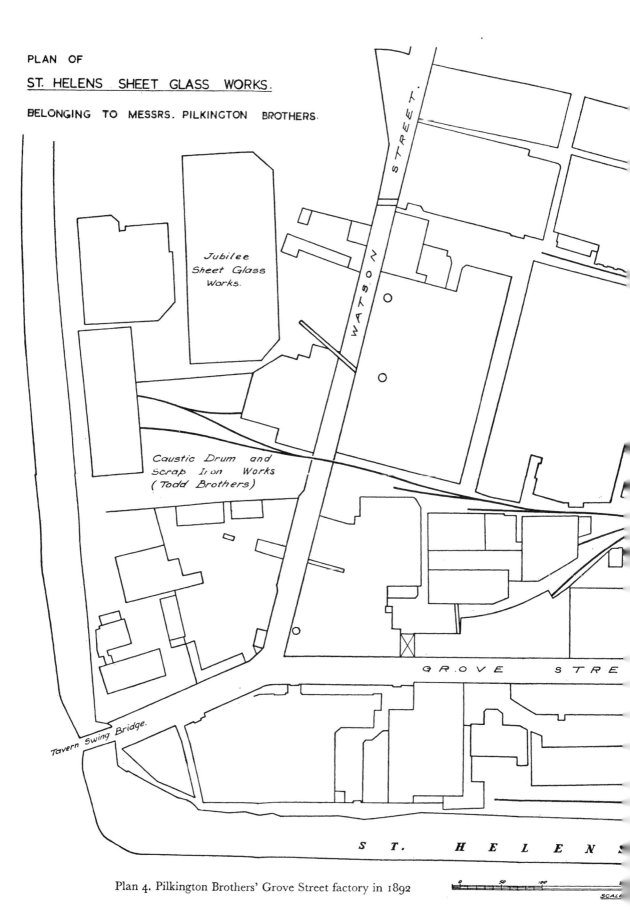

PLAN OF

ST. HELENS SHEET GLASS WORKS.

BELONGING TO MESSRS. PILKINGTON BROTHERS.

Jubilee Sheet Glass Works.

Caustic Drum and Scrap Iron Works (Todd Brothers)

WATSON STREET.

GROVE STREET

Tavern Swing Bridge.

ST. HELENS

SCALE

Plan 4. Pilkington Brothers' Grove Street factory in 1892

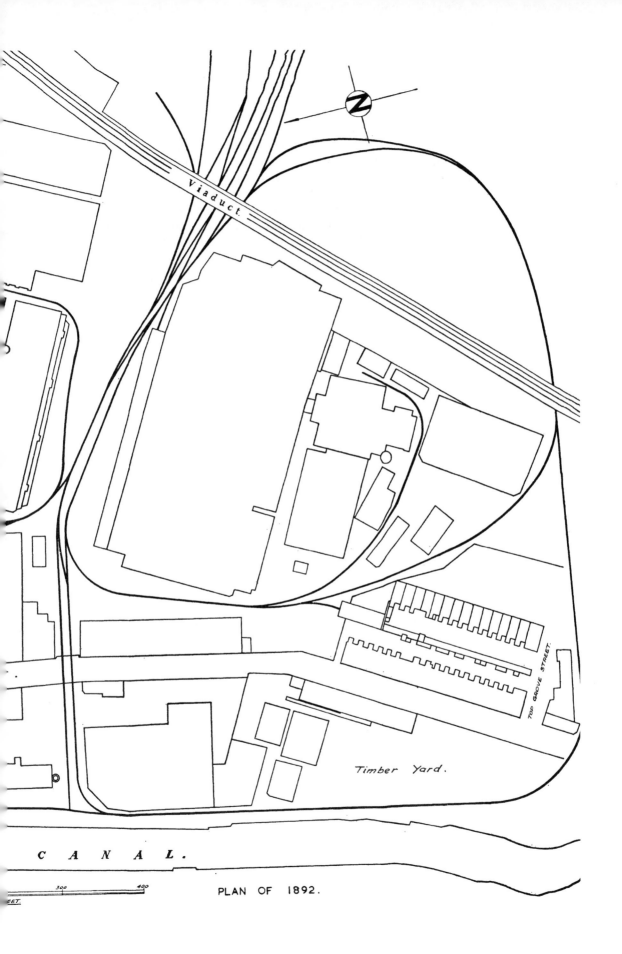

Viaduct.

TOD GROVE STREET.

Timber Yard.

C A N A L.

300   400

PLAN OF 1892.

favourable for its adoption. Pilkingtons seized their opportunity and, by moving quickly and by introducing tanks on a large scale, they obtained preferential rates of royalty. Chances, on the other hand, were content to sit back and collect information. After much pondering, they came to the conclusion that tanks could not produce a sufficiently high percentage of good quality glass to make them a worthwhile investment. This was a major error of judgment—and it was not rectified until 1892.[32] As Walter Lucas Chance later conceded:

> 'It was the adoption of the tank system for making sheet glass by their St Helens competitors . . . that finally deprived them of the predominant position which they had hitherto held.'[33]

There were other reasons, too: Chances' purchase of the Nailsea works in 1870 turned out to be a mistake, and their venture into plate glass manufacture—to be considered later in this chapter—was a costly failure.[34]

By the end of the 1870s there are clear indications that Pilkingtons had already reached the position at which they could take a more independent attitude towards Chances and Hartleys. Lucas Chance, junior, wrote to Sunderland on January 14, 1878:

> 'I . . . can quite understand your feelings of irritation at the treatment we are receiving at the hands of Pilkington Brothers and if I thought it advisable to consult my own feelings only, I should fall in with your views and say, dissolve the Association. But we cannot always allow our feelings to rule us and I am inclined to think that it will be better to swallow the annoyance and retain the Association than stand upon our dignity and throw it over. There is no doubt that it has been a substantial benefit to us in the past, checking the downward tendency of the time and putting us right when we were getting all abroad. What it has done in the past, it is competent to repeat in the future; although at present it certainly does not show symptoms of producing much fruit.'[35]

Later in the same month he wrote to the Secretary of the Association:

> 'As regards Sheet and Rolled prices, you will have to be careful what you say to Mr Richard, as from what William told me when we last met, neither Richard nor Tom (I think Tom but may have been Will. Windle) care about the Assocn. and would rather be free to do as they like but if you find Mr Richard in a humour to listen to what you have to say, you can tell him that we are dissatisfied with the evasive and offensive manner in which their people reply to our enquiries.'[36]

Richard Pilkington may have been in a humour to listen to Gwilliam, but he was apparently in no mood to co-operate, as Lucas Chance reported to Sunderland a few days later:

> 'Mr Richard's conversation with Mr Gwilliam is not of a reassuring character—but he speaks very much as he acts—independently of us all and of all arrange-

ments. I have occasion to be in London on February 7th and will write to William Pilkington and ask him if he can meet me there. I will then explain to him that an Association cannot exist without a free exchange of communications about prices and reports of underselling.'[37]

This correspondence took place when the building cycle was again beginning to move downwards over most of the country, though activity in London lagged behind that of other towns and only reached a peak in 1881. This may explain

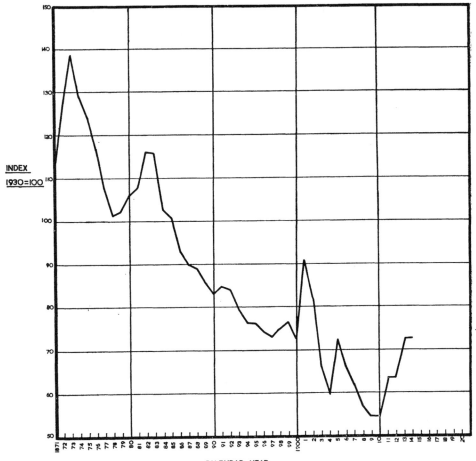

CALENDAR YEAR

INDEX OF PRICE OF WINDOW GLASS

1871-1914

Graph 8. Source: K. Maiwald, 'An Index of Building Costs in the United Kingdom, 1845–1938'. *Economic History Review*, December 1954

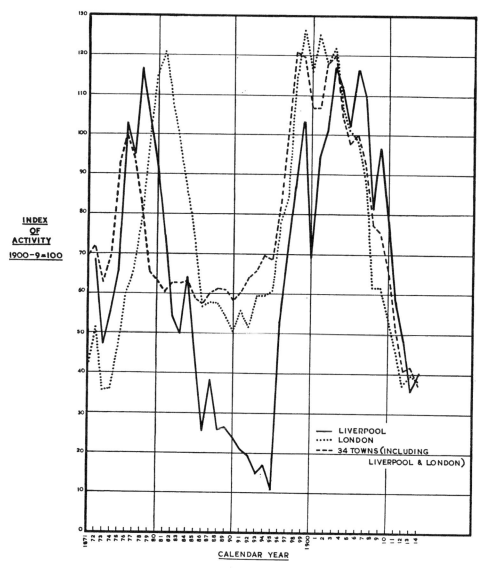

INDEX
OF
ACTIVITY

1900-9=100

LIVERPOOL
LONDON
34 TOWNS (INCLUDING
LIVERPOOL & LONDON)

CALENDAR YEAR

INDEX OF HOUSEBUILDING
1871 – 1914

Graph 9. Source: B. Weber, 'A New Index of Residential Construction, 1838–1950,'
Scottish Journal of Political Economy, June 1955

the rally in import prices in the early 1880s; but, after this, building activity fell off, and until the later 1890s there was a continuous fall in prices, interrupted only by a very slight rally in 1891-2. A steep rise in imports soon caused them to fall once more.

RETAINED IMPORTS OF WINDOW GLASS, 1889-95 ('000 CWT.)

1889	670
1890	789
1891	795
1892	947
1893	881
1894	1,061
1895	987

Source: Trade and Navigation Returns.

The competition of these years drove Hartleys out of business and put an end to window glass manufacture in the north-east.[38] The details of Hartleys' collapse and the events which led up to it are unknown. None of the firm's records has survived and newspapers and technical journals provide only the scantiest of outlines. It is quite evident, however, that the firm had continued to prosper up to the 1870s and was particularly noted in the industry for its rolled plate glass, much of which was exported. James Hartley, the founder of the business, was a powerful figure and he was ably assisted by J.J. Kayll, who had joined the firm in 1840 at the age of 19 and had been a partner since 1848. Soon after 1870 Hartley retired from active management and was succeeded by his son, John. Rolled plate glass, the speciality of the Sunderland concern, could apparently no longer be made there at a profit; after James Hartley died, in 1886, it was remarked that 'the Sunderland rough-plate glass trade may almost be said to have lived and died with him'.[39] Kayll, presumably, retired about this time and the management of the second generation was unable to carry the firm through the critical early years of the 1890s, when business was poor and Chances' new machines for making rolled plate glass came into operation. The Sunderland factory ceased to make window glass in 1894—the year when imports were particularly heavy—and was subsequently demolished.[40]

The sharp rise in building activity in the second half of the 1890s was accompanied, as was to be expected, by a further increase in window glass imports.

RETAINED IMPORTS OF WINDOW GLASS, 1896-1901 ('000 CWT.)

1896	1,142
1897	1,169
1898	1,347
1899	1,253
1900	1,129
1901	1,208

Source: Trade and Navigation Returns.

That this increase was not sustained, was chiefly due to a strike of Belgian sheet glassmakers which lasted from August 1900 to May 1901—described by *The Times* correspondent in Brussels as 'the longest industrial struggle on record in Belgium'.[41] Demand outstripped supply and, as may be seen from graph 8, the fall in import prices, arrested in 1895 and reversed slightly in 1898 and 1899, was completely reversed in 1901.

The relative prosperity which the building boom and the Belgians' misfortunes bestowed on window glass manufacture in Britain came at a time when British plate glass manufacture was in desperate straits. These years were decisive ones for Pilkingtons, who had, in 1873, entered this branch of the industry.

The particular problems of making plate glass by the casting process were considered in chapter two in connexion with the beginnings of the Ravenhead works at the end of the eighteenth century. Great amounts of capital were required. A large casting hall had to be built and equipped; machinery provided for grinding and polishing; and warehousing was also a costly item where large and expensive plates of glass were concerned. From the start the manufacture of this type of glass was confined to a few large factories. By the second half of the nineteenth century most of them were already being operated by one or two powerful concerns.

On the continent of Europe the long-established St Gobain Company owned four of the seven factories in France and operated the only two plate glassworks of importance in Germany.[42] It was said that St Gobain 'virtually controlled the manufacture of plate glass on the continent of Europe, and, to a large extent, its production and prices throughout the world'.[43] Plate glass manufacture in Belgium began much later than in France or England. The first factory had been built at Sainte-Marie-d'Oignies (Hainaut) in 1840. A second, at Floreffe (Namur), built in the mid-1850s, was followed by others at Roux (1869), Courcelles (1870) and Auvelais (1875).[44] By 1880, they were controlled by a syndicate which also operated two of the three French factories outside the St Gobain empire.

In England the various plate glass factories continued to be operated by independent concerns, though it seems likely that, by the 1850s and 1860s, a certain amount of discussion was taking place among them. Of the companies formed in the first half of the nineteenth century—some five in number—two had built their works in the St Helens area, the other three being located respectively on the Tyne, on the Thames and in the Birmingham area. (The Thames Plate Glass Company does not appear to have survived beyond 1868.) Of the two St Helens factories, one, at Pocket Nook, was owned by the Union Plate Glass Company and the other, at Sutton Oak, was owned by the London and

Manchester Plate Glass Company.[45] By the later 1860s these two factories and
that at Ravenhead were said to be responsible for two-thirds of Britain's output.[46]
By then, however, serious difficulties were being experienced at Ravenhead. In
1868 the London and Manchester company acquired the factory on a 99-years
lease at a rent of £6,200 per year.[47] The manager of Ravenhead was able to
claim, in the later 1870s, that the two factories were then producing more than
half the total output of plate glass in the kingdom.[48]

In 1873 Chances and Pilkingtons, who had both been previously bound
by the rolled plate agreement not to make this kind of glass,[49] decided to set up
as plate glass manufacturers.

Pilkingtons' decision to enter this branch of the industry was taken at a
Board meeting on February 13, 1873:

> 'Plate Works. Discussed the question of site and general question at considerable
> length. W. P. and W. W. P. went last Saturday over a site near Blackbrook [two
> miles to the east of St Helens] which seemed very likely and we decided at once to
> make further inquiry as undoubtedly this is the time to go into that Trade.'

They eventually decided on a site, not at Blackbrook, but close to Gerard's
Bridge and only about a mile from their existing works. The elevated position,
on a slope of Cowley Hill, was a particularly suitable one. The grinding process
left much waste sand, and this could be disposed of more easily from the grinding shed when it was situated at a little height. The extent of the site—over 120
acres—left plenty of lower-lying space in the immediate vicinity for lodging this
sand. The railway from St Helens to Rainford, which passed by, provided good
rail communication.

Pilkingtons discovered from Gwilliam, the secretary of the window glass
manufacturers' association, that H. C. Lockhart, manager of the Birmingham
Plate Glassworks, was likely to be interested in taking charge of their own new
venture. The Birmingham Company was then the property of two men who
were anxious for 'some Capitalists to come forward' and buy them out. (The
London and Manchester Company had been interested and Chances were, in
fact, soon to take over.) With financial control of the Birmingham works hang-
ing in the balance, Pilkingtons were probably justified in their conclusion that
Lockhart's position was 'evidently not a permanent one'. He was persuaded to
come to St Helens with the offer of a five-year agreement rising to £1,500 per
year, and started to superintend building at Cowley Hill on October 1st.[50]

The factory took about three years to build. It consisted at first of a large
casting hall with three thirty-pot furnaces in the centre and annealing kilns
along each side. Adjoining the casting hall were a matching room, a grinding
shed, smoothing and polishing rooms and a warehouse. At the end of March
1876, Lockhart was instructed to start recruiting the necessary labour, 'the
wages to be based on the Sutton rates [London and Manchester Plate Glass

Company], but men not to be taken from Sutton'. (Pilkingtons seem to have been on very good terms with William Blinkhorn, manager of the Sutton factory.) Much of the specialized labour which was taken on at Cowley Hill came, as Lockhart had done, from Birmingham. In order to accommodate the newcomers, cottages owned by Pilkingtons were 'overhauled', others were bought, and yet others were specially built.[51]

By July 1876, all was in readiness to cast the first plate. According to an eyewitness, John Kerr, 'they made a very poor job of it. They could not stow it straight and when trying to push it up and down, they set the wooden table on fire and that was the end of the plate'.[52] This was on July 14, 1876. The next casting was, however, a success. Grinding, smoothing and polishing started in the following month. In the week ended August 26th, some 9,000 sq. ft. of rough plate glass were cast, 7,500 sq. ft. ground, 4,500 sq. ft. smoothed and 2,000 sq. ft. polished. The Board, however, soon began to complain about Lockhart's poor qualities as a manager, and, on March 20, 1877, matters came to a head:

> 'General Management. Expressed to Lockhart our opinions individually and together as to his mismanagem[t] of the Works. Resolved to dispense with his further services and informed him that we should do so at once, and that tomorrow we should send him a cheque for £2,250, the 1½ years' salary due to him per agreement.'

The Board then called in the departmental managers, one by one, and told them that they intended to manage the Cowley Hill works themselves in future in the same way as they did Grove Street. Output continued to rise rapidly, and by 1878 it was on a scale comparable with that of Ravenhead. Patent plate glass was also made for a time at Cowley Hill in 1877: the cotton mill was closed in March and the men transferred, but in November the Board decided to give up patent plate manufacture, Chances agreeing to supply this product at preferential rates.[53]

Windle Pilkington turned his attention to devising technical improvements at the new factory when the problems arising out of the introduction of tank furnaces had been solved. In 1879 he devised a new form of movable crane for carrying the pots from furnace to casting table.[54] He also improved the grinding process by introducing machinery in which the iron-faced grinding surface was made sufficiently large to cover the whole plate of glass. This did away with the ridges which had been produced when the grinding surfaces were smaller than the glass itself.[55] In 1880 he went on to design new apparatus for smoothing. The machine then in use was fitted with runners which moved over the same curvilinear path and so produced an uneven surface. By causing the runners to traverse different paths, this defect was avoided.[56] Also in the same year he improved the method of heating the annealing kilns by introducing the gas at their

William Windle Pilkington

Richard Pilkington

15 The second generation:
Richard Pilkington's sons

Richard Pilkington as
a young man of about 28

16 An artist's impression of Pilkingtons' two St Helens factories in 1879. *Above*, the Plate Glassworks at Cowley Hill

Below, The Grove Street factory

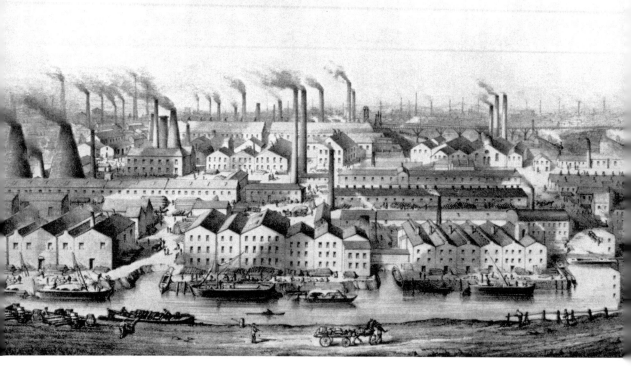

crown and thus providing a more uniform heat throughout.[57] A patent which he took out in 1886 envisaged the use of an overhead gantry for transporting the pots to the casting table, a clear advance upon the device he had patented in 1879.[58]

A diary kept from 1885 by J. H. Dickinson reveals how closely the partners watched technical changes elsewhere in the industry at this time. There are many entries concerning visits to Liverpool to consult J. T. King, who advised them on matters of patent law. Between the middle of 1888 and 1890 most of these journeys were concerned with a complicated patent taken out by Melchior Malevez, a Belgian, for circular grinding discs which enabled the glass to be ground, smoothed and polished on the same movable table.[59] Pilkingtons first heard of these discs in July 1887, and experimented with them for the following two years.[60] On October 14, 1889, Malevez himself visited the works and had conferences with Richard and Windle Pilkington, J. T. King and Douglas Herman. On October 17th and 18th the four men were in London conferring with Malevez and his agents, and soon afterwards Pilkingtons acquired the patent rights.[61] The long process of installing Malevez machinery was begun at Cowley Hill during the summer of 1890 and the new equipment, powered at first by steam engines, shafting and rope drives, was in use by the end of the year. It proved more expensive than the old method at first, but, by February 1893, was starting to pay its way. By November 1893, the old method had been entirely superseded. While the Malevez equipment was being installed at Cowley Hill, Windle Pilkington, as we have noticed (page 150), was trying to develop a lehr which would anneal plate glass, but his attempt had to be abandoned on account of the great expense involved.[62] Pilkingtons were not to have a continuous lehr at Cowley Hill for another ten years. Tanks could not be used for making plate glass and it was not until after the First World War that a satisfactory equivalent was devised to replace pot furnaces.

The weekly production figures show how successful Pilkingtons' venture into plate glass manufacture became.

AVERAGE WEEKLY PRODUCTION OF PLATE GLASS AT THE COWLEY HILL WORKS (SQ. FT.)

		Cast	Ground	Smoothed	Polished
Month of December	1876	21,000	18,000	16,000	14,000
January–December	1877	32,750	22,100	20,810	20,730
,,	1878	48,600	32,120	28,410	28,100
,,	1879	59,400	43,600	38,100	37,550
,,	1880	69,000	51,900	46,400	45,000
,,	1881	77,700	56,900	50,900	49,000
,,	1884	76,700	67,300	63,800	61,000
,,	1885	78,400	71,500	68,500	65,600
,,	1886	78,800	70,600	67,300	65,000
,,	1888	83,100	75,800	73,000	70,900

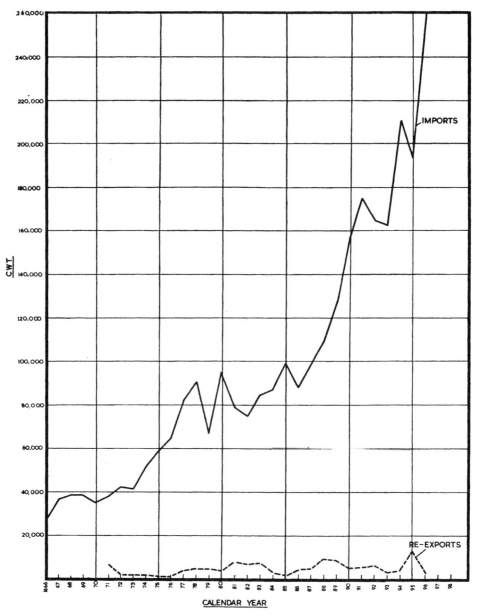

IMPORTS AND RE-EXPORTS OF PLATE GLASS.

1866-1896

Graph 10. Source: British Trade and Navigation Returns

162

Their success at Cowley Hill was in striking contrast to Chances' utter failure at Birmingham. The Birmingham works had to be closed for fifteen months while costly new plant was installed, and when this came into operation, later in 1875, the glass produced was of poor quality and there was a high proportion of breakages. In 1876 the factory ran at a loss of £20,000. With prices falling, it was decided to stop production altogether in July 1877. Glass was never cast there again and the works were eventually disposed of in 1889. The venture was later described by the historian of Chances as 'disastrous'.[63]

While Pilkingtons were establishing themselves as producers of plate glass and increasing their sales, more and more of this type of glass was also being imported from the continent. The market was growing quickly. Greater competition in business generally and particularly in retail trade—the growth of department stores and multiple shops, for instance—were all accompanied by more attractive displays of goods and, to show these off to best advantage, plate glass windows became the fashion. Large mirrors also gained a larger market; plate glass in this form was an essential feature of the late Victorian gin palace, for example. The market for plate glass, in fact, was growing in the last quarter of the nineteenth century in much the same way as the market for window glass had grown twenty-five years before. Foreign manufacturers made every effort to cater for this growing demand—and, by cutting retail prices, to stimulate it—in much the same way as they had done, and were still doing, with window glass.

Imports rose quite sharply in the mid-1870s, more than doubling between 1873 and 1878. They did not move upwards again until after 1887 when they rose more steeply than they had done in the 1870s.

IMPORTS OF PLATE GLASS, 1887–1901 ('000 CWT.)

1887	99	1895	193
1888	109	1896	259
1889	128	1897	252
1890	156	1898	281
1891	176	1899	246
1892	164	1900	316
1893	162	1901	464
1894	211		

Source: Trade and Navigation Returns.

The figures show that competition increased in four mounting waves. The first reached a crest in 1891, the second in 1894, the third in 1896 and the last—and by far the highest of all—in 1901. This strong intensification of foreign competition was chiefly the result of new factories being opened on the continent. It was made all the more severe by the growth of plate glass manufacture in the United States, formerly a very important market for all European producers.

The United States had possessed no effective plant for the manufacture of polished plate glass until the 1870s, but from then onwards this branch of the industry grew very rapidly;[64] there were sixteen factories at work in 1890. In 1895, after a period of very fierce price-cutting, the Pittsburgh Plate Glass Company took over ten of these, thereby obtaining control of 80 per cent. of the total American output.[65] This giant concern promptly set up jobbing houses in most of the cities of the United States in order to sell direct to the consumer.[66] This development, together with the Dingley Tariff of 1897—more severe on the cheaper types of plate glass than had been the McKinley Tariff of 1890[67]— was followed for a few years by a further sharp fall in the value of American imports.

AMERICAN IMPORTS OF CAST PLATE GLASS, 1890–1900 ('000 DOLLARS)

Year	Polished but unsilvered	Polished and silvered
1890	931	250
1891	1,351	183
1892	888	119
1893	830	154
1894	450	75
1895	684	16
1896	773	34
1897	285	22
1898	162	·5
1899	233	·4
1900	226	12

Source: U.S. Treasury, Bureau of Statistics cited in U.S. Census Reports, 1900, vol. IX, 985.

The growing self-sufficiency of the United States led to the utter collapse of British plate glass exports to that country. They were worth £107,000 per year in 1880–4, £89,000 in 1885–9, £18,000 in 1890–4, and a mere £3,000 in 1895–9. Competition elsewhere was intensified and total British plate glass exports to all foreign markets slumped from £251,000 per year in 1885–9 to £93,000 in 1895–9.[68] Belgium, the United States' chief supplier, also suffered severely, and this caused the Belgians to ship more to Britain than they would otherwise have done. According to the official Belgian returns, plate glass exports to the United States were worth 7½ million francs in 1890 and only 1½ million francs in 1898; in the same period, Belgian shipments to Britain rose from 5 to 15 million francs.[69] The British manufacturer not only lost an important transatlantic market as a result of the growth of the American industry, but also had to contend with much heavier Belgian competition at home.

One British company after another collapsed. The Tyne Plate Glass Company failed in 1891, having lost the whole of its capital of £89,000.[70] The Union Plate Glass Company Ltd., which owned the Pocket Nook works at St Helens, began to install Malevez machinery at the end of 1891 but closed its factory at the beginning of the following year. Production of plate glass appears to have re-started, but seems to have stopped for good in 1897.[71] The London and Manchester Company, capable of making 65,000 sq. ft. of glass per week at its Sutton Oak works and a further 26,000 sq. ft. at Ravenhead, also introduced Malevez machinery; but this did not prevent their losing nearly £83,000 in the two years ending August 1893, and £60,000 in the following year. The Sutton works were closed for a period and the lease of Ravenhead surrendered.

While cheap foreign glass was either destroying or crippling all the other English plate glass concerns, Pilkingtons, by contrast, were extending their Cowley Hill factory. A new casting hall was built in 1896–7 and other extensions made between 1893 and 1897. Kilns of a new type were installed, capable of annealing glass in three, instead of four, days. Electrical 'transporters' were ordered in 1893 and 'electric casting machinery' for the new casting hall a few years later; Pilkingtons were one of the early firms to use electricity as a source of power.[72] At first, they had to employ handymen as electricians, such a division of labour being then a novelty. Among the wiremen early in the present century was a young man called Walter Citrine.

Both the Ravenhead and Sutton Oak works came to life again for a time in the mid-'90s, the former controlled by their owners, the British Plate Glass Co. Ltd., and the latter operated by a new limited company which took its predecessor's name. But the much fiercer foreign competition at the turn of the century soon drove them both out of business for good. Pilkingtons acquired their property. They bought Ravenhead from the British Plate Glass Co. Ltd. in 1901 for £93,000, and, when they had 'knocked off the "fancy" things made there',[73] these works were used to supplement the capacity of Cowley Hill. The Sutton Oak works of the London and Manchester Plate Glass Co. Ltd., reported to be losing £200 per week towards the end of 1902, stopped production in June 1903.[74] The factory fell into Pilkingtons' hands for £82,000 in July 1905.[75] It was used only for warehousing, being disposed of later for purposes other than glassmaking.

How did Pilkingtons manage to survive when all their longer-established rivals succumbed?

Detailed accounts, available from 1894 onwards, give a clear answer. Pilkingtons were then the only plate glass manufacturers who also made sheet, rolled plate and cathedral glass, all of which continued to yield substantial profits. Annual output of sheet remained at between sixty and seventy million feet between 1895 and 1903, and remained profitable throughout the period, particularly in 1901 and early 1902 when prices rose very considerably as a result of the lengthy strike in the Belgian window glass industry.[76] Output of both rolled plate and cathedral glass, both highly profitable, doubled between 1895 and 1903.

PROFITS ON PILKINGTONS' SHEET, ROLLED PLATE AND CATHEDRAL
GLASS IN THE YEARS ENDED JUNE 30, 1895–1903

Year ended June 30	£
1895	54,356
1896	99,962
1897	114,493
1898	168,974
1899	199,689
1900	237,705
1901	275,892
1902	236,187
1903	163,127

Clearly, profits from these branches would have been sufficient to offset losses on plate glass even if these had been quite severe. In fact, although we do not know what may have happened before the middle of 1894, from that date onwards Pilkingtons' plate glassworks at Cowley Hill usually made a profit, and often quite a handsome one.

OUTPUT OF, AND PROFITS ON, PILKINGTONS' PLATE GLASS IN
THE YEARS ENDED JUNE 30, 1895–1903

Year ended June 30	Footage	Profit £
1895	3,727,736	Loss 4,579
1896	3,830,120	49,174
1897	3,613,218	53,235
1898	3,683,229	35,747
1899	4,494,873	27,793
1900	4,727,234	41,147
1901	4,769,234	54,303
1902	4,962,233	13,991
1903	5,159,496	Loss 4,477

These profits on both sheet and plate glass are largely explained by comparatively low manufacturing costs resulting from the innovations and improvements which have been the central theme of this chapter. Unfortunately we lack details of Pilkingtons' costs before 1895 and possess none of their competitors' for purposes of comparison, apart from those of the Ravenhead works after they were taken over in 1901. These, however, indicate quite clearly what was happening in plate glass manufacture. Between 1895 and 1903, during which years Pilkingtons invested no less than £100,000 at Cowley Hill, their costs there fell from 9·17d per foot to 7·36d.[77] At Ravenhead—where, according to the Pilkington Board, kilns were 'wrong and out of date and everything else'[78]—the cost of production in 1902 was 11·75d and in 1903 12·73d.[79]

Pilkingtons may also have obtained some small advantage, so far as plate glass was concerned, from having a controlling interest in a small plate glass factory on the continent. This concern was brought to their notice by Herman. At the end of 1890 he received an invitation to invest in 'a new works about to be erected near the Belgian frontier at Maubeuge in France', which he passed on to the Board. The partners looked into the prospects of the company, a French concern with head office in Paris, and decided to invest in it. By the beginning of 1892 they had put over £26,000 into the undertaking, which then consisted of one 16-pot furnace and five grinding and four polishing machines. The venture, as was to be expected, lost money at first but then began to return a modest profit. While the partners were, as usual, loud in their complaints of inefficient management and, in 1898, were wondering whether to sell the works, they eventually decided against such a course. Maubeuge provided a return on capital, it was a source of information about what was happening on the continent, and it was to prove a valuable diplomatic asset.[80]

It was at Herman's suggestion, too, that Pilkingtons became interested in a Belgian sandfield in order to safeguard their supplies of silver sand, of which their annual consumption was about 13,000 tons by 1900. At the end of that year Herman drew the Board's attention to the recently-formed Anglo-Belgian Silver Sand Company which owned property at Moll, twenty-eight miles north-east of Louvain. By 1903 Pilkingtons had invested £7,000 in the concern and had lent it a further £11,000 on mortgage. The company passed into Pilkingtons' hands completely in 1907.[81]

These economies and advantages on the manufacturing side, however, do not by themselves completely explain Pilkingtons' success, though they may go much of the way towards doing so. A great deal continued to depend on the effectiveness of the firm's selling arrangements, particularly at a time when competition was becoming far more intense. No sales ledgers have survived from this period, so it is impossible to try to present a detailed picture of what was happening on the selling side of the business; but the Board minutes do, nevertheless, give a clear indication of the main developments. Sales pressures at home were being increased; but, of far greater importance, was the growth of markets overseas.

At home, new warehouses were added to the four existing ones (Birmingham, Bristol, Leeds and Sheffield): Glasgow (1868), Bradford (1872), Newcastle (1880) and Nottingham (1885).[82] In London Pilkingtons continued to sell for a long time only direct to glass merchants and, though they had an office at 26 Bridge Street, Blackfriars, there was no London warehouse until 1889. The firm's general warehousing policy came under review at a meeting of the Board on July 2, 1874:

'Discussed at length the policy of our warehouse system and whether it is advisable to enlarge their spheres and add lead or any other branches to glass or whether it would be better to contract their range and reduce them to a simple office like our London one. Admitted that when our glass wanted first introducing to the market then a secured outlet like a whouse was a *good* thing but when our make is in the market and is liked and sought, the expediency of a whouse is naturally altered.'

No action was then taken but, a year later, when the Birmingham warehouse had shown a small nett loss, it was decided that

'the orders from the country should be sent as much as possible, in fact entirely, direct to the works, keeping the whouse as much as possible as a store for the use of the town and in the town to stop retail and deal as exclusively as possible with the 1st and 2nd class men only'.

The Bristol warehouse, too, was to be used 'as much as possible as a town store'. Glasgow was put on the same footing in 1876, all the books of the three warehouses being then sent to the works. After this the emphasis was placed upon warehouse building at St Helens and the development of office accommodation there: a completely new head office was opened in 1887.[83]

The St Helens office and warehouses were by that time also handling a considerable volume of export business. This was probably quite a recent development, for very little of Pilkingtons' glass appears to have been exported before the 1870s. In America, particularly, Chances seem to have maintained the ascendancy which dated from their early years, when they had the advantage of William Chance's American connexions and their own New York depot. In 1868, for instance, when Pilkingtons heard that a person competent to act for them happened to be going to America, they got into touch with him 'relative to our doing a trade with Boston'. They gave him the address of a merchant house there which bought plate glass from Ravenhead but added: 'We fear they are Chances' agents'. In 1873, while the Belgian manufacturers were temporarily handicapped by a fuel shortage, Pilkingtons sent one of their travellers, Scott, to America for four months and, in the following year, John Salmond, who had previously been employed at their warehouse in Birmingham and at their London office, was sent right across the United States to make business contacts. He did not, however, consider the American market sufficiently promising to justify his remaining there as Pilkingtons' agent, and he returned home to become manager, and later proprietor, of James Hetley and Co., the London glass merchants.

In 1879 Pilkingtons engaged J. Thorpe, who had previously worked for the Wearmouth Company, 'to travel through the States and Colonies' and Richard Pilkington himself was in America seeking orders from March until May of that year. Unfortunately we have no record of how Thorpe covered his extensive assignment, soon made even larger by his being sent to the East. He visited Japan in 1882, and, a year later, Shanghai. In 1890 he was responsible for opening a depot at Montreal. A second followed at Toronto in 1893. He then concentrated his activities in Canada, going to the States once a month; higher tariffs and developments in America's own industry had made it more difficult to sell glass there. Meanwhile, from the 1880s, orders also came in on some scale from South America, one in 1888 for £2,900 worth of sheet glass and 70,000 ft. of rolled plate being so large that it had to be given special consideration by the Board.[84] Sales were also continued to Australia where, as we have seen (page 127), an agency had been operating since the fifties, though there is no evidence of a companion agency in New Zealand until 1894. In South Africa, R. H. Pritchard went to Cape Town in 1882 as the first agent there, and in 1894 there were Pilkington offices in both Cape Town and Durban. In the Middle East, there was an agency in Egypt from 1892.

Much of Pilkingtons' trade with the continent seems to have been handled by H. and E. Lion of Hamburg. Selling in northern Europe against Belgian competition was particularly difficult. As H. Lion pointed out—rather obviously, perhaps—while he was on a visit to St Helens in 1878, 'he could sell large quantities of sheet, rolled, and plate in Holland, Norway, Sweden, Denmark and Russia if we could meet the foreign prices'. In 1882 and 1883, Adams, one of Pilkingtons' representatives, visited Holland, Spain and Italy and, from then onwards, separate agencies came to be formed in the various countries. By 1894, in addition to an office in Hamburg, Pilkingtons had depots in Paris and Naples. Italy seems to have provided quite a flourishing market at that time, if one may judge from the number of agencies—in Palermo, Bari, Rome and Turin, as well as in Naples itself.[85]

All these efforts to supplement the exports of merchants in London and Manchester by sales of their own direct to the countries concerned, were of crucial importance to Pilkingtons during these years. Their export department grew rapidly; by the end of the 1880s, the work had to be divided into two sections. One dealt with the European countries (apart from France) and such Middle East and Far East trade as did not pass through the hands of export merchants. The other handled sales to France, North and South America, and British possessions abroad. The effect of all this sales promotion in distant parts of the world may be seen clearly from the figures on the next page of home and foreign sales from 1877 to 1887.

Confronted by increased difficulty in selling plate and sheet glass on the home market, Pilkingtons developed outlets overseas where they were still able to find new customers. We do not know the relative profitability of their home and foreign sales nor do we know what happened after 1887; but it would seem reasonably safe to assert, on the basis of these figures, that Pilkingtons owed their survival to growing profits from exports as well as to lower production costs. The greater volume of glass handled by their shipping office at Drury

Buildings, Liverpool, made an essential contribution to the profitability of the business and this allowed the partners to keep on expanding it.

In the middle of 1872, just before the firm embarked upon large-scale expenditure—building the plate works and extending the sheet works—it was decided to call in an outside accountant 'to put the accounts upon the best commercial footing'. They engaged Arthur W. and Reginald A. Wenham, partners in the London firm of Wenham, Angus and Company. The Wenhams presented twice-yearly balance sheets from 1874 and began to undertake a continuous audit ten years later. Unfortunately none of the balance sheets prior to 1894 has survived. The estimated capital value of the concern in 1873 is, however, known from a partnership agreement of that year and the value in 1894 is also known, because the firm then transformed itself into a company. The figure for 1873 was £202,551; that for 1894, £800,000 in ordinary shares plus £600,000 in debentures (representing loans). The whole of this £1,400,000 was provided by the Pilkington family. Private valuations such as these are not always very meaningful. Even so, an estimated increase from £200,000 to £800,000 within twenty-one years indicates a remarkably high rate of reinvestment (particularly at a time of falling prices); and the advance of £600,000 on loan shows the extent to which the partners were prepared to throw their private savings into the business.

According to the 1873 agreement, which was binding for twenty-one years, all profits in excess of £12,000 a year were to be ploughed back. The capital was held by the four partners in equal amounts and if it was necessary to increase it, they were each to make equal contributions until the required sum was raised. Each partner was to devote his full time to the business and for this he was to receive a salary of £20 per week. Again, this agreement may not have

PILKINGTONS' SALES, HOME AND FOREIGN, 1877-1887

Year	Plate		Sheet		Rolled Plate		Total	
	Home £	Export £	Home £	Export £	Home £	Export £	Home £	Export £
1877	68,887	6,056	201,095	11,041	41,798	2,125	311,780	19,222
1878	93,531	8,138	182,244	6,693	38,239	2,178	314,014	17,009
1879	108,953	27,268	161,862	17,073	37,455	7,260	308,270	51,601
1880	117,477	39,660	172,450	39,655	40,442	7,585	330,369	86,900
1881	119,210	48,642	190,913	42,171	45,789	9,205	355,912	100,018
1882	144,227	60,272	192,339	52,816	56,661	13,954	393,227	127,042
1883	142,326	65,110	222,791	56,068	70,364	18,496	435,481	139,674
1884	139,026	82,015	232,282	53,006	73,936	12,954	445,244	147,975
1885	128,375	87,231	214,989	47,361	62,766	14,697	406,130	149,289
1886	121,365	88,175	195,555	71,160	60,781	15,954	377,701	175,289
1887	121,588	140,240	202,851	78,116	64,020	22,290	388,429	204,646

Source: Statement on loose sheet in Board Minutes, 1881–91.

been so meaningful as it would seem. We know that the £20 salary was doubled after the plate works were opened, and it is possible that bonuses may have been shared over and above the £12,000: this certainly was the practice after 1895. Nevertheless this agreement does suggest a considerable degree of dividend restraint to which the rapid growth of the firm's capital value is further testimony. And the extent of the loans in 1894 shows that much of what was distributed found its way back again into the business.[86]

A clause in the agreement permitted any partner to give the whole or part of his interest to his sons when they reached the age of twenty-one. For taking part in the management of the firm, the sons were to share the salary of their fathers. In accordance with this clause, Roby Pilkington, the senior member, introduced his two sons, William Lee Pilkington and George Herbert Pilkington, on March 17, 1885, each of them being given one-tenth of his share. In July 1894, when the twenty-one-year term had expired, Pilkingtons was transformed into a limited company under the Companies Act of 1862. Although in law the private limited company did not come into existence until a later Act of 1907, in fact a number of undertakings became private companies before that time merely by not offering any shares to the public.[87] This was the course followed by Pilkingtons who informed their clients in a circular letter that 'the change is simply made for family reasons; no shares are offered to the public and no alteration whatever is made in the management of the business'.[88] The ordinary share capital was divided into 8,000 ordinary shares of £100. The Companies Act required that there be a minimum of seven members. The four senior partners therefore took the opportunity to introduce four other sons, Henry William Pilkington and Richard Austin Pilkington (twin sons of Windle Pilkington) and Ernest Sinclair Pilkington and Arthur Richard Pilkington (sons of Richard Pilkington). The senior partners were each allotted 2,000 ordinary shares and £150,000 of debenture stock to be divided, if desired, with their sons. The allocation of the shares was as follows:[89]

William (Roby) Pilkington	1,600 ordinary shares and £120,000 of debentures
Thomas Pilkington	2,000 £150,000
William Windle Pilkington	1,960 £150,000
Richard Pilkington	1,960 £150,000
William Lee Pilkington	200 £15,000
George Herbert Pilkington	200 £15,000
Henry William Pilkington	20 nil
Richard Austin Pilkington	20 nil
Ernest Sinclair Pilkington	20 nil
Arthur Richard Pilkington	20 nil

From 1894 no further calls needed to be made upon the private resources of directors until after the First World War. The profits of the company from the works and colliery, from rents of property and interest on investments, were sufficient in themselves to provide all the capital needed after the directors and shareholders had taken their due: 5 per cent. interest on debenture stock, 5 per cent. dividend and an annual bonus. When all these payments had been made and much ploughed back into the concern, there still remained a residue which was invested, as company savings, chiefly in foreign rails, government bonds and public utilities. These rose from £85,000 in the year 1896–7 to £355,000 in 1902–3. Shares in the Maubeuge factory by then accounted for about £30,000 of these totals.

DISPOSAL OF PROFIT IN THE YEARS ENDED JUNE 30, 1896–1903

Year ended June 30	Profit	Directors' salaries, fees and expenses	Income tax	Debenture interest £30,000 and	Bonus on shares	Balance retained in company for development
1896	£186,343	£18,880	£ 1,768	dividend £40,000	£ 10,000	£ 85,695
1897	209,125	17,801	965	paid	30,000	90,359
1898	248,870	17,654	2,549	annually	50,000	108,667
1899	267,439	16,128	2,808		60,000	118,503
1900	334,497	16,827	5,769		120,000	121,901
1901	394,746	15,760	12,344		120,000	176,642
1902	295,197	17,010	13,582		90,000	104,605
1903	196,197	17,274	14,286		40,000	54,637

While foreign competition had driven most other British manufacturers out of business, Pilkingtons' financial position remained very sound indeed.

CHAPTER 11

LABOUR RELATIONS AND WELFARE
SERVICES IN THE LATER YEARS OF THE
NINETEENTH CENTURY

AFTER the labour troubles of the mid-1840s, Pilkingtons went for many years without any further disputes. But, with foreign competition growing more severe and glass prices falling, it was inevitable that some attempt should be made to cut labour costs and this led to further collisions between Pilkingtons and their employees. These occurred, however, during the 1870s and were dealt with so firmly—some would say ruthlessly—that, when trade unionism in the country as a whole became more militant towards the end of the century, the movement found little or no response among those employed at the Grove Street factory.

An entry in the Board Minutes on January 8, 1863, calls 'a fair blower's average about 35/- crown and 45/- sheet . . .' Although this was approximately the same rate as the English blowers had been receiving fifteen years before, it represented a fall in real wages, for the cost of living had moved upwards in the interval. These were the highest paid men. At the other end of the scale, boys starting work at Pilkingtons earned only 2/6 per week. One of them was James Sexton, who was later to become well-known as a trade union leader. He worked at Pilkingtons for four years before running off to sea.[1]

At the end of the 1860s a growing number of complaints about the quality of Pilkington glass kept arriving at the works and there was evidently some slackness on the part of the glasshouse managers. Two of the partners returned from a visit to Belgium in June 1869 more than ever convinced that their blowers and flatteners—the skilled workmen upon whom the firm was completely dependent for the size and quality of its product—were not working so efficiently as they had done in the past. The Board thereupon

'Carpeted all the managers and explained to them what had been seen in Belgium lately by W. P. and W. W. P., how far faster the men worked from one end to the other and hence our inabiltiy to compete with them; further, that we work now much more slowly than we used to do.'[2]

173

In an effort to raise standards, a bonus was offered to those who produced a high proportion of number one quality glass.

At the same time a reduction was made in the number of people employed outside the glasshouses and the wages of the rest were reduced. Despite this cut, Thomas Pilkington could still complain, in the following March, that wages were 'excessive in almost all departments connected with the Yard'. More men were laid off and others demoted. At least one of them refused the new terms which were offered:

> 'Told T. Glover that we had decided to put him to the trowel again when he at once replied that he had been expecting it as the work and reduced staff wouldn't warrant his remaining in his present position; but though he should be willing at any time to take the trowel to work *piece work* for us, he should decline to take it otherwise. This, of course, settled the matter and he goes.'[3]

Attention was now given to the wages of the glassmakers themselves. What appears to have been a new standard was introduced for calculating wage rates: 100 pieces of 15 oz. to the foot and sized 50″ x 35″, safely delivered to the warehouse. This was a man's average production per shift. Heavier weights per foot were based on 46″ x 34″ and were counted as more than one piece at the standard rate. 26 oz. glass sized 46″ x 34″, for instance, was to count as two pieces for wage purposes. There were also bonuses for larger sizes. Blowers were divided into three categories according to their skill and experience. The best were to be paid at a rate of 14/– per 100 standard pieces (56/– per week of four shifts at the average output), the second grade 13/– (52/–) and the third 11/– (44/–). Flatteners were also divided into two classes and were to receive 8/– or 7/– per 100. Gatherers were to be paid 6/8 per 100.

As we have no information about wage rates for the 1850s and 1860s, nor any lists of earnings, it is not possible to estimate the effect of these changes. The rates were, in fact, increased slightly after they had been tried out, the 11/– basic for third-class blowers being put up to 11/6 and the others advanced proportionately. Windle Pilkington estimated that, with this addition, the new rates would not cut any earnings by more than 15 per cent. and most would be reduced very much less than that. The men claimed the cuts would *average* 23 per cent. Of significance, perhaps, were the inducements to blow larger sizes, the decision to pay only for pieces safely delivered to the warehouse, and, above all, the division of these skilled employees into different categories. The lot of sheet glassmakers was probably a little harder than it had been in the boom years of the mid-1840s when their labour was in such great demand. As we have noticed, the standard was then the smaller piece measuring 40″ x 30″ and 13 oz. to the foot; for 425 cylinders of this standard the blower could earn in a week 53/8.

The new conditions provoked the most protracted strike in Pilkingtons' history. The sheet glass blowers stopped work on April 19, 1870, and the other glassmakers had to be laid off. The firm maintained a token output, using younger managers and apprentices, for over six months. When the strike eventually ended, on November 5th, the men came back on their masters' terms. Towards the close of the following month the Board was able to record 'a great improvement in the character of the glass altogether now.'[4]

In 1872, when, on the one hand, the cost of living had been driven up by high fuel prices and, on the other, the demand for glass was strong and the price rising, Pilkingtons advanced the basic rate from 11/6 to 12/6. A further increase of 10 per cent. was given in the following October, plus a bonus of 10 per cent. on all pieces above 400 per week. Soon afterwards, £200 was distributed among the office staff who had had no increases and could earn no overtime pay. This caused the recipients, thirty-six in number, to send a letter of thanks to their employers. In it they wrote of Pilkingtons' consideration for them:

> 'Your thoughtfulness and liberality in the present trying times of high prices, felt by all classes of the community, comes with double force to your servants who have thereby been enabled to look calmly on what were previously our difficulties; which, added to your general kindness to us in the past, tends to confirm our conviction of the interest taken in our welfare by yourselves.'[5]

The office staff was still very small in the early 1870s; and there do not appear then to have been more than two hundred sheet glassmakers (blowers, flatteners and gatherers) and were probably not more than another fifty skilled men at work in the rolled plate factory and other glassmaking departments. Yet, in 1876, 1,500 people were employed altogether at Grove Street.[6] The ratio of glassmakers to others, at one to six, was perhaps somewhat greater than it had been in the 1840s; yet the overwhelming majority of Pilkingtons' employees still worked outside the glasshouses. No lists of earnings for this period have survived, so we do not know how these employees fared. The Board Minutes refer, at one extreme, to sorters earning about 30/- per week, and, at the other, to apprentices receiving just a few shillings. All these people, who did not actually make glass, were working a 55½-hour week in the early 1870s: from Monday to Friday 6 a.m. to 5.30 p.m. and on Saturday from 6 a.m. to 12 noon, with intervals for meals.[7] For them, and for the glassmakers, there were three days' holiday in the year: Christmas Day, Good Friday and the Friday of Newton Race Week in June. (This last holiday was changed to Whit Monday about 1880.) August Bank Holiday—a half-holiday at first—was taken from 1882. Departmental managers sometimes had a week's holiday with pay, but the partners did not encourage this. When, for instance, one manager, who earned £5 10s od per week, was away and his work was done by a deputy who was paid £3, the Board decided to subtract the difference between the two wages from his holiday pay and added:

'Last year paid him in full but holydays are becoming more the fashion and it behoves us to check the tendency.'[8]

So long as pot furnaces were used, glassmakers had to work intermittently, ten hours on followed by twenty-four hours off while the pots were being re-charged. With the coming of tanks during the 1870s, work could continue throughout the week but the week-end rest was still preserved. We do not know for certain how the shifts were arranged at the start. It is clear from the con-tracts, however, that each glassmaker worked six shifts per week at the tanks and, since it was claimed that he could produce 20 per cent. more glass from these shifts than from four ten-hour shifts at pot furnaces, the shifts were evi-dently of eight hours' duration. According to the accounts which reached Chances (page 149), glassmakers worked three eight-hour shifts in rotation.[9]

These changes in working hours may have been a contributory cause of a second strike which occurred in 1878. It came soon after three 10 per cent. wage cuts. While prices generally were falling quite quickly, those of imported glass (as may be seen from graph 8 on page 155) were rising slightly, and it was perhaps on the strength of this that the St Helens district branch of the Sheet Glassmakers' Association demanded an advance. It was re-fused and the strike began on August 9th. This was only a partial stoppage, however, for thirty-two blowers, eight flatteners and ten gatherers refused to support the strike. It was never really effective and it eventually petered out in the middle of November, the men again returning on their masters' terms. As they came in, they were obliged to sign six-months contracts. This would appear to have been a shorter term than had obtained before the strike; it was certainly very much shorter than from six to seven years common in the middle of the century. These new contracts were arranged so that they expired at different dates, which meant that only a small section could, in future, strike at any one time without breaking their agreements. In 1879, as the contracts came up for renewal, the men were re-bound at a lower rate of pay. At the beginning of the year, when the Board considered the new rates, they decided that they should be 'the lowest that can possibly be gone to'. In fact, the basic rate for third-class blowers was reduced to 10/–, 1/6 less than it had been after the 1870 strike. The contracts also included a clause which made glassmakers liable to fines of up to 10/– for each day's absence without good cause. There was also another clause obliging all hand blowers to average, over six shifts per week, one hundred feet per hour, the average being reduced to ninety feet during the hot months of June, July and August. When the non-strikers came to be bound at these new low rates, they were granted a bonus for life of £5 per year, subject to their being 'steady and sober' and behaving to the firm's satisfaction. There were no more strikes at Grove Street after this.[10]

Pilkingtons soon saw that they had gone too far in cutting wages. Several of their men left for America and, although some are said to have returned from the United States 'disgusted', a 10 per cent. advance was agreed to in April 1880, because 'the American makers were trying to seduce [the others] into going over there. . . . Some advance here might cause them to turn a deaf ear to the temptation'. In July, when Chances cut wages by 10 per cent., Pilkingtons refused to follow suit because of rumours that 'a lot of our men are going to America as soon as they light up there again'. (The American glassworks were closed from May to July because of the hot weather.) The 10 per cent. cut was considered again on two occasions during the following twelve months, but no action was taken.[11]

The American glassmakers soon became concerned about the effects of this influx of foreign labour. In 1884 St Helens became the centre of a determined effort to organize the British glassmakers, instigated by the American Knights of Labor.[12] One of the Knights' branches—or Local Assemblies as they were called—had its headquarters in the glassmaking centre of Pittsburgh. This was Local Assembly number 300. It was, in fact, more than a local branch, for it enrolled window glass workers throughout America. L.A. 300 became concerned at the number of skilled glass workers who were arriving from Europe and entering American factories at wages below the current rates. In 1880, two of their members, James L. Michels and John Fetters, were sent to Europe

'. . . for the purpose of making an investigation into the condition of the window glass workers in Europe, and, if possible, ascertain why so many window glass workers come to America under contract for less than current wages, and, if possible, have the European workers form a union and establish a closer communication between America and the old country, in order to protect the interests of all window glass workers.'

This mission does not appear to have had any success in Britain, but its activities may, perhaps, have had some bearing upon the formation in August, 1882, of the Belgian *Union Verrière*.[13] In the following year this union sent money to help strikers in the United States, and the year after that, 1884, the Americans, in their turn, helped the Belgians to strike successfully for higher wages.[14] This *liaison* led, in June 1884, to a conference at Charleroi, attended by Isaac Cline and Henry Burtt, President and Secretary of L.A. 300, to found a Universal Federation of Glass Workers. Later in the same month, Cline, Burtt and representatives from France, Belgium and Italy, appeared at St Helens. Their conference, held at the White Lion Inn and attended by some three hundred people, was, in fact, the first Universal Convention. It was addressed by Cline, Oscar Falleur and Chery Desguin of the *Union Verrière*, F. Barr of the French association of glassmakers, and delegates from Sunderland and Spon Lane.[15] At a further meeting, held on a Sunday morning a few days later, the delegates are said to have attracted an audience more than twice as large.[16] The local chairman, named Rigby, was an employee of Pilkingtons. They promptly dismissed him and when a union deputation waited upon Windle Pilkington to ask why, he (according to the Board minutes) 'gave them some good advice and told them that we were determined to oppose it in any way that it interfered with us'.[17]

In the following November, A. G. Denny, another member of L.A. 300, came over to consolidate the work of Cline and Burtt. L.A. 3,504 was formed as the Knights' Local Assembly for British window glass workers, with headquarters at Sunderland, and a 'preceptory', or branch, at St Helens. The branch appears to have had a certain limited success in enrolling members. In February 1885, for instance, twenty were enrolled at the society's club house, the Sefton Arms Hotel.[18] In that month, too, its secretary, Joseph Norbury, an ex-miner who had just left Pilkingtons after three-and-a-half years' service with the firm, was prominent in an attempt to form a local Trades Council. Also among the trade unions interested in setting up this body was a Plate Glass Workers' Society, which had recently been largely responsible for a strike at the Pocket Nook works.[19] The St Helens branch of L.A. 3,504 kept alive for a few years longer. The Universal Convention was again held in the town in 1886 and 1888. On the latter occasion, Pilkingtons asked the Chief Constable to keep close watch upon both their meetings and upon the firm's two factories.[20] But, despite these efforts to rally Pilkingtons' men, the union made no headway at St Helens. Norbury, the branch secretary, turned out to be an alcoholic and became an increasing liability. And Pilkingtons themselves would have no truck at all with the union. *The American Glassworker*, in its issue of September 11, 1885, had contrasted the 'tyrannical vigilance of the Pilkingtons' with the attitude of 'the Chance Brothers and Messrs Hartley', who 'have at different times treated our committee with great kindness'. At the end of March 1887, the secretary of L.A. 3,504 reported to the head of the Knights in America that, whereas they were 'in good organized condition' at the other factories, at St Helens 'what with the tyrannical disposition of the capitalist and the general depressed condition of the men (through that curse Drink) we are not able to make any progress whatever. . . . Messrs Pilkington Bros are continually discharging our members for no other reason than that they belong to our Society'. His successor as secretary, writing to Beatrice Potter in 1891, attributed the failure at St Helens to Pilkingtons' staggered contract system.

The intention of all this trade union activity had been to recruit the highly skilled and relatively well-paid sheet glassmakers. At the end of the 'eighties came the spread of New Unionism among the unskilled. In 1889 the United Plate Glass Society started to enrol plate glassmakers, for the greater part unskilled men. By June of that year they claimed to have eight hundred members but only one hundred of these were said to belong to the Cowley Hill works.[21] The union appears to have gained support among Pilkingtons' employees during the following year, however, for at the end of June 1890 the men stopped work at Cowley Hill on the grounds that their wages were being gradually reduced. The strike dragged on until November but in the end the strikers had to return on their masters' terms.[22] While the great factory lay idle, the Board took the opportunity to press ahead with installing the Malevez machinery,[23] and when the strike was over they were able to claim a rebate on the St Helens town rates of one-third on account of the twenty-week stoppage.[24]

While this strike was in progress, an attempt was made to organize the labourers at Sheet Works, much on the lines of the Chemical and Copper Workers' Union which had just been formed at St Helens. In October 1890 there were said to be eight hundred members.[25] In the following year a Sheet Glass Flatteners' Society is mentioned for the first time.[26] To what extent these developments indicated any real spread of trade unionism at Grove Street is far from clear. There are certainly signs that the first eager enthusiasm was not sustained. When one of Pilkingtons' sheet glass blowers was asked in 1895 whether the workers were organized in any way, he replied in the negative.[27]

The firm's recreational activities continued to grow with the increasing number of employees. A new sports ground was opened at City Road in the mid-'70s when the adjacent Cowley Hill factory came into use. Meanwhile, as urban St Helens gradually spread outwards, the original home of the Recreation Club had to retreat before the ever-advancing builders. The first ground in the vicinity of the cotton factory had to be given up in 1877 when the firm surrendered its lease, and a new field was taken in Boundary Road. When this was acquired by the Corporation and became part of Queen's Recreation Ground, the Club removed to its present home in Ruskin Drive, opened in 1901.[28]

Until the 1880s cricket stood unchallenged as the most popular outdoor sport and it continued to have a wide appeal. In 1893, for which year a fixture book survives, the club was able to send three teams into the field every Saturday. Two of them used the Boundary Road ground and the third played at City Road. By this time, however, the summer game had a winter counterpart which enjoyed an even larger following. The rugby section was formed in 1879, and in 1884 the 'Recs' (as the team came to be known) joined the West Lancashire and Border Town Rugby Union. From then onwards the teams that came to play at Boundary Road—particularly the fierce rivals from Wigan —drew large crowds.[29]

In 1891 a club was formed for those employees who wished to ride that newfangled creation, the bicycle. The firm bought a number of cycles at cost price and sold them to members of the club who paid in weekly instalments.[30]

The oldest of Pilkingtons' welfare services, the school, continued to give part-time education to the apprentices. The schoolmaster for twenty-one years until his death in 1887 was Edward Fidler, who taught his often unruly pupils in premises at Eccleston Street.[31] When Pilkingtons gave up their Eccleston Street property, the school was removed to the old mill, close to the Grove Street works.[32] During the winter the Recreation Section sponsored various lectures, an early form of adult education. A coffee room at Sheet Works was agreed upon by the Board at the end of 1874 and a dining room in 1888. The Navigation Inn, acquired by Pilkingtons in 1890 and later converted into a staff café and recreation rooms, served as an excellent centre for such purposes. Early in the following century a works canteen was opened in a building opposite the General Office in Grove Street.[33]

The firm's medical services date from 1882. Although there had previously been arrangements between Pilkingtons and various doctors in the town for medical attention in case of accidents at the works, the employees had been obliged to rely on one or other of the town's numerous friendly societies for assistance in case of illness. Towards the end of 1881, the glassblowers, who already ran such a sickness and burial society among themselves, asked if they might hold meetings at the works instead of at a public house. Pilkingtons agreed but asked them to consider extending their club to all the other employees at Grove Street. Within a short time J. H. Dickinson, representing the firm, was negotiating with local doctors to attend nearly 1,200 employees and their wives and families. Pilkingtons, who had previously paid £40 a year to doctors for attending accident cases, now gave £50 to the club instead. They were soon contributing £100 to keep it solvent. By 1884 there were complaints —they have a distinctly modern ring—that 'yard men' who belonged to the firm's club and to another one outside, were taking every opportunity to be ill, for then they 'really got more money than if they had been at their work'. The Board commented: 'Much more sickness now than before the Club existed. No doubt some rascality exists'. By the end of the 1880s the club's income exceeded £2,000 a year. Local doctors continued to be employed until 1905 when the club appointed a doctor of its own. These arrangements did not apply to the Cowley Hill works where Pilkingtons continued to pay for medical attention in cases of accident and the men had their own contributory accident fund.[34]

Pilkingtons had no pensions scheme in operation until the inter-war years. Yet they often granted small pensions to their employees, and sometimes also to widows of employees. These grants, however, were by no means an automatic reward for long service. On one occasion, for instance, the Board noted that an elderly employee had

'been applying for assistance in shape of a pension and has written saying that he has been 50 years with the Firm, etc. Don't think him entitled to anything; been a regular black sheep.'[35]

But Pilkingtons did continue to employ him for several years longer on lighter work, instructing the younger blowers.

It is impossible for anyone to be impartial about labour relations, whether they be in the past or at the present-day. The reaction of each reader to this chapter will depend upon his own particular background. To some, Pilkingtons will appear to have been extremely harsh in their dealings at this period. To others, they will appear very fair employers, far ahead of their times in their encouragement of welfare services. Whatever conclusions may be reached, there can be no doubt that Pilkingtons' extremely exacting labour policy at this time made an essential contribution to the rapid growth of the concern and this enabled the firm to provide work for more people and better jobs for existing employees. As Pilkingtons told their men a few years before the end of the century:

'We have put forth immense energy in placing agencies, travellers and warehouses to intercept and take orders; and while others have either gone back or shut up, we have kept you at full work. While large works at St Helens have been out and men getting nothing, you have been at work.'[36]

Wage increases could not, in these years, be passed on to the consumer. It is true that, at least from the mid-1890s when balance sheets become available, from £100,000–200,000 per year were distributed among the Pilkington family. How much of this sum could have been distributed among employees without weakening the firm—bearing in mind that it was from these profits that further family investment was to be forthcoming after the First World War? If £15,000 had been paid out in any one year at the end of the nineteenth century to the 2,000 employees at Grove Street and the 1,000 at Cowley Hill, it would only have raised each man's pay by 2/– per week, 10 per cent. or less of the wages of all but juveniles.

The *régime* at Pilkingtons at the end of the nineteenth century must have seemed hard to many who lived through it, despite the general fall in the cost of living—though not so hard as it would appear to those who look back from the higher living standards of the present day. It must have been extremely irritating at times; on one occasion, for instance, the partners even went so far as to forbid domino-playing at the recreation club on the grounds that 'dominoes have a gambling tendency'.[37] There was never any doubt who was in control of the business; but the minutes of the Board show quite plainly that these rulers knew a great deal about the men who were subject to them and understood the ways in which their minds worked.

CHAPTER 12

COLLIERY AFFAIRS

PILKINGTONS' coalmining activities, unlike their venture into the chemical industry, came under the direct control of the Board at Grove Street. The St Helens Colliery was an integral part of Pilkington Brothers and William (Roby) Pilkington was responsible for its management. It is appropriate, therefore, that we should devote a brief chapter to events at the Pilkingtons' colliery from the later 1850s, when they began to work the coal measure in the immediate vicinity of the works.

Although coal was certainly being wound at the St Helens Colliery in 1861,[1] complimentary remarks from a mines inspector on 'the very judicious way in which the coal had so far been opened out' make it clear that some of the seams were still being prepared for working two years later, in 1863.[2] Perhaps Pilkingtons' decision at the beginning of the latter year to join the South Lancashire Coal Association may be taken as a sign that their mining activities had by then reached a scale when affiliation to that body had become desirable.[3]

As the workings became more extensive, official approval regarding their safety turned to censure. Complaints were made about their ventilation. At the end of 1863 an inspector asserted that the mines contained gas and 'could not be efficiently worked as at present'. He suggested that the remedy would be 'either a reconstruction of the air courses or sinking a new shaft'.[4] The Board favoured the latter, and it was decided to sink a new pit to the southward, not far from the main entrance of the Ravenhead plate glassworks. From there it would be possible to get the higher quality Rushy Park and Little Delf coals as well as to improve the ventilation system in their existing workings by means of an underground tunnel.

Work on the new pit began early in 1864. On March 17th the shaft was twenty-four yards down.[5] McGill, the manager, acquired a steam engine from Chorley for £120 to pump out the water which flooded in as the men continued boring and sinking deeper into the ground. By September a winding engine had also been bought.[6] By May of the following year, 1865, £7,000 had already been spent on the new pit and there was a year's work ahead before the Rushy Park mine could be reached. A further £3,100 were spent during these next twelve months.[7] The Little Delf mine, which lay a short distance below the Rushy Park seam, was entered early in 1867.[8] Meanwhile the ventilation tunnel was being cut. The Board Minutes of December 20, 1866, include the note: 'Doing well in the Tunnel at Ravenhead pit: expect to get it through in one month's time'. This, however, was an optimistic estimate for it was not until May 9, 1867, that the Board could record: 'Connected tunnel with Little Delf from New pit at Ravenhead May 1st'. Further work had still to be done; the minutes of May 17th, for instance, mention the driving of a tunnel to connect the Rushy Park and Little Delf seams. It was not until the end of the year that the forty workmen were entertained to a spread at one of the local hostelries, the customary conclusion to such an operation.[9] The new colliery was named after Princess Alexandra who had paid a visit to the nearby Ravenhead works in 1865.[10]

At the beginning of 1866 Pilkingtons engaged a new colliery manager at a salary of £200 a year in place of McGill. This was Francis France, then a young man in his middle twenties. He came from the Mains Colliery, Wigan, with the highest recommendations,[11] and was soon said to be 'doing very well'. Roby Pilkington thought it was 'a fortunate thing our getting him as many laxities had crept in down below'.[12] France continued in charge of the firm's colliery affairs until his death, thirty-seven years later.[13]

He was joined soon after his arrival by William Hopton, who had previously managed the nearby Croppers Hill Colliery, which had recently closed. Hopton, an older man, who had made a careful study of underground ventilation over a number of years, set about improving the flow of air in the workings even before the new tunnel was completed. He remained with Pilkingtons until 1870.[14] In an autobiographical volume, published years later, he recalled that when he went to the St Helens Colliery,

'the ventilation . . . was very bad. Only 19,000 ft. of air per minute passed through the workings and the mine gave off much explosive gas. The lamps in several parts were unsafe to work with, and the inspector found it necessary to stop some part of the mine. Gas came out of the workings now and then and filled the safety lamps hundreds of yards along the main pony roads. As soon as possible, however, I changed the up-cast shaft and split the ventilating current in parts; this increased the air from 19,000 to 40,000 feet per minute. The men then felt more safe and when I left the colliery [four years later] over five hundred miners presented me with a gold watch.'[15]

Events soon brought about a merger between the St Helens and the Ravenhead Colliery.[16] The latter was situated immediately to the south of the glassworks between the original pits of the St Helens Colliery and the newly-opened Alexandra Pit. The two concerns collaborated to maintain pumping engines at the disused Gerard's Bridge Colliery in order to keep their own coals dry,[17] but came into dispute over the right to work a certain seam.[18] Such a collision was inevitable when two companies were working in such a confined area. A merger was most desirable. In this matter Pilkington Brothers were in a much stronger position to take the initiative than were Bromilow Haddock & Co. Ltd.,[19] the proprietors of the Ravenhead Colliery. Roby Pilkington, lord of the manor of Sutton from 1860, had acquired extensive coalmines in that township from the heirs of the Bold family.[20] This allowed considerable extension of the St Helens colliery's workings to the southward. The fourteen acre piece of ground, leased by the firm in 1872, was available for surface extensions if required. On the other hand the Ravenhead company appears to have encountered some financial difficulties. It sustained losses on the year's working in 1869, 1870 and 1871[21] but was, presumably, saved by the great boom that developed after that.

The depression following the boom, however, hastened the amalgamation. By the beginning of 1876 the *Colliery Guardian*'s Liverpool correspondent reported 'the coal trade almost stagnant . . . prices drooping [*sic*] and, with a reduction offered, no more business resulting. . . . A reduction in wages must come and even with that, short time during the summer appears inevitable'.[22] As summer approached—on April 27th to be exact—there was an extraordinary meeting of the members of the Ravenhead Colliery Co. Ltd. to consent to the sale of their shares to a representative of the St Helens Collieries Co. Ltd., a company in process of formation which was to conduct both the Ravenhead and the St Helens collieries. The Ravenhead shareholders were to receive three £50 shares in the new company for each of their existing £100 shares together with £10,950 in 5 per cent. debentures.[24] The St Helens Collieries Co. Ltd. was registered on July 12th with a share capital of £500,000.[25] On the following day the directors of the new company held their first meeting. In addition to the four Pilkington partners, there were present: David Bromilow, H. J. Bromilow and James Haddock—the sons of William Bromilow and Thomas Haddock, founders of Bromilow, Haddock and Co.—and David Gamble, the chemical manufacturer, who became a director of the Ravenhead Colliery some time after his marriage to James Haddock's sister, Elizabeth. The minutes show that the old Ravenhead directors only attended these meetings for two years. After 1878 directors' meetings were confined to members of the Pilkington family.

Pilkingtons' fuel requirements were, by the 1870s, very considerable. In 1872, for instance, they burned about 75,000 tons at the Grove Street works. With later extensions there and the new factory at Cowley Hill, the glassworks' demand must have increased greatly from then onwards. Output from the two collieries could easily meet this demand. In 1880 the St Helens Colliery produced over 91,000 tons in six months and the Ravenhead nearly 112,000. The latter continued to make a loss but the former remained profitable. And this was after Pilkingtons had obtained coal for their glassworks at preferential rates.[23]

At their second meeting, on July 20, 1876, the directors resolved that Pilkingtons should be supplied with fuel at the lowest prices in each month. On
August 3rd coal cost the firm 8/– a ton, blend 7/– and slack—used in the Siemens gas producers—only 4/4. The price for slack was 5d a ton less than that
quoted to Bibby's Copper Works even closer to the collieries than Pilkingtons.
The advantage of this cheap fuel becomes even more evident in a minute
recorded on November 10, 1876:

> 'Messrs Chance Bros. of Birmingham would not take any more of our coal at the
> price quoted . . . 10/9 per ton delivered in our wagons.'

There could hardly be more eloquent testimony to the importance of Pilkingtons' coalmines to their glass business.

It was customary for the coal proprietors of the St Helens district to operate a
brickworks in conjunction with their collieries, the clay brought up from underground being well suited for brickmaking. The directors of the Ravenhead
Colliery Ltd., for instance, decided in 1872 to start such a brickworks and 'to
mix the stuff from the Pits with the field clay'.[26] Pilkingtons had a brickworks
before this: it is referred to in the Board Minutes in 1865.[27] Two years later
Thomas Pilkington was urging 'that we should make the most of the present
opportunity to get rid of the machine and works altogether, being neither worth
our time nor trouble',[28] but a new manager, Isaac Whitehead, was engaged[29] and
the brickworks appears thereafter to have become a more profitable concern. Its
original location, according to an old employee, George Blake, who remembered
it in the early 1870s, was 'near Groves's Colliery, between the dam and Sherdley
Road'.

CHAPTER 13

INTERNATIONAL, TECHNICAL AND OTHER
DEVELOPMENTS, 1900-1914

A FTER the ten-month strike of Belgian sheet glassmakers in 1900-1, this branch of the industry entered a new phase. The Belgian manufacturers, who had previously undercut their way into the world's markets, now became more favourably disposed towards curbing competition and securing a measure of stability. It is significant that, immediately after the great strike had ended, the American Window Manufacturers' Association (which controlled most of the United States' production[1]) saw fit to send a representative to Brussels to propose the formation of a Belgian glass syndicate in which the Americans were to hold upwards of one-third of the capital. The Belgians' sympathetic reaction to his overtures was indicative of the new situation. The attitude of the men, reported *The Times* correspondent, was 'largely responsible for the readiness with which Belgian manufacturers have responded to the advances made by the trust'.[2] Despite optimistic forecasts, however, these particular negotiations seem to have come to nothing. Belgian exports of window glass in 1902 reached a record figure, and shipments to Britain rose to nearly 1,450,000 cwt. In the following year there was a slight fall, due to a reduction in demand from the main consuming countries.[3] This course was accelerated in the following year (1904); in the case of Britain, the building cycle was by then swinging sharply downwards, as may be seen from graph 9 on page 156. Belgian manufacturers tried to reduce their labour costs, and this brought their glassmakers out on strike once again. This second strike also dragged on for nearly a year. It ended, on June 1, 1905, with the men being obliged to return to work on their masters' terms.[4]

It was now the Belgian industry's turn to go through a period of crisis. In the following three years the British Consul-General in Brussels sent home the most gloomy reports on its condition. Profits were very low and several concerns failed. The majority of suppliers of raw materials combined to 'fix more or less regular prices, while the manufacturers are to a certain extent the victims of circumstance in the state of workmen's organizations. . . . It is estimated in some quarters that unless the window glass makers take a decisive step towards co-operation, the present situation of low prices and small returns will continue for a considerable period before the previous prosperity of the industry can be re-established'.[5] Already, in May 1906, the possibility of forming an association to regulate sales and prices was being considered,[6] but the only outcome appears to have been a syndicate, formed at the end of 1906, to regulate exports to the growingly important markets of the East and to Canada.[7] This step does not appear to have been then accompanied by understandings relating to other markets, and prices in Britain continued to fall until 1909, as may be seen from graph 8 on page 155. In that year, however, there was a 15 per cent. increase in wages in Belgium[8] and the price of Belgian glass was put up. British prices also began to rise after this, and in 1913 were one-third higher than they had been four years before.

The level of Belgian imports into Britain after 1906 remained remarkably steady and considerably below the peak of 1902.

IMPORTS OF WINDOW GLASS, 1902–13 ('000 CWT.)

	Total	Retained
1902	1,448	1,406
1903	1,386	1,355
1904	1,081	1,058
1906	1,389	1,374
1907	1,290	1,283
1908	1,225	1,217
1909	1,192	1,181
1910	1,211	1,202
1911	1,215	1,205
1912	1,332	1,321
1913	1,239	1,230

Source: Trade and Navigation Returns.

While the rise in Belgium's window glass imports was interrupted, Pilkingtons increased their output. Production of sheet glass, which had been running at between sixty and seventy million feet from 1895 to 1903, rose to between seventy and eighty million in the following decade, reaching eighty-four millions just before the First World War. Belgian competition still remained severe; but it was no longer on the increase.

In rolled plate and cathedral glass and in plate glass itself (polished plate), the changed circumstances in Belgium led to direct arrangements between British and foreign manufacturers.

It was in rolled plate and cathedral glass that Chances' great strength still lay. In 1895 they had begun to negotiate with the Glasgow [Rolled] Plate Glass Company, which operated their patent under licence, for the formation of a joint limited company. (This Glasgow concern, on the Forth-Clyde canal at

Firhill, had been built in 1872, the leading promoter being Anthony Dixon Brogan, a man who had previously had Dumbarton connexions.) The talks between Chances and the Glasgow firm failed at that time but were successfully resumed in 1907. At first the vendors, Brogan and Mallock, were retained as managers but in 1911 Chances took over the works entirely.[9]

In 1904, Chances acted as intermediaries between the continental manufacturers of rolled plate and cathedral glass (who in that year had formed La Convention Internationale des Verres Spéciaux) and the other two makers of these products in Britain, Pilkingtons and the Glasgow firm. Although the actual agreement of August 1904 does not survive, it is clear from correspondence at Chances[10] that it came into force at the beginning of 1905; concerned imports of these types of glass into Britain and involved payment of compensation to the continental manufacturers (£5,600 in the first year and £6,300 in the second); applied also to the South American market in the first instance, and was, in 1906, extended to certain other neutral markets. The agreement lapsed in 1910 but liaison between Britain and the Continent was not entirely lost: in 1912, Chances, feeling the full effects of Pilkington competition, sold some of their shares to the St Gobain Company.[11]

Pilkingtons' records do not suggest that this Anglo-Continental agreement of 1905–10 bestowed any particular benefit upon them. Production of both rolled plate and cathedral glass continued to grow substantially but prices did not rise; indeed, in the case of cathedral glass, they continued to fall. Of much greater importance were reduced production costs after the manufacture of tank-made cathedral glass was begun at Ravenhead in 1903–4.

An international association of manufacturers of plate glass was also formed in August 1904. This arose out of a meeting in Brussels attended by representatives of the plate glassworks of Belgium (including the Courcelles factory which was American-owned), Germany, France, the United Kingdom, Italy, Austria-Hungary and the Netherlands. The Plate Glass Convention, then formed, set up a central office in Brussels. Prices were soon advanced by 25 per cent.,[12] and in 1907 the British Consul-General in Belgium reported that the Convention had decided 'to keep the supply at a level with the demand and do away with the bad results of over-production by settling upon certain days when work shall not be carried on during the month'.[13] In the following year, when exports to America, which had picked up since 1900, fell off once again,[14] M. Delloye of the St Gobain Co. proposed another method of regulating output to representatives from factories in the United Kingdom, Austria, Belgium, France and Germany, who met at the Grand Hotel in London. Each company was to be allowed to operate a fixed area of grinding surface. This stimulated efficiency in that it encouraged manufacturers to improve their grinding methods. There was much haggling by each concern to obtain as large a quota as possible. While this was proceeding, Pilkingtons made the most of their bargaining counters. At Maubeuge they possessed a factory within the continental manufacturers' own ring fence. In Britain they owned the former London and Manchester Company's works at Sutton Oak which, if brought back into production, could upset the syndicate's plans. The foreign manufacturers certainly showed some fear of what they referred to as 'le Manchester'.[15] Pilkingtons' success in these negotiations is indicated by the considerable fall in plate glass imports in and after 1908 when compared with those of previous years.

IMPORTS OF PLATE GLASS, 1901–13 ('000 CWT.)

1901	464	1908	328
1902	413	1909	331
1903	451	1910	308
1904	478	1911	332
1905	420	1912	352
1906	390	1913	443
1907	406		

Source: Trade and Navigation Returns.

The rise in imports after 1910 suggests that arrangements with the plate glass Convention broke down in that year, about the same time as the collapse of the rolled plate and cathedral glass syndicate. Pilkingtons' production figures would seem to confirm this for, after growing rapidly from 1908–11 when imports had levelled off, they themselves then levelled off while imports grew. The Ravenhead works, acquired by Pilkingtons, as we have seen, in 1901, made a useful contribution to their plate glass output; but it was from Cowley Hill that most of the additional production came.

PILKINGTONS' OUTPUT OF PLATE GLASS DURING THE YEARS ENDED JUNE 30, 1904–14

Year ending June 30	Footage (i) at Cowley Hill	(ii) at Ravenhead
1904	5,308,045	1,450,210
1905	5,522,453	1,676,721
1906	6,282,328	2,044,734
1907	7,022,198	2,422,908
1908	8,524,394	2,238,551
1909	10,320,843	2,430,832
1910	11,828,663	2,456,688
1911	13,925,992	2,397,030
1912	12,309,611	2,199,726
1913	14,093,125	2,779,238
1914	13,436,589	572,429

During these years the Cowley Hill works became very profitable and were, for a time, contributing more to the company's profits than was the Grove

Street factory. While price stability was certainly partly responsible for this, the chief explanation is to be found in lower production costs.

PROFITS OF THE GROVE STREET AND COWLEY HILL WORKS DURING THE YEARS ENDED JUNE 30, 1904–14, TOGETHER WITH AVERAGE PRICES AND COSTS OF PLATE GLASS IN THE FIRST HALF OF EACH YEAR.

Year ending June 30	Profit from Grove Street £	Profit from Cowley Hill £	Average price of plate glass d. per ft.	Average cost of plate glass d. per ft.
1904	139,392	6,898	10·91	10·22
1905	185,400	Loss 5,432	9·51	9·59
1906	182,536	38,531	10·32	9·39
1907	142,176	88,331	10·97	8·15
1908	88,999	97,588	10·53	7·68
1909	79,282	126,351	10·21	7·25
1910	85,368	170,801	10·60	7·31
1911	76,289	195,802	9·63	6·46
1912	80,339	137,321	9·70	6·77
1913	149,636	147,606	9·99	6·87
1914	158,420	145,786	11·43	7·67

Greater efficiency at Cowley Hill was the result of much carefully invested capital. As we have noticed, £100,000 were spent on these works in the nine years from 1895 to 1903. To this sum, in the eleven years from 1904 to 1914, nearly £620,000 were added. The most important single innovation was the substitution of lehrs for annealing kilns. For this, Cecil Pilkington, one of Windle Pilkington's sons, was responsible. He had joined the firm in 1897 after having been educated at Shrewsbury and Oxford, where he read Natural Science. Although several plate glass lehrs had already been built in the United States,[16] none had as yet come into use in Europe. In February 1901, assisted by Leonard Lackland, a graduate of Liverpool, Cecil Pilkington began work on a pilot plant at the recently-acquired Ravenhead works, using a tray lehr for these experiments. With the aid of an electrical recording pyrometer, one of the first to be used in Britain, he was able to regulate the temperature fall in the tunnel with sufficient accuracy to produce properly annealed glass. The pilot plant at Ravenhead having served its purpose, in 1904 a larger Cruickshank rod-type lehr was built at Cowley Hill with great secrecy.[17] This reduced the time of annealing from four days to four or five hours. The original lehr was subsequently modified and others built. By 1907 there were three in operation. Before 1914 thermo-couples and resistance pyrometers had been introduced.[18]

Technical improvements were also made in the other stages of plate glass manufacture. Grinding machinery was given particular attention and this became all the more important immediately after 1908, when the quota system was introduced, based on a fixed grinding area. At the end of 1905, Pilkingtons embarked upon a £100,000 scheme for making the finishing processes more efficient and considerable additions kept being made to the scheme, which involved a large amount of electrification.[19] The old 22 ft. diameter grinding tables were gradually replaced by tables of 35 ft., each driven by its own electric motor, and the footage was thereby increased from 400 to 1,060 per table. The pot capacity of furnaces was increased from sixteen to twenty. Potmaking itself was improved. French clays, imported *via* Maubeuge, began to be used about 1905, and from 1907 Edwin Hopkinson's systematic research and development transformed potmaking into a scientific process. Casting, too, came in for attention. In November 1913, the firm paid £3,000 for the use of a Belgian-designed *défourneuse*, an electrically-operated crane equipped with tongs for gripping each pot and carrying it to the casting table. Two such cranes were installed; but they were cumbersome, and further improvement was later made by suspending the pot tongs from an overhead crane. Improved mechanization of the roller and table enabled plates to be cast which were not only longer but also more uniform in thickness. This meant much less waste, and a further saving in grinding time. $\frac{3}{4}''$ plate, which had previously been cast 12 mm. thick to allow for surface irregularities, could now be made 10·6 mm. thick and was later cast even thinner.

Progress was also made in embossing, brilliant cutting, bevelling and bending. Bending and embossing were introduced at Cowley Hill in 1900. This work had previously been undertaken by dealers, but so many of them were by this time using foreign glass—the London firm of Farmiloe even had their own schooner to bring it over—that Pilkingtons decided to go into competition with them. Henry Enever, a London glass bender, joined the firm in 1902 and reorganized the bending department which had been started three years before. New kilns were built which reduced the time taken to bend a plate of glass from twenty hours to an hour and a half. The introduction of the Offenbacher machine also speeded up the process of bevelling straight edges.[20]

Until 1909 the large, cumbersome and very fragile plates of glass had to be carried by hand without any mechanical assistance. In that year a flexible pneumatic grip was introduced and at the end of 1911 the sum of £619 was allocated for purchasing 'cranes etc. in connexion with the scheme for putting the glass on horses and running the horses to the table'.[21] The pneumatic grip was not satisfactory and in 1913 F. B. Waldron, the engineer at Cowley Hill, invented sucker pads, exhausted by a vacuum pump and suspended from an overhead crane. St Gobain held a patent for a similar, but inferior, device—it was never used in England—but they agreed, for a small consideration, not to interfere with what was being done at Cowley Hill.[22]

Most of the new machinery for the cranes, as well as for the grinding and polishing, was worked by electricity. The old power station with its gas engines could not meet the increasing demand, and it was decided to install a completely new 4,500 kw generating set. After three weeks of frantic activity and much last-minute anxiety, this was finished in time to be started up on July 8, 1913, by King George V.

Pilkingtons' sheet glass factory was increased further in size around the turn of the century and, in 1904, a Belgian writer was able to describe it as 'la plus puissante . . . du monde entier'.[23] These extensions at Grove Street were made possible by the closing of the Ravenhead spur of the canal, permitted by Act of Parliament in 1898. The construction of Canal Street on part of the site enabled the firm to make out a good case for closing that part of Grove Street which ran through the works; the two streets ran parallel to each other and there was no need for both. The filling in of the canal also gave access across Canal Street to Greenbank, and between 1899 and 1902 Pilkingtons made some fifty purchases of property in the Greenbank area. The timber yard was removed to this new site. The vacated timber yard and the closed section of Grove Street left room for the erection of a fourth warehouse and more tank furnaces; there were twenty-three altogether by this time. Some of the pot and block makers, who had previously occupied twelve pot rooms at the otherwise disused Eccleston Street factory, moved down to Grove Street in 1899 and others went to Cowley Hill. The people of St Helens were no longer regaled with the sight of large glassmaking pots being carried through the town on specially-constructed chariot-like vehicles.

If the later nineteenth century witnessed great changes in furnace design and in annealing, the early twentieth was to see considerable changes in the methods by which the molten glass was blown into cylinders. The forerunner to these, as we have noticed (page 146), was an appliance to assist glassmakers to blow the heaviest of cylinders, which was developed by Windle Pilkington, with the assistance of John J. Wenham, in 1870–1. But in 1887 there was only one such machine per tank and by 1900 there were only two. It was not until George Hyde, the works manager, with the assistance of Joseph Wilson, a fitter, had developed a lighter machine[24]—known as 'the bicycle'—that machine blowing became general.

Of much greater importance was the introduction of what came to be known as the drawn cylinder process. This had two results: much larger cylinders of window glass could be made than before and fewer skilled glassmakers were needed.

A flanged metal disc (or 'pipe') on the end of a large blowpipe was dipped into molten glass in a specially constructed pot which was filled from a tank before each drawing with sufficient glass to make one cylinder. As this bait was slowly raised between guiding shafts, it drew up the glass with it. Compressed air, passed through the blowpipe, was blown in at such a rate as would maintain

17 Pilkingtons' head office photographed from across the Canal, *c.* 1900

18 The drawn cylinder process. (Inset shows the start of the draw of a cylinder
and the main illustration lowering a finished cylinder.) (Copyright Pilkington
Brothers Limited)

the diameter constant. By this method, a cylinder of glass could be drawn 25' long and 24" diameter. Later types of machine were able to manufacture cylinders of more than 40' long and 30" diameter. (By comparison, hand blown cylinders were usually about 5' long and 12" diameter.) These machines only blew the glass; afterwards the giant cylinders had to be cut up into smaller lengths, flattened in the usual way and then annealed.

The development of this process to the point where it could be used commercially was beset by difficulties. Three conditions had to be satisfied if it was to be successful. The molten glass in the pot had to be kept at exactly the right temperature; the bait had to be raised at exactly the right speed; and the air had to be blown in at exactly the right rate. Satisfactory results were achieved only after expenditure of much time and vast amounts of capital. But it was the time and capital of a huge American combine and not of Pilkingtons.

John H. Lubbers, an American who had been a glass flattener, began experiments in the early 1890s and subsequently took out several patents for drawing cylinders. He succeeded in interesting the American Window Glass Company in his ideas and they financed his research. In 1903 the American Window Glass Machine Company was incorporated as a subsidiary to acquire Lubbers' patents and develop the process for commercial use. Pilkingtons were already in touch with the promoters of the new machine in June 1903 but, as a result of independent advice from someone who had just returned from America, they decided not to proceed with negotiations until Lubbers, whom their informant described as 'a clever man but generally drunk', had developed his machine further.[25] After two years' work, some glass was being produced by the machine which could compete with that blown by hand.[26] But Windle Pilkington, who went to America to see the process in operation, returned with the opinion that the glass produced was not yet of sufficient quality for the British market.[27] Further development was required. The General Manager of the American Window Glass Company later confessed that 'millions of dollars' were spent in perfecting the machine; a loss had been piled up 'that would have staggered a banker.'[28]

Pilkingtons preferred to bide their time and observe these costly experiments as onlookers. Windle Pilkington later explained to the men how the firm 'kept a watch upon what was going on and had the glass over to look at it. They themselves [i.e. the Americans] continued to work in the United States and occasionally took orders in Canada where the glass seemed more suitable than for European markets'.[29] A change in the British patent laws, however, which required that a patent be worked within three years if it was to remain valid,[30] caused the Americans to make overtures to Pilkingtons. As Windle Pilkington explained:

'In 1906 they tried to get the Canadian Tariff raised to shut out European glass but fortunately they have not been successful. After the passing of the new English Patent Act they approached us to ask if we would purchase their patent for England. They had either to work the patent here themselves or let someone else do so, and so they approached us first informing us that they were negotiating with several other people. At their invitation, Mr Cecil went over to see the process, and on his return we settled that if we could come to terms (which would prevent their upsetting the glass trade here) it was the best thing to do. This was not easy, as they had no interest in the glass trade here and their one idea was to get their process worked as widely as possible.'

The Board minutes give further details of these negotiations, though not of the agreement that was eventually reached. The report of Cecil Pilkington, to which his father referred, was given to the other directors on November 24, 1908. It resulted in a telegram being sent to J. Thorpe, Pilkingtons' agent in Canada, which read:

'Go Pittsburgh. Tell American Window Glass Co. we are prepared to consider proposition. Get terms exclusive and non-exclusive rights.'

A draft agreement was drawn up on February 2, 1909, and at the Board meeting on April 2nd, Cecil Pilkington and Edward Cozens-Hardy were authorized 'to proceed to the U.S.A. and finally to settle and conclude the negotiations and arrangements with the Window Glass Machine Company and American Window Glass Company, with full power to make such variations in the agreement of February 2, 1909, as they may think desirable. . . .' The formal agreement was signed by the two directors on April 22nd and a licence was granted to Pilkingtons five days later giving them the right to work the drawn cylinder process in Britain and Canada.[31]

Pilkingtons lost little time in setting up an experimental machine. This was built in the rolled plate department at Grove Street in October 1909, under the supervision of R. F. Taylor. Several improvements were made to the American model by Windle Pilkington,[32] notably the replacement of the block tap, employed for regulating the inflow of compressed air, by a needle valve. Eight machines were brought into commercial operation on May 2, 1910, and others were started in April 1912. There was no question, at this stage, of the machine-made glass driving the hand-blown glass off the market, because the quality of the former was poor. As the manager of an American hand-operated plant put it: 'The machines make more poor glass . . . but they make so much more glass that they can pick out a great deal of good glass and sort it very carefully.'[33]

Pilkingtons' development of the American model appears to have led to some friction between them and the licence owners. In March 1912, a supplemental agreement was negotiated. This took account of 'certain questions of dispute and differences of opinion', and included as its first clause:

'Pilkington Brothers Limited shall grant to the Empire Machine Company (a subsidiary of the American Window Glass Company) free from royalty, the exclusive licence in all parts of the world outside of the United Kingdom of Great Britain and Canada to manufacture, use or sub-licence the use of all patents for improvements relating to the cylinder process (including kiln firing), which are now or hereafter may be owned or controlled by Pilkington Brothers Limited . . .'

It continued:

'As to any future improvements in said cylinder process which may be made or acquired by Pilkington Brothers Limited . . . the said Pilkington Brothers Limited shall, before publishing the same or taking any steps which would impair the right to obtain patents upon said improvements in other countries, communicate the same to the Empire Machine Company, with notice stating in what countries Pilkington Brothers Limited have applied or intend to apply for patents upon such improvements . . .'

The fourth clause of the supplemental agreement related to Pilkingtons' right to work the process in Canada. Entries in the Board Minutes make it clear that the firm was apprehensive lest their failure to do this should lead to the invalidation of their patent rights there. On June 8, 1911, for instance, the minutes refer to:

'Canadian working. Macmaster's opinion. Not safe to stand as we are—must work it twice a year—get them to work it over there.'

According to the supplemental agreement:

'Pilkington Brothers Limited shall at their own expense carry out such workings in Canada of all patents relating to the cylinder process owned by the Empire Machine Company . . . as may be required by a statement of the steps reasonably necessary to comply with the requirements of the Canadian patent laws as agreed between the patent attorneys of the Empire Machine Company and Pilkington Brothers Limited, or, failing such agreement, as settled by a disinterested patent agent or attorney nominated by the Senior Justice of the Canadian Court of Exchequer.'

On November 18, 1912, a letter was read to the Board 're Taylor and Railton's account of Canadian sites'. A site was eventually selected on the Niagara peninsula, at Thorold. Detailed plans were considered by the Board on April 1, 1913, the cost—£50,000—being then considered 'very high'. The factory was completed just before the outbreak of the First World War.

Canada also became increasingly important as a market for glass made at St Helens as Pilkingtons' export drive was further developed. Under its recently-introduced tariff, the dominion gave preference to British imports and had become Britain's most important single oversea market for glass. Exports of all kinds of glass to Canada increased in annual value from just over £50,000 in the early 1890s to £237,000 in 1906. Of this, plate glass exports, worth some £28,000 a year in 1890–4, were worth £65,000 in 1906.[34] Pilkingtons built new Canadian depots. In addition to those at Montreal and Toronto, dating from before 1900, they opened new warehouses at Vancouver in 1903, Winnipeg in 1906 and Calgary in 1912. In South America, where the company had a particularly resourceful agent, Thomas Holt, a warehouse was put in hand at Buenos Aires in 1907.[35] In Europe, a depot in Rome was added to those in Paris and Naples.

As the scale of the company's business grew, so the size of the office staff increased. In 1909 additional office accommodation was approved.[36] Within the expanding office, much specialization was taking place. The order department, for instance, was separated from the ledger work.[37] A careful system of costing was gradually evolved and costing was elevated to the status of a separate department in 1913, much to the resentment of many of the die-hards who could see no point in (what they looked upon as) taking money out of one pocket only to put it into another. On the sales side, greater emphasis was laid upon the standardization of qualities. When one new employee went to work as a cutter at Cowley Hill in 1902, he found that—

> 'the men working at the various tables had not (officially) the remotest idea what quality of glass each was turning out, there then being no such policy of standardization of quality. Each sorter and cutter had his own ideas of quality and worked to them in his own way.'[38]

Such a haphazard method of working was replaced by strict standards, which must have given greater satisfaction to customers. So, too, did the practice, introduced early in the present century, of sending specialists from the works—not the office—to attend to complaints.

The early years of the twentieth century also witnessed the three sounds which have become so familiar in the modern office: the clatter of typewriters, the ringing of telephone bells and the chatter of girls' voices, none of which was often heard prior to 1900. At the beginning of 1907, Pilkingtons decided to employ 'two typewriting girls'.[39] This number was soon increased and by 1912 the firm was turning more and more to the new source of labour. A Board minute passed in the autumn of 1912 has a distinctly modern flavour about it:

> 'Telephone. Partners not to be unreasonably troubled. Someone of good education needed in telephone room to take confidential partners' messages. Question of having a girl for this was discussed—also of employing more girls generally and of using them for the night work.'

The firm's trainee system appears to have originated during this period. One such trainee, who came to Ravenhead in 1912, was R. M. Weeks, now Lord Weeks. He had just graduated at Cambridge and was singled out by the University Appointments Board as the type of man for whom Pilkingtons were looking. Two years later, when the firm was seeking an agent for the United States market, they again decided to find and train 'a new man of university type'.[40] With the continued growth of the business, Pilkingtons came to lean more and more heavily upon these men.

During the period from July 1903 to July 1914 all of Pilkingtons' factories were highly profitable, the only loss being that already noticed at Cowley Hill in 1904–5. Even the newly-acquired Ravenhead works, which had lost over £30,000 from the time it was taken over early in 1901 up to July 1903, started to make a profit from then onwards. Most of this came from the cathedral glass made there rather than from plate glass.

Although profits were higher during this period than in the previous years, the bonuses on shares were considerably smaller. In the eight years 1895–6 to 1902–3, £520,000 had been distributed in bonuses; in the eleven years 1903–4 to 1913–14, £500,000 were distributed in this way.

DISPOSAL OF PROFIT IN THE YEARS ENDED JUNE 30, 1904–1914

Year ended June 30	Profit	Directors' salaries, fees and expenses	Income tax	Debenture interest £30,000 and ordinary dividend £40,000 paid annually	Bonus on shares	Balance retained in company for development
1904	£172,564	£16,980	£13,123		Nil	£72,461
1905	255,218	16,297	11,960		£ 60,000	96,961
1906	319,808	17,100	8,157		60,000	164,551
1907	341,963	18,105	8,941		20,000	224,917
1908	306,223	17,287	12,241		30,000	176,695
1909	256,992	13,956	13,955		10,000	149,081
1910	322,960	15,557	17,442		40,000	179,961
1911	375,492	16,403	15,202		60,000	213,887
1912	331,926	17,220	13,773		70,000	160,933
1913	432,685	18,313	18,195		110,000	216,177
1914	400,026	15,896	19,512		40,000	254,618

Not only was less distributed to shareholders, but company investment in stocks and shares ceased to rise as it had formerly done. Of the total so invested, which reached £471,000 in the peak year 1911–12, less than £100,000 was placed in other glass manufacturing enterprises. Half of this (£52,500) was in the Empire Machine Company, some £35,000 was in Maubeuge and some £10,000 in four other continental concerns. The rest was invested in other business enterprises and in public utilities, particularly in North and South America.

These years saw the active direction of the company pass from the second generation of the Pilkington family to the third. Roby Pilkington died in April 1903[41] and his brother, Thomas, became a consultative director from the end of 1898, spending much of the rest of his life on his estate in the north of Scotland and at Bournemouth, where he died in 1925[42]. This left their two younger cousins, Windle and Richard, as the senior partners at St Helens. Richard Pilkington died in March 1908[43] and his elder brother, Windle, in March 1914.[44] Three of the four partners of the second generation left substantial fortunes, each over £500,000: Richard Pilkington £692,858 gross; Windle Pilkington £589,785; and Thomas Pilkington £688,578. Roby Pilkington left only £107,658 but he, presumably, had transferred most of his fortune to his sons before his death. He had already begun to do so in 1885, as we have noticed (page 171).

While much of Pilkingtons' success was due to the vigorous sales promotion abroad, for which Thomas and, particularly, Richard Pilkington were responsible, it is Windle Pilkington who emerges as the outstanding partner of the second generation. In his fifty-six years at the works, he was responsible for making Pilkingtons the most technically advanced glass firm in the country at a time when technological progress was a prerequisite of survival. Though he took out, in all, more than fifty patents, he cannot be called an inventor in the sense that Siemens or Bessemer were inventors; but he was an astonishingly successful developer and improver. To him alone must go the credit for Pilkingtons' early development of tank furnaces; and from this innovation was derived the firm's advantage in sheet glass manufacture which helped it to weather the crisis at the turn of the century when the competition in plate glass became much fiercer. Windle Pilkington, together with his brother, Richard, also played a very active part in local affairs. After nearly thirty years' service, he became a Lieutenant-Colonel in the Volunteers in 1888 and, on his retirement in 1902, was succeeded by his brother. Between them they established Pilkingtons' link with the volunteer forces which has since become a tradition; the close connexion between certain of the directors and employees of the company is still maintained with the Territorial Army. Both brothers took an active part in local government, becoming Mayors of St Helens (in Richard Pilkington's case for three years) and were rewarded for their services by being made aldermen and freemen. Richard Pilkington became M.P. for the Newton Division from 1899 to 1906. Windle Pilkington was a pillar of the local Congregational Church, as his father had been before him. He was well known for his benevolence. As a young man he helped to found a Ragged School in the town, and was later an enthusiastic supporter of the Y.M.C.A., the St Helens Hospital and the St Helens and District Nursing Association.

Roby Pilkington was also interested in local affairs. He intervened effectively in the negotiations which led up to the incorporation of St Helens in 1868, but then his interest turned to politics generally rather than to local government as such. He was a very keen Conservative and was chairman of the local Conservative Association from its beginnings in 1868. He refused to stand, in 1885, as parliamentary candidate for the newly-formed borough seat, but supported the candidacy of his son-in-law, Henry Seton-Karr. Among the Salisbury Papers at Christ Church, Oxford, are two letters, dated 1889 and 1892, from Seton-Karr to Lord Salisbury, the Prime Minister, urging Roby Pilkington's claim to a baronetcy. This claim was made partly on the grounds that 'no glass manufacturer had yet been honoured with a baronetcy, though representatives of nearly all the other great mercantile firms had been so honoured', and partly because it was to Roby Pilkington's support that the Conservative Club of St Helens 'owed its existence and present financial soundness'. 'Peerages', Seton-Karr added, 'have often been given for smaller services than his'. He was at pains to stress that these approaches were entirely unsolicited by his father-in-law, 'who is the last man to advocate his own merits'. Confirmation of this was contained in a third letter, which followed soon after the second. This informed Lord Salisbury that 'for urgent family reasons'—which are not disclosed—his father-in-law would decline the honour even if it were offered.[45]

The departure of the second generation from the company changed, for a time, the balance of participation in the business by the two branches of the family. In the third generation of directors, the descendants of Windle and Richard Pilkington were much more strongly represented than were those of their cousins, Roby and Thomas. The change came about in this way. Both of Roby Pilkington's sons, William Lee Pilkington and George Herbert Pilkington, retired from active management at the beginning of 1907, aged 60 and 59 respectively, though both were brought back from their retirement during the First World War. The only representative from this branch of the family came from the fourth generation. This was G. H. Pilkington's son, Geoffrey Langton Pilkington, who, after an education at Eton and Oxford, entered the works in 1909 at the age of 24. Thomas Pilkington's eldest son, Thomas (b. 1876), was killed in the Boer War and only his second son, Alan Douglas Pilkington, who had also been to Eton and Oxford, joined the firm. He entered it in 1904 and became secretary of the company from 1907-8 and again from 1913-19.[46] There were thus only two members of this side of the family in the business at this time.

On the other side of the family, three of Richard Pilkington's sons went into the firm: Arthur Richard, William Norman (who took the place of another brother, Ernest Sinclair, who joined the army at the time of the Boer War and did not return to the firm[47]) and Guy Reginald, who arrived at the same time as Geoffrey Langton Pilkington, in 1909.[48] Only two of Windle Pilkington's four sons lived to succeed him in the business. Henry William, who, like his twin, Richard Austin, joined the firm in 1894, soon fell ill with lung trouble, and had to retire. This was a shock to everyone, for he had previously seemed very fit and strong; at Oxford, for instance, he had distinguished himself both as an athlete and as a rowing man. He did not recover from his illness and died in December 1902.[49] Windle Pilkington was unable to turn to his third son, Sidney, for Sidney, an artist, was known to be delicate. He died in 1905.[50] In these circumstances the youngest son, Alfred Cecil, was brought in as we have seen.[51] Windle Pilkington later introduced a brother of his daughter-in-law into the business as his third nominee—the first director not to bear the name of Pilkington. In 1903 his son Austin had married Miss Hope Cozens-Hardy, younger daughter of Sir Herbert Hardy Cozens-Hardy of Letheringsett Hall, Holt, Norfolk, then a Lord Justice of Appeal, shortly to be made Master of the Rolls, and, in 1914, to be created the first Baron Cozens-Hardy. In October 1908, Mrs Austin Pilkington's brother, Edward Herbert Cozens-Hardy, became a member of the Board. He was an electrical engineer by profession and partner in O'Gorman and Cozens-Hardy, consulting engineers of London, who already advised Pilkingtons on electrical matters. The new director was to succeed to the barony on the death of his elder brother in 1924. He joined the Board just after the death of Richard Pilkington had deprived the company of its commercial head; and shortly after his arrival, there was a further alarm when Austin Pilkington, who had become his uncle Richard's right-hand man on the commercial side, became seriously ill and, on his recovery, was advised to live abroad 'for some considerable time' as the only hope of recovery.[52] For yet another of Windle Pilkington's sons to be struck down in this way came as a considerable shock; but, fortunately, a prolonged residence in Colorado was effective and the patient recovered. He attended Board meetings again in the summer of 1912 and, in the autumn of that year, on his return to the U.S.A. for a further period, he was able to pay several visits to Canada in connexion with the new factory about to be built there. Had he died, the company would have been deprived of a member of the family whose abilities were to be of particular value during the war and, particularly, during the 1920s. As it was, he was sufficiently recovered to return to England for good on the death of his father in 1914 and thereafter to play an incessantly active part in developing the company's affairs.

The founders of the firm had no difficulty in choosing successors, for they both had numerous healthy sons. For the second generation, the problem of the succession was more difficult and control tended to fall more into the hands of the successors of Windle and Richard Pilkington. Whereas William Pilkington had been the more active of the founder partners, by the third generation it was upon the descendants of his elder brother, Richard, that chief responsibility for the firm's continued prosperity was to fall.

CHAPTER 14

EPILOGUE, 1914-1959

T HE purpose of this book has been to set down, as fully as surviving records permit, the story of Pilkington Brothers and the manufacture of window and plate glass in Britain up to 1914. From that year onwards we are dealing with events involving people who are still alive. Many of these later events are still too near to us to be viewed in just perspective. They must remain to be described *in extenso* by some future historian. For the present they may be presented in brief outline only.

The First World War interrupted the deluge of Belgian glass and turned a buyers' into a sellers' market: Pilkingtons' difficulties then lay in manufacturing, not in selling, their glass. Sources of high quality sand, needed for plate glass, had to be found and developed within Britain to replace supplies which had previously come from Belgium. A drive to recruit new labour, the employment of women on a larger scale, and much overtime were all needed to overcome the severe manpower shortage occasioned by the demands of the armed forces and munitions factories. Pilkingtons' very close connexion with the Territorial Army resulted in the immediate mobilization of hundreds of their employees and of members of the Pilkington family. Part of the Cowley Hill works was turned into a shell factory and some of the profit from making these munitions was devoted to building and equipping an emergency hospital at Ravenhead which received its first convoy of wounded early in 1917. By the close of that year more than £40,000 had been spent by Pilkingtons on this hospital.

The war saw the beginning of a new chapter in labour relations. The National Amalgamated Union of Labour (later a part of the General and Municipal Workers' Union) was recognized by the company in 1917 and, in August of the following year, the St Helens Plate and Sheet Glass Joint Industrial Council came into being, at first as a district council under the national council which the Ministry of Reconstruction had formed to cover the whole of the glass industry, and then, with the collapse of the national council, as an independent body. These developments were of first importance. They led to a much closer understanding between management and labour during the difficult times that followed the war.

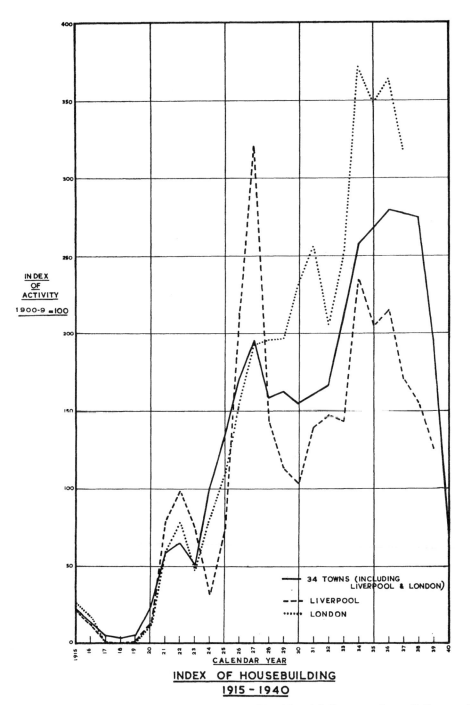

INDEX
OF
ACTIVITY

1900-9 = 100

400

350

300

250

200

150

100

50

0

34 TOWNS (INCLUDING
LIVERPOOL & LONDON)

- - - LIVERPOOL

······ LONDON

1915 16 17 18 19 20 21 22 23 24 25 26 27 28 29 30 31 32 33 34 35 36 37 38 39 40

CALENDAR YEAR

INDEX OF HOUSEBUILDING
1915 – 1940

Graph 11. Source: B. Weber, 'A New Index of Residential Construction, 1838–1950,'
Scottish Journal of Political Economy, June 1955

The post-war boom broke at the end of 1920. By that time—so the Joint Industrial Council was told—Belgian glass production had again reached its pre-war level. Pilkingtons entered a further period of intense competition and radical technical change. Competition cut prices, pared away profits, and made saving all the more difficult just when technical change made necessary a high level of investment. Under these circumstances it was particularly fortunate that the market for both sheet and plate glass grew rapidly. As may be seen from graph 11, housebuilding, stimulated by subsidies, had, by 1924, passed the average for the years 1900–9 (years of high activity) and, even in the darkest years of the depression, was 50 per cent. higher than the 1900–9 average. In addition, the growing motor industry provided a new outlet. At first, the few open tourers required only a small amount of plate glass for their windscreens; but, as the number of cars multiplied and the closed saloon became more popular, much larger quantities of glass went to the motor manufacturers and eventually sales of plate glass to them exceeded those for building. Moreover, the motor industry soon began to require safety glass, first laminated and then toughened. The fitting of safety glass in windscreens of British cars became compulsory from the beginning of 1932. Pilkingtons, by failing to acquire the Triplex Safety Glass Company Ltd[1] when that processing company was still a small and struggling concern, lost an opportunity to control the supply of glass to their most promising market, an opportunity which was taken elsewhere by their American and European counterparts. Nevertheless, Triplex soon became Pilkingtons' largest customer, and, in 1929, the two companies joined forces to form a Pilkington subsidiary under the name of Triplex (Northern) Ltd. In 1955 Pilkingtons surrendered control of this subsidiary in return for a greater interest in Triplex itself.

The technical changes of these years occurred first in plate, and then in sheet, and finally in the invention and development of float, glass. Plate glass, as we have seen, was made by a discontinuous process of casting from pots, then grinding on large circular discs, and finally polishing on the same discs. Glass manufacturers had long looked forward to the day when they could flow a ribbon of glass from a tank; in England, for instance, Chances had carried out large-scale experiments with Henry Bessemer in the middle of the nineteenth century;[2] but the search for this ideal had always ended in failure. A successful continuous process was eventually developed by the Ford Motor Company at Detroit. Their consumption of glass had grown to such proportions by the end of the First World War that Henry Ford decided to manufacture it himself. At Fords, intermittent production was, of course, unthinkable, and C. W. Avery, who was put in charge, started to experiment with methods of flowing glass continuously from a tank.[3] By the end of 1921 he had solved all the mechanical problems; but the tank was giving him a great deal of trouble and most of the glass produced was not up to standard. It was at this juncture that

Pilkingtons, who, as sheet glass manufacturers, already knew a great deal about tanks, made contact with Fords and were able to improve their glassmaking technique.

Meanwhile, as a result of F. B. Waldron's experiments at Cowley Hill, a continuous grinding and polishing system was being developed there. A continuous sequence of cast iron tables carried the rectangular plates of glass under a series of grinding heads with subsequent polishing under the same continuous line. One side of the glass was dealt with at a time. The first experimental model was running at the beginning of 1920, but much development lay ahead; it was not until May 1923 that this machine finally went into service. It featured in the negotiations between Pilkingtons and Fords. In return for technical assistance and details of this grinding and polishing machine, Pilkingtons obtained rights to the flow process, which they developed to their own needs.

This gave Pilkingtons an international advantage in plate glass manufacture by the middle of the 1920s. They were determined to keep this lead and were soon at work on further developing the finishing processes. What was needed was a machine which could grind and polish the ribbon of glass on both sides simultaneously as it emerged from the lehr and before it was cut into plates. A twin grinding process was finally developed in the early 1930s and came into service in 1935 at the Doncaster works (to be mentioned later) and in 1937 at Cowley Hill. The twin grinder first ran at 45″ per minute, but it was later improved until the ribbon of glass passed through it at the rate of 200″ per minute. It came to be used by all the principal manufacturers in the world for the greater part of their plate glass production, its use being essential to successful competition. These technical advances further consolidated Pilkingtons' powerful position as sole British producer by putting a premium on the size of glass manufacturing units. Today, the total plate glass demand of the British Commonwealth can be supplied from three tanks. The great size of the minimum economic unit and the capital risk positively forbid new starters in the industry unless they command very great resources.

The continuous rolling process was also soon in use for the manufacture of figured rolled patterns. A new method of making wired glass was developed, the wire netting being laid on a thin ribbon of glass on to which was fed a layer of molten glass, the whole then being passed between rollers. From the early 1930s only special colours, patterns, and thicknesses of figured rolled and rolled plate glass were still made by the old table method. The new process not only made glass more cheaply, but made it of better quality.

Continuous production of sheet glass did not reach St Helens until 1930. In this case, Pilkingtons lagged behind their competitors. There were already in existence two types of machine capable of making window glass by what came to be called the flat drawn process. In both of them the ribbon of glass was drawn straight out of the tank, thus avoiding the cylinder stage and the consequent splitting and flattening. In the Fourcault system, patented early in the century by Emile Fourcault, a Belgian, the glass was drawn upwards through a vertical lehr. In the Colburn system, invented in the United States by Irving W. Colburn and improved, after 1911, with the help of M. J. Owens, the ribbon of glass was carried upwards from the tank for a short distance and then, while still soft, bent over a roller and passed into a horizontal lehr. The Libbey-Owens Company was formed in 1916 to exploit this process on a commercial scale.[4]

Pilkingtons were in touch with Fourcault at an early stage in his experiments. In September 1903, they heard that his machine was drawing a sheet sixteen inches wide and twenty feet long but there were many defects in the glass. Windle Pilkington and his son, Austin, visited Charleroi towards the end of 1903 and, as a result of the visit, the Pilkington Board

> 'agreed to pay £8,000 for the machine for rolled plate, cathedral, fluted, and other kinds of glass except sheet glass and polished glass for the "British Empire". In return for our taking this risk, we are to have a royalty of half the rate compared to any other manufacturer in England, Germany, France and Belgium—outside these countries we pay the lowest royalty charged. As to the making of sheet, we have the option for 12 months. They asked £40,000 for the whole thing, but kept off sheet as much as possible. Austin will go over again before agreement finally drawn up . . .'

Something must have happened soon after this which caused Pilkingtons to have second thoughts about the proposed agreement. At the end of the following April, Fourcault wrote asking Pilkingtons to make up their minds before May 1st. They evidently did not sign any contract but, early in 1905, when Fourcault was said to be making 'something like 5,000 ft. per day' and the process was claimed to be 'a success for thin plate as well as sheet', negotiations were re-opened. On this occasion, however, Fourcault was distinctly unfriendly. According to the Pilkington Board Minutes, he 'had said they were rid of a very bad contract when we refused their offer'. Again, nothing seems to have come of the talks and Fourcault's efforts to develop this process continued for years after this before the machine could be relied upon to produce saleable glass. In 1907, for instance, the Pilkington Board noted that he was 'having a lot of trouble. His best run is 98 hours'.[5]

It was not until after the First World War—the early 1920s, in fact—that Pilkingtons began to feel the effect of competition in flat drawn glass made in Belgium, chiefly by Fourcault machines. The eventual introduction to Britain of the developed Fourcault process was not undertaken by Pilkingtons but by the British Window Glass Company, formed in 1919 with Clarence Hatry as its chairman. The company built a factory at Queenborough on the Isle of Sheppey, but went into liquidation at the end of 1924. The Queenborough factory was later acquired by Sheet Glass Ltd., who started to make Fourcault

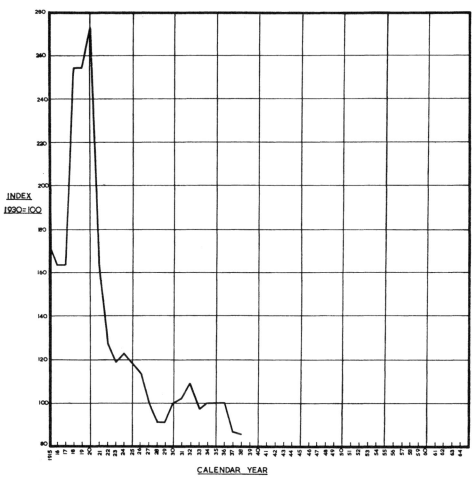

INDEX
1930=100

CALENDAR YEAR

INDEX OF PRICE OF WINDOW GLASS
1915 - 1938

Graph 12. Source: K. Maiwald, 'An Index of Building Costs in the United Kingdom, 1845–1938'. *Economic History Review*, December 1954

glass there in 1928; but the venture was unprofitable and production was stopped after a few months.

The competition of Belgian glass—much of which was sold, after 1927, through a single Fourcault *Comptoir*—drove prices down and down, as may be seen from graph 12. Pilkingtons, however, did not respond to this by installing either of the new processes. Cecil Pilkington, who was in charge of technical matters and had himself carried out various pilot experiments on flat drawn glass, was not at all convinced that the Fourcault machine was ideal; and an attempt in 1928 to acquire the British rights of the Colburn process failed. Pilkingtons had tried to reduce costs and improve quality by changing over from hand blowing and concentrating on their drawn cylinder production,[6] erecting a large new tank for this purpose in 1928. As output in Belgium continued to increase—much of it the product of recently-established factories outside the *Comptoir*—Belgian manufacturers themselves began to find the pace too stiff. Over-production led, in 1930, to the dissolution of the *Comptoir* and the formation of *L'Union des Verreries Mécaniques Belges* to take over all the Fourcault factories and control their production.[7] At St Helens, sheet glass manufacture could only be continued by subsidizing it out of profits from other departments: thus, again, Pilkingtons' strength lay in the diversification of their activities. At the turn of the century sheet glass remained profitable when plate glass ceased to be; now the position was reversed. But this economic drain could not go on for long; sales of an obsolescent product continued to fall. Pilkingtons were on the verge of abandoning sheet glass manufacture altogether when the successful development of a third continuous process completely changed the position.

This, the invention of an American of Russian origin named Slingluff, had been developed, during the 1920s, by the Pittsburgh Plate Glass Company, already the giant of the American plate glass industry before 1914, but not then particularly interested in sheet glass manufacture. This process differed from those of Fourcault and Colburn in an essential feature—the method of drawing the ribbon of glass from the tank—but was like the Fourcault machine in that it had a vertical lehr, thus being economical in the use of ground space. Cecil Pilkington was convinced that this was fundamentally a good process and Pilkingtons arranged to work the P.P.G. process in Britain. The first experimental attempts to draw glass at St Helens were made in March 1930; and as early as April 1931 Austin Pilkington could confidently describe the P.P.G. machine as 'really a winner'. In the following November the first four machines went into commercial operation. The drawn cylinder process was then rapidly abandoned; by the middle of 1933 all Pilkingtons' sheet glass at St Helens was made by P.P.G. machines.

Very soon the new sheet glass process was turning loss into profit; and the return to protection strengthened Pilkingtons' position still further. Sheet and plate glass were not included in the Abnormal Importation Orders of 1931; but, in March 1932, they became subject to an *ad valorem* import duty of 10 per cent. and, shortly afterwards, this 10 per cent. duty was raised to 15 per cent., at which figure it has remained ever since. The tariff encouraged Sheet Glass Ltd. to re-start their Fourcault machines at Queenborough; but, by the end of the year, losses were said to have reached £75,000,[8] and, in May 1933, the factory passed into Pilkingtons' hands. Pilkingtons continued to make Fourcault glass there.

The float process, the broad outline of which was made public in January 1959, extended the lead which Pilkingtons already held in plate glass manu-facture and also raised interesting possibilities concerning the future of all flat glass. Just as the *flow* process of the 1920s put an end to casting glass from pots and made possible continuous production of high quality glass, so the *float* process of the 1950s has taken the manufacture of this kind of glass a stage further by putting an end to surface grinding. It is a remarkable innovation, involving basic changes in methods of production and drawing scientists and technicians in the glass industry into hitherto unexplored territory.

Although, as we have seen, Pilkingtons had, during the inter-war years, greatly improved the method of finishing plate glass, first by the introduction of continuous grinding and then, in the 1930s, by the development of the twin grinder, the fundamental disadvantages involved in these finishing processes—dating back to the beginnings of cast plate glass manufacture in France at the end of the seventeenth century—still remained. The machinery for grinding and polishing had been made more efficient, but the whole principle of producing glass with an uneven surface and then removing these imperfections by grinding was obviously far from satisfactory. And, in the end, the polished plate glass was not so brilliant as naturally fire-finished glass which had been allowed to cool down on its own without touching anything solid while it was still soft. In plate glass manufacture the soft glass had to be passed between rollers to be formed into a ribbon in the first place. The imperfections of the roller surface were inevitably imprinted on the glass, leaving it rough and obscured. How could these imperfections be removed without grinding and polishing? Only if the glass were re-heated and allowed to cool without touching anything solid. How could this be done?

Pilkingtons—and no doubt manufacturers in other countries—had for long been pondering over this question. It began to attract the attention of a new-comer to the company, Alastair Pilkington, a member of a branch of the family which had not previously been connected with the glass industry. He joined Pilkingtons in 1947 after taking a Mechanical Science degree at Cambridge, and, in 1950, took charge of production at one of their plate glass factories. In October 1952 he began to explore the possibilities of using liquid metal as a means of supporting the uneven and obscured ribbon of glass which emerged from the rollers. In his own words:

19 The twin grinder and polisher at the Cowley Hill works in 1944. (Copyright Pilkington Brothers Limited)

20   The flat drawn process. (Copyright Pilkington Brothers Limited)

'The basic idea is a continuous ribbon of glass moving out of the melting furnace and floating along on the surface of molten metal at a strictly controlled temperature. Because the glass has never touched anything while it is soft except a liquid, the surface is unspoiled—it is the natural surface which melted glass forms for itself when it cools from liquid to solid. Because the surface of the liquid metal is dead flat, the glass is dead flat, too. Natural forces of weight and surface tension bring it to an absolutely uniform thickness.'

Within a few weeks of the original idea, the first series of tests was started and, by March of the following year, 1953, it was proved that the glass could be fire-finished by floating on a liquid metal. It remained to be seen, however, whether glass of sufficiently good quality could be made, free from any distortion. A new plant was built early in 1954 to produce a 12″ ribbon but, although the surface was considerably better than that of the first pilot run, it was still far from perfect. Nevertheless the Board had confidence in the soundness of what was being attempted. In September 1954 it was agreed to give the highest priority to further experiments. A plant capable of making a ribbon 30″ wide was designed and built in the remarkably short time of three months at a cost of £50,000. The results were, again, promising and, after a full report had been received in April 1955, the Board decided to take the decisive step and build a full-scale production unit to make float glass 100″ wide. This took two years to design and build and was started up at Cowley Hill in April 1957. Here unforeseen difficulties of formidable proportions appeared. Instead of making saleable glass within a month or two, as had been expected, more than a year of anxiety and struggle followed before good glass was produced, the big continuous plant swallowing vast sums of money all the time. To quote Alastair Pilkington again:

'. . . If we had known in 1955 the truly formidable problems that we still had to meet and beat, we almost certainly would not have decided to go ahead so boldly. . . . The fact is that the chemical and physical equilibrium problems between hot liquid glass and hot liquid metal and hot atmosphere break absolutely new ground from the technological point of view. No one outside the firm could help much, and we did not want to go outside anyway, because of secrecy. Most of the success achieved has been the result of hard slogging by our development and research teams.'

The first really good float glass was at last made in July 1958. This early output went to Triplex, Pilkingtons' associate and largest single customer, who agreed to use it in the manufacture of their safety glass. It was carefully tried out by them and conformed to their strict standards. When he announced, in January 1959, that float glass was already being used, Sir Harry Pilkington was at pains to stress that they had not then seen the best float glass nor the cheapest. Years of development still lay ahead before the full commercial advantages of the new product could be realized. It was clear, however, that the cost of a float glass plant was considerably less than one for plate glass and, moreover, it occupied very much less space. (The twin grinder, together with its associated polisher, was 1,100 ft. long.) In addition to savings in capital cost, and therefore of capital charges, there would also be savings on operating costs. This would enable high quality glass to be sold very much more cheaply once the heavy expenses of development had been met, and British glass would be able to compete much more effectively in world markets. It was, as Sir Harry Pilkington put it, 'the biggest stride forward for very many years'.

Pilkingtons spent over four million pounds between 1952 and the end of 1958 on the development of the float process. This was a special example of the continued growth of heavy capital expenditure on technical improvements. Heavy capital investment was a feature of the inter-war, as well as of the post-war, period; and, in addition to expenditure on new plant, smaller amounts of money had to be produced for the majority share in Triplex (Northern) Ltd. and the purchase of Sheet Glass Ltd. Moreover, immediately after the First World War, requiring additional space for extending plate glass manufacture, Pilkingtons had built at Kirk Sandall, near Doncaster, a new factory and a complete village to house those who worked there. This factory had come into operation at the end of 1922, just when the development of the flow process made its newly-installed plant obsolete. Further capital outlay was called for.

In 1919 the company's capital was £810,000 in ordinary shares and £600,000 in 5 per cent. debentures. Compared with the capital at the time of incorporation in 1894, this represented an increase of only £10,000 in ordinary shares, which had been made in 1916. By 1919, however, considerable reserves had been accumulated and, in October of that year, part of these were capitalized, the total authorized issue being increased to £3,240,000 and the issued share capital being written up to £2,430,000. In May 1920, in order to raise the extra money for post-war expansion, an issue was made for cash at par to existing holders of a further £762,000 in ordinary shares. At the same time Pilkingtons offered to members of the family, their friends and managers of the company, £600,000 6½ per cent. mortgage stock at £95 per cent., redeemable in May 1925. Only about half of this latter sum could be raised from these sources, however, and, by 1921, it was evident that even more money would be needed than had originally been contemplated. A loan, with a limit of £750,000, was obtained from the Bank of England. Four years later, in 1925, in order to repay the 6½ per cent. mortgage stock, discharge the remaining liability to the Bank of England and provide funds for further expansion, Pilkingtons issued £1,000,000 5¾ per cent. debenture stock to the Prudential Assurance Company Limited, again at £95 per cent., to be repaid by instalments. The final repayment was made in 1947. A further £200,000 was borrowed, in 1937, from the Norwich Union Life Assurance Society at 4 per cent. per annum. The last repayment of this loan, too, was made in 1947. In September 1936, the original 1894 issue of 5 per cent. debentures was increased to £720,000 by a capitalization of profits satisfied by the issue to shareholders of £120,000 debentures. This series of debentures was repaid at the end of 1947 and was replaced by an issue of £635,000 4¾ per cent. debentures. As a result of a rearrangement of capital and a further bonus issue of shares, the share capital of the company at March 31, 1958, has been increased to an authorized amount of £6,036,750. Of this £5,988,750 has been issued, £2,796,750 in ordinary shares and £3,192,000 in preference shares. The 4¾ per cent. debenture stock outstanding at the same date was £396,600. From the late 1920s onwards Pilkingtons made continuous and heavy provision for plant obsolescence and replacement as well as for ordinary wear and tear, and this enabled them not only to pay off these loans but also to finance their own expansion without having again to tap outside resources. Oversea subsidiaries have, however, borrowed temporarily or issued redeemable debentures; but this was usually necessitated by exchange regulations which prevented the free transfer of funds. With this minor exception, and that of the Norwich Union loan of 1937, the whole of Pilkingtons' expansion during the past thirty years has been financed by themselves.

This expansion was in scale, scope, and geographical extent. In scale, total output of plate and sheet glass was vastly increased and some of the greater output of sheet came from a new factory in Pontypool. The Government had refused a German company financial assistance to manufacture in Britain on condition that Pilkingtons put up plant to provide employment in one of the distressed areas. Pilkingtons built this plant at Pontypool at the end of the 1930s with some reluctance, for the existing capacity at St Helens was quite sufficient for their needs.

In scope, perhaps the most important new lines introduced in more recent years have been Vitrolite (1933), high voltage toughened glass insulators for power lines (1934), cathode ray tubes for television receivers (1949), and two products originally made by Chances, Fibreglass and optical glass. The manufacture of glass fibres—almost a complete new industry in its own right, with products for heat, sound and electrical insulation, and for plastic reinforcement —was begun in a small way by Chances at their Glasgow works in 1930. At the end of the war the Pilkington subsidiary, Fibreglass Limited, built a glass wool plant at Ravenhead, St Helens (1944), and this was followed by a complete new factory for glass textiles at Possilpark, Glasgow (1948). An existing factory was bought and re-equipped for plastic reinforcement manufacture at Valley Road, Birkenhead, in 1957. As for optical and spectacle glass, Chances, who had long experience in this field, and Pilkingtons set up a shadow factory for their manufacture at Sheet Works, St Helens, in 1939. Since June 1957, optical and ophthalmic glass has been further developed by the adoption for the first time in Britain of a continuous process, under licence from the Corning Glass Company, at a newly-built factory near St Asaph in North Wales.

Finally, in geographical extent, two large sheet glass factories were opened in 1951 at Springs, near Johannesburg, and the other at Scarborough, a suburb of Toronto. Pilkingtons also became the largest shareholders in two glassworks, at Llavallol, near Buenos Aires (1938), and at Asansol, in Bengal (1954). They also came to own, or control, three safety glass processing plants in Australia— at Adelaide (1936), Geelong (1937) and Villawood, near Sydney (1956); one in South Africa at Port Elizabeth (1935); one in the Argentine at Llavallol (1938); one in Brazil at Sao Paulo (1946); and one in New Zealand at Lower Hutt (1952). They have held since 1933 a large shareholding in Duplate (Canada) Ltd., by far the largest safety glass manufacturer in Canada and a company with many other activities. On the other hand, the Thorold factory, built just before the First World War to safeguard the drawn cylinder patent in Canada, was closed in 1924, and the Maubeuge factory, which had been rebuilt after that war, was sold to the St Gobain Company in the mid-1930s as part of the general settlement with some of the continental manufacturers and was then closed.[9] Pilkingtons' distributing organization in Canada has expanded rapidly and now comprises over twenty warehouses and a central processing works.

Although Pilkingtons remained, throughout this expansion, a family concern, the size of the organization inevitably changed its character. Control became more remote and the directors were no longer personally known to most of the employees who worked for them. In 1931 there was a notable change in the organization which fully recognized these altered circumstances. At that time a very large share of the company's direction was in the hands of three people— Austin Pilkington, his brother Cecil Pilkington, and Lord Cozens-Hardy. In place of this overall control by a triumvirate was substituted greater individual responsibility. Certain directors, each allocated particular duties, were formed into an Executive Committee and became responsible for the day-to-day running of the company. From time to time they were joined by the other directors and met as a fully-constituted Board to discuss matters of policy. Austin Pilkington and Cecil Pilkington then joined the ranks of the elder statesmen, putting aside their executive *role* but continuing to play a very active and important advisory part on the Board right up to the end of the 1940s. Lord Cozens-Hardy, who had devised the new arrangements, became chairman of the Executive Committee—a position he held until 1939—and his dominant personality shaped the course it was to follow for the next two decades.[10] This administrative reorganization in practice ended the partnership phase in Pilkingtons' development. Although the partnership had, in law, come to an end in 1894, it lingered on in spirit until 1931.

CHAIRMEN OF THE BOARD AND OF THE EXECUTIVE COMMITTEE
SINCE 1931

Chairmen of Pilkington Brothers Limited

July–December 1931:	W. N. Pilkington.
1932–49:	G. L. Pilkington
1949–	Sir Harry Pilkington.

Chairmen of the Executive Committee

1931–March 1939:	Lord Cozens-Hardy (Third Baron)
April–September 1939:	R. M. (later Lord) Weeks
Sept. 1939–Aug. 1, 1947:	G. L. Pilkington
August 1, 1947–	D. V. Phelps

The reorganization provided an opportunity for introducing to the Board two members of the staff who were not qualified as owners of shares to be directors. They were John Dickinson, who had joined the company in 1905 and succeeded his father as legal adviser in 1917, and W. S. Tunnock, who had also followed his father at the Glasgow warehouse, where he had begun as an office boy in 1891. The permissible number of directors not share-qualified has since been increased to three. The original two such directors have had five successors, three of whom, like W. S. Tunnock, have come from Scotland. This provision, which was perhaps overdue, added much to the strength of the Board at a time when it was clear that the shareholding members of the family themselves, although continuing to play a very active part in the conduct of the company, could not carry the whole burden effectively.

It is necessary to refer to two or three other ventures undertaken by the company since 1930. Pilkingtons' old rivals, Chances of Spon Lane, Smethwick, had, as we have seen, failed to maintain their former position in the industry and had, in 1912, sold some of their shares to the St Gobain giant.[11] By 1933 they had abandoned sheet glass manufacture altogether. Walter Chance, then chairman of the company, saw that the time was coming when its character would have to change. If there was to be a change in ownership, it was his wish that the company should pass to a concern with similar traditions and background. He therefore approached Pilkingtons in 1936 and suggested an immediate purchase of a large part of Chances' shares with the obligation of purchasing further shares, as these might be offered, until control was fully transferred. Agreement on these lines was reached, and the final stage arrived when Chances passed completely into Pilkingtons' ownership in 1955.

A somewhat similar arrangement was made, about the same time, with Mr Jobling-Purser, the owner of the Sunderland concern of James A. Jobling, the manufacturers of Pyrex. Pilkingtons acquired a sixth of the shares on the understanding that they would acquire the remainder when the vendor wished them to do so. This request came, quite suddenly, in 1949, when Pilkingtons were heavily committed in expanding their glassmaking activities elsewhere. In the following year, therefore, they sold a controlling interest to Thomas Tillings and later sold the remaining 40 per cent. to the Corning Glass Company.

Another post-war sale—this time a compulsory one—was that of Pilkingtons' valuable colliery interests, nationalized in 1947.

A venture of Pilkingtons, which did not turn out successfully, was their entry into the plastics industry. This was in the mid-1930s when there was considerable unemployment at St Helens and the company wanted to make use of space at the Eccleston factory of Triplex (Northern) Ltd., which had been freed with the switch from laminated to toughened glass. In 1936 the business of H. E. Ashdown (Birmingham) Ltd. was purchased and its plant gradually removed to Eccleston where, in the event, new buildings had to be put up. Manufacture was first undertaken by the Triplex partner but was so unprofitable that they insisted on either closing down or selling out to Pilkingtons. Pilkingtons took over for a further twenty years but eventually, after a long run of mixed fortune, decided that there were other and better outlets for their energies. They stopped plastic moulding altogether in 1957 but continued to supply important raw materials to the whole industry through Fibreglass Ltd.

During the inter-war years the company's research was conducted on a larger scale and placed on a more permanent basis. Thanks very largely to the initiative of Professor W. E. S. Turner and his promotion of the Glass Technology Department at Sheffield University[12] and the Society of Glass Technology with its *Journal*—all products of the First World War—the technical side of glass manufacture attracted attention in the university and among academics as well as in the factory and among skilled glassmakers. An increasing number of science graduates and other highly qualified men came to Pilkingtons from all quarters and, during the 1920s, team work, under Cecil Pilkington's direction, was important in improving existing methods and developing new ones. After the reorganization of 1931 a technical committee was formed to co-ordinate research in the various works and to establish a separate Research Laboratory. This was opened in 1938.

The inter-war years, and particularly the turbulent period between the early 1920s and the early 1930s, were full of opportunities for labour disputes at Pilkingtons. Technical changes called for reorganization of the labour force, causing, as often happens, numerous cases of individual hardship. The unprofitableness of sheet glass at the end of the 1920s was reflected in the company's wages policy. The resumption, in 1926, of working to four o'clock on Saturday afternoons, instead of one o'clock (which had been the case since 1920), was a further possible cause of trouble, and the reaction to the appearance of time study experts in 1933 might easily have been even more vigorous than it was. That none of these circumstances led to strike action was due chiefly to the regular consultation which took place between members of the Board and employees' representatives. Verbatim reports of some of these meetings show some very frank speaking indeed on both sides; but they also reveal mutual respect. Since 1914, the only important and widespread stoppage due to labour action was in the General Strike of 1926.

Various insurance schemes and social services undoubtedly strengthened the spirit of accord which arose from regular joint consultation. On the initiative of Austin and Cecil Pilkington, a compensation scheme was introduced for skilled blowers displaced by the drawn cylinder process. A staff superannuation fund came into force at the beginning of 1918 and a workmen's pension scheme followed in 1925. Both of these schemes—quite early examples of their kind—were contributory, and the company paid the same amount into the two funds as did its employees. The introduction of both these schemes involved setting aside large additional sums of money so that pensions could begin to be paid at once. The original arrangements, of course, have been greatly enlarged and improved. By 1958, the funds' trustees were responsible for administering £6¼ millions.

Meanwhile, a Welfare Department, formed in 1920, was increased in size, and branches established at the various works. Dental and medical facilities were provided, and optical, physiotherapy, chiropody and rehabilitation services were later added. In 1945 an Education Department was formed to organize training courses and continuation classes. At the same time, the company continued to encourage those who studied on their own, money prizes being awarded to any who passed professional examinations. Pilkingtons' interest in university education was shown in 1926 when three Pilkington Scholarships were endowed—one by Mr and Mrs Austin Pilkington personally and the others by the company—for the benefit of students from the Cowley schools at St Helens. Pilkingtons also continued to encourage their employees' social activities and sports. It is believed that theirs was the first industrial recreation club to celebrate its centenary (1947).

Pilkingtons has never lacked enterprise; each generation has added its own impetus to the growth of the concern and its own ideas of how to exercise its responsibilities both to those who work for it and to the community in general. Extensive administrative reorganization, the introduction to the Board of members of the staff, heavy reinvestment and a constant search for new opportunities —all these have contributed to the company's remarkable growth in recent times. Largely under the management of the fourth generation, it still remains in essence a family concern with some of the personal touch and personal knowledge that is characteristic of smaller family businesses. The sole survivor for many years in a growing industry of no little importance, it is still able, despite its size, to move quickly and intimately when decisions on commercial or labour matters are required, without waiting for the agreement of others. And the discovery and development of the float process are proof that initiative and enterprise are very strong on the technical side. It is no longer a company of purely local significance, and this has been shown by the larger part its directors and others have played in the economic and industrial life of the nation. Its importance is to be seen not so much in the size of the parent company's ordinary share capital—£6,000,000—or the number of employees within the organization—nearly 25,000—but rather in the multitude of people in many countries who have come to depend on it. Today Pilkington Brothers Limited ranks as one of the most notable private companies in the world, and, with increasing demand for its growing range of products, the future would seem to hold opportunities as rich as any that have offered in the past.

THE PILKINGTON PEDIGREE

It has not been possible to discover with certainty when the Pilkingtons first went to live at the White House, Horwich. According to the Deane and Horwich Registers,[1] two uncles of the successful claimant of 1759 were baptized at Horwich on October 9, 1670, and February 23, 1671/2. His grandmother died in giving birth to the second of these children and was buried on February 22, 1671/2. The contrast between these three entries in the space of less than eighteen months and the absence of any earlier Pilkington references in the registers suggests that Richard Pilkington moved into the Horwich district in, or just before, 1670, at a time when nonconformity, of which he was a strong supporter, was making great strides in that neighbourhood.[2] He may have gone there from the Bolton direction, as his marriage with Mary Hardman of Great Lever, a township to the south-east of Bolton, may indicate. Possibly a James Pilkington, described as the son of Richard Pilkington of Sharples, who was baptized at Bolton on October 7, 1655, was his first son. Possibly, too, the entry in the Bolton baptismal registers on January 20, 1627/8, referring to Richard Pilkington, the son of James Pilkington of Sharples, recorded his own baptism. This is the view taken in Burke,[3] but it can only be a surmise. All the chapel registers for miles around contain numbers of Pilkington entries and it is therefore quite impossible, in the absence of family papers, to reach any certain conclusions. To the genealogist, a glut is often a more severe handicap than a dearth.

Any attempt to trace the family pedigree back into the previous century and beyond is certainly to enter far into the land of conjecture. Richard Pilkington who married Mary Hardman may or may not have been a collateral descendant of the lords of the manor of Pilkington who had lost their Lancashire estates after Sir Thomas Pilkington had sided with Richard III at Bosworth.[4] Similarly, the Horwich family may or may not have been related to the Pilkingtons who held part of the manor of Rivington. Though this Rivington branch was wise enough not to become embroiled in the Wars of the Roses, its fortunes dwindled during the sixteenth century. The Pilkingtons of Rivington gained distinction in numbering among their members the Right Reverend James Pilkington, the saintly Elizabethan Bishop of Durham.[5] But their earthly affairs went ill: after mortgaging their interest in the manor in 1601, they sold it in 1611.[6] Lieutenant-Colonel John Pilkington, after a very careful study of the Pilkington pedigree, came to the conclusion that 'most of the persons bearing the name [of Pilkington] have emanated from the original stock which settled in the vill de Pilkington';[7] but he was obliged to admit his inability to trace the Horwich branch of the family beyond the early seventeenth century.[8] The more recent and no less painstaking research of Captain Richard Pilkington, M.P., has also failed to supply the missing link.[9] Until further evidence comes to light, it is necessary to preserve an open mind on the subject.

WAGES LISTS FOR THE WEEKS ENDING
12 AND 19 MAY, 1849

Crown Houses	Week ending May 12, 1849			Week ending May 19, 1849		
	£	s.	d.	£	s.	d.
W. Blanshard	2	17	9	2	17	9
W. Ashall	1	1	0	1	1	0
T. Fury	1	1	0	1	1	0
J. Pemberton		5	0		5	0
W. Hunter	1	0	10	1	4	11
His Son		8	11		11	1
R. Cooper	1	8	9½	1	14	4½
D. Dale	1	8	9½	1	14	4½
W. Jones		5	11		8	1
W. Clare	1	1	6	1	1	6
P. Cowens		8	7½		9	7½
F. Railton		8	11		11	1
T. Roughley		18	0		18	0
R. Henderson		9	7½		9	7½
W. H[enderson]		7	0½		5	7½
T. Ashall	1	4	10	1	4	10½
R. Pemberton		13	8		13	7
Glass d. 2 [sic]		8	9		8	9½
J. Farr		8	7½		8	7½
C. Sidney	1	1	0	1	1	0
J. Dobson	1	12	0½	1	17	8½
His Son		5	11		8	1
W. Brotherton	1	5	8½	1	10	2
W. Benson	1	12	0½	1	17	8½
W. Brown	1	12	0½	1	17	8½
J. Holt	1	12	0½	1	17	8½
W. Radcliffe	1	5	2	1	9	7
W. Hudspeth, senior	1	6	3½	1	14	6½
G. Lunt	1	3	1	1	7	2
J. Hussy		19	6		19	6
J. Cookson		15	0		15	0
—. Short				1	10	0
W. Short		15	0		15	0
G. S. J. Edmondson	1	10	0			
D. Edmondson		5	7½		7	1½
T. Dutton	1	2	8	1	2	8½

Crown Houses (contd.)	Week ending May 12, 1849 £	s.	d.	Week ending May 19, 1849 £	s.	d.
T. Henderson		5	7½		5	8½
J. Kenmore	1	11	3	1	11	10½
J. Atkinson	1	11	3	1	11	10½
J. Hall	1	2	8	1	2	8½
J. Lockhart	1	11	3	1	11	10½
T. L[ockhart]	1	12	1½	1	17	8½
D. L[ockhart]	1	0	11	1	3	1
Glass d. 3 [sic]		10	3		10	4½
G. Forber		10	11		13	1
W. Hewitt		13	4	1	1	7
E. Hazledon	1	5	2½	1	5	3
E. Vose		17	7½		17	7½
W. McConnell	1	7	11	1	8	6½
E. McMullen	1	10	7	1	15	7½
J. Gallagher	1	5	8½	1	10	2
J. Marsh [? J. Nash]	1	11	3	1	11	10½
G. Greaves	1	5	2	1	9	7
J. Phillips		18	9		18	9
W. Birchall	1	9	8	1	9	8
R. Catterall		19	6		19	6
J. Pinnington	1	1	0	1	1	0
H. Pownall	1	4	9½	1	4	11
T. Gregson	1	1	0	1	1	0
J. Holding	1	7	11	1	8	6½
E. H[olding]		6	11		9	1
C. H[olding]	1	4	7			
J. Holt	1	11	3	1	11	10½
R. Hudspeth	1	7	11	1	9	7
W. Milburn				1	5	3
T. Fildes				1	4	9
	£66	17	0	£73	12	0
Low & Helsby		9	0		13	6
H. Taylor	1	12	1	1	7	0
J. Appleton		15	0		16	6
W. Pownall		14	0		14	0
W. Livesley		13	0		13	0
B. Jones		13	0		10	0
J. Cowens		12	0		11	0
E. Risley		15	0			
W. Woodyer		11	6		12	0
W. Arnold		4	0		4	0
A. Spratt	1	0	0			
W. Hewitt		9	0		8	8
E. Lyon		5	7½			
W. Ewin		9	0		9	0

Crown Houses (contd.)	Week ending May 12, 1849			Week ending May 19, 1849		
	£	s.	d.	£	s.	d.
W. McCully		10	6		12	0
W. Robinson		10	6		8	6
M. Ford		5	0		5	0
J. Case	1	0	3	1	0	3
G. Pris		6	0			
J. Atherton		14	0		14	0
J. Mercer		4	0		14	0
S. Wilcox		10	0		10	10
H. Taylor		12	0		12	0
J. Burrows		17	6		12	6
J. Richardson		12	0		12	6
A. Back		12	0		14	6
P. Ashall		12	0		13	0
W. Patterson		13	6		14	2
J. Cole		10	0		10	0
E. Brownbill		10	0		5	10
J. Culshaw		10	0		10	0
W. Critchley		10	6		10	0
J. Mather		13	6		16	2½
A. Dixon		13	6		16	4½
W. Iveson		13	6		14	0
J. Peak		13	6		14	0
E. Atkinson		18	0		18	8
W. Morris		13	6		14	0
T. Boardman		10	0		10	0
J. Murfy [sic]		14	6		14	6
M. M[urphy]		14	7½		15	2
G. Sixmith		7	6			
E. Glover		19	6		12	0
E. Stanistreet		16	0		13	0
Clay Grinding		6	0			
E. Birchall		5	0		5	7½
J. Short		10	0		10	10
J. Hulme		12	0		10	0
W. Henderson		6	8		8	2
J. Benson		12	0		10	0
J. Parr		6	4		7	8
Glass prs.		9	2		9	1
J. Jameson					8	8
W. Dale					5	7½
N. Maxwell					8	7½
J. Rea					10	0
A. Telford					9	0
W. Wills					11	0½
	£30	16	9	£30	10	0

French (or Sheet) Houses	Week ending May 12, 1849			Week ending May 19, 1849		
	£	s.	d.	£	s.	d.
Gaspard and Son	4	3	0	3	10	0
C. Etheridge	2	17	9	2	11	1
E. Hall	2	14	10	2	7	8
Auguste	3	15	0	3	8	0
Ferdinand	2	18	0	2	11	6
Beck	3	6	6	3	3	6
Adam	3	18	0	3	16	6
Aikin				2	16	10
Geo. Dixon	1	0	2		8	0
Jno. Lockhart	1	18	4	1	1	9
Tattens		11	3	1	5	8
Raper		15	0	1	6	4
Thos. Mather	1	9	5	1	3	4
Thos. Carlisle	2	6	7	1	11	8
Jas. Tickle	3	10	0	3	18	7
Hypolite	4	4	0	4	4	0
Eugene	3	18	6	3	14	0
Geo. Fog	3	6	0	3	10	0
Zelere	3	5	6	3	9	0
W. Dixon	2	4	4	2	13	0
Merryfield	2	1	7	1	15	0
Jas. Rose	1	5	1	2	2	10
Jas. Grieves	3	2	6	2	15	0
L. André and L. Lourd				2	2	0
A. Hartley	2	0	0	2	0	0
J. Edmondson	2	0	0	2	0	0
Thos. Hudspeth	2	0	0	2	0	0
Jno. Taylor	1	16	7	1	9	10
T. Jones	2	4	2	2	0	0
J. Wright	1	17	4	1	11	2
Jno. Bibby	1	17	0	1	14	5
Jos. Owen	2	5	0	1	10	0
W. Edmondson	1	3	10	1	8	4
Wm. Owen	1	9	8	1	10	6
Wm. Scott	1	4	9	1	3	0
Frank Hodgson	1	5	0	1	5	0
John Scott		15	0	1	2	6
Rd. Glover	1	0	0	1	3	8
Joseph Scott	1	2	0		12	11
Frederick Vose	1	10	0	1	5	0
J. Harper		18	0		18	0
T. Ryan	1	0	0		16	0
B. Jones		3	0		3	0
J. Brotherton		6	0		6	9
W. Gaskell		18	0		18	0
His Son		3	0		3	0
W. & G. Ashall		6	0		6	0

APPENDIX 2

French (or Sheet) Houses (contd.)	Week ending May 12, 1849			Week ending May 19, 1849		
	£	s.	d.	£	s.	d.
J. & W. Hunter		6	0		6	0
W. Glover	1	3	0	1	4	0
J. Anders					8	5
R. Vose		5	0		5	0
A. Broadhurst		18	0		18	0
T. & P. Anders		6	6		6	0
J. Cowens		3	0		3	0
W. Butler		3	0		3	0
J. Bridge		16	0		16	0
I. Frodsham		3	0		3	0
J. Battersby		3	0		3	0
J. & T. Roughley		7	3		7	6
J. Makin		3	0		3	0
W. Jones		3	0		3	0
C. Henderson	1	2	3	1	1	2
P. Henderson		3	0		3	0
R. Wilson		3	0		3	0
J. & C. Hodgson		6	0		6	0
R. Appleton		3	6		3	0
J. Kitchin		3	0		3	0
J. Matthews		3	0		3	0
J. Holland		3	0		3	0
H. Tickle		13	6		13	6
W. Tickle		8	3		8	3
S. Leyland		4	0		4	0
W. Monks		3	0		3	0
J. Raper		12	0		12	0
T. W.					3	0
J. Prescott		6	0		6	0
J. Meredith		8	9		9	3
T. Meredith		5	3		4	6
W. Meredith		3	0		3	0
S. Colville	1	12	9	1	11	2
J. Appleton	1	14	0	1	9	4
J. Nash		19	4		17	3
R. Thompson		13	5	1	4	5
His Son		3	0		3	0
B. Holt	1	3	11	1	4	8
W. Hall	1	3	11	1	4	8
J. Owen	1	1	0	1	1	0
T. Welsh	1	1	0	1	1	0
T. Rose	1	1	0	1	1	0
J. Edmondson		7	6		8	0
J. Holt	1	12	8	1	12	8
His Son		3	0		3	6
J. Wear		18	0		18	0
J. Baily	1	7	8	1	7	8

French (or Sheet) Houses (contd.)	Week ending May 12, 1849			Week ending May 19, 1849		
	£	s.	d.	£	s.	d.
T. Travers		18	0		18	0
E. Vose		3	0		3	0
W. Mulvaney		13	5		13	0
F. Mulvaney		6	0		6	0
W. Mulvaney					3	0
R. M. Moss		3	0			
W. Moss		12	0		12	0
W. Yates						9
W. McCully					5	2
G. Lidiate		12	0		12	0
J. Dixon		14	2		19	10
R. Dixon		3	0		3	0
J. Edmondson		13	9		19	0
E. Ford		11	3		12	0
W. Milburn	1	5	2½			
J. Risley	1	2	6	1	2	6
E. Risley					15	0
W. Taylor		3	0		3	0
J. Barlow	1	1	0		19	0
W. Roughley		15	6		15	6
His Son		18	0		18	0
J. Roughley		15	0		15	0
R. Davis		18	0		18	0
R. Sudlow		10	11		11	6
A. Malcolm	1	4	2		7	11
J. Broadhurst		17	8		17	8
His Son		3	0		3	0
R. White		3	0		2	3
T. Unsworth		10	0		9	5
R. Unsworth		3	0			
T. Appleton		11	0		11	0
J. Appleton		3	0		3	0
M. Lyon		8	6		9	6
I. Lyon		3	0		3	0
D. Lockhart		3	0		3	0
J. Andrews		9	0			
J. Arnold		1	6		3	0
W. Hewitt		7	0		8	6
J. Hewitt		12	6		10	0
E. Hewitt		6	0		6	0
G. Hewitt		5	0		5	0
T. Burdice		15	0		15	0
J. Taylor		13	2		15	0
E. Grayson		3	0		3	0
R. Hardman	1	6	10	1	4	5
E. Hazleden		3	0		3	0
P. Wright		19	6		19	6

French (or Sheet) Houses (contd.)	Week ending May 12, 1849			Week ending May 19, 1849		
	£	s.	d.	£	s.	d.
S. Bate		12	6		11	0
J. Scott		6	0		6	0
I. T[aylor]		10	1		9	0
J. Taylor		3	0		3	0
J. Taylor		14	11	1	0	6
R. Lyon	1	1	0	1	1	0
His Son		8	4		8	0
R. Bate		3	0		3	0
T. Vose		12	1		15	0
E. Vose		3	0		3	0
J. Banks		12	1		10	0
L. Holland		3	0		3	0
T. & W. Greaves		5	9		5	6
J. & G. Phillips		6	0		6	0
Edward Holt					3	0
J. Andrews	1	8	8	1	8	8
His Son		7	0		9	7
J. Sherlock	1	1	0	1	1	0
W. Phillips	1	1	0	1	1	0
J. Case	1	1	0	1	1	0
His two Sons		5	0		5	0
		3	0		3	0
T. Holding	1	3	6	1	1	1
T. Case		18	0		18	0
His two Sons		6	0		6	0
3 Members of the Brogan Family		9	0		10	3
		7	0		10	7
		3	0		3	0
J. Critchley		11	1		10	8
B. & E. Holt		6	0		6	0
J. Molyneux		19	6		19	6
J. Frier		9	6		11	4
M. Dixon		3	0		3	0
W. Milburne		13	5			
J. Hudspeth		3	0		3	0
J. Livesly		18	0		18	0
J. & P. Marsden		6	0		6	0
R. Appleton		3	0			
Fines		6	0			
	£156	10	0	£156	9	4
Cutting Rooms, etc.						
Mr William Pilkington, junr.	4	4	0	4	4	0
Henry Deacon	5	18	6	5	18	6
J. Varley	2	6	0	2	6	0
W. Ross	1	18	6	1	18	6
W. Johnson	1	10	0	1	10	0

Cutting Rooms, etc. (contd.)	Week ending May 12, 1849			Week ending May 19, 1849		
	£	s.	d.	£	s.	d.
W. Sothern	1	0	0	1	0	0
J. Fidler		13	6		13	6
W. Taylor		11	6½		11	6½
H. Johnson		11	6½		11	6½
Thomas Jenkins		16	0		16	0
J. Pagan	1	10	0	1	10	0
W. Holt & Co. [sic]	2	8	6	2	10	0
J. Alpas	1	0	0	1	3	4
W. Hardy		5	0		5	0
W. Banks		18	0		18	0
G. Houghton	1	2	6	1	2	6
H. Taylor	1	10	0		2	6
B. Getley	1	3	0	1	3	0
R. Haslom		5	3		8	3
W. Waterworth		4	9		5	6
Glass Polishers	2	1	5	2	5	0½
T. Webster		5	0		5	7½
W. Edmundson		18	0		18	0
W. Woodward		13	0		13	0
His Son		3	0		3	0
J. Smith		17	0		17	0
B. Appleton		18	0		18	0
J. Seddon		3	0		3	0
J. Prescot		3	0		2	10½
E. Lyon					5	0
B. Webster					1	6
J. Ford		6	0		5	9
H. Nash		3	0		2	10½
J. Bickerstaff		7	0		7	0
W. Ross		4	0		4	0
W. Holt, junior		2	10½		3	0
J. Houghton		2	10½		3	6
P. Holden		5	3		6	0
M. Seyer		9	0		8	7½
T. Rigby		9	0		9	4½
A. Holt		16	6		18	0
H. Arnot		18	0		18	0
M. Brogan & Co. [sic]	2	5	0	2	5	0
J. Vass		3	0		3	0
J. Dixon		12	0		12	0
W. Appleton		13	0		13	0
W. Maxwell	1	10	0	1	11	3
J. Scott		3	0		3	0
Jno. King		18	0		18	0
	£46	5	6	£46	1	1

Joiners, etc.	Week ending May 12, 1849 £ s. d.			Week ending May 19, 1849 £ s. d.		
W. Wharton	1	15	10	1	13	10
H. Hunter		16	6		19	6
Rd. King	1	1	0	1	5	4½
Jas. Houghton	1	0	0	1	4	2
J. Grayson		19	6	1	2	6
T. Clarkson		17	0	1	0	6½
Thos. Webster		18	0	1	0	3
M. Owen	1	1	0	1	6	3
H. Wharton	1	0	0	1	5	0
Richd. Atkinson		3	0		3	7½
Thos. Forshaw		7	0	1	5	4½
Thos. Colquitt	3	6	2½	3	5	3
Johnson	2	6	3	3	6	2
Isaac Vose	1	0	2	1	2	0
Jno. Vose	1	0	0	1	0	0
Will Vose, senior	1	11	3		16	8
Will Vose, junior	1	4	1	1	1	3
Jas. Bromilow		12	6	1	0	0
Jas. Vose	1	0	5		14	7
Thos. Woodward		18	8		16	4
W. Cooke		14	0		14	0
W. Wilson		4	8		4	8
J. Staples	1	11	0	1	7	0
J. Mather	1	7	8	1	3	8
His Son		3	10½		3	4½
J. Murray		19	3		15	9
P. Leigh		5	4		4	6
T. Glover	1	11	6½	1	3	8
H. Blundell	1	8	5	1	3	10
E. Evans	1	9	4	1	4	9
T. Latham	1	2	11	1	2	0
W. Greenholgh		17	4		16	0
T. Burrows	1	2	2	1	0	0
T. Bibby	1	2	9	1	1	0
J. Taylor		16	8	1	7	2
M. Dale		5	0			
J. Chapman	1	3	11½	1	8	1½
J. Blundell	1	2	6		14	0½
J. Gilday		6	0		14	0
A. Vass	1	5	0	1	8	1½
R. Young	1	1	6	1	5	4
G. Evans	1	10	3		3	8
J. Burrows		13	0		12	6
J. Holland	1	2	0	1	2	0
A. Spratt				1	0	0
	£46	4	6	£47	7	10

Staining Room	Week ending May 12, 1849			Week ending May 19, 1849		
	£	s.	d.	£	s.	d.
R. Edmundson	2	2	0	2	2	0
W. Gardner	1	15	0	1	16	5½
W. Arthur		16	10½		18	0
J. M. Kethney	1	4	2	1	4	2
Myatt		10	10		12	1
Jas. Edmondson		14	0		12	0
W. Edmondson		8	8		7	0
Eliz. Edmondson		7	0		6	0
J. Hall		10	6		9	0
Eliz. Parr		6	3		6	3
M. Davidson		5	10		5	0
Ann Williamson		5	10		5	0
Mary Atkinson		5	10		5	0
Overtime		16	6			
	£10	9	3½	£9	7	11½

Summary of Totals						
Crown Houses	66	17	0	73	12	0
	30	16	9	30	10	0
French (or Sheet) Houses	156	10	0	156	9	4
Cutting Rooms	44	5	6	46	1	1
Joiners	46	4	6	47	7	10
Staining Room	10	9	3½	9	7	11½
	£355	3	0½	£363	8	2½

STATEMENT ISSUED BY PILKINGTONS DURING THE LABOUR CRISIS OF 1845

TO THE GLASS-MAKERS AT THE ST HELENS CROWN GLASS WORKS

In order to prove our desire to terminate all disagreement and to cultivate to the utmost that mutual good will which has heretofore subsisted between ourselves and our workmen, we are induced to lay before them a plain statement of facts, from which we will leave it to their own good sense to decide, whether all parties are not likely to gain both present comfort and future profit, rather by arranging in a friendly manner anything in their present position which may seem capable of improvement, than by continuing a contest on the legality of a power never hitherto considered unjust, and which our workmen themselves have deliberately given us.

It is well known that RICHARD PEMBERTON entered into an Agreement to serve us for seven years. It is said by his advisers that this Agreement is bad in point of law. But whether good or bad, is he not bound as an honest man to keep his word with us? He had the benefit of the Agreement for a time, but then he shewed us letters from Dumbarton wishing him to become a Manager of works there. One object of the Agreement was to prevent a frequent change of hands, yet we consented to his leaving us in order to improve his circumstances, provided he prevented any loss to us by finding another blower equal to himself. He failed to do this, but offered us instead a sum of money, which we refused. He then absconded from our employ. To submit to this would have been to give the Dumbarton Company free permission to select and engage all our best men, just as it might suit their convenience. We therefore gave them notice, that if they employed PEMBERTON, they must either pay us £100 as a compensation, or expect us to bring an action against them. Could there be any injustice in this? PEMBERTON's Agreement with us was only a few months old, and we had paid £152 10s od for leave to engage his Father when his Agreement had only seven months to run. He did not return, however, and after waiting two months we felt ourselves obliged to send for him to Scotland, and, much against our inclination, to cause him to be committed to prison. From thence he has been discharged, not from any defect in the Agreement, which we are assured by most eminent Counsel cannot be set aside; but, because a single Judge considered the Justice's Warrant of Commitment informal.

Now it must be observed, that our real ground of complaint is not against our workmen, and scarcely against RICHARD PEMBERTON, but against the Dumbarton Company. If they interfere with our rights, may we not claim compensation? But it is said that the Agreement is bad in law. This we deny. But if it were, would not the law prevent many a workman from earning bread for himself and his family, at a time when his work perhaps hardly pays his employer? At such a time, the master hopes that under an Agreement, he may at a future day turn his workmen to good account, and the workman trusts to his master's liberality to advance his wages according to the times. The workman for a present benefit runs the risk of future loss, just as the tradesman often pays much more than the usual rate of interest for a sum of money, either to enable him to make still greater profits, or to prevent serious loss. The law allows it, and trade could not go on without it. It must be remembered too, that though at the present moment Crown Glass Makers are much sought after, there is great reason to fear that the introduction of Foreign Glass at a lower duty, and the increased production of other kinds of Glass, may shortly produce a very serious change for the worse, and we would ask, whether our workmen would rather run the risk of sharing adversity with strangers or with old acquaintances? If they have stood by us in the summer, may they not expect us to stand by them in the winter?

Though, as we have shewn, there is no injustice in the Contracts, yet when the question of Bounty or Binding Money was named to us, we did not refuse it as we might have done, on the grounds that our men were already bound, and that we had raised their wages considerably beyond the rates we had agreed to pay. But having heard that some were desirous of breaking their Contracts, and knowing that others who had formerly received Bounty Money had not completed their term of service, we proposed to give the whole sum asked for, not at once, but divided into annual payments to be made on each New-year's day during the several contracts. Many expressed themselves perfectly satisfied with this plan, none to our knowledge objected to it, and we considered the matter settled. If however the immediate payment of the sum in question would terminate all discontent, we are not disposed to withhold it from any who may apply for it.

It is true that in making this offer our motives may be doubted, and that it may be insinuated by those whose interest it is to keep alive ill feeling, that we doubt the validity of our Contracts. But we have to state that our rights have been unjustly assailed; that we will not yield them up to threats or intimidation; and that we are firmly resolved to maintain not only those rights, but also that proper discipline, obedience, and order in our Works which are one great object of the Contracts, and without which not only the Master but every good and steady Workman might suffer from the misconduct and irregularity of others. At the same time we have no animosity or ill feeling towards any one in our Works. It is our duty and our study, and we have always considered it our interest, to promote the happiness and welfare of all, and whatever grievances may be properly made known to us, we are most willing to redress them.

We trust these remarks will be received with the same good feeling by which they are dictated,—that all disputes may cease and be forgotten,—and that the harmony and tranquillity which we have always endeavoured to establish, may in future reign amongst us undisturbed.

RICHARD AND WILLIAM PILKINGTON

St Helens Crown Glass Works,
October 7, 1845.

P.S. It may perhaps be said that this address should have been issued earlier; we feared however that our motives might be misconstrued, and we hoped, that as we had been led to expect, our men would have laid their wishes before us. A season of affliction too has lately come upon us which absorbed almost our whole thoughts, but we have great satisfaction in acknowledging the good conduct and respectful demeanour observed by *all* our Workmen upon this occasion of general mourning and regret.

BESSEMER'S EXPERIMENTS WITH GLASS,
1841-1851

Bessemer, that most prolific patentee, had been interested in glass for some years before 1847. In 1841 he had taken out a patent (in association with a man called Schonburg) for improving the manufacture of plate and flint glass[1] and at the end of that year the two inventors tried to interest the proprietors of the Ravenhead Plate Glassworks in this patent but without success.[2] Bessemer's fertile brain later turned its attention to the manufacture of window glass. The improvements he suggested in this field foreshadowed in several respects the later mechanization of the industry. He proposed to pass a long sheet of glass ladled from the pots through two sets of rollers, the first set having a roughened surface to exert the necessary drawing effect and the second being either smooth or patterned according to the type of glass required. The lehr, placed next to this rolling machine, was to be in the form of an inclined plane down which the long sheet or sheets of glass could slide. When annealed, the glass was to be smoothed and polished by an endless belt 'charged with polishing material'. The lehr was not to be coal-fired but indirectly heated by hot air conveyed by cast iron pipes from the founding furnace 'after the practice in heating air for hot blast in the manufacture of iron.'[3]

Bessemer's ingenious suggestions attracted Robert Lucas Chance, who persuaded the firm to advance £250 for these experiments.[4] He later visited Baxter House, St Pancras, where Bessemer was working, in order to witness a demonstration of the rolling machine. Bessemer later claimed that on this occasion he drew a piece of glass seventy feet long and two and a half feet wide.[5] R. L. Chance was very impressed and decided to support Bessemer further. J. T. Chance, however, who was the firm's technical expert, was unpersuaded by Bessemer's preliminary experiments and refused to support the development of the patent, as did his father, William Chance. R. L. Chance and his son, Robert, were therefore left to support the venture on their own. They built and equipped works at Camden Town, partly for Bessemer's convenience and partly so that he should not have constant opportunity to observe what was being done at Spon Lane. The process, however, could not be satisfactorily developed. Bessemer became interested in other fields of research and in 1851 withdrew altogether from his association with the Chances. After further disappointments and delays, the whole project, a most costly failure, was finally abandoned in 1854. As Bontemps later commented:

> 'The whole system showed, unquestionably, immense mechanical ability but . . . complete ignorance of the qualities inherent in the substance of glass.'[6]

EXPORTS OF BELGIAN WINDOW GLASS
TO BRITAIN AND THE UNITED STATES
1850-1913

ne following figures, derived from each year's *Tableau Général du Commerce avec les Pays Etrangers (Statistique de la Belgique)* show the relative importance of Britain and the United States as markets for Belgian window glass.

Year	Total Exports (kgs.)	To Britain (kgs.)	To the United States (kgs.)
1850	11,672,300	1,812,540	3,429,234
1851	14,681,002	1,980,241	5,213,099
1852	16,443,568	1,865,896	4,948,538
1853	20,607,865	2,965,150	7,878,668
1854	27,261,609	4,306,675	11,112,534
1855	21,763,996	2,835,586	6,946,189
1856	24,303,458	3,056,073	7,819,029
1857	27,551,166	8,513,491	7,076,634
1858	22,634,377	4,912,032	6,032,627
1859	27,188,823	5,726,552	8,077,377
1860	30,227,965	5,469,406	9,868,672
1861	24,045,726	6,167,356	4,420,338
1862	25,616,910	7,459,588	3,084,442
1863	30,940,096	9,370,274	2,345,426
1864	35,501,712	10,972,019	6,151,775
1865	40,625,500	Details not available	
1866	41,584,103	14,800,157	11,891,138
1867	41,366,271	12,646,108	13,837,148
1868	38,678,083	16,370,666	6,369,425
1869	45,893,254	19,251,934	9,906,036
1870	40,847,233	18,098,478	8,167,166
1871	28,721,705	12,714,007	5,402,929
1872	23,963,568	11,080,802	1,695,256
1873	63,747,861	21,862,388	15,160,074
1874	80,649,334	25,385,960	17,608,240
1875	80,546,576	27,909,622	16,862,710
1876	74,668,468	30,820,145	9,985,220
1877	76,160,658	27,960,457	11,504,458

Year	Total Exports (kgs.)	To Britain (kgs.)	To the United States (kgs.)
1878	78,134,823	33,518,731	9,440,314
1879	84,214,180	33,792,907	11,697,414
1880	93,430,744	32,250,567	26,687,139
1881	97,482,670	30,482,198	24,673,384
1882	97,061,079	30,315,334	24,055,675
1883	105,366,016	27,580,461	31,305,405
1884	110,429,066	30,130,403	35,537,945
1885	109,554,284	32,501,334	27,357,853
1886	107,849,996	30,420,877	27,705,097
1887	122,973,617	33,340,095	34,821,889
1888	130,783,734	34,347,920	39,115,838
1889	123,096,892	30,325,464	35,768,859
1890	129,460,725	31,144,210	38,254,777
1891	132,440,106	31,469,189	34,366,256
1892	134,254,750	30,655,563	34,033,022
1893	136,151,772	30,194,272	28,705,934
1894	136,384,483	39,242,026	26,733,177
1895	132,026,884	42,178,808	19,961,650
1896	153,476,414	48,474,269	23,219,431
1897	149,251,775	52,723,267	19,411,432
1898	154,300,287	58,785,687	21,456,178
1899	170,092,136	58,727,783	23,474,624
1900	133,201,083	46,626,930	16,752,340
1901	127,447,281	43,745,729	17,007,893
1902	171,370,275	59,896,030	24,796,583
1903	168,950,067	55,406,752	25,232,269
1904	118,298,868	40,049,278	12,725,051
1905	152,332,184	47,695,530	9,884,478
1906	212,041,397	59,932,027	13,542,562
1907	181,783,001	50,292,671	11,404,511
1908	155,711,414	48,023,977	7,528,393
1909	186,239,587	46,075,327	8,589,105
1910	213,507,116	46,869,009	12,022,891
1911	204,663,350	49,243,016	9,253,329
1912	217,265,095	53,757,151	8,115,372
1913	205,561,684	47,241,594	8,698,647

EXTRACT FROM THE SIEMENS' FURNACE PATENT SPECIFICATION OF 1870

' . . . Another part of the Invention has reference to an improved construction of and mode of working glass pots or tanks of glass furnaces. Heretofore the materials have been first charged into glass pots or tanks then melted down and then worked out completely, after which they have been recharged and the process repeated, thus entailing considerable loss of time through the intermittent nature of the work. Now the present improvement has for its object to render the process of glass making a more uniform and continuous one, and consists in constructing the glass pots or tanks with three separate compartments, in one of which the materials are introduced continuously or at short intervals, and from which the materials as they melt are caused to flow into the next compartment where the operation of melting is completed, and whence the glass flows into a third compartment where it is worked out continuously. To produce this circulation of the melted glass through the three compartments, advantage is taken of the gradually increasing specific gravity of the glass as it becomes more and more heated. Thus, when this invention is applied to glass pots the first compartment communicates with the second one through a small vertical passage into which the melting materials as they descend in the compartment by virtue of this increasing specific gravity enter through a hole at the lower end, and in rising up in the passage eventually flow over into the second compartment. Here as the melted glass accumulates, that portion thereof which has become most highly heated and is consequently in the most fluid and clarified condition again descends by virtue of its increasing specific gravity and finds its way through an aperture at the bottom of the third compartment in which it rises, and whence it is worked out in the usual manner. This latter compartment is provided with a cover having a working aperture as in ordinary glass pots.

In applying the Invention to tank furnaces the tank is divided in its length into three compartments by means of transverse partitions or bridges provided with air passages in communication with vertical air shafts for effecting a circulation of cold air through the same. Into the hindmost of the compartments the

crude materials are introduced and as they melt they pass through the apertures at the bottom of the first bridge into vertical channels formed in the same
in which the melted glass rises and then flows over the bridge into the second or
middle compartment where the operation of melting is completed. Lastly the
glass flows from this compartment through the apertures in the bottom of the
second partition into the front or working compartment. The heated air and
gas ports are arranged along each side of the tank so that the flames play across
the same, thus allowing the requisite temperature to be maintained in each
compartment by means of a regulated admission of the gas and air effected by
making the ports of different dimensions. For this purpose also a division wall
provided with air passages is carried right across the furnace at the hindmost
partition, thereby entirely separating the heating chamber to the hindmost
compartment from that of the other compartments, in which a greater heat is
maintained. The gas and air ports are continued backwards through the brickwork of the furnace and are closed outside by means of slabs, by removing
which the glass tank may be rendered accessible through such ports at any
point of its length.'

BIOGRAPHICAL NOTES ON THE DIRECTORS
OF THE COMPANY

---

(1) *Present Directors*. (See also Chart V, page 212)

LORD COZENS-HARDY.   Fourth Baron of Letheringsett.
Born 1907.
Educated at Winchester and Worcester College, Oxford.
Was a Trainee with J. & J. Colman Ltd., a business with which his family has a close connexion; joined the Firm in 1932; Director 1937, and has always taken a special responsibility for Personnel and Welfare matters.
During the Second World War was responsible for the Company's Civil Defence arrangements.
Is a J.P. and a D.L. for Lancashire.
He is Chairman of the Prescot Magistrates.

ALAN MEREDYTH HUDSON DAVIES
Born 1901.
Educated at Bancroft's School and King's College, Cambridge.
1924 Industrial Investigator with the National Institute of Industrial Psychology.
1928 Assistant Commercial Manager, Imperial Chemical Industries Ltd., Billingham-on-Tees.
1933 Joined H. P. Bulmer & Co. Ltd., cider makers, Hereford, becoming Works Director in 1936.
1941 Chairman of the Birmingham Manpower Board (Ministry of Labour and National Service).
1946 Joined the Firm as Managing Director of Fibreglass Limited.
1952 Director of Pilkington Brothers Limited.
He is a member of the Council of Liverpool University.

GEORGE MCONIE

Born in 1903.

Educated at Greenock Academy, Allan Glen's School, Glasgow, and Glasgow University, where he took an Engineering Degree.

After six years in the Shipbuilding industry he joined the Firm in 1927. He was for a number of years primarily associated with the introduction of methods of work control; he became the Works Manager at Doncaster in 1937 and subsequently Manager of Triplex (Northern) Limited in 1938, and Ravenhead Works in 1939.

From 1941-3 he was seconded to the War Office as Civil Adviser to the Director-General of Army Equipment, General Weeks. Returning to the Firm he was Manager at Doncaster from 1945-52 (becoming a local Director in 1949). Returning to St Helens he became Manager of Cowley Hill in 1952, became a sub-Director in 1954 and a Director in 1958.

LANCELOT ROGER PERCIVAL

Born in 1906; grandson of Thomas Pilkington.

Educated at Eton and Trinity College, Oxford.

Represented Oxford in the low hurdles and Great Britain in the 400-metre hurdles event at the 1928 Olympic Games.

Joined the Firm in 1928, becoming a Director in 1936, being associated always with the Commercial side of the business.

Mobilized in 1939, he served throughout the war in Anti-Aircraft Command, being awarded the M.B.E. He was released with rank of Major, and returned to work on the Commercial side of the business. He has been a J.P. for Lancashire since 1952.

Partly on account of his own athletic ability, he has always been closely connected with the various activities of the Firm's recreational undertakings.

DOUGLAS VANDELEUR PHELPS

Born in 1904; grandson of Thomas Pilkington.

Educated at Harrow and Magdalen College, Oxford.

Joined the Firm in 1927, becoming a Director in 1934.

In 1947 succeeded Mr Geoffrey Pilkington as Chairman of the Executive Committee; also Chairman of Chance Brothers Limited, Fibreglass Limited, and a Director of the Westminster Bank Limited.

Mobilized with the Territorial Army in 1939, he went to the Staff College, Camberley, in 1940, and served in staff appointments throughout the war in the United Kingdom and the War Office, Middle East and Italy.

From 1947-51 he commanded the local Territorial Regiment, and from 1951-4 he commanded an Anti-Aircraft Brigade with the rank of Brigadier.

He was appointed an A.D.C. to King George VI and subsequently to the Queen.

He is now Vice-Chairman of the West Lancashire Territorial and Auxiliary Forces Association.

He has been a J.P. for St Helens since 1937 (Chairman of the Bench since 1956) and a D.L. for Lancashire since 1953.

He is Chairman of the National Health Executive Council for St Helens.

ARTHUR COPE PILKINGTON

Born in 1909; younger son of Arthur Richard Pilkington.

Educated at Charterhouse and Royal Military College, Sandhurst. He was for four years a Regular Officer in the Coldstream Guards.

In 1934 he joined the Firm on the commercial side, becoming a Director in 1946.

Recalled to the Coldstream Guards from the Reserve of Officers in 1939, he served throughout the war as a Regimental Officer and was awarded the Military Cross in 1945, retiring with the rank of Major.

Returning to the Firm in early 1946 his main interest was with the Company's Export Sales, and later he assumed principal responsibility for the Sales and Commercial direction of the Firm and has travelled widely on the Firm's business. He is a Director of Triplex Holdings Limited and Triplex Safety Glass Company Limited.

DAVID FROST PILKINGTON

Born 1925.

Educated at Clifton, Upper Canada College, Toronto, and Trinity College, Cambridge, where he took a degree in Mechanical Sciences.

1945–7 R.N.V.R. finishing as Sub-Lieutenant E. Before leaving the Service he was offered a permanent commission in the R.N.

1947 Joined Pilkington Brothers Limited. Became Works Manager at Pontypool in 1953, a sub-Director in 1955, and a Director in 1959.

GEOFFREY LANGTON PILKINGTON

Born in 1885; son of George Herbert Pilkington.

Educated at Eton and Magdalen College, Oxford.

Joined the Firm in 1909. Became a sub-Director in 1910 and a Director in 1919.

He became Chairman of the Company after the reorganization in 1932 and remained as such until 1949; he became Chairman also of the Executive Committee in 1939 and retained this appointment until 1947.

Having joined the Lancashire Hussars in 1911, he served in England and in Egypt until 1916 when he transferred to the Royal Flying Corps. He raised and commanded 611 (West Lancs.) Squadron, Royal Auxiliary Air Force, from 1937 and was mobilized with it in 1939. He being then 54 years of age had to hand over the command of this Fighter Squadron to younger hands, but he ultimately became its Honorary Air Commodore.

He is a D.L. for Lancashire.

He has for many years been a noted gardener, for some time his main interest being the raising of bearded irises.

He is a member of the Council of the Royal Horticultural Society.

GUY REGINALD PILKINGTON

Born in 1881; youngest son of Richard Pilkington.

Educated at Clifton and Trinity College, Cambridge.

He joined the Firm in 1909 after a short period with Sutton Manor Collieries, near St Helens, in which his father was a shareholder.

He became a sub-Director in 1910 and a Director in 1919.

Mobilized with the Territorial Forces in 1914 he won the D.S.O. in 1917 and was severely wounded. Re-joined the Territorial Association after the war; he commanded the 5th South Lancs. from 1928–34.

He retired from the Executive direction of the Company in 1937, but remained a Director.

He has taken an active interest in municipal affairs as a member of the St Helens Borough Council for many years, and is still an Alderman.

A J.P. from 1934–56, he was Chairman of the Bench from 1954–6.

He is President of the St Helens Y.M.C.A. and a member of the National Council of Y.M.C.A.'s.

LAWRENCE HERBERT AUSTIN PILKINGTON

Born in Colorado, U.S.A., in 1911; second son of Richard Austin Pilkington.

Educated at Bromsgrove School and Magdalene College, Cambridge.

After a spell in Labrador with the Grenfell Mission, he joined the Firm in 1935; he was Manager of the Queenborough Works from 1937–9. He became a sub-Director in 1940 and a Director in 1943. Always associated primarily with the manufacturing side of the business, like his grandfather, William Windle Pilkington, and his uncle, Cecil Pilkington before him, his particular interests have been in the development of the Firm's research organization.

He has been closely associated for many years with the British Glass Industry's own Research organization based on Sheffield University, and was Chairman of the British Glass Industry Research Association from 1953.

In 1956 Sheffield University conferred an Honorary LL.D. on him in recognition of this work.

LIONEL ALEXANDER BETHUNE (ALASTAIR) PILKINGTON

Born 1920.

Educated at Sherborne School and Trinity College, Cambridge, where he began to read for a Mechanical Science degree, but his studies were interrupted by war service. He was commissioned in the Supplementary Reserve of the R.A. in 1938 and posted to Egypt a week after war was declared. He fought in the Desert, Greek and Crete campaigns, and then, having been taken prisoner in Crete, spent four years in Germany. On his return to Cambridge after the war, he gained three blues, for tennis, squash and fives, and, in 1947, he was Fives Doubles Amateur Champion of England.

1947 Joined Pilkington Brothers Limited. 1950–2 Production Manager and Assistant Works Manager at Doncaster. 1955 Director.

SIR HARRY PILKINGTON

Born in 1905; eldest son of Richard Austin Pilkington.

Educated at Rugby and Magdalene College, Cambridge.

Joined the Firm in 1927; associated wth the Sales side of the business, he became a Director in 1934 and succeeded Mr Geoffrey Pilkington as Chairman of the Company in 1949.

He has been a J.P. for St Helens since 1937.

He was Chairman of the Executive Committee of the National Council of Building Material Producers from 1944–52 and subsequently its President.

Since 1952 he has been a member of the British Productivity Council and also of the Dollar Exports Council.

He received a Knighthood in the New Year Honours of 1953.

From April 1953 to April 1955 he was President of the Federation of British Industries. In this capacity he became a member of the Council of European Industrial Federations of which he was President from 1954–7.

Since 1955 he has been a Director of the Bank of England.

In 1956 he became Chairman of the National Advisory Council on Education for Industry and Commerce, succeeding Lord Weeks in this post.

Government tasks he has undertaken include: in 1952, a single-handed investigation into methods and costs of School Buildings; in 1953, Chairmanship of a committee appointed by the Minister of Fuel and Power which led to the setting up of the National Industrial Fuel Efficiency Service in 1954; a member of a small committee to settle some of the troubles that arose over Crichel Down.

In 1957, at the personal request of the Prime Minister, he undertook the Chairmanship of the Royal Commission on Doctors' and Dentists' Remuneration.

He is a member of the Board of Triplex Holdings Limited.

He has lived since his marriage in 1930 at Windle Hall, St Helens, which has been a Pilkington family home continuously since the 1820s and he takes a fairly active part in many local activities in St Helens.

Manchester University conferred its LL.D. degree on him in 1959.

JAMES BONAR WATT

Born in 1896.

Educated at Allan Glen's School, Glasgow.

He joined the Firm in 1914, going soon afterwards to the new Thorold factory in Canada; he served in France during the First World War with the Canadian Artillery and returned to the Company in Canada after that war.

In 1923 he came back to the Sheet Glass Works at St Helens and was prominently associated with the successful and successive developments of mechanical Sheet Glass processes until he became Works Manager of the Sheet Glass works in 1938. He became a sub-Director in 1949 and a Director in 1950.

In 1951 he succeeded Mr James Meikle in his responsibilities both as Production Director and for the firm's Industrial Relations.

In 1955 he became a member of the North West Regional Gas Board.

LORD WEEKS

Ronald Morce Weeks, first Baron of Ryton, was born in 1890, and educated at Charterhouse and Caius College, Cambridge, where he was captain of the University Association Football XI.

1912 Joined Pilkington Brothers Limited as one of their first technical trainees. Served throughout the First World War, was mentioned in despatches three times and won the D.S.O., M.C. and Bar.

1920 Manager of Cowley Hill. 1928 Director. 1939 Succeeded Lord Cozens-Hardy as Chairman of the Executive Committee, but only held this position for a short time owing to the outbreak of war.

1934–8 Commanded the Fifth Battalion South Lancashire Regiment T.A. 1939 G.S.O.1 66th (Territorial) Division. 1940 Brigadier, General Staff at G.H.Q., Home Forces. 1941 Director-General of Army Equipment; Major-General. 1942 Deputy C.I.G.S. as Lieutenant-General with a seat in the Army Council. K.C.B. 1943. 1945 Deputy Military Governor and Chief of Staff, British Zone Control Commission for Germany.

1945 Retired from the Executive Committee of Pilkington Brothers Limited, but retained his seat on the Board. Became Director of Vickers Limited and Chairman of that Company from 1948 to 1956. His Vickers' connexion took him on to the Boards of a number of other concerns, including the English Steel Corporation, Palmers, Hebburn and Company Limited, Associated Electrical Industries Limited, and a number of engineering and kindred companies in the Dominions. He is a Director of the Royal Exchange Assurance and the

Hudson Bay Company. He was for a number of years a Director of the Westminster Bank, but he resigned on his appointment, in 1957, to succeed Lord Bruce of Melbourne as Chairman of the Finance Corporation for Industry.

Activities of a more benevolent nature include Directorship of Remploy Limited, Vice-Chairmanship of King George's Memorial Trust Fund, Chairmanship for some years of the National Advisory Council of Education for Industry and Commerce. He is President of the British Scientific Instrument Research Association. He is an Hon Fellow of Caius College, Cambridge, Chairman of the Governing Body of Charterhouse, and an Hon LL.D. of Liverpool University.

(2) *Former Directors*

LORD COZENS-HARDY

Edward Herbert Cozens-Hardy, third Baron of Letheringsett, born June 28, 1873. Educated at Rugby and the Royal Technical College.

Having served a pupilage with Brush, he went into partnership, in 1898, with Col. O'Gorman, the firm of O'Gorman and Cozens-Hardy acting as consultants in the young and rapidly growing electrical engineering industry. It was as a consulting engineer that he came into touch with Pilkington Brothers Limited in the early years of the present century in connexion with the electrification schemes at the Cowley Hill factory. His sister married Mr R. A. Pilkington in 1903 and he himself joined the Board in October 1908. His father, Sir Herbert Cozens-Hardy, in turn Lord Justice of Appeal and Master of the Rolls, was created the First Baron in 1914 and he succeeded to the title on the death of his elder brother in 1924.

He played a particularly active part in the life of the Company in the inter-war period and was responsible for the internal reorganization of 1931. He was Chairman of the Executive Committee from its formation until 1939. He retired altogether from the company in March of that year but returned as a member of the Board at the outbreak of war and continued to serve the Company in that capacity until his death on October 22, 1956.

He was for many years a J.P. for Lancashire, being Chairman of the Prescot Magistrates and Chairman of the Standing Joint Committee for the County, and a Deputy Lieutenant for Lancashire for nearly forty years. He was also a J.P. for Norfolk.

JOHN HERBERT DICKINSON

Born in 1870.

Joined the Firm as its first resident solicitor in 1905, his father, though unqualified, having looked after much of the firm's legal business before him with the title of 'Agent'.

Mobilized with the Territorial Force in 1914, he was awarded the M.C. and Bar for acts of gallantry and leadership, the Bar at the age of 43.

In 1931, together with Mr W. S. Tunnock, he became one of the first two non-share qualified Directors and served as a Director until 1937 when he retired.

He died in 1958.

JAMES MEIKLE

Born in 1890.

Educated at Allan Glen's School, Glasgow, and the Royal Technical College, Glasgow.

He served his early years with Allen Maclellan, Mavor & Coulson, and with the electricity undertaking of Glasgow Corporation.

He joined the Firm in 1914 as an Electrical Engineer; he became Assistant Works Manager at Doncaster in 1926 and at Cowley Hill in 1929. He succeeded the then Major R. M. Weeks as Manager of Cowley Hill in September 1931. He became an Executive Director in 1937. When Colonel Weeks was mobilized in 1939 Mr Meikle became the Firm's principal Production Director and so remained until he retired from executive work in 1951. He was prominently associated not only with the technical aspects of manufacture but also with the Firm's industrial relations, and he was Chairman of the St Helens Group of Manufacturers from 1939–51.

He retired from the Board finally in 1953.

ALFRED CECIL PILKINGTON

Born 1875; youngest son of William Windle Pilkington.

Educated at Shrewsbury and Christ Church, Oxford. He was brought into the Company in 1897 and followed very much in his father's footsteps as the technical expert on the Board. He played a dominating part in the management of the works and in labour matters generally until 1931 when he moved to Oxford. He continued to give advice, as a member of the Board, and was always available for consultation on all matters of policy, whether general or manufacturing.

He retired from the Board in 1950.

His interests have been mainly scientific. This scientific bent later found an outlet in farming when he developed a large and up-to-date farm on the outskirts of Oxford.

ARTHUR RICHARD PILKINGTON

Born 1871.

Entered the Firm in 1892 and became a Director when Pilkington Brothers became a limited company in 1894. Gained practical experience on the manufacturing side of the business and then moved to the commercial side. He became Chairman of the Company in 1914, but a few years later his health broke down and he died in January 1921.

He had led an active life outside the works, in the South Lancashire Regiment from 1896 to 1904; as a J.P. (from 1903); as a member of the St Helens County Borough Council (1906–9), and, in particular, as a warden of the St Helens Parish Church. He was keenly interested in farming.

RICHARD AUSTIN PILKINGTON

Born February 8, 1871.

Educated at Shrewsbury and Christ Church, Oxford.

Immediately after leaving Oxford he joined the Firm and became a Director when Pilkington Brothers was formed into a limited company in 1894. In about 1908 he had a severe illness and was advised to live abroad 'for some considerable time' in order to recuperate. He went to Colorado and recovered completely. He was attending Board meetings once more in the summer of 1912 and, in the autumn of that year, was able to leave for Canada in connexion with the new factory about to be built there. He continued to take a very active part in the direction of the Company and was even able to serve in the Army for a time during the First World War, despite his past medical history and despite the fact that he was at that time already forty-five years of age.

In 1921, on the death of Arthur Richard Pilkington (see above), he became Chairman of the Company and continued in that position until 1931. He then retired from active management, though he continued to play an important advisory role as a member of the Board until shortly before his death in 1951.

Prior to 1931 he was for a long time the Senior Sales Director and was personally known to almost every important customer in the Commonwealth. He was particularly interested in social matters. Inside the Company, he was always on the side of social reform; outside it, he spent much time in public affairs. He was particularly interested in local education, was a member of the St Helens Education Committee for many years, and in 1921 became its Chairman. The endowment of the Pilkington Scholarships (see page 215) was on his initiative, and for about twenty-five years was the only Independent member on the Town Council. He was particularly interested in the work of the Y.M.C.A. and the London Missionary Society, of both of which he was an active and very successful national treasurer for many years. Like his ancestors, he was a Congregationalist, and of a tolerant and broad mind, and few good causes in St Helens looked to him in vain for help in one way or another. He was a J.P. in the town for some fifty years.

His private interests were very widespread and included reading, gardening and mountaineering. He was an exceptionally active man and very fond of the open air.

WILLIAM NORMAN PILKINGTON

Born July 26, 1877.

Educated at Clifton and Trinity College, Cambridge. While at the university he captained the Rugby Football XV, played in international matches, and was first string in the hundred yards against Oxford in 1897 and 1898.

He joined Pilkington Brothers Limited in place of his brother, Ernest Sinclair Pilkington, who joined the Army at the time of the Boer War and did not return to the Company. Director 1905.

Concerned himself with local affairs, becoming a member of St Helens County Borough Council and Rainford U.D.C. (of which he was for a time Chairman), and a J.P. He was also President of the St Helens Y.M.C.A. and a member of the Y.M.C.A.'s National Council. He took a deep interest in the life of the Church of England both in St Helens and Rainford.

He joined the Prince of Wales's Volunteers in 1900, rising to the rank of Major by 1912. He served with distinction throughout the First World War, being awarded the D.S.O. and Bar. He was gazetted Lieutenant-Colonel in 1920, and it is as Colonel Norman Pilkington that he is usually remembered. He retired from command of the Battalion in 1928.

He was Chairman of the Company from July to December, 1931, during the reorganization of the Board, and remained as a Director until his death on February 8, 1935. His hobbies included cricket, golf, and shooting.

JOHN TILBURY

Born in 1887.

Was apprenticed to the London and North Western Railway in the office of the Superintendent of the line at Euston in 1902.

Served in the R.E. (Railway Transport Establishment) throughout the First World War. He was mentioned in despatches and commissioned in 1916.

He joined the Firm on demobilization in 1919, becoming Manager of the Railway Department in 1922, then transferred to the Sales Department in 1924; Manager of the Export Department in 1928, and of the Home and Export Departments in 1935. He became a sub-Director in 1938, a Director and member of the Executive Committee in 1944, and retired in 1950.

WILLIAM STUART TUNNOCK

Born in 1877.

Educated at Glasgow High School.

Joined the Firm as office boy at the Glasgow warehouse in September 1891, his father then being Pilkingtons' Scottish Agent. He himself became Scottish

Agent early in the present century and remained in this position until 1912 when he went to Canada in connection with the beginnings of window glass manufacture there. On his return from Canada at the end of 1915, he was sent to investigate trade conditions in New Zealand. He subsequently revisited Canada regularly. He was Secretary of the Company from 1919 until 1932, having become a sub-Director in 1920. During this period he was Mr R. A. Pilkington's right-hand man on the sales side of the business. In 1931 he became one of the first two non-share-qualified Directors, serving on the Executive Committee until 1938 and on the Board until 1940, when he retired through ill-health.

He died in 1947.

THE EARLY HISTORY OF THE FLOW PROCESS: PILKINGTONS' ASSOCIATION WITH THE FORD MOTOR COMPANY DETROIT

———————————

C. W. Avery, whom Henry Ford placed in charge of his plate glass plant at the end of the First World War, had been a student at the University of Michigan and was subsequently Edsel Ford's teacher of manual training at Detroit University School before entering the service of the Ford Motor Company.[1] Just before the First World War he had been chiefly responsible for creating Ford's precisely-timed continuous vehicle production line.[2]

About glassmaking Fords knew nothing when these experiments began. One of their employees who happened to be in charge of windscreen assembly was sent to the local library by Avery and told to 'read up on glass'.[3] He was accompanied by the Assistant Superintendent of the Highland Park plant, W. C. Klann, on whose account, together with that of Avery himself, we rely for the description of how the process was developed. Klann continues:

> 'We sent for a little crucible from Germany. It was about a month before we got the crucible back and it only held about a pint. It was about an inch thick. We got some burners and put it [sic] underneath the heat and mixed our sand and our glass and lead and arsenic and everything else. We mixed it all and it came out a piece of black glass as black as a telephone. . .
>
> Then we sent to England for a crucible. . . It held about four pounds of glass, enough to make a piece of glass about one foot square. With that we made our first white glass . . .'

These experiments began, apparently, in 1919.[4] When they had been completed, Avery decided to build a furnace about twelve feet long and, beneath it, a pit, ten feet deep, into which the ribbon of glass could be poured. After eight months' work, however, they still—in Klann's words—'couldn't use the glass no how'.[5]

The dismissal, in January 1921, of a certain Edward Donner, who had been particularly concerned with this stage of research, brought an indignant letter from him, complaining of Avery's being 'so wrapped up in the development of the plate machine, which contains some of his (Avery's) personal ideas'.[6] Perhaps it was at this point that Henry Ford's continued financial support, despite the disappointing results, made all the difference between success and failure. Avery recalled later how, having spent 1,500,000 dollars, he went to Ford, hardly expecting to receive a further grant. 'If this experiment works', he urged, 'we will save many times the money we have spent'. To which Ford replied: 'What do you mean—*if* it works? It *must* work. Forget the money you have spent and go back and make it work'.[7]

Avery persisted, and by the end of 1921 he had solved all the mechanical problems. He had devised a method of flowing glass successfully; but most of the glass produced by the tank was not up to standard and the rest was quite unusable.[8]

At this point Pilkingtons began to hear about these developments. R. F. Taylor, who had been their representative in North America and was himself a technical man, heard various rumours just before he sailed for home in December 1921, and additional information came *via* J. E. Harrison, Pilkingtons' manager in Canada.[9] Pilkingtons decided to send R. F. Taylor on a visit to Detroit, together with F. B. Waldron, the mechanical engineer at Cowley Hill.

When they called on Avery, the two Pilkington representatives were perturbed to find that the American plate glass concerns and the St Gobain Company had already been there before them. But, once more, Pilkingtons' unusual position as makers of both plate and sheet glass gave them a particular advantage. Plate glass manufacturers elsewhere had little working knowledge of tanks and had thrown cold water on Avery's work, claiming that plate glass could never be made in a tank. R. F. Taylor, who knew about tanks, took no such superior attitude. As soon as he saw Avery's plant, he realized at once that here was a development of major importance and he told the inventor so and congratulated him. His enthusiasm contrasted so markedly with the coolness shown by the earlier visiting glass experts that an accord was immediately established between Pilkingtons and Fords. Taylor and Waldron returned so St Helens with their exciting news. The Board at once decided to conduct experiments on one of the tanks at Grove Street 'to roll a sheet about 6 ft. wide. The making of the drawings and machinery for the experiments [were] to be done by Mr Waldron and the experiment to be carried out by Mr LeMare in consultation with Mr Railton.'[10]

Behind these experiments stood Cecil Pilkington, the director responsible for technical development. He was already quite sure in his own mind that glass suitable for plate glass manufacture could be made in a tank, and the pilot experiments, carried out during the summer of 1922, justified his confidence.

Pilkingtons now knew that a wide ribbon of glass could be produced (Fords had only been concerned with a narrow ribbon for car windows) and were impressed by the smoothness of the surface, which would lead to great economies in grinding. On October 10, 1922, the Board authorized the expenditure of £10,000 on continuous casting plant in the Rolled Plate department at Grove Street and ordered that preparations be made to install the new process at Cowley Hill. In the following months Austin Pilkington, accompanied by R. F. Taylor and W. S. Tunnock, then secretary of the company, visited Fords to discuss the next step. Negotiations proceeded remarkably smoothly. Fords' flow process, though making a satisfactory ribbon of glass, was still not making good glass; Pilkingtons knew they could remedy this by work on Fords' tank. Fords, in the meantime, although they used some of their own glass, despite its sub-standard quality, still had to buy much of their requirements from other manufacturers and Austin Pilkington, the director in charge of sales, was able to promise Fords to supply them from St Helens. Finally, Pilkingtons had been developing a grinding machine and this became a good bargaining counter in the negotiations. Fords were themselves developing a continuous grinder of a sort—the glass, mounted on small trucks, travelled at intervals under a series of grinders and polishing heads—but this machine was inferior to the one then being developed at St Helens. Fords were also rather anxious about their patent rights on this machine and were glad of the chance to settle these legal points.

Pilkingtons had thus much to offer Fords in return for their flow process: the technical knowledge to improve the tank, the Waldron grinding equipment and, in the interim, a reliable supply of glass. On December 12, 1922, the Board heard the result of the visit to Detroit 'and arrangements arrived at for interchange of experience. It was reported that drawings of the Waldron Grinder had already been mailed, that further particulars were ready to be sent to Mr Avery . . .' Pilkington experts—notably E. B. LeMare and J. H. Griffin—went to assist Fords at Detroit and, at St Helens, the new continuous plant was installed at Cowley Hill.

ABBREVIATIONS USED IN FOOTNOTES

L.R.O.   Lancashire Record Office, Preston
P.R.O.   Public Record Office, London
J.S.G.T.   *Journal of the Society of Glass Technology*
H.M.C.   Historical Manuscripts Commission
Cal. S.P.D.   Calendar of State Papers Domestic
D.N.B.   *Dictionary of National Biography*
B.P.G.M.   Minutes of the British Plate Glass Company

Unless otherwise specified, all documents referred to are
among the archives of Pilkington Brothers Limited.

CHAPTER I

THE FAMILY BACKGROUND

[1] L.R.O., will of Richard Hardman, dated February 20, 1658/9, and proved at Chester in 1661.

[2] Ronald Stewart-Brown, *A History of the Manor and Township of Allerton* (Liverpool 1911), 29. The following account of events at Allerton is chiefly based on this source.

[3] *Whitworth's Manchester Advertiser*, April 3, 1759; *Liverpool Chronicle*, April 6, 1759. A rather fulsome letter, signed by T.P., printed in the latter paper on April 13, dealt at length with John Hardman's outstanding qualities.

[4] L.R.O., DDPi 9/2. In 1761 Lawrence Haslam, a weaver of Wigan, successfully advanced his claim through Elizabeth Hardman but in 1763 it was decreed that this share should go to James Russell of Darcy Lever who had a prior claim. Richard Pilkington and James Russell thereafter succeeded in warding off all other claimants.   [5] *Ibid.*

[6] P.R.O., Palatinate of Lancaster Records, Chancery Records, Bills, P.L. 6/82/38, June 9, 1761.   [7] *Ibid.*

[8] Thomas Hampson, *Horwich: Its History, Legends and Church* (Wigan, 1883), 179–80; L.R.O., DDPi 9/2. For Richard Pilkington's ancestors, see Appendix I.

[9] Hampson, *op. cit.*, 158, 159, 164, 175.

[10] See also *Historical Gleanings of Bolton and District*, Ed. B. T. Barton (Bolton, 1883), III, 198 *seq.*

[11] The various court cases arising out of claims against Richard Pilkington's right to the manor of Allerton must have taken up much time and energy. In June, 1761, Richard Pilkington was even obliged to bring an action against Lawrence Haslam and others to restrain them from hewing down trees on the estate. Richard Pilkington's Bill is to be found among the Palatinate of Lancaster Chancery Records at the Public Record Office, P.L.6/82/38 and the answer of Haslam and others in P.L.7/170.

[12] L.R.O., DDPi 7/1, 8/5. Deeds January 10, 1778, May 1, 1781.

[13] L.R.O., DDPi 7/1.

[14] Evidence of Richard Pilkington (b. 1763) to the Commissioners of Enclosure of Horwich Moor (Bolton Reference Library). I owe this reference to Mr J. Charnock of Horwich.

[15] *Manchester Mercury*, April 4, 1786.

[16] The diary is among the Pilkington Papers at the Lancashire Record Office.

[17] Archibald Sparke, *Bibliographia Boltoniensis* (Manchester, 1913), 114.

[18] L.R.O., DDPi 7/1. Deed of January 10, 1778.

[19] See below.

[20] L.R.O., DDPi 8/5. Deed of May 1, 1781.

[21] A. P. Wadsworth and J. de L. Mann, *The Cotton Trade and Industrial Lancashire* (Manchester, 1931), 488.

[22] L.R.O., DDPi 8/7. Deed of June 28, 1784.

[23] L.R.O., DDPi 2/1. 23 Geo. III cap. 77, An Act For the More Effectual Encouragement of the Manufacture of Flax and Cotton in Great Britain.

[24] Bucking consisted in the repeated pouring of a solution of alkali and soap in water over cloth at blood heat. The cloth was then crofted, or laid out in the open air. Bucking and crofting was continued ten to sixteen times, the strength of the lye being increased and then decreased. The cloth was then soured (with dilute sulphuric acid) and soaped. The processes of bucking, crofting, souring and soaping were then repeated.

[25] Wadsworth and Mann, *op. cit.*, 178.

[26] L.R.O., DDPi 5/9. Letter from William Talbot of Liverpool dated October 29, 1793.

[27] S. H. Higgins, *A History of Bleaching* (1924), 82 *et seq.*

[28] L.R.O., DDPi 1/4. Richard Pilkington to Samuel Rathbone, Bill for Lancashire Assizes, March, 1794.

[29] On January 27, 1792, Robert Walmsley of Bolton, fustian manufacturer, was bound to Richard Pilkington for a loan of £250 (L.R.O., DDPi 4/2). On April 11, 1793, Walmsley and James Pilkington of Horwich, described as a whitster (i.e. a bleacher), agreed to become co-partners trading under the name of Walmsley and Pilkington with a warehouse in Spring Gardens, Bolton. James Pilkington was to bring £650 to the partnership within three months (DDPi 10/10). The two became bankrupt on August 7, 1795, and were discharged on December 22, 1800 (DDPi 10/13).

[30] L.R.O., will of Richard Pilkington, proved on December 4, 1797.

[31] According to Richard Pilkington's will, the Liverpool estates were to be sold to 'Mr Wakefield and others'. They eventually passed to William Roscoe (Stewart Brown, *op. cit.*, 65).

[32] Diary, September 20, 1796.

[33] L.R.O., will of Richard Pilkington senior proved on October 27, 1788, and that of his son on December 4, 1797.

[34] L.R.O., DDPi 8/11, 8/14. Leases to John Hopwood, bleachers, 1804 and 1817.

[35] *Manchester Mercury*, October 10, 1797.

[36] L.R.O., DDPi 5/4, 5/9.

[37] L.R.O., DDPi 8/11. Lease of 1804.

[38] Manchester Reference Library, MS. Fee Book and House Expenses of Dr Guest of Bedford Leigh, *sub* October 8, 1788.

[39] Cecil Wall, *The History of the Surgeons' Company 1745–1800* (1937), 90.

[40] Wall, *op. cit.*, 83–4. For the experiences of a Lancashire doctor's son while walking the London hospitals in 1743–4, see *A Lancashire Doctor's Diary 1737 to 1750* (Southport, 1895), 12–18.

[41] St Helens Reference Library, Parr Poor Law Papers, Doctors' Account Book, August 3, 1781.

[42] St Helens Congregational Church, Bond dated March, 1788.

[43] L.R.O., Land Tax returns (Windle Township).

[44] L.R.O., DDPi 5/9. William Pilkington to Richard Pilkington, May 30, 1790.

[45] Diary of Richard Pilkington, January 6, 1794.

[46] L.R.O., DDPi 5/8.

[47] The last bill from Pilkington and Walker to the Overseers of the Poor of Parr was settled in April, 1813. In that month the Overseers accepted the services of Walker and Gaskell. (Doctors' Account Book among the Parr Poor Law Papers at St Helens Reference Library.) William Pilkington was for a time in partnership with William Atherton of Rainford, in respect of his wine and spirit business. The partnership was dissolved on May 12, 1810 (*London Gazette*, August 25, 1810).

[48] The indentures of apprenticeship are preserved among the archives at Pilkington Brothers Ltd.

[49] Library of H.M. Customs and Excise, Treasury and Excise Papers, *125*, 540–4. Petition of William Pilkington junior, December 23, 1825.

[50] L.R.O., DDPi 5/9-19.

[51] Library of H.M. Customs and Excise, Treasury and Excise Papers, *125*, 540–4. Petition of William Pilkington junior, December 23, 1825.

[52] Seventh Report from the Commisioners of Excise Inquiry (British Spirits) 1834 [7] XXV, 16–17.

[53] 6 Geo. IV cap. 80. The duty was reduced from 10/6 per wine gallon to 7/– per imperial

gallon, equivalent to 5/10 per wine gallon (Hansard's Parliamentary Debates, new series, XIII, cols. 133–4, April 22, 1825.)

[54] About a dozen firms in England distilled what were known as Plain British Spirits. These were sold to rectifiers, of whom there were 108 in England in 1832. Of these firms there were seven in Liverpool, nine in Manchester, one at Bolton, one at Warrington besides William Pilkington & Sons at St Helens. The rectifiers redistilled the Plain British Spirits and compounded them with certain herbs, berries and seeds to add flavour (7th Report from the Commissioners of Excise Inquiry (British Spirits) 1834 [7] XXV, 29, 234–6; article on Messrs Octavius Smith and Co's distillery in the *Penny Magazine*, XI, 303–4.)

[55] *St Helens Newspaper*, September 21, 1872; petition December 23, 1825.

[56] Petition, December 23, 1825.

CHAPTER 2

THE HISTORICAL BACKGROUND TO THE FLAT GLASS
INDUSTRY IN BRITAIN

[1] J. U. Nef, *The Rise of the British Coal Industry* (1932), I, 359.

[2] S. E. Winbolt, *Wealden Glass* (Hove, 1933), 53. See also the same writer's contributions in *J.S.G.T.*, vols. XVI (1932) and XX (1936).

[3] Minutes of the British Plate Glass Company (henceforward referred to as B.P.G.M.), April 12, 1815. The local sand was, of course, used for grinding.

[4] Kurgliga Biblioteket, Stockholm, MS. M.260. J. L. Robsahms dagbok over en resa i England, 1761. I owe this reference to Mr M. W. Flinn.

[5] 23 Eliz. cap. 5. For a recent discussion of this subject see G. Hammersley, 'The Crown Woods and Their Exploitation in the Sixteenth and Seventeenth Centuries', *Bulletin of the Institute of Historical Research*, 30 (1957), 148 seq.

[6] William Hyde Price, *The English Patents of Monopoly* (Cambridge, Mass., 1906), 107–8.

[7] Rhys Jenkins, 'The Reverberatory Furnace with Coal Fuel, 1612–1712', *Transactions of the Newcomen Society*, XIV (1933–4), 68.

[8] T. S. Ashton, *Iron and Steel in the Industrial Revolution* (Manchester, 1924), 10.

[9] State Papers Domestic, James I, vol. 162, No. 64 (April 16, 1624), cited in Albert Hartshorne, *Old English Glasses* (1897), 424; debate in the House of Commons, May 7, 1621, Notestein, Relf and Simpson, *Commons Debates 1621*, New Haven 1935, III, 196.

[10] Simon Sturtevant, *Metallica* (dated May 22, 1612) in *Dud Dudley's Metallum Martis* ed. Bagnall (Wolverhampton 1854), 8; *The Loseley Manuscripts* ed. Alfred John Kempe (1836), 493.

[11] Part of the following account is a version of Warren C. Scoville's observations on the glasshouse *à l'anglaise* in his volume *Capitalism and French Glassmaking 1640–1789* (University of California Publications in Economics 1950), 41–2. For wood-fired furnace designs, *ibid.*, 37–8, and Georgius Agricola, *De Re Metallica* (1556), translated by Herbert Clark Hoover and Lou Henry Hoover (London, 1912), 584 *et seq.*

[12] D. R. Guttery, *From Broad Glass to Cut Crystal* (1956), 38.

[13] State Papers Domestic, July 27 and 28, 1610, cited in Price, *op. cit.*, 71.

[14] Nef, *op. cit.*, I, 222; Scoville, *op. cit.*, 42.

[15] Glasier's Petition, April 15, 1621, Notestein, Relf and Simpson, *op. cit.*, VII, 547; Price, *op. cit.*, 68.

[16] Petition Against Mansell's Patent, Alford Papers cited in Notestein Relf and Simpson, *op. cit.*, VII, 540.

[17] Several Dutch glassmakers settled in England in the 1530s and 1540s and are believed to have blown window glass in Southwark (*Letters of Denization and Acts of Naturalisation 1509–1603*, ed. William Page, Publications of the Huguenot Society, VII (1893), xiv). M. S. Guiseppi in the *Victoria County History of Surrey* (1905), II, 298, reached the conclusion that the old art of making window glass was never, in fact, lost. Possibly the Bungards were writing about Normandy, or crown, glass.

[18] For these families, see H. S. Glazebrook, *Collections for a Genealogy of the Noble Families of De Hennezel, etc.* (privately printed 1872).

[19] *Cal. S.P.D. 1547–80*, 297; Hartshorne, *op. cit.*, 393–6; *Cal. S.P.D. Addenda, 1566–79*, 34; R. H. Tawney and Eileen Power, *Tudor Economic Documents* (3 vols. 1924), I, 302–7; George Longe to Burghley, 1589, Lansdowne MSS. 59/72, transcribed in Hartshorne, *op. cit.*, 403.

[20] E. Graham Clark, 'Glass-making in Lorraine', *J.S.G.T.*, XV (1931), 111–3.

[21] S. E. Wimbolt, *op. cit.*; L. F. Salzman, *English Industries in the Middle Ages* (Oxford, 1923), 183–6; M. S. Guiseppi in the *Victoria County History of Surrey*, II (1905), 295–6.

[22] MSS. of Rye Corporation, 1579, 1581 (*H.M.C.*, 13th Report, Appendix Part IV, 62–3, 75–6); *Cal. S.P.D.*, April 25, 1574; *Victoria County History of Surrey*, II, 298.

[23] S.P.D., Jas. I, vol. 162, No. 64, transcribed in Hartshorne, *op. cit.*, 424.

[24] Longe to Burghley, October 3, 1589 (Lansdowne MSS. 59/75, transcribed in Hartshorne, *op. cit.*, 402).

[25] Alford Papers transcribed in Notestein, Relf and Simpson, *op. cit.*, 543.

[26] *Registre de l'Eglise Wallone de Southampton* (Publications of the Huguenot Society, vol. IV) contains references to Buckholt glassmakers and Hartshorne, *op. cit.*, 171–2, a report on excavations. For glassmaking on the North Staffordshire–Shropshire border, see T. Pape, 'Medieval Glassworkers in North Staffordshire', *Transactions of the North Staffordshire Field Club*, LXVIII (1933–4), 74–121.

[27] Newent Parish Registers, 1599 and 1601, cited by A. W. Cornelius Hannen, 'Glass-making', *Scottish Antiquary*, VII, 151; J. Stuart Daniels, *The Woodchester Glass House* (Gloucester, 1950).

[28] For this proclamation, see Hartshorne, *op. cit.*, 413–4.

[29] New Letters Patent were issued on January 19, 1614–5, granting a monopoly of the use of the new furnace to Thomas Percival and nine others, mostly courtiers.

[30] *D.N.B.* summarizes most of the known facts about Mansell.

[31] James Howell, *Epistolae Ho-Elianae* (5th ed. 1678), 68.

[32] *Loseley Manuscripts*, 493.

[33] State Papers Domestic, Jas. I, Vol. 162, No. 63, transcribed by Hartshorne, *op. cit.*, 426–30.

[34] Sturtevant, *Metallica*, 110.

[35] The following is based upon Mansell's own account, written in 1624 (State Papers Domestic, Jas. I, Vol. 162, No. 63, printed in Hartshorne, *op. cit.*, 427). The Scots at this time were very touchy about this export of their coal to what was, apart from the union of thrones, a foreign land. The matter was raised before the Scottish Privy Council (*Register of the Privy Council of Scotland* ed. Masson, X, 277, 372, 382–3). The same source also contains useful information about the Scottish glass patent and the glasshouse at Wemyss, the rivalry of which was a constant worry to Mansell in the earlier years of his patent (XI, 138–9; XII, 374, 428, 439–40, 451–2, 772).

[36] In December 1615, an agreement was made between Sir Percival Willoughby and Sir Robert Mansell whereby Willoughby leased to Mansell a great barn as Wollaton for seven years with dwelling house and garden adjoining them in the occupation of Jacob Henzey and John Squire, two glassmakers. He also contracted to deliver at the barn as much coal as Mansell's workmen should require to use in the two glassworks lately erected in the barn. On July 23,

1617, arrangements were being made to build a glasshouse and furnace near the coalpits at Awsworth. (H.M.C., MSS. of Lord Middleton, *69*, 499–500.) It is difficult to know whether either of these ventures was connected with Mansell's main effort or whether they were merely smaller furnaces, intended to supply a local market. The first coal-fired 'glassworks', housed in a barn, was obviously a very makeshift affair. The second one, where both glasshouse and furnace were to be specially built, may have borne a closer resemblance to the new model.

[37] S.P.D., Chas. I, vol. 282, No. 99, transcribed in Hartshorne, *op. cit.*, 432. Some glass had been exported from Newcastle at the end of the sixteenth century in very small quantities and the suggestion has been made that this was in the form of bottles. Whether they had been made in the Newcastle area, is not clear. (Nef, *op. cit.*, I, 180; Alexander Nesbitt, *Notes on the History of Glass-making*, privately printed 1869, 128.)

[38] Nef, *op. cit.*, I, 25.

[39] Newcastle Reference Library, details of the parish register of All Saints, Newcastle. Edward Hensey, described as servant to Sir Robert Mansfield, was buried on February 11, 1617/18. Other references to glassmakers occur on July 8, 1619, January 1, 1620, and October 15, 1620.

[40] S.P.D., Jas. I, vol. 162, No. 63, cited in Hartshorne, *op. cit.*, 430.

[41] *Ibid.*, 427. An agreement dated 1678 gave glassmakers permission to dig clay at Bichfield, Northumberland (*Proceedings of the Society of Antiquaries of Newcastle-upon-Tyne*, I, new series (1884) 127). This may have been the neighbourhood where Mansell obtained his clay. On the other hand, leases of glasshouses in Newcastle itself, dated June 7, 1658, and October 20, 1679, include the right to dig clay for the use of the glasshouses. (Archivist's Section, Town Clerk's Department, Newcastle, 43/2/50; 46/2/50.)

[42] S.P.D., Jas. I, vol. 162, No. 63, cited in Hartshorne, *op. cit.*, 430.

[43] Cal. S.P.D., Chas. I, September 15, 1640; T. S. Willan, *The English Coasting Trade, 1600–1750* (Manchester, 1938), 98–9.

[44] *Journals of the House of Commons*, II, 523, 529, 530, 596 (April 12, 15, May 31, 1642); Price, *op. cit.*, 78.

[45] *Extracts from the Newcastle-upon-Tyne Council Minute Book, 1639–56* (Newcastle, 1920), 54, 74–5. For the site of Mansell's glasshouses, recital in lease dated June 7, 1758, Archivist's Section, Town Clerk's Department, Newcastle, 43/2/50.

[46] *Chorographia or a Survey of Newcastle-upon-Tyne, 1649* (reprinted Newcastle, 1818), 40.

[47] Thomas Salmon, *South Shields, Its Past, Present and Future* (South Shields, 1856), 21.

[48] The Rev C. E. Adamson, 'John Dagnia of South Shields, Glassmaker', *Proceedings of the Society of Antiquaries of Newcastle-upon-Tyne*, New Series, VI (1894), 163.

[49] P.R.O., Chancery Records C5.284/96. Bill from Zachariah Tizack of Howden Pans, broad glassmaker, dated February 28, 1697/8.

[50] Guttery, *op. cit.*, particularly chapter 5.

[51] *The City and Country Purchaser's and Builder's Dictionary or the Complete Builder's Guide* originally written by Richard Neve (3rd ed. 1736) *sub* Glass.

[52] *Craftsman*, April 30, 1743, quoted in Francis Buckley, 'Glasshouses on the Tyne in the Eighteenth Century', *J.S.G.T.*, X (1926), 43. Isaac Cookson was living at Newcastle when his father, William Cookson of Penrith, drew up his will prior to his death in 1712 (*Newcastle Daily Chronicle*, May 20, 1897). For eye witness accounts of the Newcastle glasshouses, see Basil Cozens-Hardy (ed.), *The Diary of Silas Neville, 1767–1788* (1950), 158, and B. Faujas de Saint Fond, *A Journey Through England and Scotland to the Hebrides in 1784* (Glasgow, 2 vols., 1907), I, 133.

[53] 13th Report of the Commissioners of Excise Inquiry (Glass), 1835, [15] XXXI, Appendix 7.

[54] *Ibid.*, Appendix 23.

[55] State Papers Domestic, James I, Vol. 162, No. 63, cited in Hartshorne, *op. cit.*, 431.

[56] Thomas May, 'On the Altar and Other Relics Found during Recent Excavations (1895–6)

on the site of the Roman Station at Wilderspool', *Transactions of the Historic Society of Lancashire and Cheshire*, XLVIII (1897), 16–17.

[57] L. R. Salzman, *English Industries of the Middle Ages* (Oxford, 1923), 186; Maurice B. Ridgway and George B. Leach, 'Further Notes on the Glasshouse site at Kingswood, Delamere, Cheshire', *Chester Archaeological Society Journal*, XXXVII, Part 1 (1948), 133–40; Maurice H. Ridgway, 'Coloured Glass in Cheshire', *Transactions of the Lancashire and Cheshire Antiquarian Society*, LIX (1947), 41–84, LX (1948), 56–85.

[58] J. A. Twemlow, *Liverpool Town Books* (Liverpool, 1918), II, 549–51, 708, 789, 974; *The House and Farm Accounts of the Shuttleworths of Gawthorpe Hall, 1582–1621*, Chetham Society, old series, *35* (1856); L.R.O., Quarter Sessions Records (Recognizances).

[59] The Register was printed by the Lancashire Parish Register Society in 1902. I am grateful to the late F. A. Bailey for drawing my attention to this source.

[60] In the vicinity of St Helens, for instance, there are two names which denote that glasshouses were once worked nearby: Glasshouse Close near Carr Mill, and Glasshouse Farm near Lea Green. There is no trace whatsoever in any records relating to these furnaces.

[61] J. P. Earwaker, *East Cheshire Past and Present* (1877), I, 405–6n. [62] *Ibid.*

[63] For information concerning Shirdley Hill sand, P. G. H. Boswell, *A Memoir of British Resources of Sands and Rocks Used in Glass-Making* (London, 1918), 64, and the same author's paper on 'British Glass-Sands: Their Location and Characteristics', *J.S.G.T.*, I (1917), 20–4. A map showing the geographical extent of this sand is to be found in Wilfred Smith, *A Physical Survey of Merseyside* (Liverpool, 1946), 23.

[64] Thomas Baines, *History of the Commerce and Town of Liverpool* (1852), 715.

[65] Evidence of Thomas Holt to the Committee of the Whole House on Orders in Council 1812 [210] III, 292. The glass industry at Bristol appears to have grown up in much the same way. A historian of the port wrote in the early 1790s that 'The call for window glass at home, at Bath and in the Towns about Bristol; in the Western Counties, Wales, and from North to South wherever Bristol Trade extends, and the great quantities sent to America, employ several houses for this article'. (Quoted by Professor MacInnes in *The Trade Winds*, ed, Parkinson, 1948, 65.)

[66] Pearce Davis, *The Development of the American Glass Industry* (Cambridge, Mass., 1949), chapters 3 and 4.

[67] *A Collection of Letters for the Improvement of Husbandry and Trade* (ed. Houghton), No. 198, May 15, 1696. This list appears to have been connected with the recently-introduced excise duty on glass. It has been reproduced by J. N. L. Baker in *A Historical Geography of England Before AD 1800* (ed. Darby) (Cambridge, 1936), 420.

[68] Liverpool Town Books, October 23, 1721; Chadwick's Map of Liverpool (1725); George Skene's observations of 1729, published in *The Miscellany of the Spalding Club* (Aberdeen, 1940), II, 132; Francis Buckley, 'Old Lancashire Glasshouses', *J.S.G.T.*, XIII (September, 1929); C. P. Hampson, 'History of Glass-making in Lancashire', *Transactions of the Lancashire and Cheshire Antiquarian Society*, XLVIII (1932), 70–1. It seems unlikely that glassmaking was carried on in Liverpool on any scale before the middle of 1724, when St Nicholas's Church registers first begin to include glassmakers. (Transcripts at L.R.O.)

[69] L.R.O., transcripts of Warrington Registers.

[70] *St James's Evening Post*, December 12–14, 1745, quoted in R. C. Jarvis, 'The Rebellion of 1745. The Passage Through Lancashire from Contemporary News-Sheets', *Transactions of the Lancashire and Cheshire Antiquarian Society*, LVI (1941–2), 144.

[71] King's College, Cambridge, MS. PC 2/132. Survey of the Manor of Prescot, 1721. Quoted in a paper on 'Early Glassmaking in Prescot', read to the Prescot Historic Society in 1946 by Mrs R. H. Hughes, the manuscript of which is in the possession of the Society. I am also indebted to the late F. A. Bailey for information about glassmaking in Prescot.

[72] *Craftsman*, June 22, 1734, quoted in Buckley, *J.S.G.T.*, *13* (1929), 239.

[73] *Selections from the Diary of Nicholas Blundell* ed. T. Ellison Gibson (Liverpool, 1895), 153–4.

[74] *The Travels Through England of Dr Richard Pococke* ed J. J. Cartwright (Camden Society 1888, New Series *42*, 209, *sub* June 12, 1751).

[75] King's College, Cambridge, MS. PC 2/132 quoted in Mrs Hughes's paper.

[76] *Blundell's Diary*, (ed. Gibson), 177.

[77] Memorandum dated 1774 and written by Zachariah Leaf, quoted by Mrs Hughes.

[78] In the possession of the Prescot Historic Society. See also J. R. Harris, *Economic and Social Developments in St Helens in the Latter Half of the Eighteenth Century* (M.A. thesis, Manchester University, 1950), 207.

[79] W. A. Tonge (ed.), *Marriage Bonds of the Ancient Archdeaconry of Chester*, Record Society of Lancashire and Cheshire, *82* (1933), 177. The name appears as Lease, obviously an error in transcription. A John Leaf, glassman, son of John Leaf of Warrington, glassmaker, became a freeman of Liverpool on September 5, 1694.

[80] L.R.O., will proved at Chester, May 7, 1713.

[81] In 1712 John Leaf held half an acre of land in Woods's Tenement, adjacent to Ravenhead Estate. The Abstract of Title among the Ravenhead Deeds, shows that the Thatto Heath Bottleworks also stood in a part of Woods's Tenement.

[82] It is impossible to say to what extent the local clays were used at this time. Clay was certainly an ingredient used in bottlemaking. It may have been used for pot-making, though it must have been very inferior to Stourbridge clay. Yet it must be remembered that local clays were used for this purpose quite frequently. One of the advantages of a glasshouse at Maryport, for instance, so late as 1760 was that clay for making pots could be found within two miles (*Newcastle Journal*, July 5, 1760, quoted in Francis Buckley 'Cumberland Glasshouses', *J.S.G.T.* **X**, 385). The St Helens clays were specifically mentioned as a bargaining point in an agreement of September 29, 1779, between John Mackay of Ravenhead and three men who were about to establish a copper works on Mackay's estate. They were to be supplied with 'all such Fire Clay as they may want and have occasion to make use of it at their . . . Smelting and Refinery Works'. (L.R.O. Gerard Papers, DDGe (M) 830.) I am indebted to Dr J. R. Harris for this reference. For use of local clay at the Ravenhead works early in the nineteenth century see p. 261 n.131.

[83] J. N. L. Baker in his chapter on 'England in the Seventeenth Century' in *An Historical Geography of England Before 1800* (ed. Darby) (Cambridge, 1936), 419, has observed that the most important glassmaking centres, with the exception of London, were situated near to salt workings.

[84] T. C. Barker, 'Lancashire Coal, Cheshire Salt and the Rise of Liverpool', *Transactions of the Lancashire and Cheshire Historic Society*, *103* (1951), 83–101.

[85] Notestein, Relf and Simpson, *op. cit.*, II, 366; S.P.D., Jas. I, vol. 162, No. 63, cited in Hartshorne, *op. cit.*, 428, 430.

[86] *The Plate Glass Book* by a Glass-house Clerk (1757), xxiv.

[87] *A New and Complete Dictionary of Arts and Sciences*. By a Society of Gentlemen (1754), 1442.

[88] Scoville, *op. cit.*, 28–32, 39–41, 47 note 25. A description of the St Gobain works is also to be found in *The Universal Dictionary of Trade and Commerce from the French of the Celebrated Monsieur Savary . . . With Large Additions and Improvements by Malachy Postlethwayt Esq.* (1751) *sub* Glass.

[89] British Patent 268 of 1691.

[90] *Calendar of State Papers Domestic*, May, 1690–October, 1691, 537, 540.

[91] *London Gazette*, June 6, 1692, quoted in Buckley, *The Glass Trade in England in the Seventeenth Century*, 46.

[92] *Post Man*, February 13, 1700/1, quoted *ibid.*, 59.

[93] Guildhall Library, Broadsides 13/49, 50. *The Case of Mr Gumley and his Partners, Proprietors of a Glasshouse over against Hungerford Market* (1706); *The Answer of the Proprietors of the Bear Garden Glasshouse to the Case of Mr John Gumley and Partners* (1706).

[94] This section is based upon the evidence given by various witnesses to the House of Commons on the bill for the incorporation of the British Cast Plate Glass Manufacturers, February 24, 1773 (*Journals of the House of Commons*, XXXIV). A correspondent described methods of blowing, *casting*, grinding and polishing plate glass at Southwark in the *Universal Magazine*, November, 1747, and June, 1748.

[95] When the Bill was first introduced into the Commons by Herbert Mackworth on January 25, 1773, it aroused much opposition and was said to introduce a dangerous precedent. The Attorney General thought that it 'contradicted every rule of justice, of legal compensation and every established notion of trade and commerce' (*The History Debates and Proceedings of Both Houses of Parliament*, VII, 420).

[96] The best kinds of barilla consisted of ashes of a plant of the goosefoot family, *salsola sativa*, extensively grown in Spain, Sicily and Teneriffe and contained about 20% alkali (C. T. Kingzett, *The History, Products and Processes of the Alkali Trade* (1877), 70). Scottish and Irish kelp, the ash of seaweed, contained 10% alkali.

[97] British Patent 760 of 1761.

[98] T. C. Barker and J. R. Harris, *A Merseyside Town in the Industrial Revolution* (Liverpool, 1954), 35.

[99] Abstract of Title, Ravenhead Estate. Ravenhead Deeds.

[100] *Gore's General Advertiser*, May 24, 1771, cited in Barker and Harris, *op. cit.*, 44.

[101] L.R.O., Gerard Papers, DDGe (M) 830.

[102] The proprietors mentioned in the petition to Parliament of January 25, 1773, were: Charles Fitzroy, the Honourable Robert Digby, Peregrine Cust, Thomas Dundas, John Mackay, Philip Affleck, Henry Dagge, James Bourdieu, Angus Mackay, Henry Hastings, Ranald Macdonald and Samuel Chollett. General Sir James Affleck later claimed that 'the concern itself originated with my family' (B.P.G.M., May 20, 1829). For Philip Affleck, see the *Dictionary of National Biography*.

[103] David Garrick of Hampton, Middlesex, lent Mackay £12,000 on July 2 and 3, 1776 (Abstract of Title, Ravenhead Estate).

[104] James Christie in his evidence to the House of Commons Committee was reported to have said that 'a large quantity of such crates would be exported to the East Indies and elsewhere, though at present he knows of no exportation from England while a very considerable one is carried on from France'. It would be tempting to see in the promotion of the new firm the hand of the East India interest wishing to deny the French East India company an advantage they possessed through the St Gobain works.

[105] 13 Geo. III cap. 38.

[106] Date stone at Ravenhead; B.P.G.M., April 22, 1829. For an interesting account of the works, see *An Illustrated Itinerary of the County of Lancaster* (1842), 89–99.

[107] Communication from John Grant, Waltham Place, May 3, 1793 (Treasury and Excise Papers, *26*, 240, at the Library of H.M. Customs and Excise).

[108] Scoville, *op. cit.*, 81–2.

[109] The grave is to be found in the old burial ground, Windleshaw, St Helens. His will, dated November 17, 1787, with a codicil dated November 28, was proved on April 17, 1788, at Chester. He signed himself G. La Bruyère. His executors were the Rev Joseph Emmott of Fazakerley, Thomas West of Croppers Hill and George Mackay of Ravenhead.

[110] Library of H.M. Customs and Excise, Treasury and Excise Papers, *26*, 240.

[111] George Mackay (see above p. 50) reported to the House of Commons (*Journals* XL, 806–7, April 7, 1785) that they had only been able to reduce the level of waste 'in cases where wood

alone had been constantly burnt, which on account of the expense, the company cannot afford to do'. He added, however, that the saving was not great. The chief causes of waste he mentioned were: more frequent breakage of the pots because of the great heat; lading from the furnace to the cuvettes; metal adhering to the bottom and sides of the cuvette; metal forced over the end of the table by the roller; and unevenness and losses in squaring.

[112] An attempt was made to tax the French glass industry during the American war in 1781. But the proprietors of St Gobain appealed and were allowed to compound for 150,000 livres a year from which the amount of glass provided for the use of the royal palaces and the amount exported were to be deducted (Evidence of Alexander Black, June 18, 1784, *Journals of the House of Commons*, XL, 223).

[113] 17 Geo. III cap. 39. The duty was raised from 9s 4d to 18s 8d.

[114] Treasury and Excise Papers February 12, 1779, *19*, 455–6.

[115] *Ibid.*, 482. Memorial dated April 26, 1779.

[116] *Journals of the House of Commons*, XL, 226.

[117] *Ibid.*, 806.

[118] 27 Geo. III cap. 28. This Act was related to the Eden Treaty of 1786.

[119] Treasury and Excise Papers, *26*, 237.

[120] Birmingham Reference Library, Correspondence in the Boulton and Watt Collection.

[121] Treasury and Excise Papers, *26*, 240.

[122] B.P.G.M., April 19, 1809.

[123] *Journals of the House of Commons* XLIX, 349, 413, 467, 570.

[124] Ravenhead Deeds. Indenture September 30, 1794, between the Governor and Company and Thomas Oakes.

[125] *Journals of the House of Commons* LIII, 288; 38 Geo. III cap. XC. Unlike the previous Act of 1773, this Act is not generally available in print but the original document can be consulted at the House of Lords Record Office. It names the following as Governor and Company of the British Plate Glass Manufacturers: Philip Affleck, Paul Benfield, Walter Boyd, John Grant, Henry Grant, Thomas Oakes, Philip Stowey, the Rt Hon Thomas Lord Dundas, Sir John Call Bart., Robert Digby, William Mills, John Pybus, Robert Sherbourne, John Burnall, Henry Errington, James Affleck and Alexander Aubert. For Boyd and Benfield, see S. R. Cope, *The History of Boyd, Benfield and Co.* (London Ph.D. Thesis 1947.)

[126] Letter from Robert Sherbourne, April 20, 1829 (B.P.G.M., April 22, 1829).

[127] B.P.G.M., April 19, 1809.

[128] *Ibid.*

[129] Treasury and Excise Papers, *35*, 263–4. Memorial from the British Plate Glass Manufacturers, October 15, 1801.

[130] Treasury and Excise Papers, *26*, 422–4 (February, 1794); 34 Geo. III cap 27.

[131] B.P.G.M., April 12, 1815. Sherbourne also used local clay to some extent as well as that from Stourbridge. In 1809, for instance, £511 was spent on Stourbridge clay and £874 on furnace bricks made of Stourbridge clay. In addition, £67 was spent on Whiston clay. In 1811 £202 was spent on Rainford clay and in 1813 £190 on Rainford and Whiston clay.

[132] B.P.G.M., April 19, 1809.

[133] The information in this paragraph is taken from the minute and account books of the British Plate Glass Company, now at Pilkington Brothers Ltd.

[134] *Gore's General Advertiser*, April 29, 1790.

[135] Ravenhead Deeds. Abstract of Title of Ravenhead Estate.

[136] L.R.O., Land Tax Returns (Sutton Township), 1781. John Mackay was also partner in a glass enamelling business in Liverpool (P.R.O., P.L.6/88/42).

[137] *Journals of the House of Commons*, XL, 806; Boulton and Watt Papers.

[138] *Gore's General Advertiser*, April 19, 1792; Buckley, 'Old Lancashire Glasshouses', 240.

[139] Barker and Harris, *op. cit.*, 110.

[140] A marble slab was originally used and marver is the anglicization of the French for marble, *marbre*.

[141] Believed to be the anglicization of pontil.

[142] There has been a change in the meaning of this word. At the time of which we are writing, flashing was the name given to the process of rotating the piece of glass on the end of the punty. The term is now used to mean the applying of a thin layer of an opaque or coloured glass to a clear glass while both glasses are in a molten condition.

[143] Anthony Becku to Sir William Cecil (Lansdowne MSS. 59/76 quoted in R. H. Tawney and Eileen Power, *Tudor Economic Documents*, 1924, I, 306).

[144] *Cal. S.P.D. William and Mary, 1694–5*, January 5, 1693/4.

[145] *Collections of Letters for the Improvement of Husbandry and Trade*, May 15, 1696.

[146] 13th Report of the Commissioners of Excise Inquiry (Glass), 1835 [15] XXXI, Appendix 23. Evidence of Thomas Dunn, November 4, 1833.

[147] Lease from Millicent Fraser and John Gladstone to Bell, October 5, 1822; Library of H.M. Customs and Excise, Excise Trials, *647*, 17.

CHAPTER 3

AN UNPROMISING START

[1] For an account of the operation of the window tax, see pp. 96–8.

[2] Parliamentary Return 1830/1 [124] XI.

[3] B.P.G.M., May 10, 1826.

[4] T. C. Barker and J. R. Harris, *A Merseyside Town in the Industrial Revolution* (Liverpool, 1954), 197–200, 203.

[5] L.R.O., will of William Pilkington proved at Chester, April 4, 1832.

[6] L.R.O. Cross Papers, DDCS 37/20. Lease dated December 26, 1826. It was to take effect from February 2, 1827, and to last for 13 years.

[7] L.R.O., will proved at Chester, April 4, 1832.

[8] For these activities, see Barker and Harris, *op. cit.*, 181 *et seq.*

[9] Abstract of Title of St Helens Crown Glassworks.   [10] *Ibid.*   [11] *Ibid.*

[12] This draft, dated May 18, written in a copper-plate hand, is preserved among the archives at Pilkington Brothers Ltd. A careful search has failed to reveal the final articles of co-partnership.

[13] *St Helens Newspaper, St Helens Standard*, September 21, 1872.

[14] This was stated as a fact by Abraham Hartley, a glassmaker at the works from 1836, in an interview published in the *St Helens Lantern*, January 3, 1889.

[15] According to a note in William Pilkington's handwriting, the initial cost of the first house and the price of the land totalled £9,189 9s 4d. The dimensions of the cone are given on a plan of the works, 1856.

[16] See above, footnote 142.

[17] Interview with William (Roby) Pilkington, *St Helens Lantern*, June 7, 1888.

[18] *St Helens Newspaper*, September 21, 1872. According to the census returns for 1851 at the Public Record Office (H.O. 107/2195) Kenmore, then aged 54, was born at Midford, Northumberland, and his wife came from Scotland. Their daughter (22) was born in St Helens.

[19] Henry Deacon, *The Manufacture of Blown Window Glass* (Liverpool, 1855), 17.

²⁰ The following account is based upon Exchequer Records at the Public Record Office, P.R.O., E.159/733/Mich. 8 Geo. IV, m. 299; Excise Trials at the Library of H.M. Customs and Excise, February 16, April 25, June 14, 21, November 29, 1828, and May 7, 1830; and a leading article in the *Liverpool Mercury*, January 16, 1829.

²¹ Indenture December 21 and 22, 1827, cited in Abstract of Title.

²² Indenture May 1 and 2, 1828, cited in Abstract of Title.

²³ *London Gazette*, April 22, 1828.

²⁴ *Liverpool Mercury*, January 19, 1838. Bell's will, dated April 29, 1836, and proved at Chester May 21, 1838, was sworn at less than £600. Thomas Bell, described in the 1841 census return as having been born in Lancashire, was not mentioned at all in the will.

²⁵ *St Helens Newspaper, St Helens Standard*, September 21, 1872.

²⁶ Note in William Pilkington's hand upon a list of production figures, 1827–40.

²⁷ Bromilow Papers, Black Park, Chirk. Adam Bromilow to James Bromilow, June 27, 1829. I am grateful to Col H. A. Bromilow for permission to consult this correspondence.

²⁸ Abstract of Title. Indenture of February 2 and 3, 1829.

²⁹ When Richard Pilkington was formally admitted to the partnership in 1835, it was stated that half of William Pilkington's interest was held in trust for his elder brother. The correspondence between the two in 1831 makes it clear that Richard Pilkington was already actively engaged at the works at that time.

³⁰ *The Annual Register's* obituary of Peter Greenall (1845, 296–7) states that he himself was a partner in Parr's 'in which he had acquired a large fortune', but there is no confirmation from any other source of this assertion.

³¹ This paragraph is based on James Frederick Chance, *A History of the Firm of Chance Brothers and Co.* (privately printed 1919), 1–3.

³² For the Nailsea works, see A. C. Powell, 'Glassmaking in Bristol', *Transactions of the Bristol and Gloucestershire Archaeological Society*, XLVII, 252 *et seq*. Lucas had previously been a member of a bottlemaking firm in Bristol. His father, a cooper, had gone there from Hanbury in Worcestershire. The Lucases no doubt already knew the Chances who had lived nearby, at Bromsgrove, since the fifteenth century. (Information from Sir Hugh Chance, who is engaged in writing a monograph about the Nailsea works.)

CHAPTER 4

THE COLLAPSE OF A COMPETITOR AND THE STRUGGLE FOR SURVIVAL

¹ Thirteenth Report of the Commissioners of Excise Inquiry (Glass), 1835, 29.

² J. F. Chance, *op. cit.*, 55.

³ Unless otherwise stated, this account is based upon Excise and Treasury Papers, England 1829/30, T.E. 1432 at the Library of H.M. Customs and Excise, and Supplementary Statements and Proofs on the Part of the Petitioners (n.d.) among the Cross Papers at the L.R.O.

⁴ Thirteenth Report of the Commissioners of Excise Inquiry (Glass), 94.

⁵ L.R.O., Cross Papers, DDCS 14/59, J. U. West to William Rowson, September 25, 1833.

⁶ *Gore's General Advertiser*, January 14, 1830.

⁷ L.R.O., Cross Papers, DDCS 14/30.

⁸ Thirteenth Report of the Commissioners of Excise Inquiry, 133. Evidence of Robert Lucas Chance; Bromilow Papers, Black Park, Chirk, letters from General Gascoyne, October 14, 1832, March 1, 1833; James Bromilow to General Gascoyne, October 29, 1832.

[9] L.R.O., Cross Papers, Mackay West and Co.'s Arbitration. King's Bench, Michaelmas, 1834.

[10] L.R.O., Cross Papers, DDCS 14/68.

[11] *Wigan Gazette*, October 8, 1836.

[12] L.R.O., Cross Papers, draft Deed for Settling Disputes, January 23, 1837.

[13] The fiat of Bankruptcy was dated September 28, 1837.

[14] See p. 122.

[15] J. F. Chance, *op. cit.*, 3–4; Library of H.M. Customs and Excise, T.E. 5010, Memorial of William Chance, February 1, 1832.

[16] *The First Statistical Account of Scotland*, IV (1792), 23, VIII (1793), 596; *The New Statistical Account of Scotland*, VIII (1845), 9–11, 49–50; 13th Report of the Excise Commissioners Inquiry, Appendix, 139, 143; J. Arnold Fleming, *The Art of Glass Making* (Dumbarton, 1934) and *Scottish and Jacobite Glass* (Glasgow, 1938), 154–63. I am also indebted to Miss Aileen Grierson of the Vale of Leven Academy, for permitting me to see her thesis on the history of Dumbarton and for making inquiries for me in that neighbourhood.

[17] Notestein, Relf and Simpson, *Commons Debates 1621*, VII, 547.

[18] Agreement between the Glass-sellers' Company and various glassmakers, September 1, 1684 (MS. 5556 at Guildhall Library, London).

[19] W. H. B. Court, *The Rise of the Midland Industries 1600–1838* (Oxford 1938), 124–6.

[20] See p. 40.

[21] Quarto notebook containing details of correspondence and meetings during the 1780s. This is now in the possession of Mr Guy L. Chater of the old-established firm of Joseph Chater and Sons, who kindly permitted me to look at it.

[22] The following account is based on the Manufacturers' Association minutes, some of which are preserved among the archives of Chance Brothers Ltd. and some among those of Pilkington Brothers Ltd.

[23] Minutes of Manufacturers' Association, September 19, 1828.

[24] William Pilkington to Richard Pilkington, November 3, 1834.

[25] In January and February, 1836, several manufacturers met to consider the complaints of Mr Bower of Hunslet, but refused to take any decision until Mr Bower himself attended to substantiate his claims.

[26] There was, however, a meeting of Lancashire manufacturers only on December 15, 1832, at Warrington. They fixed a minimum price for the sale of squares.

[27] William Pilkington to Richard Pilkington, April 29, 1831.

[28] Joseph Chater and Sons. Letter from J. W. Bell, January 23, 1828.

[29] William Pilkington to Richard Pilkington, April 23, 1831.

[30] William Richardson and Company were proprietors of the North Tyne Glass Manufactory, Newcastle. Their works were opened about 1825. (Petition dated September 29, 1825, Newcastle Archivist's Section, Town Clerk's Department, document number 11/21/49.)

[31] William Pilkington to Richard Pilkington, April 29, 1831.

[32] William Pilkington to Richard Pilkington, August 4, 1834.

[33] *Ibid.*

[34] William Pilkington to Richard Pilkington, November 3, 1834.

[35] William Pilkington to Richard Pilkington, December 18, 1838.

[36] William Pilkington's eldest daughter, Mary, married Henry Chater in 1850.

[37] William Pilkington to Richard Pilkington, December 8, 1838.

[38] These figures are taken from a list of production figures drawn up by William Pilkington about 1840.

[39] R. C. O. Matthews, *A Study in Trade-Cycle History: Economic Fluctuations in Great Britain, 1833–1842* (Cambridge, 1954), 115.

[40] Reference is made to this second house by William Pilkington in a letter dated November 3, 1834.

[41] The figures in this and the following paragraph are from lists drawn up by William Pilkington about 1836 and 1840.

[42] Thomas Pilkington formally retired from the partnership on June 28, 1836 (*London Gazette*, July 8, 1836).

[43] Board Minutes, December 8, 14, 1880; May 23, 1882.

[44] Letter from William Pilkington, March 8, 1836. The recipient is not known.

[45] Account Book of William Pilkington and Sons.

[46] See p. 113.

[47] Greenall Whitley and Co. Ltd., St Helens. Rent Book. The Cross Papers at the L.R.O. contain letters about Millbrook House, written by William Pilkington in 1836 and 1850.

CHAPTER 5

THE INTRODUCTION OF A NEW TECHNIQUE

[1] See p. 51.

[2] *Official Descriptive and Illustrated Catalogue of the Great Exhibition of the Works of Industry of all Nations, 1851* (1852), 525; G. Bontemps, *Guide du Verrier* (Paris, 1868), 231–3; Scoville, *op. cit.*, 8–9.

[3] Samuel Parkes, *Chemical Essays* (1815), III, 446.

[4] Although diamonds came into general use in England, the Belgians always employed splitting irons (Report on Belgian and French Glassworks in 1859 at Chance Brothers Ltd.). The diamond cuts had to be made inside the cylinder.

[5] Treasury and Excise Papers, *125*, 423, January 27, 1758.

[6] 17 Geo. III cap. 39, sec. 26.

[7] D. R. Guttery, *From Broad Glass to Cut Crystal: A History of the Stourbridge Glass Industry* (1956), 96.   [8] *Ibid*, 98–9.

[9] British Patent 2812 of 1805.

[10] 13th Report of the Excise Commissioners Inquiry (Glass), appendix p. 95.

[11] Treasury and Excise Papers, T.E. 9651. Memorial submitted by manufacturers of window glass, 1830.

[12] Treasury and Excise Papers, T.E. 5010. Memorial from Chance and Hartleys, June 6, 1835.

[13] *Ibid*; J. F. Chance, *A History of the Firm of Chance Brothers and Co.* (privately printed 1919), 6.

[14] Treasury and Excise Papers, T.E. 5010.

[15] Treasury and Excise Papers, T.E. 5010. Memorial from Chance and Hartleys, June 6, 1835.

[16] *Ibid*, letter from Gervase Oldham, Collector at Stourbridge, May 19, 1832.

[17] J. F. Chance, *op. cit.*, 5–6; speech by James Hartley reported in a supplement to the *Sunderland Times*, November 6, 1866; Bontemps, *op. cit.*, 375.

[18] J. F. Chance, *op. cit.*, 6.

[19] Chance Brothers Ltd., Board Minutes, October 15, 1835. For exports to North America between 1837 and 1843, see Parliamentary Return, 1844 [200] XLV.

[20] 5 & 6 Wm. IV Cap. 77, sec. 5; 1 & 2 Vict. Cap. 44.

[21] J. F. Chance, *op. cit.*, 26.

[22] British Patent 7177 of 1836.

[23] Chance Brothers Ltd., Board Minutes, December 29, 1837.

[24] British Patent 7618 of 1838.

[25] 56 Geo. III cap. 8, sec. 6; 13th Report of the Excise Commissioners Inquiry (Glass), 6, 29, 133.

[26] Chance Brothers Ltd., J. T. Chance to W. Chance, junior.

[27] *Leeds Intelligencer* quoted by the *Mechanics Magazine*, XXXII (1839/40), 192; J. F. Chance, *op. cit.*, 7.

[28] Chance Brothers Ltd., J. T. Chance to Wren and Bennett, May 12, 1840.

[29] Chance Brothers Ltd., J. T. Chance to A. B. Goss, September 5, 1840.

[30] Chance Brothers Ltd., J. T. Chance to Messrs Clough, December 24, 1839.

[31] Chance Brothers Ltd., J. T. Chance to William Chance, January 28, 1841.

[32] J. F. Chance, *op. cit.*, 20–1.

[33] Printed statement from Wear Glassworks, Sunderland, on the proposed glass duties, 1841, in a scrapbook kept by James Hartley or J. J. Kayll, now in the possession of Mr Michael Brett, Secretary of the Plate Glass Merchants' Association, London; Treasury and Excise T.E. 7653. Memorial of window glass manufacturers, received February 1839.

[34] *St Helens Lantern*, January 3, 1889.

[35] P.R.O., H.O. 107/516.

[36] This inscription is reproduced in the *St Helens Lantern*, Christmas edition, 1888.

[37] Chance Brothers Ltd., J. T. Chance to Wren and Bennett, September 14, 1842.

[38] Chance Brothers Ltd., Board Minutes, March 8, 1843.

[39] Chance Brothers Ltd., J. T. Chance to Wren and Bennett, September 14, 1842.

[40] B.P.G.M., July 27, 1842.

[41] Chance Brothers Ltd., J. T. Chance to Wren and Bennett, March 24, 1846.

[42] For the general background to Deacon's life, see J. Fenwick Allen's memoir in the *Chemical Trade Journal*, September 18, 1889, later printed in that writer's *Some Founders of the Chemical Industry*.

[43] At Pilkington Brothers Ltd.

[44] British Patent 10,686 of 1845.

[45] *Artizan*, September 1, 1864.

[46] British Patent 9815 of 1843.

[47] British Patent 11,384 of 1846.

[48] J. F. Chance, *op. cit.*, 31–2.

[49] See p. 107.

CHAPTER 6

YEARS OF CONTRAST

[1] H. A. Shannon, 'Bricks—A Trade Index, 1785–1849', *Economica*, 1934, 304; R. C. O. Matthews, *A Study in Trade-Cycle History* (Cambridge, 1954), 116.

[2] Some of the Minutes of the Manufacturers' Association are to be found among the archives at Pilkingtons and others at Chances.

[3] For plus, see p. 110.

[4] See p. 63.

[5] *Liverpool Mercury*, September 19, 1845; *Manchester Guardian* and *Manchester Courier*, September 20, 1845; *Annual Register* 1845, 296–7.

[6] For a survey of the relevant legislation, see the Thirteenth Report of the Excise Commissioners Inquiry (Glass), 3–10; Stephen Dowell, *A History of Taxation and Taxes in England* (4 vols. 1884), III, 194–203; W. R. Ward, 'The Administration of the Window and Assessed Taxes, 1696–1798', *English Historical Review*, LXVII (1952), 522–542.

[7] Thirteenth Report of the Excise Commissioners Inquiry, 138.

[8] *The Economist*, July 19, 1845.

[9] Thirteenth Report of the Excise Commissioners Inquiry, 137–8.

[10] See p. 135.

[11] Chance Brothers Ltd., Board Minutes, October 22, 1833.

[12] Treasury and Excise Papers, T.E. 9651. Memorial from Chance Brothers and Co., February 24, 1842.

[13] A. P. Wadsworth and J. de L. Mann, *The Cotton Trade and Industrial Lancashire* (Manchester, 1931), 489.

[14] Peter Drinkwater to Boulton and Watt, April 3, 1789, cited in W. H. Chaloner, 'Robert Owen, Peter Drinkwater and the Early Factory System in Manchester', *Bulletin of the John Ryland Library*, 37 (1954), 89.

[15] Return 1831 [124] XI; 1841 [303] XXIV; G. R. Porter, *Progress of the Nation* (1847), 537.

[16] Return 1846 [223] XXV.

[17] This paragraph owes much to discussion with Professor W. Ashworth. I am also grateful to Miss V. Hole, of the Building Research Station, for helpful advice.

[18] *The Times*, April 14, 1845; return of window duty, 1846 [223] XXV.

[19] 8 & 9 Vict. cap. 6.

[20] Return of the Reduction of the Excise Department . . . together with Information . . . respecting the Effects produced by the Repeal of the Duty on the manufacture of Glass, 1846 [109] XLIV.

[21] 7 & 8 Vict. cap. 84.

[22] *The Builder*, January 11, 1845.

[23] Chance Brothers Ltd., R. L. Chance to J. T. Chance, July 8, 1845.

[24] Return, 1846 [109], XLIV.

CHAPTER 7

A LABOUR CRISIS

[1] For the introduction of gatherers in sheet glass manufacture, see G. Bontemps, *Guide du Verrier* (Paris, 1868), 117, 273–5; J. F. Chance, *A History of the Firm of Chance Brothers and Co.* (1919), 33.

[2] L.R.O., Cross Papers. Cases arising from the disputed contracts at the St Helens Crown Glass Works, 1845–6.

[3] Lecture by James Hartley, *The Journal of the Society of Arts*, February 17, 1854.

[4] *Rules and Regulations of the British Crown Glass Makers' Society Agreed Upon at a General Meeting of Delegates from Spon Lane, Smethwick, Birmingham, St Helens, Old Swan, Eccleston and Newton Glass Works* (Birmingham 1846).

[5] See Appendix 2.

[6] L.R.O., Cross Papers, William Pilkington to Rowson and Cross, November 27, 1845.

[7] Interview with Thomas Gerard, *St Helens Lantern*, January 3, 1889.

[8] *St Helens Lantern*, June 7, 1888. See also p. 142.

[9] Chance Brothers Ltd., R. L. Chance, junr. to R. L. Chance, July 19, 1845.

[10] L.R.O., Cross Papers.

[11] Parliamentary Return, 1846 [109] XLIV.

[12] *Ibid.*

[13] This and subsequent paragraphs dealing with the labour difficulties of the firm in 1845 and 1846 are based upon a mass of documents discovered at the office of Henry Cross & Son, successors to Rowson and Cross who were the firm's solicitors at this time. These documents now form part of the Cross Papers at the Lancashire Record Office.

[14] I owe this information to Miss Aileen Grierson of the Vale of Leven Academy.

[15] By 4 Geo. IV, cap. 34, sec. 3.

[16] See Appendix 3.

[17] For these Birmingham works, see J. F. Chance, *op. cit.*, 61–2.

[18] See p. 106.

[19] L.R.O., Cross Papers. William Pilkington to William Cross, September 3, 1845.

[20] Appendix to the Fourth Report of the Children's Employment Commission, 1865 [8357] XX, 276.

[21] 'A Day at a Glass Factory', *Penny Magazine*, June 29, 1844. This account of Cooksons' works in South Shields and Newcastle contains one of the best descriptions of window glass-making at that time.

[22] The agreements of 1839 and 1845, both printed, are among the Cross Papers at the L.R.O. That of 1833, in William Pilkington's handwriting, is among the papers at Pilkington Brothers Ltd.

[23] L.R.O., Cross Papers.

[24] These are reproduced as Appendix 2.

[25] L.R.O., Cross Papers.   [26] *Ibid.*

[27] Royal Society of Arts, *Abstract of Proceedings*, April 14, 21, June 9, 1847.

[28] H. Logan, 'Early Days of the Recs. Club', *Cullet*, January, 1929.

[29] Both William (Roby) and Thomas Pilkington played for a St Helens side in a match against an All England XI in May, 1853 (*Wigan Times*, May 13, 1853).

[30] Appendix to the Fourth Report of the Children's Employment Commission, 1865, 274. Evidence of William Pilkington.

[31] *Liverpool Mercury*, July 23, 1850.

[32] *Liverpool Mercury*, January 23, 1849.

[33] Appendix to the Fourth Report of the Children's Employment Commission, 1865, 275.

[34] *The Builder*, April 5, 1851. According to a resolution of the Board on March 17, 1864, these fines were from that date onwards to be returned after a lapse of time in cases of good conduct.

[35] Second Report of the Children's Employment Commission, 1843, b. 55. Evidence of Thomas Percival, manager of Messrs. Molyneux and Well, Flint Glass Manufacturers, Manchester.

[36] Third Report of the Children's Employment Commission, 1864, 191.

[37] *Liverpool Mercury*, May 21, 1847.

[38] *Cullet*, July, 1931.

[39] *Cullet*, April, 1932.

[40] Mrs Boyes subsequently married Richard Fildes, the leading grocer and draper in the town, himself a widower. Her previous husband, who had died, had been a captain in the Royal Navy.

[41] According to addresses printed in the *Proceedings of the Institution of Mechanical Engineers*, he was living in various parts of London between 1864–6, at Darlington until 1869 and at Birmingham until 1872. His name does not appear in the *Proceedings* after this. He died in 1894.

⁴² List of students at the Royal College of Chemistry, evidence to the Royal Commission on Scientific Instruction, 1872 [C. 536] XXV, 359.

⁴³ Obituary, *St Helens Newspaper*, March 20, 1914. This school, founded in Birmingham by Thomas Wright Hill, was developed by his sons Rowland (the author of penny postage) and Matthew Davenport (the criminal law reformer). It was moved from Hazelwood, near Birmingham, to Tottenham in 1827. For information about the curriculum and method of training, see R. L. Archer, *Secondary Education in the Nineteenth Century* (Cambridge, 1921), 90–6.

⁴⁴ Katherine Chorley in her book *Manchester Made Them* (1950), 128–134, has much to say in praise of Lawrence Pilkington, a neighbour of hers in her youth. For Alfred Pilkington's obituary, see *St Helens Newspaper*, December 12, 1896.

⁴⁵ Recollections of James Marsh, Richard Pilkington's successor as superintendent, *St Helens Newspaper*, May 3, 1890.

CHAPTER 8

THE REMOVAL OF BRITISH COMPETITORS

¹ *Journal of the Society of Arts*, February 17, 1854.

² Henry Chance, 'On the Manufacture of Crown and Sheet Glass', *Journal of the Society of Arts*, February 15, 1856; Walter Lucas Chance in J. F. Chance, *A History of the Firm of Chance Brothers and Co.* (privately printed, 1919), 277.

³ Warrington Public Library. Rate books.

⁴ P.R.O. C.101/5393 and 5394. I am grateful to Mr J. M. Hemphill for drawing my attention to these papers among the Chancery Master's Exhibits.

⁵ The leading shareholders were: George Bennett of Liverpool, wine merchant, who held 423 shares; John Blakeway Tipton, of Birkenhead, merchant, who held 277 shares; Oswald Airey, of Liverpool, chemist, who held 213 shares; Arthur Latham of Liverpool, merchant, who held 155 shares; John Sothern of Liverpool, merchant, who held 150 shares; Robert Falk of Cleveland Square, Liverpool, and Thomas Corlett of the North and South Wales Bank, who each held 130 shares; William Crosfield, wholesale grocer—also described as 'original proprietor'—who held 122 shares; and Andrew Kurtz, the manufacturing chemist of Liverpool, who held 100 shares. (P.R.O., C.101/5393.)

⁶ See p. 37. For obituaries of Isaac Cookson, see *Annual Register* and *Gentleman's Magazine*, 1851.

⁷ Chance Brothers Ltd. Postscript to a letter written by R. L. Chance to James Chance, July 31, 1845. For a full account of this factory, see 'A Day at a Glass Factory', *Penny Magazine*, June 29, 1844.

⁸ L.R.O., Cross Papers. Richard Shortridge to William Pilkington, November 15, 1845.

⁹ I am much indebted to Dr Michael Thompson of University College, London, who has placed at my disposal this information from the Ridley family diary at Blagdon Hall, Seaton Burn.

¹⁰ Thomas Salmon, *South Shields, Its Past, Present and Future* (South Shields, 1856), 22.

¹¹ Quoted in *The Builder*, April 21, 1849.

¹² George B. Hodgson, *The History of South Shields* (Newcastle, 1924), 246; J. Collingwood Bruce, *A Handbook to Newcastle-on-Tyne* (1863), 258. (The latter acknowledged the assistance of Hartley and Swinburne in compiling the handbook.)

[13] *Report of the 32nd Meeting of the British Association held at Newcastle-upon-Tyne in August and September, 1863* (1864), 56.

[14] *Newcastle Journal*, May 25, 1886.

[15] British Patent 11,891 of 1847.

[16] J. F. Chance, *A History of the Firm of Chance Brothers and Co.* (1919), 52–3; Henry Chance, 'On the Manufacture of Crown and Sheet Glass', *Journal of the Society of Arts*, February 15, 1856; C. R. Fay, *Palace of Industry 1851* (Cambridge, 1951), 16. Chances had already supplied glass to Paxton for Chatsworth Observatory (see p. 86).

[17] *Journal of the Society of Arts*, February 17, 1854.

[18] James Hartley to William (Roby) Pilkington, December, 1854. This letter was sent on to Chances and is printed in J. F. Chance, *op. cit.*, 78.

[19] J. F. Chance, *op. cit.*, 78.

[20] Manufacturers' Association Minutes, February 28, March 5, 1845; *Gore's Directory*, 1845; plan of Old Swan Glassworks, 1851, in P.R.O., C101/5393.

[21] Conveyance, August 31, 1846. Hadland also acquired Bells' Ravenhead Flint Glassworks (Abstract of Title, John and Edward Cannington).

[22] Mortgage deed, February 24, 1847.

[23] Rate Books of the St Helens Improvement Commission, in the possession of St Helens Corporation.

[24] J. F. Chance, *op. cit.*, 78n; schedule dealing with the Eccleston Crown Glassworks.

[25] Appendix to the Fourth Report of the Children's Employment Commission, 1865, 275; agreement between Hartley and Pilkingtons.

[26] J. F. Chance, *op. cit.*, 79.

[27] Walter Lucas Chance in J. F. Chance, *op. cit.*, 278.

[28] J. F. Chance, *op. cit.*, 46.

[29] Chance Brothers Ltd., William Pilkington to R. L. Chance, June 23, 1855.

[30] John Henry Lane, *Newton-in-Makerfield: Its History* (Newton 1914–6), II, 163–4; Chance Brothers Ltd., John Reynell to William Chance, July 26, 1833.

[31] Chance Brothers Ltd., William Pilkington to R. L. Chance, June 23, 1855.

[32] *Ibid*, and Note on Newton Glassworks at Chance Brothers Ltd.   [33] *Ibid*.

[34] Chance Brothers Ltd., Robert Gardner to Chance Brothers, March 12, 1855.

[35] Chance Brothers Ltd., William Pilkington to R. L. Chance, June 23, 1855.

[36] Chance Brothers Ltd., memorandum of agreement between Robert Gardner and William Pilkington, July 4, 1855.

[37] Papers at Chance Brothers Ltd.

[38] Chance Brothers Ltd., memorandum made by Mr Swinburne at Sunderland, July 13, 1855. There is no further evidence of the Bristol company's co-operation.

[39] Chance Brothers Ltd., James Hartley to R. L. Chance, January 30, 1856.

[40] Chance Brothers Ltd., James Hartley to J. T. Chance, July 23, 1856.

[41] Joshua Bower, born in 1773, the founder of this firm, started work as a carpenter and in the Leeds Directory of 1817 is described as 'ironmonger, joiner and builder and crown glass manufacturer'. In later life, besides being a considerable glassmaker, he became one of the largest toll farmers in England and at one time is said to have possessed nearly all the tolls between Leeds and London together with some in Hampshire, Dorset, Wiltshire and elsewhere. He also owned coalmines. He died at Hunslet on September 7, 1855, leaving his son, also named Joshua, to continue his window glass business until 1860. (R. V. Taylor, *The Biographia Leodiensis*, 1865, 455–6.)

[42] Chance Brothers Ltd., indenture dated May 31, 1861.

[43] Prospectus of the Albion Glass Co. Ltd. 10,000 shares were to be issued at £1 each. R. T. Wolstenholme was named as the secretary and directors had still to be appointed. The

prospectus is not dated but it was received by Hartleys on September 12, 1861, and was pasted into a scrapbook kept by them. This is now in the possession of the Secretary of the London Plate Glass Merchants Association who kindly permitted me to consult it.

[44] Henry Chance, 'On the Manufacture of Plate, Crown and Sheet Glass', in *The Resources, Products and Industrial History of Birmingham and the Midland Hardware Districts*, ed. Samuel Timmins (1866), 149.

[45] 'The "piece" is "blocked" and blown as if for sheet, until it would be ready for opening, but the closed end forms the top of the shade, and the workman's object is to give it an agreeable form. He manages this by heating it, and allowing it to cup in, again heating when the sides become more softened, and then, according to circumstances, blowing out the depression with the end more or less elevated or hung down. By these means he destroys the pointed form resulting from the swinging, and, according to his skill, gives a more or less elegant curve to the "top". The "cap" is then removed and the open end of the "shade" squared in the same way as the cylinders.' (*The Manufacture of Blown Window Glass.*)

[46] *Ibid.*

[47] A copy of this book is preserved among the firm's archives. There is also one in the Bodleian Library, Oxford.

[48] See one of Henry Peet's editorial notes in his *Liverpool in the Reign of Queen Anne 1705 and 1708* (Liverpool, 1908), appendix p. 128.

[49] Deeds at Pilkington Brothers Ltd.

[50] Information from Mr G. Scott, Representative of Pilkington Brothers Ltd. in Australia. According to the official trade and navigation figures, exports to Australia at this time comprised about one-fifth of the total of British exports of window glass.

[51] Lecture by R. B. Edmundson, published in *The Builder*, April 8, 1854.

[52] B.P.G.M. January 10, 24, 1844. *Manchester Guardian*, February 14, 1844.

[53] Notebook of Robert Whyte. We have based the following paragraph on this source unless otherwise stated.

[54] L.R.O., Tithe Award (Windle).

[55] *St Helens Intelligencer*, July 12, 1856.

[56] *Liverpool Mercury*, October 11, 1844.

[57] Library of H.M. Customs and Excise, T.E. 4168. This enquiry was occasioned by an attempt to sell New South Wales sand in this country.

[58] See, for instance, Board Minutes, April 2, 15, July 23, August 11, September 1, 1869 (Windle); March 2, 1871 (Carr Mill and Moss Bank); February 19, 1874 (Eccleston and Rainford); October 30, 1879 (Rainford).

[59] *Report of the Royal Commission on Noxious Vapours*, 1878 [C.2159] XLIV. Evidence of William Windle Pilkington, q.11,080.

[60] British Patent No. 8,000 of 1839.

[61] L.R.O., DDCS 14/101. William Pilkington to Rowson and Cross, May 2 1845.

[62] T. C. Barker and J. R. Harris, *A Merseyside Town in the Industrial Revolution* (Liverpool, 1954), 342–3.

[63] John Fenwick Allen, *Some Founders of the Chemical Industry* (Manchester, 1906; 2nd ed. 1907). These memoirs had previously appeared in the *Chemical Trade Journal* of 1889 and 1890. The article on Henry Deacon was published in the issue of September 18, 1889.

[64] D. W. F. Hardie, *A History of the Chemical Industry in Widnes* (I.C.I. Ltd. General Chemicals Division, 1950), 25.   [65] *Ibid.*, 23–4.

[66] D. W. F. Hardie and R. Dickinson, 'Gaskell-Deacon 1853–1953', *General Chemical Division News*, I.C.I. Ltd., August, 1953.

[67] L.R.O., Cross Papers. Deed of Dissolution of the Pilkington-Deacon Partnership, June 15, 1855. The following paragraph is also based on this source.

[68] Patent of William Gossage (422 of February 21, 1854) and patent of J. H. Johnson (1504 of July 8, 1854).

[69] L.R.O., Cross Papers, William Pilkington to William Cross, June 2, 1855.

[70] Article by John Blundell, *Cullet*, July, 1931.

[71] Hardie, *op. cit.*, 61.

[72] Board Minutes, March 9, 16, June 22, 1865.

[73] First Report of the Rivers Pollution Commission, 1870 [C.109] XLIV, vol. II, 132.

CHAPTER 9

COMPETITION FROM BELGIUM AND CONSOLIDATION AT ST HELENS

[1] V. Lefebvre, *La Verrerie à Vitres et Les Verriers de Belgique depuis le XVe Siècle* (Publications de l'Université de Travail de Hainaut, 1938), 48. For a comprehensive bibliography of writings on the Belgian glass industry, see R. Chambon, *L'Histoire de la Verrerie en Belgique* (Brussels, 1955), 261–81.

[2] *Statistique Générale de la Belgique, Exposé de la Situation du Royaume, 1851–60* (Brussels, 1865), 138.

[3] James Frederick Chance, *A History of the Firm of Chance Brothers and Co.* (Privately printed 1919), 32.

[4] Report from Lord Howard de Walden. Correspondence with Her Majesty's Missions Abroad Regarding Industrial Questions and Trades Unions, 1867 [3892], LXX, 5–6.

[5] Library of H.M. Customs and Excise, T.E. 5263. Memorial dated March 2, 1837.

[6] Library of H.M. Customs and Excise, T.E. 9651. Memorial dated April 15, 1841.

[7] Library of H.M. Customs and Excise, T.E. 9651. Memorial from Chance Brothers and Co. dated February 24, 1842.

[8] Customs Tariffs of the United Kingdom from 1800 to 1897, 1898 [C.8706] LXXXV.

[9] For the details, see appendix 5.

[10] Henry Chance, 'On the Manufactures of Plate, Crown and Sheet Glass', in *The Resources, Products and Industrial History of Birmingham and the Midland Hardware District*, ed. Samuel Timmins (1866), 150.

[11] The Association then had a London office. It was first situated at 14 Old Jewry Chambers and later at Adelaide Chambers, 52 Gracechurch Street.

[12] Pilkington Brothers, Board Minutes, September 21, 1865.   [13] *Ibid.*, February 9, 1866.

[14] Chance Brothers Ltd. R. L. Chance to Richard Pilkington, August 30, 1877.

[15] J. F. Chance, *op. cit.*, 94.   [16] *Ibid.*, 283.

[17] Minutes of the Manufacturers' Association, April 5, 1865. The Minutes of this meeting and those of December 13–14, 1865, and September 27, 1866, are the only ones relating to the years after 1845 which remain at Pilkington Brothers Ltd.

[18] Pilkington Brothers, Board Minutes, October 15, 1866.

[19] *The Brierley Hill Advertiser*, November 30, 1872, June 5, 1873; *Birmingham Daily Gazette*, November 12, 1872. Bowen was to fail for a third time in 1872.

[20] J. F. Chance, *op. cit.*, 106–7.

[21] *Proceedings of the Institution of Mechanical Engineers*, 1863, 268–80.

[22] See p. 268 n.41.

[23] British Patent 2959 of 1869.

[24] Board Minutes, May 17, 24, June 14, November 15, December 20 ,1866.

[25] C. William Siemens, 'On a New Construction of Furnace, Particularly Applicable Where Intense Heat is Required', *Proceedings of the Institution of Mechanical Engineers*, 1857, 103–11.

[26] *Ibid*. British Patents 2861 of 1856 and 1320 of 1857.

[27] C. William Siemens, 'On a Regenerative Gas Furnace as Applied to Glasshouses, Puddling, Heating, etc.' *Proceedings of the Institution of Mechanical Engineers*, 1862, 22.

[28] British Patent 167 of 1861.

[29] Siemens, 'Regenerative Gas Furnace', 29; J. F. Chance, *op. cit.*, 86.

[30] The following is based upon the Board Minutes at Pilkington Brothers Ltd.

[31] These two letters are preserved at Chance Brothers Ltd.

[32] Appendix to the Fourth Report of the Children's Employment Commission, 275.

[33] See p. 127.

[34] Appendix to the Fourth Report of the Children's Employment Commission, 275.

[35] Board Minutes, March 21, 1867.

[36] Board Minutes, July 10, 1872.

[37] For the transport monopoly, its rates, and the Act of 1864, see T. C. Barker and J. R. Harris, *A Merseyside Town in the Industrial Revolution* (Liverpool, 1954), 342–3, 351.

[38] *A Brief History of Efforts Made by Traders in the St Helens and Widnes Districts in Connection with the Retention and Continuation of the Special Rates First Authorized Under the St Helens Canal and Railway Act of 1864* (booklet issued by the Association in February, 1950).

[39] *St Helens Standard*, February 20, 1869.

[40] Obituaries are to be found in the *St Helens Standard* and *St Helens Newspaper* on January 1, 1870, and September 21, 1872.

CHAPTER 10

EXPANSION ONCE MORE

[1] Board Minutes, January 21, April 2, 1869; October 19, November 9, December 8, 1870; January 4, 1883; December 7, 1891.

[2] Board Minutes, June 10, 25, 1869; July 12, 27, August 25, 1871; May 31, June 6, 13, July 10, August 23, 1872.

[3] Board Minutes, May 13, June 25, 1869; March 23, 1870.

[4] Board Minutes, December 8, 1870, February 23, October 19, 1871; January 4, 1872; British Patent 207 of 1871.

[5] Board Minutes, May 21, October 19, 1868; July 28, August 11, 18, October 1, 27, November 10, 17, 1869.

[6] British Patents 1513 of 1870; 2152 and 3478 of 1872.

[7] The Siemens' knowledge of the behaviour of glass was derived from practical experiment rather than from theory. They believed, for instance, that the specific gravity of glass increased with its temperature. See the extract from the 1870 patent specification printed as appendix 6.

[8] Interview with James Taylor, published in *Cullet*, January, 1934. James Taylor, the son of Henry Taylor, for many years manager of Pilkingtons' sheet glass warehouse, became the father of Sir Hugh Taylor, Professor of Physical Chemistry at Princeton.

[9] Chance Brothers Ltd. Statement of one of Pilkingtons' teasers who applied for a job at Spon Lane.

[10] Chance Brothers Ltd. Statement of Sample, a teaser from Pilkingtons, August 31, 1876.

[11] Chance Brothers Ltd. Statement of Thomas May, February 13, 1877.

[12] Chance Brothers Ltd. Statement of Matthew P. Elliott, May 7, 1877.

[13] Chance Brothers Ltd. C. W. Siemens to Chance Brothers, October 29, 1875.

[14] Chance Brothers Ltd. Henry Chance to James Chance, February 2, 1877.

[15] Old memorandum book, February 7, 1874.

[16] *Ibid.*, March 4, 1878.

[17] Chance Brothers Ltd. Statement of Thomas May, February 13, 1877.

[18] Chance Brothers Ltd. Statement of Sample, August 31, 1876.

[19] Chance Brothers Ltd. Dated June 24, 1876.

[20] *Ibid.*, and Statement of Matthew P. Elliot.

[21] Statement of Sample.

[22] These sites were then occupied by the Bridgewater Chemical Works (advertised for auction in the *St Helens Newspaper*, May 3, 1884) and Forster's Navigation Boiler Works. Between the two lay Todds' St Helens Ironworks, the site of which was acquired by Pilkingtons in 1896.

[23] Board Minutes, June 27, 1878.

[24] Pearce Davis, *The Development of the American Glass Industry* (Cambridge, Mass., 1949), 122.

[25] Statement of Alexander Makin; Board Minutes, March 12, 1889; April 14, September 15, 22, 1891; March 29, 1892; Board Minutes (Plate), May 21, 1891.

[26] J. F. Chance, *op. cit.*, 128. See also pp. 117–8. I am also grateful to Sir Hugh Chance for information on this subject.

[27] Board Minutes, April 17, 1894; March 12, 1895; November 25, 1897.

[28] Under Lee Pilkington's patents, 15,162 of 1892 and 15,792 of 1894.

[29] Deeds at Pilkington Brothers Limited; Board Minutes, February 6, 1873, May 28, 1875, September 24, 1875.

[30] R. Chambon, *L'Histoire de la Verrerie en Belgique* (Brussels 1955), 181.

[31] British Trade and Navigation Returns. Belgian trade figures show a considerable fall in window glass exports to Britain in 1871 and 1872. (See appendix 5.)

[32] J. F. Chance, *op. cit.*, 127.

[33] *Ibid.*, 279.

[34] *Ibid.*, 106–110.

[35] Chance Brothers Ltd. R. L. Chance to J. J. Kayll.

[36] Chance Brothers Ltd. R. L. Chance to Gwilliam, January 25, 1878.

[37] Chance Brothers Ltd. R. L. Chance to J. J. Kayll, January 29, 1879.

[38] Mattesons' Wearmouth Glassworks was turned into a public company. 200 shares were issued and £100 called up on each. On December 31, 1875 (presumably this was very soon after the public company had been formed) T. G. Matteson owned 15 shares. All but one of the other shareholders—Ephraim Sadler of Eccles, near Manchester—came from Sunderland. They were: J. Fawcett, T. Gibson, and Rd. Lewis, shipowners; W. Moore, gentleman; and R. Preston, slate merchant. (MS. notes in scrapbook kept at Hartleys, now in the possession of the Secretary of the London Plate Glass Merchants' Association.) It is not clear when glass ceased to be made at this factory. Its closing is reported in the Pilkington Board Minutes on June 27, 1878, but there is also a later reference, on February 29, 1882, which shows that it was then in operation again.

[39] Article on James Hartley in a series on Commercial and Industrial Pioneers (newscuttings at Newcastle Reference Library, 11,275; source not stated). The rest of this paragraph is based upon newscuttings in the possession of the Secretary of the London Plate Glass Merchants' Association and information provided by Sunderland Public Library.

[40] William Waples, 'Glassmaking and Glazing', a short manuscript written by a Sunderland man in 1952.

[41] *The Times*, May 22, 1901.

[42] For St Gobain's interest in the Stolberg factory, see Rondo E. Cameron, 'Some French

Contributions to the Industrial Development of Germany, 1840–70', *Journal of Economic History* XVI, No. 3, September, 1956, 307–8.

[43] Joseph D. Weeks, Report on the Manufacture of Glass in *Report on the Manufacturers of the United States at the Tenth Census* (June 1, 1880), 73. The information in this paragragh is based on this source unless otherwise stated.

[44] *Statistique Générale de la Belgique, Exposé de la Situation du Royaume, 1841–50* (Brussels, 1852), section iv, 140; companion volume covering 1851–60 (Brussels 1865), III, 140; companion volume covering 1876–1900 (Brussels, 1902), 299. R. Chambon, *L'Historie de la Verrerie en Belgique* (Brussels, 1955), 174, 178, 182.

[45] For these factories, see T. C. Barker and J. R. Harris, *A Merseyside Town in the Industrial Revolution* (Liverpool, 1954), 216–221, 361–363.

[46] William Pilkington in *The St Helens Newspaper*, July 13, 1867.

[47] Deeds of the Ravenhead works.

[48] Evidence of John Crossley to the Royal Commission on Noxious Vapours, 1878 [2159], XLIV, q. 10,997.

[49] Pilkington Board Minutes, May 9, 1863. It was then rumoured that Hartleys intended to make plate glass, but Pilkingtons did not credit this report 'especially as we are bound by agreement not to make plate (Chance, Hartley and ourselves)'.

[50] Board Minutes, March 20, July 3, October 2, 1873.

[51] Board Minutes (Plate), March 28, 1876, *et seq.*

[52] *Cullet*, July, 1932.

[53] Board Minutes, March 8, 22, 28, November 14, 1877.

[54] British Patent 4283 of 1879.

[55] British Patent 2434 of 1879.

[56] British Patent 1154 of 1880.

[57] British Patent 26 of 1880. There is no doubt that these last three patents were used by the firm, for J. H. Dickinson refers in his diary to payments of royalties to Windle Pilkington for them.

[58] British Patent 5748 of 1886.

[59] British Patent 6028 of 1888.

[60] Board Minutes (Plate), July 20, 1887, *et seq.*   [61] *Ibid.*, November 7, 1889.

[62] Windle Pilkington took out several patents for improvements in plate glass annealing kilns. They were numbers 927 and 17,204 of 1890; 6,524, 6,694 and 10,661 of 1891. Although the results of these experiments were not unsatisfactory, the lehr had to be built of an awkward shape because (according to F. E. Slocombe) the existing buildings could not be removed without great cost. The firm was unwilling to incur this additional expenditure and the whole scheme had to be dropped. William (Windle) Pilkington also took out the following patents during the years 1890–3:

21,181 of 1891. Melting and fining of plate glass.
1,222 of 1891. Forming molten glass into sheets.
6,525 of 1891. Improved apparatus for rolling glass.
19,441 of 1891. Forming molten glass into sheets (a second patent).
4,542 of 1893. Making hollow articles in blown glass.
4,543 of 1893. Reflectors.
8,758 of 1893. Forming molten glass into sheets (a third patent).
15,719 of 1893. Lanterns for lamps.

[63] J. F. Chance, *op. cit.*, 106, 108–110.

[64] For the background to the glass industry in America, see Pearce Davis, *The Development of the American Glass Industry* (Harvard, 1949) and Warren C. Scoville, *Revolution in Glassmaking* (Harvard, 1948).

[65] U.S. Tariff Commission, Report No. 123 (second ser.). Flat Glass and Related Glass Products (1937), 82.

[66] U.S. Census Reports, 1900, vol. IX, 964.

[67] For the rates, see U.S. Tariff Commission, *op. cit.*, 97.

[68] Report of the British Tariff Commission (1907), vol. VI, table 12.

[69] These figures are derived from each year's *Tableau du Commerce avec les Pays Etrangers* (*Statistique de la Belgique*).

[70] George B. Hodgson, *The History of South Shields* (Newcastle, 1924), 246.

[71] *St Helens Newspaper*, December 26, 1891, February 6, October 15, 1892. Board Minutes (Plate), February 4, 1892. According to Hudson A. Binney, manager at Sutton Oak, in a statement published in the *St Helens Newspaper* on November 27, 1903, the Pocket Nook works ceased to make plate glass about five years before that date. Rolled plate glass was, however, made there until the company went into liquidation in 1904. (Chance Brothers Ltd., Letter Books M., K. A. Macaulay to Glasgow Plate Glass Co., March 26, 1897, to Richard Pilkington, January 30, 1904, and to George Crowther, April 8, 1904.)

[72] Board Minutes (Plate), January 5, 1893, March 31, 1896.

[73] Board Minutes, March 13, 1901.

[74] *St Helens Newspaper*, May 29, June 12, 26, 1903, and deeds; Board Minutes, November 1, 1902. Only 300 people were employed at this time compared with 1,500 in 1889.

[75] Board Minutes, July 10, 15, 1905.

[76] For the background to this strike, see H. de Nimal, 'L'Industrie du Verre à Vitre en Belgique et la Crise Actuelle', *Revue Economique Internationale*, June, 1904.

[77] Biannual accounts.

[78] Board Minutes, June 3, 1901.

[79] Biannual accounts.

[80] Board Minutes, December 23, 1890; November 19, 1891; February 18, 1892; September 20, 1894; December 15, 1898; May 2, 1899.

[81] Board Minutes, December 19, 1900; September 17, December 24, 1901; January 14, 1902; January 20, May 19, 1903; October 4, 1904; September 10, 1906; May 14, 1907; June 17, 1908.

[82] Board Minutes, January 30, 1868; March 5, 1875; December 30, 1884; deeds at Pilkington Brothers Limited.

[83] Board Minutes, March 4, 5, 1875; March 3, June 27, 1876; January 22, 29, 1889.

[84] Pilkingtons' pioneer representative in this market was a man called Dickinson.

[85] Information from Pilkingtons' Sales Department; correspondence in the possession of Mr Hugh Salmond of James Hetley and Co.; Board Minutes, January 10, 16, 1868; July 31, 1873; December 12, 1878; February 14, April 2, May 29, September 12, 1879; August 31, September 19, 1882; January 16, 1883; January 10, April 3, 1888; May 2, 1899; Board Minutes (Plate), June 7, 1883.

[86] Articles of partnership, package 5, Secretary's Papers, Pilkington Brothers Limited; Board Minutes, August 27, 1872; October 22, 1874; January 16, 1877; January 9, 1880; February 21, 1884.

[87] C. A. Cooke, *Corporation Trust and Company* (Manchester, 1950), 181.

[88] A copy of the letter is to be found in the diary of J. H. Dickinson.

[89] The agreement, dated July 5, 1894, is to be found in package 5 among the Secretary's papers.

CHAPTER 11

LABOUR RELATIONS AND WELFARE SERVICES IN THE
LATER YEARS OF THE NINETEENTH CENTURY

[1] *Cullet*, October, 1933; *Sir James Sexton, Agitator* (1936), 27–8.
[2] Board Minutes, July 2, 1869.
[3] Board Minutes, March 23, 1870.
[4] Board Minutes, April 6, 13, 20, November 9, December 22, 1870; November 2, 1877; *Liverpool Courier*, May 11, 1870; *St Helens Newspaper*, July 16, October 15, 1870; *Liverpool Mercury*, August 9, 1878.
[5] Letter at back of Board Minutes, 1870–3.
[6] Board Minutes, April 20, 1876.
[7] Board Minutes, January 12, 1872.
[8] Board Minutes (Plate), September 15, 1881.
[9] Board Minutes, November 22, 1877; contracts of 1878.
[10] Board Minutes, August; November 7, 12, 21, 1878; January 29, February 14, June 19, November 4, 1879; *St Helens Newspaper*, August 10, November 9, 1878; *Birmingham Daily Mail*, November 9, 1878; J. F. Chance, *A History of the Firm of Chance Brothers and Co.* (privately printed 1919), 116; information from George Blake. The bonus lists, still preserved, show that one employee was still benefiting from his action forty-two years later, in 1920.
[11] Board Minutes, March 5, April 29, July 6, December 28, 1880; March 1, 1881.
[12] Henry Pelling, 'The Knights of Labor in Britain, 1880–1901', *Economic History Review*, vol. ix, No. 2 (December, 1956), 313–331. This article draws upon the Knights of Labor Papers now at the Library of the Catholic University of America. This and the next two paragraphs are based entirely on this source unless otherwise stated. For a recent discussion of the activities of the Knights of Labor among American window glass workers, see Charlotte Erickson, *American Industry and the European Immigrant, 1860–85* (Cambridge, Mass., 1957), Chapter 8.
[13] V. Lefebvre, *La Verrerie à Vitres et Les Verriers de Belgique depuis le XVᵉ Siècle* (Hainaut, 1938), 63.
[14] *Ibid.* British Parliamentary Paper, 1888 [C.5269] XCVIII, 20.
[15] *St Helens Newspaper*, June 21, 1884.
[16] *St Helens Newspaper*, June 28, 1884.
[17] Board Minutes, July 9, 1884.
[18] This was stated in a case of alleged assault and intimidation, reported in the *St Helens Newspaper*, August 1, 1885.
[19] *St Helens Newspaper*, February 28, 1885.
[20] Diary of J. H. Dickinson, April 5, 1888.
[21] *St Helens Newspaper*, June 22, 1889.
[22] *St Helens Newspaper*, June 28, September 6, November 8, 1890.
[23] Statement of W. J. Fillingham.
[24] Diary of J. H. Dickinson, December 18, 1890.
[25] *St Helens Newspaper*, October 11, 18, 1890.
[26] *St Helens Newspaper*, September 26, 1891.
[27] *St Helens Newspaper*, May 4, 1895.
[28] H. Logan, 'Early Days of the Recs Club', *Cullet*, January, 1929; Board Minutes, November 2, 1898, January 22, 1901.

[29] T. C. Barker, 'Early Sports Clubs at St Helens', *Cullet*, Spring, 1952.

[30] *St Helens Newspaper*, April 4, 1891.

[31] *Prescot Reporter*, May 14, 1887; *St Helens Newspaper*, May 21, 1887; John Kerr in *Cullet*, July, 1932.

[32] Reminiscences of John Edmundson, *Now Thus, Now Thus*, 75.

[33] Deeds; *Liverpool Daily Post*, April 18, 1891; information from Charles Green; Board Minutes, December 30, 1874; April 17, May 1, 1888; January 7, 1890.

[34] Board Minutes, October 27, 1881; January 3, 10, April 11, 18, May 2, 1882; February 7, 1888; January 29, 1889; March 8, April 19, 1898; January 18, 31, February 8, 10, 21, March 7, 1905.

[35] Board Minutes, September 29, 1886.

[36] Notes in Board Minutes (1891–1900).

[37] Board Minutes, June 26, 1868.

CHAPTER 12

COLLIERY AFFAIRS

[1] *St Helens Weekly News*, August 10, 1861. The St Helens Colliery is not listed in a local directory of 1858.

[2] Board Minutes, March 12, 1863.

[3] Board Minutes, January 8, 1863. For this Association, see T. C. Barker and J. R. Harris, *A Merseyside Town in the Industrial Revolution* (Liverpool, 1954), 248.

[4] Board Minutes, December 24, 1863.

[5] Board Minutes, March 17, 1864.

[6] Board Minutes, September 2, 1864.

[7] Board Minutes, May 25, 1865; November 15, 1866.

[8] Newscutting at Pilkington Brothers Ltd., dated December 30, 1867.   [9] *Ibid.*

[10] *Ibid.* For Princess Alexandra's visit to Ravenhead, see the *St Helens Standard*, November 4, 1865.

[11] Board Minutes, January 25, 1866; obituary notice, *St Helens Newspaper*, February 20, 1903.

[12] Board Minutes, May 17, 1866.

[13] *St Helens Newspaper*, February 20, 1903.

[14] W. Hopton, *Conversation on Mines* (Manchester, 8th edition, 1886), 325–6.

[15] Board Minutes, September 14, 1870.

[16] A third and larger concern, that of Bournes and Robinson, was also involved in the earlier negotiations, but withdrew after disagreement about the price at which their pits would have been taken over. Board Minutes, October 22, 1868; October 24, November 22, 1872; February 27, 1873.

[17] Minutes of the Ravenhead Colliery Co., February 11, December 15, 1869.

[18] *Ibid.*, March 19, May 15, July 24, November 20, 1873.

[19] Bromilow Haddock and Co. were incorporated under the Companies Act of September 5, 1871, with a capital of £100,000 in £100 shares (*Mining Journal*, September 16, 1871).

[20] When these coals were first put up for auction in 1848, they were said to lay under 1,100 acres of ground and to be worth £52,800. Portions of these mines were then leased to Bromilow Haddock & Co. The coalmines were, however, not disposed of in 1848 nor at later auctions in 1852 and 1859 (Sale catalogues among the Cross Papers at the Lancashire Record Office).

[21] Minutes of the Ravenhead Colliery Co. Ltd., October 24, 1872.

22 *Colliery Guardian*, February 4, 1876.
23 Board Minutes, May 7, 1872, August 5, 1880.
24 Printed notice of meeting.
25 *Colliery Guardian*, August 4, 1876; *St Helens Newspaper*, July 29, 1876.
26 Minutes of the Ravenhead Colliery Co. Ltd., March 21, 1872.
27 Board Minutes, January 5, 1865.
28 Board Minutes, March 15, 1867.
29 Board Minutes, April 5, 1867.

CHAPTER 13

INTERNATIONAL, TECHNICAL AND OTHER DEVELOPMENTS,
1900–1914

1 Pearce Davis, *The Development of the American Glass Industry* (Harvard, 1949), 175–80.
2 *The Times*, August 15, 1901. For other despatches on this subject, see the issues of August 10, 21, September 7, 10 and October 1.
3 Consular Report (Belgium) 1905 [Cd.2236] LXXXVII, 13.
4 Report of British Vice-Consul at Charleroi and of the British Consul-General at Brussels in Consular Report (Belgium) 1905 [Cd.2682], XXX, 5, 30.
5 Consular Report (Belgium) 1907 [Cd.3727] XLI, 39–41.
6 Consular Report (Belgium) 1906 [Cd.2682] CXXII, 38.
7 Consular Report (Belgium) 1908 [Cd.3727] CIX, 32.
8 Consular Report (Belgium) 1910 [Cd.4962] XCVI, 21.
9 J. F. Chance, *A History of the Firm of Chance Brothers and Co.* (privately printed 1919), 132; C. A. Oakley (ed.) *Scottish Industry* (The Scottish Council 1953), 282.
10 Chance Brothers Ltd. Manufacturers' Letters on Continental Agreement 1904–10.
11 J. F. Chance, *op. cit.*, 132, 283; information from Sir Hugh Chance.
12 Consular Report (Belgium) 1905 [Cd.2682] XXX, 30.
13 Consular Report (Belgium) 1907 [Cd.3727] XLI, 41. U.S. Daily Consular Trade Report, June 18, 1909, cited in *The Glass Industry as Affected by the War* (U.S. Tariff Commission 1918), 61. For the origins, aims, and history of the Convention up to 1929, see C. Frérichs, 'L'Entente entre les Producteurs dans l'Industrie Européenne des Glaces Polies', *Revue Economique Internationale*, January 1930.
14 For details, see U.S. Census of 1910, Vol. X, 882.
15 Information from Cecil Pilkington.
16 U.S. Census of 1900, Vol. IX, 962–3.
17 Information from Cecil Pilkington; Board Minutes (Plate), December 2, 1901; September 29, 1903; November 17, 1904; Board Minutes, August 9, 1904.
18 Information from E. B. LeMare.
19 Board Minutes (Plate), December 13, 1905; February 22, August 29, 1907; May 7, 1908; September 23, 1909.
20 Board Minutes, January 31, April 18, 25, 1899; March 7, 1905. Board Minutes (Plate), October 6, 1902; March 31, 1904.
21 Board Minutes, December 5, 1911.
22 Board Minutes, October 22, November 4, 1913; British Patents 156,919 and 156,920 (October 1919–January 1921); information from F. B. Waldron.

[23] H. de Ninal, 'L'Industrie du Verre à Vitres en Belgique et la Crise Actuelle', *Revue Economique Internationale*, June, 1904.

[24] British Patents 10,584 and 11,373 of 1906. Hyde came to Pilkingtons in 1898, having previously been employed in the engineer's department of the Great Northern Railway.

[25] Board Minutes, June 23, September 24, 1903.

[26] Warren C. Scoville, *Revolution in Glassmaking* (Harvard 1948), 190; Davis, *op. cit.*, 182–4.

[27] Statement to employees, June 22, 1909 (Board Minutes).

[28] William L. Monro in *The Glass Industry as Affected by the War* (U.S. Tariff Commission 1918).

[29] Statement to employees, June 22, 1909 (Board Minutes).

[30] 7 Ed. VII, cap. XXIX.

[31] Board Minutes, May 18, 1909.

[32] British Patents 14,283, 16,064 and 20,141 of 1910 and 9,244 of 1911.

[33] H. R. Hilton, manager of the Alleghany Window Glass Co. in *The Glass Industry as Affected by the War* (U.S. Tariff Commission 1918), 87.

[34] Report of the British Tariff Commission, Vol. 6 (1907), para. 19 and table 12.

[35] Board Minutes, April 11, 1905; August 10, September 18, 1906; June 4, 1907.

[36] Board Minutes, June 22, 1909.

[37] Board Minutes, December 30, 1912.

[38] Information from J. Tabern.

[39] Board Minutes, January 15, 1907.

[40] Board Minutes, May 5, 1914.

[41] Obituary, *St Helens Newspaper* and *St Helens Reporter*, April 17, 1903.

[42] Obituary, *St Helens Newspaper* and *St Helens Reporter*, May 22, 1925.

[43] Obituary, *St Helens Newspaper*, March 13, 1908.

[44] Obituary, *St Helens Newspaper* and *St Helens Reporter*, March 20, 1914.

[45] Christ Church, Oxford, Salisbury Papers. Letters from Henry Seton-Karr to Lord Salisbury, July 21, 1889, July 16, 29, 1892. I am grateful to the present Lord Salisbury for permission to quote from these letters and to my friend Dr J. F. A. Mason for drawing my attention to them.

[46] From July 1908 to the end of 1912 the secretary of the company was Reginald Arthur Wenham, the accountant.

[47] *Now Thus, Now Thus*, 28.

[48] Board Minutes, September 24, 1909. Both men joined the firm on twelve months' probation at a salary of £100.

[49] Obituary, *St Helens Newspaper*, December 26, 1902.

[50] Obituary, *St Helens Newspaper*, September 29, 1905.

[51] Above, p. 190.

[52] Board Minutes, September 24, 1909.

CHAPTER 14

EPILOGUE 1914–1959

[1] The Triplex Safety Glass Company Ltd. had been formed in 1912 to operate in Britain certain patents owned by the French Société du Verre Triplex. The British company opened a factory at Willesden in 1913 to produce laminated glass, but it did not manufacture the glass itself, relying for its supplies upon existing manufacturers. See Westcote R. Lyttleton, 'A

Brief Outline of the History, Development and Methods Employed in the Manufacture of Laminated Glass', *J.S.G.T.*, *13* (1929).

² For details, see appendix 4.

³ The story of these developments in Detroit, based upon the Ford archives and the eye-witness testimony of E. B. LeMare, R. F. Taylor and F. B. Waldron, is told in appendix 8.

⁴ For the Fourcault and Colburn processes, see W. C. Scoville, *Revolution in Glassmaking* (Cambridge, Mass. 1948), 168 *et seq.*, 190 *et seq.*, 330. For Fourcault and Libbey-Owens production in Belgium after 1912 and 1923 respectively, see R. Chambon, *L'Histoire de la Verrerie en Belgique* (Brussels, 1955), 199 *et seq.*

⁵ Board Minutes, September 24, December, 1903; April 26, 1904; July 23, August 18, 1905; August 8, 1907.

⁶ See p. 192, for details of this process.

⁷ *Glass*, October, 1929; February, March, 1930; June, 1931. For agreements, in 1932, between the *Union* and the Libbey-Owens *Campagnie Internationale*, see Chambon, *op. cit.*, 217–8.

⁸ *Glass*, May, 1933.

⁹ For details of these international agreements among plate glass manufacturers, see *The Report of the Canadian Combines Investigation Commission into Flat Glass* (1949).

¹⁰ For biographical details of the directors, see appendix 7.

¹¹ J. F. Chance, *A History of the Firm of Chance Brothers and Co* (privately printed 1919), 132.

¹² For Professor Turner's activities, see Arthur W. Chapman, *The Story of a Modern University* (1955), 264–73.

APPENDIX I

THE PILKINGTON PEDIGREE

¹ I am much indebted to Mr J. Charnock of Horwich for these references and for assisting me with his extensive knowledge of the Horwich district.

² According to the ecclesiastical records at Chester, the year 1669 was marked by numerous meetings of Nonconformists in the neighbourhood, and Horwich Chapel was said to have been a conventicle (*Victoria County History of Lancaster*, V, 8). After the Toleration Act, Richard Pilkington was among those who signed a petition (dated July 29, 1689) asking that Horwich Chapel be exempted from the penalties to which dissenting chapels were then liable (L.R.O., Quarter Sessions Papers, QSP 668/47).

³ *Landed Gentry* (ed. L. G. Pine, 1952), 2033–4.

⁴ *Victoria County History of Lancaster*, V, 90. The family estates elsewhere were forfeited two years later after Sir Thomas had been rash enough to rally to the cause of Lambert Simnel. Sir Thomas appears to have been killed at Stoke. His son, Roger, was able to recover most of the family estates outside Lancashire.

⁵ For James Pilkington, see *The Dictionary of National Biography* and the note in the *Victoria County History of Lancaster*, V, 289. A portrait of him is reproduced in the *Transactions of the Historic Society of Lancashire and Cheshire*, new series, IX (1893), 196. His will is printed in *Publications of the Surtees Society*, XXXVIII (1860), 8–10.

⁶ *Victoria County History of Lancaster*, V, 290.

⁷ Lieutenant-Colonel John Pilkington, 'The Early History of the Lancashire Family of Pilkington and Its Branches, From 1066 to 1600', *Transactions of the Historic Society of Lancashire and Cheshire*, new series, IX (1893), 161–2. The complete paper occupies pp. 159–218. See also

John Harland, *Genealogy of the Pilkingtons of Lancashire* (ed. William E. A. Axon), printed for private circulation 1875.

⁸ Regarding James Pilkington of Sharples, believed to have been the father of Richard Pilkington who married Mary Hardman, he wrote: 'his parentage is not known' (The Big Book of Col. John Pilkington now in the possession of Captain Richard Pilkington, M.P.).

⁹ Captain Pilkington issued a set of duplicated pedigrees, which he had compiled, in 1944.

APPENDIX 4

BESSEMER'S EXPERIMENTS WITH GLASS, 1841–1851

¹ British Patent 9100 of 1841.

² B.P.G.M. October 27, November 10, 24, 1841.

³ British Patents 11,317 of 1846 and 11,794 of 1847.

⁴ This account of based upon J. F. Chance, *A History of the Firm of Chance Brothers and Co.* (1919), 64–77.

⁵ Sir Henry Bessemer, *An Autobiography* (1905), 113–5.

⁶ Cited in Chance, *op. cit.*, 72.

APPENDIX 8

THE EARLY HISTORY OF THE FLOW PROCESS

¹ Ford Archives. Speech by C. W. Avery at Dearborn Inn, December 19, 1944, 1. Allan Nevins and Frank Ernest Hill, *Ford: The Times, The Man, The Company*, I (New York, 1954), 474.

² Nevins and Hill, *op. cit.*, I, 474–5.

³ Ford Archives. Reminiscences of W. C. Klann, 213–29.

⁴ Nevins and Hill, *op. cit.*, II (1957), 230–1.

⁵ Ford Archives. Reminiscences of W. C. Klann, 215.

⁶ Ford Archives, Accesssion 285, Box 9. Edward Donner to Henry Ford, January 20, 1921.

⁷ Ford Archives. Speech by C. W. Avery at Dearborn Inn, December 19, 1944, 4.

⁸ The statement that the plant was, by November, 1921, 'turning out an excellent product on an assembly line plan' (Nevins and Hill, *op. cit.*, II, 231) is confirmed neither by Pilkingtons' eye witnesses nor by Klann.

⁹ The rest of this account, unless otherwise stated, is based upon discussion with E. B. LeMare, R. F. Taylor and F. B. Waldron.

¹⁰ Board Minutes, May 8, 1922.

INDEX

For Product Safety Concerns and Information please contact our
EU representative GPSR@taylorandfrancis.com Taylor & Francis
Verlag GmbH, Kaufingerstraße 24, 80331 München, Germany